AF574690

THE HISTORY OF RAILWAYS IN BRITAIN

A

The Lion, *designed by Todd, Kitson & Laird in 1838 for the Liverpool & Manchester Railway and preserved today at Liverpool. Inside cylinders 12 × 18 inches, boiler pressure 50 lb., drivers 5 ft. (Photo: John Adams, Esq.)*

THE HISTORY OF RAILWAYS IN BRITAIN

FRANK FERNEYHOUGH

OSPREY PUBLISHING LIMITED

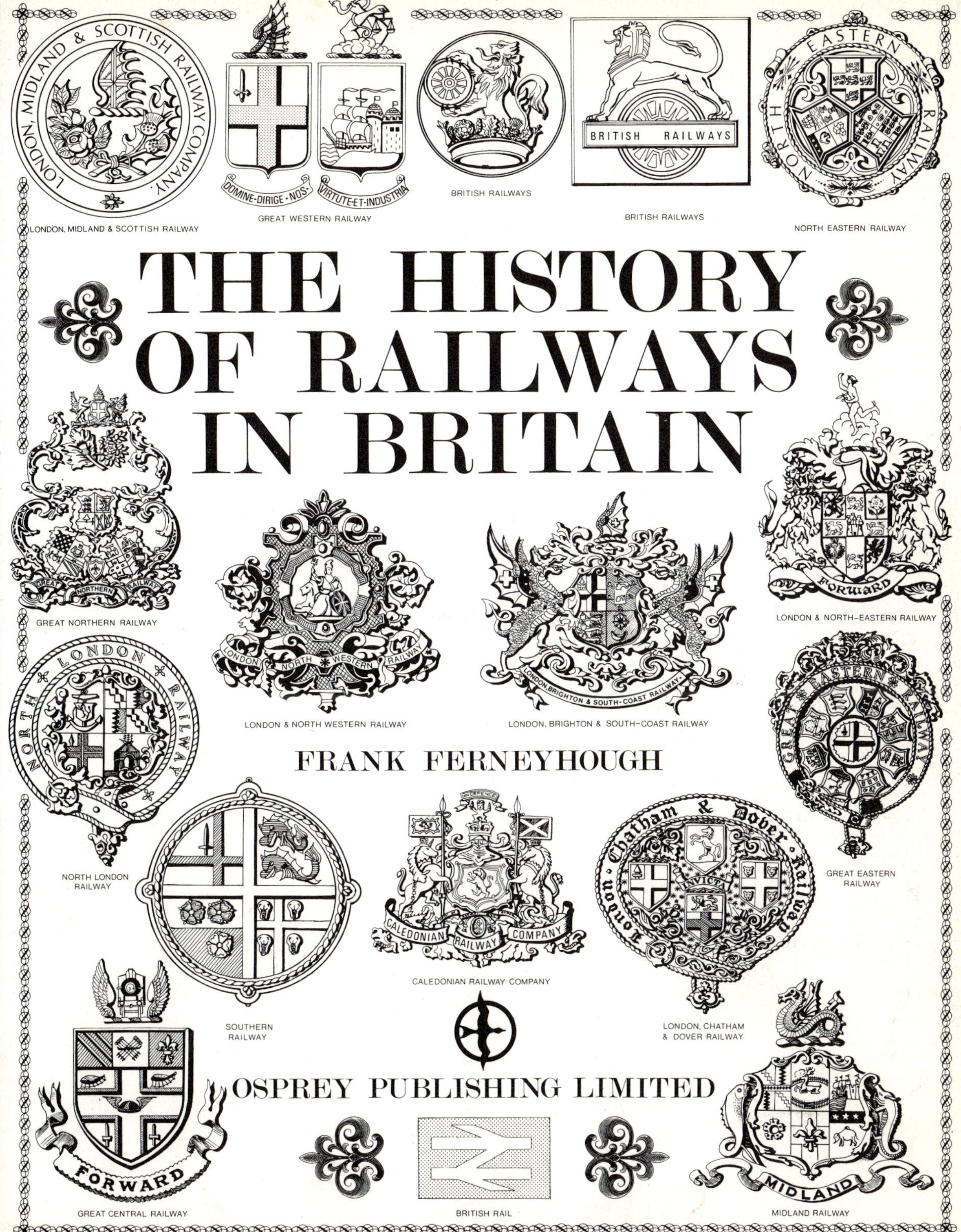

LONDON, MIDLAND & SCOTTISH RAILWAY

GREAT WESTERN RAILWAY

BRITISH RAILWAYS

BRITISH RAILWAYS

NORTH EASTERN RAILWAY

GREAT NORTHERN RAILWAY

LONDON & NORTH-EASTERN RAILWAY

LONDON & NORTH WESTERN RAILWAY

LONDON, BRIGHTON & SOUTH-COAST RAILWAY

NORTH LONDON RAILWAY

GREAT EASTERN RAILWAY

CALEDONIAN RAILWAY COMPANY

SOUTHERN RAILWAY

LONDON, CHATHAM & DOVER RAILWAY

GREAT CENTRAL RAILWAY

BRITISH RAIL

MIDLAND RAILWAY

This book was designed and produced by
Alban Book Services Limited,
147 London Road, St. Albans, Herts, England

First Published in 1975 by
Osprey Publishing Limited,
137 Southampton Street, Reading, Berks, England
Member Company of the George Philip Group

Set in 9/10pt. Times New Roman 327 and
printed on 118 gsm Nimrod paper by
W. S. COWELL LIMITED
at the Butter Market, Ipswich, England

ISBN 0 85045 060 8

LIST OF CONTENTS

ACKNOWLEDGEMENTS

THE author has received generous advice and assistance from numerous friends, colleagues and organisations and wishes to express his gratitude particularly to the following:

Peter Choules, Esq.
Cyril Crook, Esq.
John R. Day, Esq.
John Edgington, Esq.
Roger Ferneyhough, Esq. (son)
John Fogg, Esq.
Dennis Joiner, Esq.
Peter Keen, Esq.
Eric Merrill, Esq.
Roger Owen, Esq.
Ronald Owen, Esq.
David Pattisson, Esq.
Kenneth G. Pope, Esq.
Sydney Preston, Esq.

Association of Railway Preservation Societies
Daily Telegraph Information Service
House of Commons Library
London Transport Press Office
Marylebone Public Reference Library
Public Records Office, British Transport Historical Records

Illustrations:
John Adams, Esq.
British Railways Board
British Transport Films
Keith Heckler, Esq.
Herbert Hinchley, Esq.
J. M. Jarvis, Esq.
Mr. & Mrs. M. G. Powell
Science Museum
Victoria & Albert Museum
Wayland Picture Library (WPL)

BIBLIOGRAPHY

IN the preparation of this railway history, nearly 200 books, dating from the early 19th century to the present day, have been consulted, together with old magazines and newspapers, historical documents, old prints and many Statutes. For railway titles, the most comprehensive single volume is the Bibliography of British Railway History, by George Ottley (Allen & Unwin 1966), which lists 7,950 books in its 683 pages.

The best popular sources of new books are the review pages of the principal monthly railway magazines. The following brief bibliography offers a quick reference for further detailed study.

Annuals and Directories

British Railways Annual Report and Accounts (British Railways Board)

Jane's World Railways (Macdonald & Jane)

Railway and Steam Enthusiasts' Handbook, Ed. Geoffrey Body (David & Charles)

Railway Directory and Year Book (IPC Business Press)

Railway World Annual, Ed. Alan Williams (Ian Allan)

Biographies

Breath of Steam, W. G. Thorley (Ian Allan Vol. 1 1975, Vol. 2 1976)

Brunel, Isambard Kingdom, L. T. C. Rolt (Longman Green 1957, Penguin 1970)

The Thomas Cook Story, J. Pudney (Michael Joseph 1953)

Cornish Giant, L. T. C. Rolt (Lutterworth Press 1960)

Lives of the Engineers, Samuel Smiles (John Murray 1858, reprinted David & Charles 1958)

Master Builders of Steam, H. A. V. Bulleid (Ian Allan 1964)

Railway King 1800–71, R. S. Lambert (Allen & Unwin 1964)

George and Robert Stephenson, Michael Robbins (Oxford University Press 1966)

Richard Trevithick, H. W. Dickenson and Arthur Titley (Cambridge University Press 1934)

Twenty Locomotive Men, C. Hamilton Ellis (Ian Allan 1958)

General History

British Narrow Gauge Steam, M. J. Messenger (Bradford Barton 1974)

British Railway History 1830–1947, 2 Vols., C. Hamilton Ellis (Allen & Unwin 1960)
British Railways Today and Tomorrow, G. F. Allen (Ian Allan 1959)
Historical Geography of the Railways of the British Isles, Ernest Carter (Cassell 1969)
Historical Transport 1974, Transport Trust (IPC Transport Press 1974)
Light Railway and Vintage Transport Guide, Ed. Geoffrey Body (David & Charles 1974)
The Navvies, Terry Coleman (Pelican 1965)
Outline of Irish Railway History, H. C. Casserley (David & Charles 1974)
The Railways of Britain, J. Simmons (Routledge & Kegan Paul 1961)
Trains, John R. Day (Hamlyn 1969)

Locomotives and Carriages

Britain's Railway Liveries, E. F. Carter (Harold Starke 1963)
British Express Locomotive Development 1896–1948, E. C. Poultney (Allen & Unwin 1952)
British Internal Combustion Locomotives 1894–1940, Brian Webb (David & Charles 1974)
British Railways Diesels in Action, G. Weeks (Bradford Barton 1974)
British Railways Standard Steam Locomotives, E. S. Cox (Ian Allan 1966)
Diesel Traction Manual for Enginemen (British Railways Board 1962)
Electric Traction, A. T. Dover (Pitman 1963)
Handbook of Steam Locomotive Enginemen 1952 (Facsimile Ian Allan 1975)
Historical Steam Locomotives, O. S. Nock (Allen & Unwin 1957)
History of the Electric Locomotive, F. J. G. Haut (Allen & Unwin 1969)
Locomotive Panorama Vol. 1, E. S. Cox (Ian Allan 1965)
Nineteenth Century Railway Carriages, C. Hamilton Ellis (Modern Transport Publishing Co. 1949)
Preserved Locomotives in the British Isles, Ed. M. Swift (Industrial Railway Society 1970)
Railway Carriage Album, G. M. Kichenside (Ian Allan 1966)
Railway Locomotives and Other Power, Alan Williams and David Percival (Ian Allan 1975)
Short History of the Railway Carriage, R. W. Kidner (Oakwood Press 1946)
Southern Electric, G. T. Moody (Ian Allan 1968)
System of Electrification for British Railways (British Transport Commission 1956)

Management and Policy

All Change, C. McLeod (Gower Press 1970)
British Railways in Transition, D. H. Aldcroft (Macmillan 1969)
Modernisation and Re-equipment of British Railways (British Transport Commission 1955)
Railway Amalgamation in Great Britain, W. E. Simmett (Railway Gazette 1923)
Railway Commercial Practice, Vol. 1 Passenger and General; Vol. 2 Freight (Chapman & Hall 1952)
Reshaping of British Railways (British Transport Commission 1963)
Unification of British Railways (Modern Transport 1951)

Signalling

British Railway Signalling, G. M. Kichenside and A. Williams (Ian Allan 1963)
Fifty Years of Railway Signalling, O. S. Nock (Institution of Railway Signal Engineers 1962)
Railway Signalling Systems, John R. Day and B. K. Cooper (Frederick Muller 1958)
Red for Danger, L. T. C. Holt (David & Charles 1966)

Underground Railways

History of London Transport Vol. 2, T. C. Barker and Michael Robbins (Allen & Unwin 1974)
Story of London's Underground, John R. Day (London Transport 1974)
Underground Railways of the World, H. C. P. Havers (Temple Press 1966)

Unions

The Lighted Flame – History of ASLEF, Norman McKillop, (Nelson 1950)
The Railwaymen, Dr. Philip S. Bagwell (Allen & Unwin 1963)

GREAT BRITAIN
RAILWAYS IN OPERATION
1851
Miles 10 0 10 20 40 60 80 90
Kilometres 0 10 20 40 60 80 100 120 140
SHETLAND ISLANDS
ORKNEY ISLANDS
North Minch
Moray Firth
Firth of Forth
North Channel
Solway Firth
IRISH SEA
NORTH SEA
St. George's Channel
Bristol Channel
ENGLISH CHANNEL
Strait of Dover
The Wash
Isle of Man
ANGLESEY
Isle of Wight
Isles of Scilly
ABERDEEN
Stonehaven
Brechin
Forfar
Arbroath
Dundee
PERTH
Cupar
STIRLING
Alloa
Dunbar
EDINBURGH
Greenock
Airdrie
GLASGOW
Duns
BERWICK
Kilmarnock
Muirkirk
Galashiels
Belford
Kelso
Cumnock
Ayr
Sanquhar
New Cumnock
Hawick
Lockerbie
Morpeth
DUMFRIES
Gretna
Hexham
NEWCASTLE
Sunderland
CARLISLE
DURHAM
Cockermouth
Penrith
Whitehaven
Windermere
Darlington
Stockton
Whitby
Richmond
Kendal
Bedale
Northallerton
Thirsk
Scarborough
BARROW
LANCASTER
HARROGATE
YORK
Bridlington
Fleetwood
Blackpool
Lytham
PRESTON
BURNLEY
HALIFAX
LEEDS
HULL
BLACKBURN
BURY
Goole
Barton
Southport
HUDDERSFIELD
BARNSLEY
Grimsby
LIVERPOOL
Birkenhead
BOLTON
Gainsborough
Market Raisen
Warrington
MANCHESTER
SHEFFIELD
HOLYHEAD
Conway
Bangor
Mold
CHESTER
CHESTERFIELD
Rowsley
Worksop
LINCOLN
Macclesfield
Mansfield
Southwell
Newark
CREWE
Boston
DERBY
Nottingham
Grantham
Melton Mowbray
Fakenham
Lynn Regis
Wisbech
E. Dereham
Oswestry
Stamford
NORWICH
YARMOUTH
Swaffham
Wymondham
SHREWSBURY
Walsall
Tamworth
LEICESTER
Peterborough
March
LOWESTOFT
Wolverhampton
BIRMINGHAM
Thetford
Diss
Ely
Bury St. Edmunds
COVENTRY
RUGBY
Huntingdon
WORCESTER
Warwick
Northampton
Cambridge
Newmarket
Hadleigh
IPSWICH
Sudbury
Banbury
Bedford
Cheltenham
Winslow
Bletchley
Hertford
Braintree
Leighton Buzzard
Dunstable
Chelmsford
Gloucester
Cirencester
Llanelly
SWANSEA
Merthyr Tydfil
Pontypool
OXFORD
Aylesbury
Barnet
Chepstow
Didcot
Maidenhead
LONDON
BRISTOL
SWINDON
CARDIFF
Chippenham
READING
Windsor
Whitstable
Margate
Ramsgate
Bath
CROYDON
Rochester
Hungerford
Maidstone
CANTERBURY
Deal
Guildford
Reigate
DOVER
Bridgwater
Godalming
Ashford
Horsham
Tunbridge Wells
Folkestone
Salisbury
SOUTHAMTON
Hailsham
Tiverton
Chichester
Hastings
Brighton
Newhaven
Eastbourne
EXETER
Dorchester
Poole
PLYMOUTH
Redruth
Hayle
Ballymena
Antrim
BELFAST
Lisburn
Armagh
Dundalk
Drogheda
Balbriggan
DUBLIN
Kingstown
Francis K. Mason

Chapter 1

A Chronology of Railways in Britain

Opening of the Bodmin & Wadebridge Railway, Cornwall, in 1834. Musicians can be seen in the seventh and eighth wagons. A top-hatted guard sits in front of the locomotive stagecoach-fashion. (Photo: Victoria & Albert Museum)

ALTHOUGH this Chronology is mainly about the railways of Britain, the country of their birth, it includes selected events of historical importance concerning railways in many parts of the world. The history of practical railways begins with George Stephenson's line, the Stockton & Darlington Railway, which opened in 1825, to become acknowledged as the world's first proper railway in which a steam locomotive hauled loaded goods wagons and passenger carriages along a track of metal rails. But centuries before then, horse-drawn wagons on rails had been in use, chiefly in mining areas, both in Britain and Europe. James Watt, having built successful stationary steam engines in the 18th century to perform useful mechanical work, had toyed with the idea of making his engines move along the ground; but it was Richard Trevithick who built the first practical steam locomotive to run on rails over 20 years before the Stockton & Darlington opened. The first documented evidence of mechanical movement by steam power dates from Hero of Alexandria, *circa* AD 100. Since Hero's time, dreamers, philosophers and men of mathematics and science have conjectured about mechanical movement using neither horse- nor man-power. A brief chronological commentary precedes the era of Stephenson, whose railways changed the face of Britain.

THE BIRTH OF STEAM POWER

circa AD 100 — The first known mechanical movement activated by steam power is devised by Hero of Alexandria, with his *Pnéumatica*. Steam from a boiling cauldron rises through pipes into a pivoted hollow globe; the steam escapes through two exit pipes angled from the globe, and the "jets" of steam cause the globe to rotate.

c. 1698 — Thomas Newcomen of Dartmouth, Devon, is reputed to have built his first steam pumping engine before about 1698. The first practical and useful piston engine for pumping, which he invented, was erected at a colliery in South Staffordshire in 1712.

1698 — Thomas Savery of Shilstone, Devon, takes out a patent for a pump in which steam power from a boiler forces water from a reservoir through a one-way outlet valve, with a repeated action in sequence.

1748 — Baron von Kempelen of Pressburg, in what is now Czechoslovakia, experiments with a steam reactor turbine on similar lines to the simple water-wheel.

9–6–1758 — An Act of Parliament, No. 31 Geo II cXXI, is passed, authorising a horse-drawn railway of about 4 miles for the private use of Middleton Colliery to convey coal to Leeds. The line is currently operated by the Middleton Railway Trust.

1765 — James Watt, an instrument-maker of Glasgow, produces a modified and improved version of Newcomen's steam engine.

1769 James Watt obtains a patent for his "new method of lessening the consumption of steam and fuel in a fire engine" – steam boiler. Watt later joins in a partnership with Matthew Boulton, who owns a workshop.

1769 The first known European self-moving (automotive) steam engine is built in France by Cugnot, to run on the roads.

1775 James Watt's patent for his steam engine is extended by 25 years.

1800 By this time, Boulton and Watt have built about 500 steam engines, most of which were of the rotative type, the rest being pumping engines.

21–5–1801 The Surrey Iron Railway is incorporated, the first public goods railway line in the world to be sanctioned by Parliament. It opens on 26th July 1803 for horse-drawn goods traffic between Wandsworth, on the River Thames, and Croydon.

24–3–1802 A steam locomotive to run on the road is patented by Vivian and Trevithick, and is built the next year.

17–5–1803 The Croydon, Merstham & Godstone Railway is incorporated; and is opened between Croydon and Merstham on 24th July 1805.

21–2–1804 A steam locomotive on iron rails is used successfully by Trevithick on the Pen-y-darran tramroad near Merthyr Tydfil, South Wales.

29–6–1804 The Oystermouth Railway Company is incorporated and opens about April 1806 between Swansea and Oystermouth. The horse-drawn system conveys fare-paying passengers from 25th March 1807, the first railway to do so, and was known for many years as the Swansea & Mumbles Railway.

1804 Oliver Evans builds a steam carriage to run on roads in America.

27–5–1808 The Kilmarnock & Troon Railway of 9¾ miles is incorporated, the first in Scotland, the 4 ft. gauge line being opened with horses on 6th July 1812. An early Stephenson locomotive is used in 1817.

1808 Trevithick's improved locomotive, hauling a carriage, runs on a circular railway track at a public demonstration in London.

12–8–1812 The first commercial use of steam locomotives is inaugurated on the Middleton Colliery Railway which had been relaid with John Blenkinsop's rack rail. Blenkinsop and Matthew Murray's steam engines, with cogged driving wheels to engage in the toothed rail, are employed. Rack locomotives were operated on this line until 1835.

25–7–1814 George Stephenson's first "travelling engine", the *Blücher*, hauls wagons at 4 miles an hour on a trial journey on the Killingworth Railway colliery line.

28–2–1815 George Stephenson takes out a patent for his second steam locomotive.

1815 Trevithick takes out a patent for a system of fanners to produce a strong draught through the boiler fire.

1815 George Stephenson invents the blast, by which the exhaust steam from the cylinders is directed through the boiler to the chimney, the draught making the fire burn more fiercely for greater heat.

16–6–1817 The Mansfield & Pinxton Railway, in the north Nottinghamshire coalfields, is inaugurated, and goes into service on 13th April 1819. The line is taken over by the Midland Railway in 1848 and is re-opened on 9th October 1849 using steam traction.

2–7–1819 The Plymouth & Dartmoor Railway is incorporated and opens to Kings Tor on 26th September 1823, completed shortly afterwards to Princetown. The gauge is originally 4 ft. 6 in.

23–10–1820 John Birkinshaw of the Bedlington Ironworks is granted a patent for the manufacture of rolled rails.

17–6–1824 The Redruth & Chasewater Railway is incorporated, and opens on 30th January 1825. Steam traction begins in 1854. Until it was closed 90 years later, the line continued as a remarkable example of very early railway practice.

DAWN OF THE STEAM RAILWAY AGE

27–9–1825 The ceremonial opening of the Stockton & Darlington Railway, **Britain's and the world's first practical steam railway** in which a steam locomotive hauls loaded goods wagons and passenger carriages on metal rails. George Stephenson's locomotive *Locomotion* (still preserved) is used on the opening day. In the early stages, steam is used only for goods traffic. The gauge of the track was 4 ft. 8½ in., which became known as the Stephenson gauge and was adopted in many countries.

5–9–1826 The Stratford & Moreton Railway opens, the company having been formed on 28th May 1821.

–10–1826 The Monkland & Kirkintilloch Railway opens, using both steam and horse traction.

7–9–1827 The first railway in the Austrian Empire opens, with animal traction, between Budweis and Trojanov on the Linz–Budweis Railway.

1–10–1828 The first railway in France opens, with horse traction, on the St. Etienne (a coal-mining area) to Andrézieux line of 12 miles. The concession was obtained on 26th February 1823 and the line brought unofficially into service in May 1827. Passenger traffic began on 1st March 1832 and steam traction was introduced in 1844. The second line, from St. Etienne to Lyons, was built between 1830 and 1833, passengers being carried in 1831 in coal trucks drawn by horses, steam engines being used the same year. Marc Seguin's locomotive used enclosed fans to force a draught through the multi-tube boiler.

Robert Stephenson built nine locomotives for a new line from Marseilles to Avignon which was opened in sections in 1847–49.

6/14–10–1829 Trials are held along the Rainhill Level of the Liverpool & Manchester Railway, which is under construction, to find the best locomotive for the new line. Competing locomotives are the *Rocket* (George Stephenson), *Sans Pareil* (Timothy Hackworth), and *Novelty* (Braithwaite and Ericsson). The *Rocket* wins and is awarded the £500 prize on the last day.

9–10–1829 The Carbondale–Honesdale Railway in the United States of America is opened by the Delaware & Hudson Canal Company, which later became the Delaware & Hudson Railroad. The Steam locomotive *Stourbridge Lion*, built by Foster, Rastrick & Co. of England, ran a trial trip on 8th August 1829, but proved too heavy for the track. For many years afterwards, the line was worked as a gravity railway.

On 24th May 1830, a 13-mile section of the Baltimore & Ohio Railroad opened, with horse traction for regular passenger and freight traffic, the first public railway in the USA.

The **first American regular steam railway,** the South Carolina Railroad, opens on 15th January 1831, with the American locomotive *Best Friend of Charleston.* About this period, four English locomotives are used for some of the early American railways: *Delaware* and *Hudson* built in Stourbridge, and *America* and *John Bull* built by the Stephensons.

3–5–1830 The Canterbury & Whitstable Railway is formally opened, using cable traction, and on part of the line Stephenson's locomotive *Invicta* (still preserved in Canterbury). Public traffic was carried the next day.

15–9–1830 The Liverpool & Manchester Railway is formally opened, to become the first public railway specifically to carry passengers and goods in vehicles hauled by steam locomotives. The company was formed on 5th May 1826. Following the pioneer work of the Stockton & Darlington, this railway firmly establishes the new era in transport.

–7–1831 The first section of the Edinburgh

Opening of the Glasgow & Garnkirk Railway, the first section between Garnkirk and Coatbridge being completed in 1831. (*Photo: Victoria & Albert Museum*)

& Dalkeith Railway is opened, using cable and horse traction.

21–9–1831 The Garnkirk & Coatbridge Railway opens.

16–12–1831 The Dundee & Newtyle Railway opens, first with cable and horse traction, then in September 1833 with steam locomotives.

17–7–1832 The Leicester & Swannington Railway opens, to become the oldest part of the Midland Railway. A level-crossing accident on the line on 4th May 1833 results in the locomotive *Samson* being fitted with the first steam "trumpet".

4–7–1834 The Bodmin & Wadebridge Railway opens, and is acquired by the London & South Western Railway in 1847.

22–9–1834 The Leeds & Selby Railway opens carrying passengers, and goods on 15th December.

17–12–1834 The Dublin to Kingstown railway opens, the **first railway in Ireland.** It is built in the 4 ft. 8½ in. gauge, but in 1857 is converted to 5 ft. 3 in., the standard Irish gauge.

1835 Joseph Locke designs and develops a new type of rail as an improvement on rails then in use. Its additional strength allows the track to carry larger and heavier locomotives, carriages and wagons at faster speeds. The rail was "double-headed", the bottom part in cross-section having similar dimensions to the top part. Locke's rail formed the basis of the bull-head rail which, with appropriate alterations, remained in use for well over a century.

9–3–1835 The Newcastle & Carlisle Railway opens between Blaydon and Hexham and is opened throughout on 21st May 1839.

5–5–1835 The **first Belgian steam railway** opens between Brussels and Malines using two Stephenson locomotives, the *Stephenson* and *La Fléche* (The Arrow). The line is built and operated by the Belgian Government, as part of a planned State railway, the first in the world to do so.

7–12–1835 The **first German steam railway,** the Ludwigsbahn, opens between Nuremburg and Fürth, using a Robert Stephenson locomotive *Der Adler* (The Eagle).

8–2–1836 The first public railway in London opens from Spa Road to Deptford on the London & Greenwich Railway. The line is extended to London Bridge on 14th December and to Greenwich on 24th December 1838. Until 1901, trains ran on the right-hand track.

20–4–1836 The world's first narrow-gauge railway, the Ffestiniog, opens, using a 1 ft. 11½ in. gauge to carry slate traffic. Steam traction is used in 1863, and passenger traffic began officially on 6th January 1865.

21–7–1836 **Canada's first steam railway opens,** the Champlain & St. Lawrence Railroad, between Laprairie and St. John, using the Stephenson locomotive *Dorchester*.

9–10–1836 Russia's first public railway opens, the Petersburg & Pavlovsk Railway, using horse power, on a 6 ft. gauge. In 1837, steam locomotives were supplied by Robert Stephenson and Timothy Hackworth, when steam haulage was introduced. Later, the 5 ft. gauge is established as the standard for Russian railways.

3–4–1837 The Paisley & Renfrew Railway opens.

4–7–1837 The Grand Junction Railway opens throughout, to become the first British trunk railway and connects Birmingham with Warrington. Driver James Middleton takes the first train into the new Crewe station where Captain Winby is station master.

20–7–1837 The London & Birmingham Railway opens from Euston to Boxmoor; then to Tring on 16th October, to Denbigh Hall and south from Birmingham to Rugby on 9th April 1838. It is completed throughout on 17th September. Because of a heavy gradient rising from Euston to Camden at about 1 in 70, cable traction was at first used on that section.

6–1–1838 The **first steam railway to run entirely in modern Austria** is opened from Vienna to Florisdorf and Deutch Wagram.

21–5–1838 The London & Southampton Railway opens from Nine Elms in South London to Woking and is extended to Winchfield on 24th September; Winchfield to Basingstoke and Southampton to Winchester on 10th June 1839, and completed throughout on 11th May 1840. A branch line is opened to

Ireland's first line, the Dublin & Kingstown (now Dun Laoghaire) opened in 1834; a view looking towards Dublin. (Photo: Victoria & Albert Musuem)

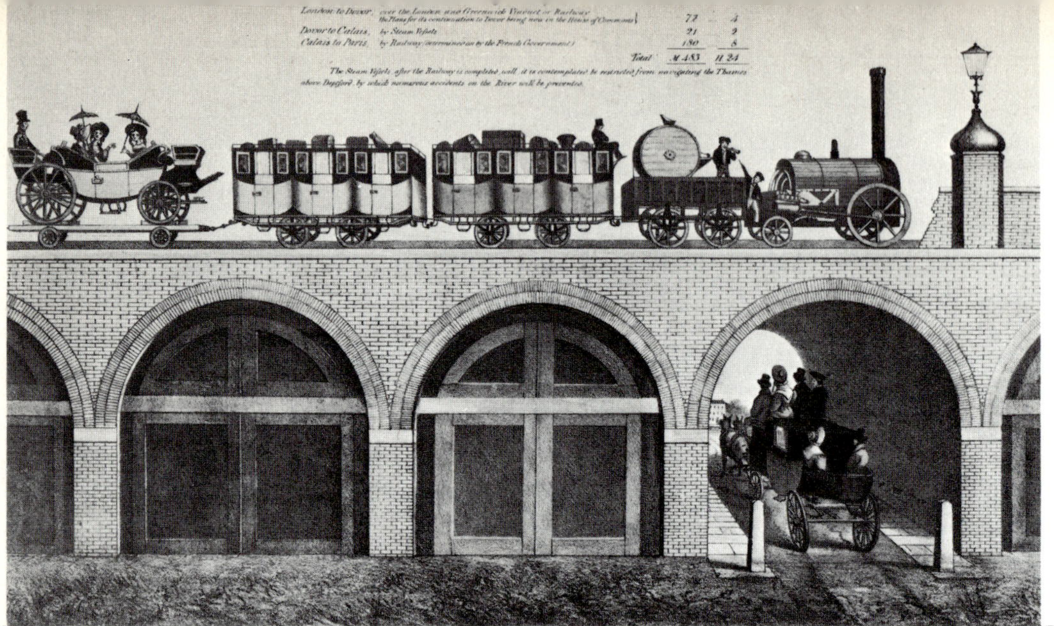

London's first railway, the London & Greenwich Railway, opened in 1836 and seen ultimately as a link between Liverpool and Paris via Dover, the 483 miles expected to be completed in twenty-four hours. The influence of stagecoach travel is still strong. (*Photo: Victoria & Albert Museum*)

Gosport on 7th February 1842, and consequently the name is changed to London & South Western.

4–6–1838 The Great Western Railway is opened from Paddington to Maidenhead via Slough (near Windsor) and is extended to Twyford on 1st July 1839 and to Reading on 30th March 1840. The section between Bristol and Bath is opened on 31st August and London to Bristol completed throughout on 30th June 1841, using Brunel's wide gauge of 7 ft. The company's Act of incorporation had been passed on 31st August 1835.

6–10–1838 The Dundee & Arbroath Railway opens, with a gauge of 5 ft. 6 in.

31–10–1838 The Sheffield & Rotherham Railway opens.

3–1–1839 The Arbroath & Forfar Railway opens, with a gauge of 5 ft. 6 in.

4–6–1839 The first section of the Midland Counties Railway opens from Derby to Nottingham, then to Leicester on 4th May 1840 and to Rugby on 30th June.

5–6–1839 The London & Croydon Railway opens.

18–6–1839 The first section of the Eastern Counties Railway opens between Devonshire Street and Romford, using a gauge of 5 ft., converted five years later to 4 ft. 8½ in. In 1840, the company built the first smoking saloons. Smoking on trains and railway property was usually forbidden.

5–8–1839 The Birmingham & Derby Junction Railway opens.

1839 The first railway hotel is opened at Euston station by the London & Birmingham Railway.

12–8–1839 The Ulster Railway opens between Belfast and Lisburn, and is completed to Armagh (later the scene of a serious disaster). It is originally in a gauge of 6 ft. 2 in., but is converted to the standard Irish gauge of 5 ft. 3 in. in 1847.

24–9–1839 The **first steam railway in the Netherlands** opens between Amsterdam and Haarlem.

4–10–1839 The **first steam railway in Italy** opens between Naples and Portici, five miles long. Italy later faces a shortage of coal and consequently becomes one of the first countries to electrify its main lines, starting in 1901.

10–10–1839 The "Bradshaw" railway timetable is published. (The last issue appeared on 10th March 1961.)

12–5–1840 The first section of the London & Brighton Railway opens between Brighton and Shoreham. It is opened from Norwood, a junction with the Croydon Railway, to Haywards Heath on 12th July 1841 and completed throughout to Brighton on 21st September.

4–6–1840 The Manchester & Birmingham Railway opens as far south as Stockport and completed to Crewe on 10th August 1842.

24–6–1840 The Birmingham & Gloucester Railway opens between Cheltenham and Bromsgrove, and throughout on 17th December. The Lickey Incline near Bromsgrove, with a gradient of about 1 in 38 for over two miles remained as one of the most severe gradients on any main line in Britain.

30–6–1840 Two new railways are opened, the North Midland and the York & North Midland, both connected at Normanton.

6–1840 An atmospheric system of traction, patented by Clegg and Samuda, is tried out at Wormwood Scrubs in London. The idea had been considered many years earlier, and was eventually given trials on the Croydon, Dublin & Kingstown, and South Devon lines, but was finally abandoned as unsatisfactory.

6–7–1840 The London & Blackwall Railway opens in a gauge of about 5 ft. and using cable haulage. George Stephenson and G. P. Bidder were the engineers. The 3½-mile line connects the City with West India Docks. "Slip" carriages are used, the rear one being disconnected to stop at an intermediate station while the remainder continue running. Electric telegraphy, supplied by Cooke & Wheatstone, is introduced, the instruments being preserved in the Science Museum in London. Steam locomotives take over *c.* 1849.

12–8–1840 The Glasgow, Paisley, Kilmarnock

Euston station, opened by the London & Birmingham Railway in 1837. For some years third class passengers on the new railways travelled in open wagons without seats. (*Photo: Victoria & Albert Museum*)

& Ayr Railway is completed.

24–8–1840 About 2,400 passengers are carried on a single excursion train run by the Midland Counties Railway.

4–1–1841 The Great North of England Railway opens between York and Darlington carrying mineral traffic, and passengers from 30th March.

1–3–1841 The Manchester & Leeds Railway opens to Normanton. It is amalgamated with other railways in 1847 to form the Lancashire & Yorkshire Railway.

5–7–1841 Thomas Cook, then aged 33, runs his first railway excursion train of open wagons from Leicester to Loughborough. Helped by his son, Cook develops the excursion business eventually to become a worldwide travel organisation.

14–6–1841 The Bristol & Exeter Railway opens to Bridgwater and is completed to Exeter on 1st May 1844.

1841 A block signalling system, using Cooke & Wheatstone's electric telegraph, comes into use at Clay Cross tunnel which is just over one mile long, on the North Midland Railway between Derby and Chesterfield. An adapted "block telegraph" system later becomes the standard on all railways.

1841 Fixed semaphore arm signals are used for the first time on railways at New Cross just outside London.

1841 Gravity-fed sanding gear for locomotives is developed by Robert Stephenson to overcome wheel slip on wet or greasy rails.

2–1–1842 The Railway Clearing House (RCH) begins its work of calculating proportions of fares and charges for journeys made over two or more railways in the scheme. The RCH gradually develops the scope of its work concerning the common interests of the many railways.

21–2–1842 The Edinburgh & Glasgow Railway opens between Edinburgh (Haymarket) and Glasgow (Queen Street) stations.

26–5–1842 The South Eastern Railway opens to Tonbridge via Redhill. It is extended to Headcorn in August, Ashford on 1st December, Folkestone on 28th June 1843, and completed to Dover on 7th February 1844.

13–6–1842 Queen Victoria, aged 23, accompanied by Prince Albert, makes her first railway journey from Slough, near Windsor, to Paddington.

2–1–1843 Swindon locomotive works open, the first important engine depot and repair shop of the Great Western Railway.

29–3–1843 The Eastern Counties Railway opens to Colchester.

1843 The Crewe works opens by the Grand Junction Railway and the local village grows steadily into a large town.

1843 Weights are added to the inside rims of locomotive driving wheels to balance the reciprocating movements, a mathematically imperfect but practical technique that becomes common practice. William Fernyhough, locomotive superintendent, Eastern Counties Railway from 1843, is the engineer credited with this innovation.

29–4–1844 Official opening of public service using atmospheric traction on the Dalkey extension of the Dublin & Kingstown Railway; the system was abandoned on 12th April 1854.

1–5–1844 The Yarmouth & Norwich Railway is opened.

10–5–1844 The Midland Railway is formed by the "Railway King", George Hudson, who amalgamated three companies: the North Midland, Midland Counties, and Birmingham & Derby Junction railways, to become the first important amalgamation and one of the most powerful railways of the time.

24–5–1844 The Newcastle & Darlington Junction Railway opens.

26–5–1844 The Dublin & Drogheda Railway opens.

12–6–1844 The Great Western Railway is extended from Didcot to Oxford.

15–6–1844 The **first steam railway in Switzerland** is opened between Basle and St. Louis (St. Ludwig). The Swiss use a German-built locomotive

The Shoreham Branch opens in 1840 as the first section of the London & Brighton Railway. This drawing was "respectfully dedicated to the Shareholders, by their Obedient Servant, W. H. Mason". (Photo: Victoria & Albert Museum)

similar in design to Stephenson's.

6–7–1844 The Bristol & Gloucester Railway opens using Brunel's wide gauge of 7 ft. On 3rd August 1846, the railway is taken over by the Midland Railway and later converted to the standard gauge.

9–8–1844 Gladstone's Railways Act is passed, making it compulsory for all railways to provide third class carriages on every line for at least one train each way each weekday at a penny a mile, and gives the Government authority, in specific circumstances, to purchase any railway.

1844 Following the pattern of other leading railways, the Eastern Counties Railway is converted from 5 ft. gauge to standard, keeping trains on the move temporarily by single-line working.

10–2–1845 The Thames & Medway Canal Company opens seven miles of railway between Gravesend and Rochester (Strood) which is later absorbed in the South Eastern Railway.

10–2–1845 The Maryport & Carlisle Railway opens the Wigton–Aspatria section, to complete the Company's main line of $27\frac{1}{2}$ miles.

5–5–1845 The London & South Western Railway opens the six-mile section between Woking and Guildford. The original plan included the use of wooden rails, and vehicle guide wheels designed by William Prosser. In the event normal practice was used and Prosser compensated with £20,000.

8–5–1845 The Railway Clauses Consolidation Act is passed to handle the mass of accumulated railway legislature, its stated objective being "to consolidate into one Act certain provisions usually inserted in Acts authorising the making of railways."

12–5–1845 The Great Western Railway opens the Gloucester–Kemble Junction line, with a tunnel 1,855 yards long cut through the Cotswold hills.

2–6–1845 The London & Birmingham Railway opens a 47-mile section of single line branching off from Blisworth to Peterborough. It halves the journey time taken by coach for the 77-mile road route.

8–7–1845 The York & North Midland Railway opens the York to Scarborough and Pickering section of 48½ miles of mostly single line. The section is built in twelve months at a cost of under £6,000 a mile.

30–7–1845 The Eastern Counties Railway open the 56-mile section between Bishop's Stortford and Brandon. Authority had been obtained for the 10 miles from Bishop's Stortford to Newport in July 1843, and for the remaining 46 miles in July 1844; this is an example of the shorter time now being taken from Parliamentary sanction to completion of new lines.

6–8–1845 The Gauge Commission begins its investigation into the problem of differing rail gauges. A historic decision is made the following year in favour of Stephenson's gauge of 4 ft. 8½ in. which is adopted as the standard British gauge; an exception is made for the Great Western Railway and associated lines which later are faced with the costly and disruptive conversion from the 7 ft. gauge.

20–9–1845 The South Eastern Railway opens a 4-mile section between Tonbridge and Tunbridge Wells; work began before the Parliamentary Act was passed, to meet the desires of property owners concerned with this short route.

24–11–1845 The London & Brighton Railway opens the 5-mile section between Shoreham and Worthing.

23–12–1845 The Sheffield, Ashton & Manchester Railway opens 4 miles between Woodhead and Dunford Bridge which includes the Woodhead Tunnel of 3 miles 13 yd., then the longest railway tunnel in the British Isles. This completes the second route through the Pennine Range.

19–1–1846 Atmospheric traction is used for regular traffic on the London & Croydon Railway between Croydon and Forest Hill. As an experiment, passengers had been carried free of charge from 27th October 1845. The system was abandoned on 4th May 1847.

6–2–1846 The South Eastern Railway opens the 14-mile Ashford–Canterbury line.

16–3–1846 The London & Brighton Railway opens the 7½-mile Worthing and Littlehampton (Lyminster) line. The L & B is extended to Chichester on 8th June.

13–4–1846 The South Eastern Railway opens the 16-mile Canterbury–Ramsgate line.

30–5–1846 The South Devon Railway of 15 miles opens between Exeter and Teignmouth.

8–6–1846 The London & Brighton Railway opens the 8-mile Brighton–Lewes line.

18–6–1846 The North British Railway formally opens between Edinburgh and Berwick a few miles south of the English border, a distance of 57½ miles.

22–6–1846 The Caledonian Railway is formed, and in 1848 opens its first lines from Glasgow to Carlisle via Carstairs and Lockerbie, and a fork from Carstairs to Edinburgh.

27–6–1846 The London & Brighton Railway opens the Lewes–Bulverhythe (St. Leonards) line of 24½ miles.

1–7–1846 The Leeds & Bradford Railway opens.

15–7–1846 The **first steam railway in Hungary** opens between Pest and Vacz, a distance of 20½ miles.

16–7–1846 The London & North Western Railway is formed, the second important amalgamation, joining the London & Birmingham, Manchester & Birmingham, and Grand Junction Railways. The Grand Junction had previously absorbed Stephenson's historic line, the Liverpool & Manchester Railway. The L & NWR later advertised itself as the "Premier Line".

20–7–1846 The Furness Railway opens between Barrow-in-Furness and Dalton and Kirby.

27–7–1846 The London, Brighton & South Coast Railway is formed by the amalgamation of the London & Brighton and the London & Croydon Railways.

4–8–1846 The Midland Railway opens a new line between Nottingham and

Lincoln, and on 2nd September the Syston–Melton Mowbray line.

22–9–1846 The Lancaster & Carlisle Railway opens to Kendal (Oxenholme) and is completed to Carlisle on 17th December.

2–10–1846 The Midland Railway opens the Peterborough–Stamford line.

1–12–1846 The South Eastern Railway opens the 4-mile line between Ramsgate and Margate (Sands).

30–12–1846 The South Devon Railway is extended for 5 miles between Teignmouth and Newton Abbot.

1846 The South Eastern Railway introduces part-interlocking for signals to aid safety at Bricklayers Arms.

1846 The "Railway Mania" year, when 272 Acts of Parliament were passed for new railways, many of which failed to reach beyond the documentation stage.

10–5–1847 The London, Brighton & South Coast Railway opens the West Croydon–Epsom line of 8 miles, the first to cope with the thousands of people who travel to Epsom for the Derby Day races.

1–6–1847 The London & South Western Railway opens between Southampton and Dorchester.

26–6–1847 The London & North Western Railway opens the Trent Valley line between Rugby and Stafford carrying goods, and passengers from 1st December.

1–7–1847 The Newcastle & Berwick Railway is completed to Tweedmouth, opening up more prospects for services through to Scotland.

14–8–1847 Atmospheric traction begins on a short section of 1 mile 646 yd. on the Paris–St. Germain Railway, but on 2nd July 1860 gives way to steam.

10–9–1847 The Caledonian Railway opens from Carlisle to Beattock and is extended to Glasgow and Edinburgh on 15th February 1848 to form an important part of the West Coast Route.

13–9–1847 Atmospheric traction is introduced by the South Devon Railway between Exeter and Teignmouth, and extended to Newton Abbot on 10th January 1848. This Brunel venture lost much money and atmospheric trains were withdrawn on 10th September. Despite the appeal of running trains by air pressure and without locomotives, the technical disadvantages were overwhelming.

1–3–1848 The Great Northern Railway opens its first section between Grimsby and Louth, and on 17th October the 59 miles between Lincoln and Peterborough. The Doncaster–Retford line of 17 miles is added on 4th September 1849.

11–4–1848 The Northern Counties Railway opens, 33½ miles between Belfast and Ballymena.

1–5–1848 The Chester & Holyhead Railway opens between Chester (Saltney Juntion) and Bangor, 58 miles. The line is completed to Holyhead on 18th March 1850 by the opening of Robert Stephenson's Britannia Bridge which is completely enclosed and spans the Menai Straits – the "Royal Mail Route to Holyhead". The Bridge was the first to be designed in which wrought iron was used for spans of 460 ft. (The bridge timber lining was set alight by youths on the night of 23rd May 1970 causing serious damage and putting it out of action for well over a year.)

5–5–1848 The South Devon Railway is extended to Plymouth.

9–5–1848 The Waterford & Limerick Railway opens for 25½ miles between Limerick and Tipperary.

22–5–1848 The Scottish Central Railway is opened between Perth and Stirling, a distance of 33 miles, a route which later will link Glasgow and Edinburgh with Inverness.

12–6–1848 The line between Morecambe and Lancaster opens, and after 1852 is operated by the Midland Railway.

11–7–1848 The London & South Western Railway is extended from its old London terminus at Nine Elms to the more central station at Waterloo.

2–8–1848 The Scottish Midland Junction Railway is opened between Perth and Forfar.

2–8–1848 The Belfast & County Down Railway opens its first section between Belfast and Holywood, and the Comber–Newtonards branch is opened on 6th May 1850.

5–9–1848 The Wilts, Somerset & Weymouth Railway opens between Thingley Junction and Westbury, a distance of 14 miles, and extended to Weymouth on 20th January 1857.

14–10–1848 The Shrewsbury & Chester Railway via Wrexham is completed, the first section having opened on 4th November 1846.

28–10–1848 The **first steam railway in Spain** opens between Barcelona and Mataro, a distance of 17 miles, near the Mediterranean coast. Robert Stephenson had visited the country three years earlier for railway consultations. Despite Stephenson's advice, Spain decided on a gauge of 5 ft. 6 in., a non-standard European gauge that remains inconveniently to this day.

1–2–1849 The Edinburgh & Hawick Railway opens to Galashiels for goods traffic. Passenger business is added on 19th February and the line completed in stages to Hawick by 29th October.

4–6–1849 The Ambergate–Rowsley line opens and is worked by the Midland Railway. The projected Midland line to Manchester with tunnels and sharp curves through the Derbyshire hills is not completed until 1867.

1–8–1849 The Midland Railway opens the Leicester–Burton line.

15–8–1849 The first passenger train crosses the High Level Bridge over the River Tyne at Newcastle and the bridge is visited on 28th September by Queen Victoria, then aged 30. The previous year (20–8–1848) a temporary bridge was opened. On 4th February 1850, the lower deck is opened as a roadway. In 1950, the bridge was scheduled for preservation as an Ancient Monument.

20–8–1849 The Manchester, South Junction and Altrincham Railway opens.

1–11–1849 Buchanan Street station in Glasgow opens for all traffic.

1–4–1850 A through route from London to Aberdeen via Perth is established with the completion of the Aberdeen Railway (Scottish North Eastern).

1–5–1850 The Buckinghamshire Railway opens, 31 miles from Bletchley to Banbury via Verney Junction, and the branch line to Oxford, the town's second station, on 20th May 1851.

18–6–1850 The South Wales Railway opens, from Chepstow to Swansea, 75 miles, with a gauge of 7 ft. that is already doomed. Grange Court to Chepstow (East), 19 miles, is opened on 19th September 1851.

7–8–1850 The Great Northern Railway opens between Werrington Junction near Peterborough to Maiden Lane near King's Cross, 79 miles, completing the East Coast route.

29–8–1850 The Royal Border Bridge across Tweedmouth is formally opened for all traffic, although goods had been conveyed across it from 20th July. It was built by the York, Newcastle & Berwick Railway and so completed the Midlands and East Coast Route to Edinburgh.

2–9–1850 The Great Western Railway opens the 24-mile Oxford–Banbury line.

26–9–1850 The North London Railway opens its first section of 5 miles between Islington and Bow.

28–10–1850 The Glasgow & South Western Railway is formed by amalgamating the Dumfries & Carlisle and the Ayrshire Railways, and at the same time completes the line from Gretna to Glasgow via Cumnock.

1850 The compounding of locomotive cylinders for the more effective use of steam is invented by J. Nicholson and tried on the Eastern Counties Railway.

13–2–1851 The South Eastern Railway opens the 28-mile line between Ashford and St. Leonards, a stretch known as the Bopeep line. The Tunbridge Wells–Robertsbridge line of 16 miles is opened on 1st September 1851, extended 16 miles to Battle on 1st January 1852, and 5 miles to

St. Leonards on 1st February.

1–8–1851 The Midland Great Western Railway is completed between Dublin and Galway.

8–12–1851 The Cork, Bandon & South Coast Railway is completed between Cork and Bandon. The Bandon–Ballinhassig section had been operating since 1st August 1849.

11–3–1852 The West Cornwall Railway opens for 7 miles between Penzance and Hayle. The Redruth–Truro section is opened on 25th August with 4 ft. 8½ in. gauge.

21–4–1852 The Shrewsbury & Hereford Railway opens between Shrewsbury and Ludlow, 27 miles.

15–7–1852 The Great Northern Railway is extended 59 miles from Werrington Junction, Peterborough, to Retford for goods trains, and on 1st August for passengers. At the London end, the line is extended for 1 mile from the temporary terminus at Maiden Lane to King's Cross, to become one of the leading main line stations in the Metropolis.

1–10–1852 The Great Western Railway opens the Birmingham (Snow Hill)–Banbury line of 42 miles in mixed gauge, to accommodate 7 ft. and 4 ft. 8½ in. gauge trains. The line is extended to Wolverhampton on 14th November 1854.

11–10–1852 The South Wales Railway is extended from Landore to Carmarthen Junction for 30 miles, and is opened to Haverfordwest (7 ft. gauge) on 16th January 1854.

1–11–1852 A "standard time" is introduced on the Great Western Railway, made possible by the erection of telegraph wires on their main routes. Until Greenwich Mean Time came into force in 1880, "local" times, taken mainly from local sundials, were used by the various railway companies, causing considerable confusion at stations where the lines of one company connected with another.

1852 The smokebox superheater for improved steam power is introduced by James Edward McConnell on London & North Western Railway locomotives.

1853 The London & North Western Railway introduce "staff" working on single lines as a safety device.

18–4–1853 The **first steam railway opens in India,** the Great Indian Peninsula Railway, between Bombay and Thana.

4–6–1853 The Oxford, Worcester & Wolverhampton Railway opens from Oxford to Evesham, and is completed to Bushbury Junction, Wolverhampton, in October 1854.

16–1–1854 A new station, the second, is opened at Paddington, the main structure of which still remains.

30–4–1854 The **first railway in Brazil** opens.

18–5–1854 The first public railway to carry passengers and goods opens in

Opening of the West Cornwall Railway at Penzance in 1852. (*Photo: W.P.L.*)

Australia, and uses horse traction: the Port Elliot & Goolwa Railway (South Australia). The **first Australian steam-operated line** is the Flinders Street–Melbourne Railway, opened on 12th September 1854. As the Australian railways develop, three main rail gauges are used: 3 ft. 6 in., 4 ft. 8½ in., and 5 ft. 3 in.

31–7–1854 The North Eastern Railway is formed by amalgamation, the main constituents being the York & North Midland, the Leeds Northern, and the York, Newcastle & Berwick Railways. The pioneering Stockton & Darlington Railway was absorbed in the NER on 1st July 1863.

1–9–1854 The **first railway opens in Norway** between Oslo (then named Christiania) and Eidsvoll, 42 miles.

12–9–1854 The Great North of Scotland Railway opens its first section between Kittybrewster and Huntly, and is extended to Keith in 1856.

1855 The Railway Clearing House, an inter-railway committee, begins to formulate the standardisation of wagons, particularly of underframes and running gear. This facilities the many amalgamations which later take place. Many other standard practices are encouraged.

1–2–1855 The world's first special postal train runs between London (Paddington) and Bristol. Passengers were not allowed until June 1869 when one first-class carriage was added.

1–6–1855 The Hereford, Ross & Gloucester Railway opens, with 7 ft. gauge.

5–11–1855 The Inverness & Nairn Railway opens; it is renamed the Inverness & Aberdeen Junction Railway and extended to Keith on 18th August 1858.

5–3–1856 The **first railway in Sweden** is opened between Nora and Ervalla; the first sections of the Swedish State Railways are opened – Gothenburg to Jonsered, and Malmö to Lund – on 1st December in the same year.

7–4–1856 The Perth & Dunkeld Railway opens.

30–6–1856 The Great Western Railway opens the Warminster–Salisbury line, with 7 ft. gauge, and on 1st September opens the Frome–Yeovil line.

28–10–1856 The **first railway in Portugal** opens between Lisbon and Carregado, 23 miles.

1856 The interlocking of signals and points is patented by John Saxby, a mechanical device to prevent a signal being turned to "clear" until the points concerned are in the correct position. The system becomes widely adopted as an aid to safety.

1–5–1857 The London & South Western Railway opens the Andover–Salisbury line.

7–5–1857 The Leicester–Hitchin Railway opens, enabling Midland Railway trains to reach London on GNR lines from Hitchin.

30–8–1857 The **first railway in Argentina** opens from Parque to Floresta, using the the 5 ft. 6 in. gauge which becomes the standard for main lines. E. B. Wilson & Co. of Leeds had built the first locomotive the previous year.

1857 The first steel rail is made by Robert Forester Mushet, a big improvement on iron rails. Early in the year, they are laid experimentally at Derby Midland station on a heavily used line and remain in service until June 1873. Their worth is proved and they come into general use. The L & NWR laid them for the first time at Chalk Farm, just north of Euston station.

25–1–1858 The East Kent Railway opens between Chatham and Faversham, the company later renamed the London, Chatham & Dover Railway.

3–5–1859 The Royal Albert Bridge, with a single line of railway crossing the River Tamar at Saltash on the Devon–Cornwall border, is officially opened at a public ceremony by Queen Victoria's Consort, Prince Albert. The bridge, considered to be Brunel's finest, was completed on

11th April and took about 12 years to build. It stands on the Exeter–Penzance main line.

4–5–1859 The Cornwall Railway is opened to Truro, to make through rail connection between London and Penzance.

1–6–1859 The main parts of the East Suffolk Railway open, to connect Ipswich with Yarmouth and Lowestoft.

3–8–1859 The Potteries, Biddulph & Congleton Railway opens, later part of the North Staffordshire Railway with headquarters at Stoke-on-Trent, the centre of the Potteries.

31–8–1859 The Cambrian Railways open the first section for passengers between Llandiloes and Newtown, carrying goods from 30th April.

1–9–1859 George Mortimer Pullman's first sleeping car begins service between Bloomington and Chicago. It was rebuilt from a coach of the Chicago & Alton Railroad. Pullman was then aged 28.

1–6–1860 The Salisbury & Yeovil Railway is completed to Yeovil.

26–6–1860 The **first railway in South Africa** opens from Durban to The Point (Natal), the Natal Railway. The 4 ft. 8½ in. gauge is used, but a few years later it is decided to build new railways to a standard 3 ft. 6 in. because of the costs in a difficult terrain. The narrow gauge remained, most of the network being built in single line.

9–7–1860 The East Kent Railway is extended from Faversham to Canterbury.

18–7–1860 The London & South Western Railway is extended to Exeter.

7–11–1860 The Dumfries & Castle Douglas Railway opens.

1860 Water pick-up apparatus is installed on the London & North Western Railway, by which a scoop lowered from the tender scoops water while the train is running at speed. It was patented by John Ramsbottom for the Company.

12–3–1861 The Portpatrick & Wigtownshire Joint Railway opens to Stranraer and is extended to Portpatrick in 1862.

1862 The Great Western Railway publishes a staff magazine, reputed to be the first true "house journal" in Britain and the first British railway staff publication. It ceases after two years and is restarted in 1888. Along with others, it is absorbed in the *British Railways Magazine* following railway nationalisation in 1948. The publication is renamed and restyled as a staff newspaper *Rail News* in July 1963 during the Beeching regime.

11–6–1862 The Inverness & Ross-shire Railway opens to Dingwall and on 1st October 1864 is extended to Bonar Bridge.

16–6–1862 The first line in the Isle of Wight opens, the Cowes & Newport Railway of 4½ miles. New lines are opened progressively: to Shanklin 23–8–1864, to Ventnor 10–9–1866, Sandown to Newport 6–10–1875, connection from Ryde line to Newport 20–12–1875, Ryde Pierhead to Ryde St. John's Road 12–7–1880, Brading to Bembridge 27–5–1882, Freshwater–Yarmouth–Newport for goods only 10–9–1888 and passengers 20–7–1889, Merston to Ventnor 1–6–1900 (part opened 20–7–1897). All lines single except for 2¾ miles between Ryde and Smallbrook Junction. Length eventually totals 45¼ route miles operated by five rival railway companies.

1–7–1862 The Shrewsbury & Hereford Railway comes under joint ownership of the GWR and the L & NWR.

7–8–1862 The Great Eastern Railway is formed by the amalgamation of the East Anglian, Eastern Counties, Newmarket, Eastern Union, and Norfolk Railways; Liverpool Street station in London opens on 2nd February 1874, to become its principal terminus.

10–1–1863 The world's first underground railway opens between Bishop's Road near Paddington and Farringdon Street in the City, the first section of the Metropolitan Railway. The track is in mixed gauge, and the carriages, hauled by steam locomotives, are lighted by gas from

Shareholders' inspection trip on the Metropolitan Railway before the official opening of the first "underground railway" in 1863. The extra rail was laid to take both broad and standard gauge trains. (*Photo: London Transport*)

the start. The line is extended to Moorgate on 23rd December 1865.

2–3–1863 The West London Extension Railway is opened with a mixed gauge, and the first scissors crossing is laid at Addison Road station in Kensington.

1–7–1863 The Stockton & Darlington Railway is taken over by the NER.

9–9–1863 The Inverness & Perth Junction Railway opens. This line joins the Inverness & Aberdeen Junction and the Perth & Dunkeld Railways to form the Highland Railway on 29th June 1865. Aberdeen joint station opens on 4th November 1867, and is rebuilt in May 1916.

10–10–1863 The first section of the Central Wales Railway opens.

1–12–1863 The **first steam-operated railway opens in New Zealand** between Christchurch and Ferrymead, in 5 ft. 3 in. gauge.

31–12–1863 The Londonderry & Lough Swilly Railway opens.

11–1–1864 The South Eastern Railway is extended to Charing Cross, the latter to become a main London terminus.

2–9–1864 The Neath & Brecon Railway opens.

2–1–1865 The Cockermouth, Keswick & Penrith Railway opens.

1–11–1865 The North London Railway opens the line between Dalston Junction and Broad Street.

1–3–1866 The Kettering, Thrapston & Huntingdon Railway opens, and is taken over by the Midland Railway on 6th August 1897.

1–9–1866 Cannon Street station and Hawkshaw's bridge across the River Thames open, the "city terminus" of the SER.

1867 The Great Eastern Railway is in financial trouble and creditors seize the company's locomotives.

1867 The first recorded dining-car service in North America on scheduled trains runs on the Great Western Railway of Canada, a line taken over later by the Canadian National Railways.

1–3–1867 The West Cornwall Railway is converted to 7 ft. gauge and allows through passenger services to run between Paddington and Penzance.

1–5–1868 The SER completes its main line to Tonbridge via Sevenoaks.

1–10–1868 St. Pancras station and the main line to Bedford is opened by the Midland Railway to gain its first London terminus. The huge hotel frontage with its ornate Gothic style dwarfs King's Cross station which is across the road.

1–3–1869 The broad gauge outer rails of the mixed-gauge Metropolitan are removed, leaving the standard 4 ft. 8½ in. track.

–4–1869 The L & NWR builds the first railway flyover at Birdswood Junction.

10–5–1869 The first USA trans-continental route is completed when two rival railroads, striving to reach the furthest, meet at Promontory in Utah.

8–7–1869 The Caledonian Railway opens its Glasgow–Edinburgh line via Midcalder, and Edinburgh Prince's Street station on 2nd May 1870.

19–10–1869 The **first railway in Romania** opens between Bucharest and Giurgiu.

23–12–1869 The Glasgow & South Western Railway opens the Greenock and Ayrshire line and Prince's Pier at Greenock.

1–2–1870 The Midland Railway opens a main line between Chesterfield and Sheffield.

14–3–1870 The London & South Western Railway is extended to Bournemouth via Ringwood, a direct line being opened on 5th March 1888.

2–8–1870 The world's first tube railway, but with cable traction, the Tower Subway in London, formally opens, following experimental working from April. Cable operation was soon abandoned, and the tube was used as a foot subway from 24th December until June 1894.

10–8–1870 The Dingwall & Skye Railway opens to Strome Ferry, but the remaining few miles to the Kyle of Lochalsh are not completed until 2nd November 1897.

25–5–1871 The Bank Holidays Act is passed granting four days a year, with the addition of New Year's Day for Scotland. (Hogmanay is celebrated on 31st December.) Much new day excursion business accrues to the railways.

29–6–1871 Trade Unions are made "legal" by the Trade Union Act and railwaymen continue their agitation for a nine-hour working day.

1–4–1872 The Midland Railway begins to carry third class passengers by all trains, an uncommon arrangement which upsets their rivals. During the year, the GER follows suit. The 1844 Act had required only one train a day to have third class compartments.

12–6–1872 The **first railway in Japan opens,** the Yokohama–Shinagawa line. The route is completed to Tokyo (then known as Yedo or Jeddo) on 14th October. Various gauges were introduced on Japanese railways, a large proportion of which were 3 ft. 6 in.

2–4–1873 The first sleeping car for first class passengers is introduced in Britain by the North British Railways for regular services on the East Coast route, from Glasgow and Edinburgh to London (King's Cross), to run on alternate nights in each direction. On 31st July, the Great Northern Railway introduces a sleeping car for this route, to give a sleeper service in both directions on consecutive nights.

26–6–1873 The Glasgow, Barrhead, and Kilmarnock line opens.

1–7–1873 The Isle of Man Railways open their first section with 3 ft. gauge.

1–6–1874 Pullman cars, luxuriously fitted and running on bogies, are introduced to Britain by the Midland Railway, for use by both first and third class passengers.

20–7–1874 The Ilfracombe Railway opens and is worked by the London & South Western Railway.

20–7–1874 The Somerset & Dorset Railway opens between Bath and Evercreech. From 1st November 1875, it is leased jointly to the London & South Western and the Midland Railways.

28–7–1874 The Sutherland & Caithness Railway completes the Highland Railway system to Wick, and to Thurso, the most northerly railway station in Scotland.

1–1–1875 The Midland Railway abolish second-class passenger accommodation from their trains, and have all their third class seating upholstered. Second class bookings are also withdrawn on the joint Midland and Glasgow & South Western on the Anglo–Scottish services. Their rivals reluctantly have to follow suit.

13–4–1875 Alexandra Docks & Railway opens – Newport and South Wales.

2–8–1875 The Midland Railway opens the Settle and Carlisle line for goods traffic, and on 1st May 1876 for passengers, when Midland trains first run to Glasgow and Edinburgh.

27–9–1875 A railway jubilee is celebrated at Darlington, a great public occasion to mark the opening of the pioneering Stockton & Darlington Railway.

1875 An electrical passenger communication system by Stroudley is fitted on London, Brighton & South Coast Railway trains for emergency use. This is the first major improvement on the communication cord running along the outside of the trains.

21–1–1876 A collision at Abbott's Ripton on the Great Northern Railway, in which 14 passengers are killed, prompts the railway to discontinue the old type of semaphore arm working in a slotted signal post; it is replaced with a centrally balanced arm designed for somersault movement.

20–6–1876 The Cornwall Minerals Railway opens for passenger traffic between Fowey and Newquay.

1–10–1876 The Glasgow & South Western Railway opens the Girvan–Challoch Junction line, and during the month the St. Enoch station in Glasgow.

1–6–1877 The last section of broad gauge railway (7 ft.) ever laid in Britain opens; it is a 4½-mile branch of the West Cornwall Railway and runs from St. Erth on the main Penzance line to St. Ives.

15–8–1877 The North Wales Narrow Gauge Railway opens.

1–10–1877 The London & North Western Railway opens the North Wall extension line in Dublin.

–12–1877 Sleeping cars, first class, come into service on Great Western Railway.

1–6–1878 The longest railway bridge in the world, the Tay Bridge, built by Thomas Bouch, is opened, the ceremonial opening on 31st May. It shortens the journey between Edinburgh and Dundee. On 28th December heavy gales blow part of it down as a train crosses, causing 78 deaths.

31–5–1879 to 30–9–1879 An electric locomotive, by Werner von Siemens, operates successfully on a passenger line in the grounds of the Berlin Trades Exhibition.

1–8–1879 Glasgow Central station is opened by the Caledonian Railway. The station is enlarged in 1906.

1–11–1879 A dining car comes into service on the Great Northern Railway on the London (King's Cross) to Leeds route.

1–6–1880 The Midland Railway opens its alternative route between Nottingham and London (St. Pancras).

1–7–1880 The Callander & Oban Railway is completed, having opened to Killin Junction in 1870 and to Tyndrum in 1873.

2–8–1880 Greenwich Mean Time becomes the "legal" standard in Britain, replacing the widely varied "local times" that impaired inter-railway connections, with the passing of the Statutes (Definition of Time) Act.

–11–1880 The first major electric lighting for a station in Britain is installed in Paddington station, GWR.

12–5–1881 The first public electric railway in the world opens at Lichterfelde near Berlin.

27–7–1881 The Swindon, Marlborough & Andover Railway opens to Marlborough, and on 5th February 1883 is extended to Andover. The line is merged into the Midland & South Western Junction Railway in 1884.

1881 Electric train lighting is introduced experimentally in a Pullman car between London and Brighton on the London, Brighton & South Coast Railway.

1–7–1882 The Swiss Gotthard Railway and tunnel are opened. The tunnel, then the longest railway bore in the world, is 9 miles 562 yd. long.

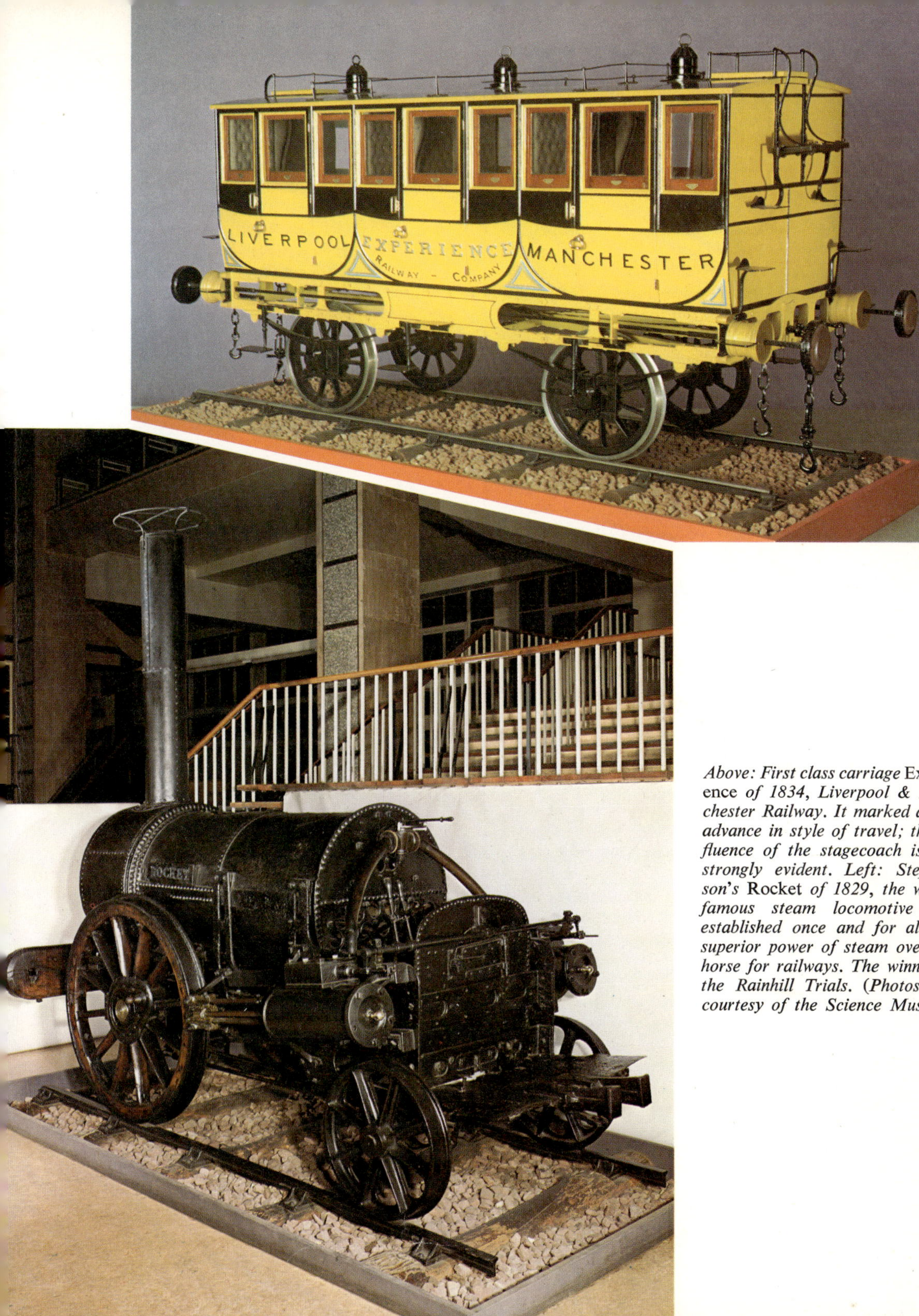

Above: First class carriage Experience *of 1834, Liverpool & Manchester Railway. It marked a new advance in style of travel; the influence of the stagecoach is still strongly evident. Left: Stephenson's* Rocket *of 1829, the world-famous steam locomotive that established once and for all the superior power of steam over the horse for railways. The winner of the Rainhill Trials. (Photos: By courtesy of the Science Museum)*

1-8-1882 The Great Northern Railway completes the Spalding–Lincoln line.

18-8-1882 The Eastern & Midland Railway is formed by amalgamation – Midland & Great Northern Joint Committee on 1st July 1893.

18-8-1882 The Post Office (Parcels) Act is passed concerning the apportionment of revenues for postal packages conveyed by train. The volume had become too large to allow for packages individually to be weighed and charged.

3-8-1883 A pioneer electric railway in Britain opens, the first section of Magnus Volk's Brighton electric railway, a unique resort attraction. It is taken over by the Brighton Corporation on 1st April 1940.

28-9-1883 The first railway in the world to be run by hydro-electric power opens, being formally inaugurated on the Giant's Causeway Railway.

15-9-1884 The **first railway in Serbia opens** between Belgrade and Nish, of 151 miles.

6-10-1884 The Metropolitan and District Railways complete the Inner Circle which connects with the East London Railway and main line stations in London.

1-7-1885 A mail train, without passengers, is inaugurated between London and Aberdeen by the London & North Western and Caledonian Railways.

20-7-1885 The Hull, Barnsley & West Riding Junction Railway opens. It becomes known briefly as the Hull & Barnsley, a name that becomes official in 1905.

7-11-1885 A through line across Canada – the Canadian Pacific Railway transcontinental – is completed, and the last spike driven, by joining the Eastern and Western sections at Craigellachie in British Columbia.

1-2-1886 The Mersey Railway opens.

15-3-1886 The Glasgow City & District Railway – some of it underground – opens and is operated by the North British Railway which takes over the line in 1887.

1-12-1886 The Severn tunnel under the Bristol Channel opens for passenger traffic, shortening the route to South Wales, and taking 14 years to build. It became, and still remains, the longest railway tunnel in Britain at 4 miles 628 yd., and is double track. The first goods train ran through on 9th January.

13-6-1887 The new Tay Bridge, built by W. H. Barlow, is opened.

1-3-1888 A steam-operated Lartigue monorail is opened by the Listowel & Ballybunion Railway in County Kerry.

July–August 1888 The "Race to the North", with vigorous competition between the East and West Coast Routes, results in substantial improvements in the Anglo-Scottish passenger train timings.

12-6-1889 The worst accident to date since records began in 1840 occurs at Armagh in Northern Ireland, when 80 people are killed in a collision. An accumulation of mishaps prompts the British Government to pass a "railway safety" Act two months later.

30-8-1889 The Regulation of Railways Act is passed. It enforces the "block" system (space interval between trains instead of time interval), the interlocking of points and signals to ensure points are safely set before the appropriate signal is turned to "clear", and the provision of automatic brakes on passenger trains. Higher safety standards were set. Several forward-looking railways were already using these techniques, voluntarily.

4-3-1890 The Forth Bridge is publicly opened, shortening the route between Edinburgh and Dundee on a double track. The cantilever bridge is 1 mile 1,006 yd. long.

1-10-1890 Following the lead of the Midland, the Great Western Railway carries third class passengers on all its trains.

18-12-1890 The first electric underground railway in the world is opened by the Prince of Wales (later King Edward VII). The new railway – the City & South London – runs under the

The first electric "tube" trains of 1890 at Stockwell station; the carriages are constructed of wood. An electric locomotive stands on the left. (Photo: London Transport)

River Thames and is between the Monument and Stockwell. It took four years to build.

–12–1891 A record is made when a six-coupled goods locomotive is erected in ten working hours at the Stratford locomotive works in London, Great Eastern Railway.

7–3–1892 The first corridor trains are introduced by the Great Western Railway on the Paddington–Birmingham–Birkenhead services, followed by the London & North Western Railway in July 1893 on a Scottish express from Euston. Corridors are put on other railways from London to the north soon afterwards, and in 1900 run on London & South Western Railway expresses.

20–5–1892 The last wide-gauge trains run on Brunel's 7 ft. track of the Great Western Railway, and the conversion of the remaining lines to Stephenson's 4 ft. 8½ in. gauge is completed by 23rd May. Total conversion over the years had resulted from one of the most costly and heartbreaking disputes of Britain's 19th century railways.

1–9–1892 The Metropolitan Railway is extended to Aylesbury.

1–11–1892 Southampton Docks are taken over by the London & South Western Railway, and become State-owned in 1948.

6–3–1893 The first electric elevated railway in the world opens on a section of the Liverpool Overhead Railway. The railway was closed on 30th December 1956.

6–11–1893 The Midland Railway opens the Dore and Chinley line for goods traffic, and passengers on 1st June 1894. The double line runs through the Dore and Totley tunnel, of 3 miles 950 yd., the next longest tunnel to the Severn.

1–1–1894 The lines of the Manchester Ship Canal open.

7–8–1894 The West Highland Railway opens between Fort William and Craigendoran and is worked by special stock of the North British Railway.

4–8–1895 Electric locomotives come into use on the Baltimore & Ohio Railroad on 3¾ miles of line near Camden. An overhead electric slot system is used, but is replaced by a third rail in March 1902.

22–8–1895 The "Race to Aberdeen" between trains from London on the East and West Coast Routes. A world speed record is achieved when the West Coast train from Euston covers the 541 miles in 512 minutes, an average speed of over 60 m.p.h. The East

Coast train from King's Cross completes the journey of 523½ miles in 518 minutes. This is the last "big race" between rival railways for such long distances.

1–10–1895 Some Great Western Railway expresses cease to stop at Swindon station for refreshments. Previously, trains were obliged to stop for ten minutes by contract with refreshment room lessees. The "stop for refreshments" was a practice gradually outdated by the increase in dining-cars on fast trains.

6–4–1896 The only rack railway in Britain, the Snowdon Mountain Railway, opens, and carries traffic regularly from 19th April 1897.

14–12–1896 The Glasgow underground railway is opened.

21–6–1897 An all-night service between Liverpool Street and Walthamstow is opened by the Great Eastern Railway.

1–8–1897 The Manchester, Sheffield & Lincolnshire Railway is renamed the Great Central Railway, ready for its London debut. The line is extended to Marylebone station and is opened for passengers on 15th March 1899 and general goods on 11th April. Coal had been carried from 25th July 1898.

A splendid six-floor hotel, the Great Central, in the Victorian idiom with winter garden, clock tower and facilities for horse-drawn carriages, was built in front of the station. In 1948 it became the headquarters of the State-owned railways.

1–8–1899 An Act of Parliament forms the South Eastern & Chatham Railway Companies Management Committee to carry out a joint working arrangement between the South Eastern Railway (having 59 per cent) and the London, Chatham & Dover Railway (41 per cent). The arrangement was back-dated to take effect from 1st January of that year.

Victorian silk top hats, "bowlers" and frock coats abound for the ceremonial opening of Marylebone station in 1899, completing the Great Central Railway extension of 92 miles from Annesley, Nottinghamshire, to London. The ceremonial lever, when pulled, admitted steam to the cylinders of engine No. 861 and started the train. (*Photo: British Rail*)

1900

1–8–1900 Dining cars and corridor coaches throughout are provided on the *Flying Scotsman* between London (King's Cross) and Edinburgh. This eliminates the booked stop of 20 minutes at York as a "lunch interval".

20–4–1902 Automatic signalling is installed between Andover and Grateley by the London & South Western Railway.

3–5–1903 The Mersey Railway, a city underground line, is electrified.

17–8–1903 The first regular road motor service is introduced by the Great Western Railway between Helston and the Lizard, in Cornwall, to connect main line trains. A branch railway line had originally been considered.

14–2–1904 The Great Northern & City Railway opens.

29–3–1904 Electrification is introduced between Newcastle (New Bridge Street) and Benton, about 5 miles, the first section of the Tyneside electrification on the North Eastern Railway.

5–4–1904 Public service of electric trains opens between Liverpool and Southport, 18½ miles, part of the Lancashire & Yorkshire Railway. Both electric and steam trains are used at the start, but a subsidence at the power station at Formby temporarily suspends the electric trains on 11th April.

9–5–1904 A notably high maximum speed of 102 m.p.h. is attained by the Great Western Railway *Ocean Mail* down Wellington Bank, hauled by the locomotive *City of Truro*.

With this engine, the train runs 128 miles from Plymouth to Bristol in 123 minutes, and hauled by the *Duke of Connaught* completes the 118-mile Bristol to London run in 100 minutes.

12–9–1905 Electric traction replaces steam on the Inner Circle line of the London Underground system, and the last steam train is withdrawn on 22nd September.

5–12–1905 Charing Cross station roof collapses, killing six people. The London terminus of the South Eastern & Chatham Railway is closed until 19th March 1906.

1–1–1906 Audible locomotive cab signalling is introduced by the Great Western Railway on the Henley double line branch of 4½ miles from Twyford on the main line, and on 1st December on the Fairford single line branch. In 1908, the system is installed on the four track line between Reading and Slough and is extended to Paddington in 1912. About that time Automatic Train Control (ATC) was added, to become standard G.W.R. practice. The basic aim of ATC was to prevent a driver missing the distant or caution signal which is set back a sufficient braking distance in rear of the next "stop" signal. The G.W.R. were pioneers in this field.

10–3–1906 The first section of the Bakerloo line (later to link Baker Street and Waterloo on the London Underground) is opened.

1–6–1906 The first Simplon tunnel opens between Switzerland and Italy and becomes the world's longest railway tunnel, 12 miles 537 yd. long. The first trial trips ran through on 25th January. The second Simplon tunnel, 22 yd. longer, opened on 16th October 1922, both operated by the Swiss Federal and the Italian State Railways.

1–11–1908 An all-Pullman luxury train is introduced between London and Brighton by the London, Brighton & South Coast Railway, and a supplementary charge is made. It is named the *Southern Belle*, and renamed in 1934 as the *Brighton Belle*. The Pullman stock is finally withdrawn in 1972, and replaced by standard modern coaches.

1–12–1909 The South London line is electrified by the London, Brighton & South Coast Railway, and is regarded as the oldest section of the present "Southern Electric" system.

17–8–1911 The first national railway strike is called, gaining additional wages and additional power for the railway trade unions.

7–8–1912 The Midland Railway takes over the London, Tilbury & Southend Railway.

1–7–1913 A through service begins between London (Charing Cross) and Paris, initiated by the South Eastern & Chatham Railway. It completes the throughout journey, connecting finally with cross-channel ship, in seven hours, only 20 minutes longer than the *Golden Arrow* speeds of a quarter of a century later. The service is postponed because of the outbreak of World War One.

4–8–1914 Because of the outbreak of World War One on this date, Britain's railways are taken over by the Government under the Regulation of Forces Act 1871. The Irish railways are taken over on 1st January 1917. The Government relinquishes control on 15th August 1921 at the time when large-scale railway amalgamations are imminent.

22–5–1915 The worst railway accident in Britain occurs at Quintinshill on the Caledonian Railway when an estimated 227 people lose their lives.

1–1–1917 Severe restrictions are imposed on railway travel because of the pressures of the war, and fares are increased by 50 per cent.

22–10–1917 The Trans-Australian Railway opens between Kalgoorlie and Port Augusta, 1,052 miles in 4 ft. 8½ in. gauge. The line includes the longest straight stretch of railway in the world, 328 miles across the Nullarbor Plain.

12–12–1917 The world's worst railway accident occurs at Modane on the French Railways in which 543 people lose their lives.

11–11–1918 The Armistice between Britain and her Allies and Germany is signed in dining car No. 2419 of the International Sleeping Car Company. The vehicle was attached to the train of Marshall Foch in Compiègne Forest, and was later preserved.

1–2–1919 An eight-hour day, demanded by the Associated Society of Railway Engineers & Firemen, is granted by the Government without the agreement of the railway companies. The concession is granted to other railway workers, followed by an agreement to standardise conditions of service on all the railways.

15–8–1919 The Ministry of Transport is created, with Sir Eric Geddes as its first Minister. Formal transfer of the transport functions, including the railway inspectorate, from the Board of Trade to the new Ministry, takes place on 23rd September.

6–2–1920 The Institute of Transport holds its first Council meeting, having been founded the previous year. Its first president is the new Minister of Transport, Sir Eric Geddes, who delivered his Presidential Address "Transport and the State" on 22nd March.

In 1926, the Institute was incorporated by Royal Charter. Its objects are to promote, encourage, and co-ordinate the study and advancement of the science and art of transport in all its branches.

19–8–1921 The Railways Act 1921 is passed, which provides for the grouping of the railways into four main-line companies. Government control ended on 15th August.

1–1–1923 The 123 separate railway companies are amalgamated and formed into four group companies: London Midland & Scottish Railway, London & North Eastern Railway, Great Western Railway, and Southern Railway. The Cheshire Lines Committee, the Midland & Great Northern Joint, and some other joint lines continue as separate entities as before.

24–4–1924 The Harwich-Zeebrugge train ferry service opens, operated by Great Eastern Train Ferries Limited.

–6–1924 Gleneagles Hotel, Perthshire, is opened by the L.M.S.R., one of the finest ever built by a British railway company, and with its splendid golf courses gained world fame. It was planned by the directors of the Caledonian Railway to rival the great spa hotels in Europe. Building began in 1913, was halted by the First World War, restarted in 1922 and completed after the Caledonian had been absorbed into the L.M.S.R. During the Second World War, the hotel was closed and was used as a rehabilitation centre for miners and for a time as a military hospital. Within fifty years, about a million and a quarter people from all over the world had stayed at Gleneagles.

1–1–1925 All the railways within the Irish Free State, are grouped into the Great Southern Railways.

1/3–7–1925 The Stockton & Darlington Railway Centenary is celebrated, in advance of the "official" opening date.

17–7–1925 Automatic train couplers are introduced by the Imperial Japanese Railways, the replacement being attained in 24 hours, following eight years of preparation.

3–5–1926 Railwaymen go on strike, officially called by the railway trade unions as part of a general strike joined by other unions in support of the miners. The general strike collapsed on 12th May but coal production and distribution were delayed for many months, with an adverse effect on the railways.

12–9–1926 The *Golden Arrow* all-Pullman service between Calais and Paris is introduced on the London–Paris through route via Dover. From 15th May 1929, the *Golden Arrow* all-Pullman runs throughout.

20–12–1926 The first underground railway in Australia opens, on a section of the Sydney City Railway.

1–5–1928 The first all-steel car trains are introduced by the London & North Eastern Railway, on the London–Edinburgh–Glasgow route; the trains are the two Pullman *Queen of Scots* sets.

1–5–1928 The world's longest non-stop run is introduced by the London & North Eastern Railway between London and Edinburgh.

24–9–1928 Third class sleeping cars are inaugurated by three of the four group companies: the London Midland & Scottish, the London & North Eastern, and the Great Western Railways.

1929 World-wide researches begin by the International Conference on the Properties of Steam. The objective is to evaluate more accurately the thermodynamics of steam in a wide range of pressures and temperatures.

1–8–1930 The Road Traffic Act is passed. Restrictions placed on the operation of commercial vehicles bring some advantages to the railways in competing for business.

13/20–9–1930 The centenary of the Liverpool & Manchester Railway is celebrated at Liverpool.

8–1–1931 Electrification of the Manchester, South Junction & Altrincham, a line owned jointly by the London Midland & Scottish and the London & North Eastern Railways. It is the first passenger railway in Britain to use the 1,500vDC system, recommended in the Weir Report.

21–6–1931 A world record railway speed of 143 m.p.h. is achieved, and maintained for 6¼ miles, between Karstadt and Dergenthin on a test run in Germany, using a Kruckenberg airscrew-driven railcar.

–9–1931 The first diesel-powered traction in the British Isles to run on a regular service is used on the County Donegal Railways. Diesel traction is introduced in Britain in December by the London & North Eastern Railway.

1931 The Great Western Railway begins to extend Automatic Train Control equipment (ATC) on all main routes, using a modified system of the installation introduced in 1906. Much of the work is completed within the year, and further installations during 1937 bring the total lines covered to about 2,850 route miles.

1–1–1933 The London to Brighton and Worthing electrification is completed on the Southern Railway. It is the beginning of a large programme and is the first main-line electrification in Britain. On the same date, the *Brighton Belle* becomes the world's first all-electric Pullman train. The cars are of all-steel construction.

12–4–1933 The first air service to be operated by a British railway company opens, to serve Cardiff–Torquay–Plymouth; and on 21st March 1934, Railway Air Services Limited is incorporated.

13–4–1933 The London Passenger Transport Board is formed by Act of Parliament, and begins its working life on 1st July managing London's train and bus services.

17–11–1933 The Road and Rail Traffic Act is passed, bringing some relief to the railways from unfair competition. Regulations introduced for the carriage of goods by road for hire or reward include A, B and C licences for different categories of road transport operation.

5–6–1935 A Government scheme is announced to promote £35 million credit (increased later to £45 million) for the improvement and electrification of London suburban railways.

27–9–1935 The first streamlined train runs in Britain and reaches high speeds. On its trial run between King's Cross and Newcastle, the L.N.E.R. *Silver Jubilee* express averages 100 m.p.h. for 43 miles, and touches 112½ m.p.h. at two places. The train went into public service on 30th September. The L.M.S.R. ran their first streamlined train in a trial from London to Glasgow on 29th June 1937. Named the *Coronation Scot*, it reached 114 m.p.h. approaching Crewe. The train, painted blue throughout, entered public service on 5th July. On 30th June, the L.N.E.R. made a trial run with its streamlined train the *Coronation* from London to Edinburgh, also entering public service on 5th July.

1938 Automatic Train Control (ATC) apparatus is installed during the year at 112 distant signal locations on the London–Southend line of the L.M.S.R. It is known as the Hudd intermittent inductive system, and is installed on the Glasgow–Edinburgh line by the L.N.E.R. on 13th August 1939.

14–3–1938 Two lines are electrified: the Wirral section of the L.M.S.R. and the Newcastle–South Shields line of the L.N.E.R.

3–7–1938 A speed record for steam in Britain, and probably in the world, of 126 m.p.h. is set up near Peterborough by the L.N.E.R. locomotive *Mallard*, class A4 streamlined Pacific 4–6–2 No. 4468, hauling a train of seven coaches weighing 240 tons.

17–9–1938 The centenary of the opening of the London & Birmingham Railway is celebrated, featuring at Euston historic locomotives and period characters in chimney-pot hats, frock coats and crinolines.

30–5–1939 The "down" marshalling yard at Toton, near Long Eaton, is mechanised, the equipment including a control tower and automatic braking of wagons.

1–9–1939 The Minister of Transport makes an Order taking over the control of the railways and certain associated undertakings because of the imminence of war. The Minister appoints the Railway Executive Committee for giving directions under the Order: Sir Ralph Wedgwood (Chairman), Sir James Milne, Sir Charles Newton, Mr. Frank Pick (later succeeded by Lord Ashfield), Mr. Gilbert S. Szlumper (later succeeded by Sir Eustace Missenden), and Sir William V. Wood.

1/4–9–1939 Massive evacuation of women and children from London and other highly vulnerable centres takes place, in which the railways are heavily engaged. Contingency preparations had been made to move some three million people. In the event, records showed the transporting of 1,220,496 (including 607,635 from the London area) in England, and 178,543 in Scotland.

3-9-1939 The ultimatum to Germany expires, and war is declared by Great Britain and France against Germany. The Railway Executive Committee takes over a specially prepared and protected tube station, which is disused, at Down Street on the Piccadilly line, as its deep-level headquarters.

5-2-1940 The Great Western Railway issues its new timetable with improved services and more restaurant and sleeping cars.

22-9-1940 The travelling postal sorting offices are discontinued; the lineside apparatus for the exchange of mail bags at high speed had been out of use since the outbreak of war.

9-5-1941 The Ministry of War Transport is formed by the merger of the Ministries of Transport and Shipping.

6-10-1941 First class travel accommodation on local lines in the London area is abolished.

8-12-1941 Restaurant car services are substantially withdrawn and 44 sleeping cars are taken out of service.

1-4-1944 The Wick & Lybster Light Railway, L.M.S.R., is closed to all traffic. The line was originally opened on 1st July 1903.

5-4-1944 All remaining restaurant cars are withdrawn by Direction of the Minister of War Transport.

1-1-1945 The Irish Transport Company (Coras Iompair Eireann) is formed by the Eire Transport Act of 29th November 1944, begins its operating life. It merged the undertakings of the Great Southern Railways Company and the Dublin United Transport Co. Ltd.

8-5-1945 VE Day, Victory in Europe, with the unconditional surrender of Germany.

15-8-1945 VJ Day, Victory in Japan, with the unconditional surrender of Japan.

1-10-1945 The travelling post offices are reinstated between Euston and Aberdeen and between Paddington and Penzance.

1-10-1945 Restaurant car services are restored on the L.M.S.R., L.N.E.R. and S.R., and on 31st December on the G.W.R. The services are gradually increased on all railways.

19-11-1945 The Government announces proposals to nationalise specific industries, including railways, canals, and long distance road haulage services.

7-1-1946 British railway fares are increased to 33⅓ per cent. above the pre-war level, on an Order of the Minister of Transport.

7-3-1946 The Ministry of Transport is reinstated, and the War Ministry is abolished on 1st April.

15-4-1946 The all-Pullman *Golden Arrow* service is reinstated by the Southern Railway. It includes the first public address installation throughout the train, and the first cocktail bar featuring plastic interior decoration.

6-5-1946 Many additional trains and higher speeds are introduced in the first post-war summer timetable for the main line railways. Travelling post offices are reinstated between Bristol and Newcastle, Bristol and Carmarthen, Edinburgh and York, Newcastle and London, and London–York–Edinburgh.

6-8-1947 The Royal Assent is given to the Transport Act 1947. It establishes the British Transport Commission, and provides for the national ownership of railways and canals from 1st January 1948 and for various road transport services later.

1-10-1947 Charges for fares and merchandise on the main line railways are raised to 55 per cent. above the pre-war level and some differentiations between passenger and goods traffic cease.

14-10-1947 Public services begin on the new Central Line tube to Newbury Park and Woodford. This involved the electrification of L.N.E.R. surface lines from Leytonstone to Woodford. The Leytonstone–Newbury Park line is in a newly completed tube, the last in the tunnel construction programme for the London area. It is also the last new construction to be brought into public use before public ownership.

THE STATE TAKES OVER

1–1–1948 The railways of Britain are nationalised. Custody of the four main line railways, the joint committees, and the minor railways which had been under Government control during the war, is transferred to the British Transport Commission. The railways are divided into six regions for operating purposes.

1–7–1948 Railway hotels and station and train catering become the responsibility of the Hotels Executive under the British Transport Commission.

10–8–1948 The Transport Act (Northern Ireland) 1948 receives the Royal Assent, incorporating the Ulster Transport Authority to take over the Northern Ireland Road Transport Board by compulsory powers; to acquire the Belfast & County Down Railway and the Northern Counties Railway by voluntary agreement; and to acquire and operate other transport services by agreement. On 1st October, the N.I.R.T.B. and the B. & C.D.R. are taken over; and the N.C.R. is managed by the new authority until 1st April 1949 when formal transfer of ownership from the B.T.C. takes place.

10–9–1948 Agreement is reached between Thomas Tilling Limited and the British Transport Commission for the purchase by the B.T.C. of all Tilling interests in passenger road transport. The bus companies concerned continue to operate under their own well-known names that are familiar to the local communities.

19–10–1948 The Rugby Locomotive Testing Station is formally opened by Mr. Alfred Barnes, Minister of Transport. Work had begun by the L.M.S.R. and L.N.E.R. in 1938, but was postponed at the outbreak of war and resumed in 1944.

30–11–1948 The Cheshire Lines Railway loses its identity (originally Cheshire Lines Committee) and is absorbed completely into the London Midland Region.

30–11–1948 The Railway Executive, which is the body that manages the railways under the B.T.C., issues an official announcement that many railway stations, goods depots and routes are involved in an extensive tidying-up programme. Inter-regional adjustments are designed to simplify supervision, to reduce administrative costs, and to avoid unnecessary duplication. The lines and stations concerned are those which penetrate from one region into the boundaries of another. In most cases, the alterations concerned competitive lines built by the original railway companies.

1–1–1949 A new organisation for the supply and maintenance of the horse stud comes into force. It provides for a chief veterinary surgeon and horse superintendent at railway headquarters, and subordinate officers in London, Birmingham, Manchester and Glasgow. Purchase and sale of horses is centralised, and facilities for horse and harness maintenance are co-ordinated. Of the total stud of 7,600 horses, most are used for local road collection and delivery services of parcels and goods, and about 200 for wagon shunting operations. (The number of horses is reduced each succeeding year, and they are phased out by 1959).

20–2–1949 For administration purposes, some lines are transferred from the London Midland to the Eastern Region: London, Tilbury & Southend line, the Tottenham & Hampstead joint line east of the site of St. Ann's Road station, and the Tilbury-Gravesend Ferry services, excluding the Gravesend Landing Stages which are transferred to the Southern Region.

–6–1949 Two 1,600 h.p. diesel electric locomotives working as one unit complete the inaugural non-stop run from London (Euston) to Glasgow.

26–9–1949 Electric traction is formally opened by Mr. Alfred Barnes, Minister of Transport, between Liverpool Street and Shenfield in the Eastern Region. The route of 20 miles is equipped with the 1,500 V overhead system. Steam locomotives haul some trains until the complete change-over on 7th November.

–10–1949 British Railways join with several European railways and decide to found a company for constructing and managing the rolling stock required for international rail transport under controlled temperature conditions. The company is founded in Brussels, is named Interfrigo, and establishes headquarters in Basle, Switzerland. The first member countries are: Belgium, France, Great Britain, the Netherlands, and Switzerland, soon joined by German and Danish State railways.

The company celebrated its 25th anniversary in October 1974, by which time there were 21 shareholder railways, its activities spread over most of Europe and the Mediterranean area. Its stock then consisted of about 20,000 refrigerator wagons (deep-freeze techniques being used), 8,000 other wagons and 340 mechanically-refrigerated containers.

2–11–1949 The first two-level (or double-deck) train runs on British Railways: a multiple-unit electric in the Southern Region between Charing Cross and Dartford. It has 1,104 seats compared with 772 normally. Seats in the compartments are arranged on two levels, but not one deck directly above the other. After extensive trials, the advantages are outweighed by disadvantages.

23–1–1950 A number of lines in the London area are transferred by the British Transport Commission from the Railway Executive to the London Transport Executive.

The Great Central Hotel was built at Marylebone to serve the new G.C.R. line opened in 1899. It was used as a departure centre for army officers setting off for France in the First World War and as headquarters of Special Operations in the Second World War. Since 1948 it has served as British Railways' headquarters. (*Photo: British Rail*)

2–4–1950 Further substantial adjustments are made to the railway regional boundaries. Among them are: the distribution of the former Great Central Railway among the Eastern, Western, and London Midland Regions, transfer of Southern Region lines west of Exeter to the Western Region; transfer of Western Region lines south of Castle Cary to the Southern Region; and transfer of the London Midland Region lines south-west of Birmingham to the Western Region.

1–10–1950 "Workmen's" tickets are renamed "early morning" tickets in the London area, disposing of an anachronism. The new tickets apply to all the services of London Transport, suburban services of British Railways in the area served by London Transport buses, and the London, Tilbury & Southend line.

30–1–1951 The first standard locomotive of British Railways is placed in service; the locomotive is a 4–6–2 wheel arrangement, is numbered 70,000, and named *Britannia*.

1–5–1951 British Railways publish jointly with *Modern Transport* a full report describing the unification of British Railways: early achievements, progress, the problems of welding the four former group companies into one network, and plans for the future system.

4–2–1952 Electric traction for freight begins on the Wath-Barnsley Junction Dunford Bridge line, a heavily graded route on which "bank" engines are required. Trains are loose-coupled and the wagons are "unfitted" – have no automatic brakes. The route is part of the Sheffield-Manchester scheme, for which the new Woodhead tunnel opens on 3rd June 1954, replacing the first and second tunnels of 1845 and 1852, the electric passenger services starting on 14th September.

11–2–1952 The body of King George VI, who died at Sandringham on 6th February, is carried by special train from Wolferton, Norfolk, to King's Cross for the Lying-in-State in Westminster. The body of His Majesty is conveyed from Paddington to Windsor in the Royal Train, and five special trains were run between Paddington and Windsor for mourners attending the funeral service.

1–5–1952 The ordinary fares on British Railways are reduced from 2.44d. a mile to 1.75d. for third class.

1–9–1952 "Workmen's" tickets are renamed "early morning" tickets on British Railways, which was done for the London area on 1st October 1950. The workmen's ticket on the railways of Britain now virtually disappears but it was retained on the Liverpool Overhead Railway until the line closed on 30th December 1956.

8–10–1952 The worst railway disaster ever experienced in England and the second worst in British history occurs in a double collision at Harrow & Wealdstone on the Euston main line. Three passenger trains are involved in which 112 people are killed and 167 seriously injured. Many are railway staff.

29–11–1952 London Transport introduce at Ealing Broadway the first push-button signalling control installation; each self-restoring button selects all points and signals for a particular route.

January 1953 British Railways, and other services of the British Transport Commission, suffer heavy loss of lines and damage to equipment during the exceptional gales and floods that swept the east coast and breached many sea walls.

8–4–1953 A fatal accident occurs on London Underground. Twelve people lose their lives and 45 are injured as an eastbound Epping train in the tunnel on the Central Line collides with the rear of a stationary train bound for Hainault.

2–6–1953 The Coronation of Queen Elizabeth II; 1,338 extra trains run to and from London at cheap fares during the six days, 29th May to 3rd June.

30-9-1953 The Railway Executive is abolished by the Transport Act 1953 which also requires the British Transport Commission to break up and sell off their road haulage undertakings.

21-11-1953 The last electro-pneumatic semaphore signal on London Transport railways is withdrawn.

1-10-1954 A pension scheme is introduced for wages grades of British Railways and other B.T.C. services.

1-1-1955 Following the Transport Act 1953, British Railways are reorganised and Regional Boards are appointed.

MODERNISATION BEGINS

24-1-1955 The modernisation and re-equipment of British Railways, to cost £1,200 million, is announced by the B.T.C. chairman.

5-6-1955 The ordinary fares on British Railways are increased from 1.75d. a mile to 1.88d. for third class.

6-3-1956 The B.T.C. decide to adopt the 25kV 50-cycle AC system of electrification with overhead equipment. It is also decided to adopt the long-established system of vacuum brake as standard for all freight and passenger rolling stock, except for electric and diesel multi-unit vehicles which will continue to have air brakes.

3-6-1956 Third class fares and accommodation on British Railways are abolished and redesignated second class.

11-6-1956 Electric traction is extended from Shenfield to Chelmsford, Eastern Region, for 9½ miles, after formal inuaguration on 8th June.

5-7-1956 The Clean Air Act is passed, in which Section 19 requires the minimising of smoke emission from railway locomotives.

1-10-1956 The Ulster Transport Authority abolishes third class accommodation and second class fares, and the third class fares are designated second class. Until this date, three classes of accommodation were available.

8-11-1956 Pneumatic tyres on trains are introduced on the Paris Metropolitan underground railway.

30-11-1956 The British Railways system of automatic train control (ATC) is approved by the Minister of Transport for use with non-electric traction. Earlier, tests had been made over the 105 miles between London (King's Cross) and Grantham.

31-12-1956 Electric traction at 1,500 V DC is extended from Shenfield to Southend Victoria for 15½ miles in the Eastern Region. The electrification was formally inuagurated on 28th December, and by the 30th electric trains had taken over most of the steam schedules.

1956 Disc brakes instead of the traditional brake blocks are put in use on passenger coaches in the Southern Region, an entirely new departure for British Railways trains.

1956 During the year, no passenger was killed as a result of a train accident. Since nationalisation, was a "nil return" also for 1949 and 1954.

1-1-1957 The State railways in Turkey and Greece adopt the system of two passenger classes; this leaves Spain and Portugal, where the rail gauge is 5 ft. 6 in., as the only major railways in Europe still providing first, second and third class travel.

April 1957 *Transport Age*, a quarterly "prestige" magazine is launched, to publicise new technical and commercial developments, particularly for freight and passenger services. It is closed by the British Railways Board after the 33rd issue in summer 1965, and bound in five volumes.

6-5-1957 Multiple-unit diesel trains are introduced between London and Hastings via Tunbridge Wells Central on the Southern Region.

2-6-1957 The first Trans-Europe-Express (TEE) railway services are introduced with self-contained diesel train sets, in a standard red and yellow livery. They are the result of collaboration between French, West German, Italian, Luxembourg, Netherlands, and Swiss railway authorities.

3–6–1957 The first 1,000 h.p. main line diesel-electric locomotive is delivered, as part of the modernisation programme.

1–7–1957 The B.T.C. (Railway Merchandise) Charges Scheme comes into force. It allows railway freight charges to be varied below permitted maximums to give a commercial advantage. Freight charges can now be based on "loadability", except for consignments of 100 tons or more, for which charges must be "reasonable".

15–7–1957 Passenger fares are raised from 1.88d. per mile to 2d., authority for which had been held by the British Transport Commission since 1953.

4–12–1957 A collision, and the fall of a bridge on a train, at St. Johns, Lewisham, Southern Region, causes 90 deaths.

23–12–1957 Agreement is reached between the B.T.C., A.S.L.E.F. and N.U.R. on the manning of diesel and electric locomotives and multiple-unit trains, which includes some "single manning."

1–1–1958 The platform ticket charge is increased from 1d. to 2d. It has remained unchanged from its introduction in July 1912.

26–1–1958 Complete automatic signalling of junctions by programming machines instead of signalmen is introduced, as a first stage, at Kennington on the Northern Line of London Transport. Camden Town followed on 14th June and Euston on 16th November.

13–2–1958 The first four-wheel lightweight diesel rail bus is delivered for rural services; and on 21st April, a battery rail car begins service on the Aberdeen–Ballater line of 43 miles in Scotland.

9–6–1958 Gatwick Airport station is opened by H.M. Queen Elizabeth II. London's second airport becomes the world's first fully-integrated rail-road-air link, which British Railways describe as a "happy juxtaposition". The station, which is within the airport, is on the direct electrified line 26¾ miles from London (Victoria) and 24 miles from Brighton. By 1972, about one-third of the 5,000,000 air passengers were using the rail service, and some 600 trains were using the station daily.

15–12–1958 The last steam locomotive to be built in Crewe works, London Midland Region, leaves to take up work. It is a 2–10–0 class 9 goods locomotive No. 92250, and is the 7,331st steam locomotive to be built at Crewe since the works opened in 1843.

1958 The largest precast hollow concrete blocks ever cast in Britain, each weighing 35 tons, are used in British Rail's first wide-span stressed concrete railway bridge, No. 23. It spans the four railway tracks on the Manchester–Stockport line, and has been built this year ready for faster and heavier trains being prepared in the 1955 Modernisation Plan. The bridge contains 64 of the concrete blocks in the girder construction. The original bridge was built in 1840 by the Manchester & Birmingham Railway for its first section between Manchester and Stockport which opened on 4th June of that year. When the line was widened by the London & North Western Railway in 1880, a second bridge was erected alongside the older one.

16–3–1959 The new 25kV AC 50 cycles overhead electric traction is introduced on the Colchester–Clacton–Walton line of 24½ miles in the Eastern Region.

20–5–1959 Formal opening by Sir Brian Robertson, B.T.C. chairman, of the Greenwood to Potters Bar widening to four tracks of the Great Northern line in the Eastern Region. The work included three new double-line tunnels and quadrupling between King's Cross and Welwyn viaduct, 21 miles 32 chains.

15–6–1959 Introduction of electric traction from Gillingham to Margate and Ramsgate via the Kent Coast line, from Sittingbourne to Sheerness-on-Sea, and from Faversham to Dover, in the Southern Region, a total of 78 route miles. The programme had been arranged four years earlier, and the lines opened on the scheduled date. It was the first stage of an extensive plan for the Southern.

20–1–1960 A two-hour test at Colchester (St. Botolph's) station proves conclusively the safety of the new 25kV overhead system. A live steam locomotive stands on the line under the overhead wires, a loop from which is gradually lowered to the steaming chimney. The "flashover" does not occur until the gap has been reduced to two inches. Railway officers, and trade union officials are present as Brigadier C. A. Langley, the Ministry of Transport's chief inspecting officer of railways, pronounces the system "perfectly safe".

18–3–1960 The naming ceremony of the *Evening Star* takes place at Swindon Works. Numbered 92220, this 2–10–0 class 9 goods locomotive is the last steam engine to be built by British Railways, and Swindon takes on modern rolling stock.

4–7–1960 Midland Pullman Services of all first class six-car diesel electric train sets painted blue, go into service between London (St. Pancras) and Manchester (Central) and between London (St. Pancras) and Leicester. The Leicester service is withdrawn on 31st December. In September, the Pullmans also enter service between London (Paddington) and Wolverhampton, and Paddington–Bristol. The multi-unit trains were specially designed for the business traveller.

–9–1960 The new trav-o-later – a moving walk-way – comes into use at Bank station for the Waterloo & City line.

9–9–1960 The last slip-coach train in Britain runs on the 5.10 p.m. Paddington–Wolverhampton, slipping the rear coach at Bicester, Western Region, while the express continues its journey.

12–9–1960 Electric services begin between Crewe and Manchester, with both multi-units and locomotives, in the London Midland Region. Semaphore signals are replaced by colour-light signals throughout the lines totalling 144 route miles, and track has been reformed. Speed limits are lifted from 75 to 90 m.p.h.

–10–1960 A new goods depot at Hither Green, Southern Region, is opened for handling continental perishable traffic.

7–11–1960 Electric trains go into service on the Glasgow suburban lines: 31 route miles at 25 kV and 20 miles at 6·25 kV, on the north side of the River Clyde. Because of accidents on 13th and 17th December, the services are withdrawn pending a Ministry of Transport enquiry and steam returns. Normal electric train services resume on 1st October 1961.

21–11–1960 Electric trains begin on the Great Eastern suburban services from London (Liverpool Street) to Chingford, Enfield Town and Cheshunt, with 21 route miles at 6·25 kV; and Cheshunt to Bishop's Stortford, and Hertford East, 24 route miles at 25 kV.

1–1–1961 The statutory obligation to issue "early morning" return tickets (previously known as "workmen's) ends, and the facility is withdrawn generally outside the London area; and on 1st January 1962 in the London area also.

10–3–1961 The "Bradshaw" monthly railway guide is published for the last time. (The first appeared on 10th October 1839.)

9–9–1961 The last steam-hauled train runs on regular passenger services on the Metropolitan line of London Transport.

6–11–1961 Some passenger-carrying electric trains begin on the London, Tilbury & Southend line from Fenchurch to Shoeburyness. On 18th June 1962, steam is withdrawn, and a full accelerated electric service is introduced.

1961 The first fully automatic half-barrier level crossings in Britain are brought into use: one at Spath, Uttoxeter, on the Stoke–Derby line, and another at Marston, Millbrook, on the Bletchley–Bedford line. In subsequent years, many more come into use.

1961 Automatic ticket issuing machines are installed in station booking offices during the year: London (Euston) Birmingham (Snow Hill), Manchester (Piccadilly), Paignton, Chelmsford, Cleethorpes, Shenfield, and Yarmouth (Vauxhall). The machines, coupled with improved accounting, are widely introduced in succeeding years, and the old-fashioned cast iron hand dating presses, familiar at booking office windows, are gradually withdrawn.

1–1–1962 Electric services begin between Crewe and Liverpool, part of the London Midland Region's Euston electrification programme.

1–1–1962 The standard weekly working time is reduced by two hours to 40 hours for salaried staff, and to 42 hours for "conciliation" grades; hours were reduced to 42 in railway workshops on 30th October 1961.

27–5–1962 Electric multi-unit trains (the "Blue Trains") come into service over 27 route miles of line south of the River Clyde: the second phase of the Glasgow suburban electrification.

1–9–1962 The functions of the Transport Users Consultative Committee (TUCC), originally formed by the Transport Act 1947, are considerably revised "to establish a procedure which could deal with largescale closures", under the Reshaping ("Beeching") Plan.

–9–1962 A modern coal concentration depot opens at Enfield Chase in Middlesex on the King's Cross–Hertford line. It is designed as a railhead to handle some 48,000 tons of coal annually, previously dealt with at thirteen local stations. The coal is conveyed from collieries in block train loads and local deliveries are made by road in special British Rail vehicles to merchants' depots at the stations from which facilities have been withdrawn. By 1974, 57 fully-mechanised and about 400 partially mechanised coal concentration depots were in use.

1–8–1962 Royal Assent is given to the Transport Act 1962 to dissolve the British Transport Commission after 15 years of its life, and to reorganise radically the nationalised transport undertakings of which British Railways are the biggest part.

20–9–1962 Work begins on the construction of the Victoria Line, the first new tube across central London for over half a century.

3–10–1962 The National Union of Railwaymen and the Confederation of Shipbuilding and Engineering Unions call a one-day strike as a protest against the closures of stations, lines and workshops.

–10–1962 An offer is made (and accepted) by the British Transport Commission, just before it is wound up, to purchase the privately held preference shares of the Pullman Company's services which are later integrated into the train catering network, but with individuality maintained in the service. This is 88 years after the Midland Railway first introduced into Britain the luxury carriages built by the American George Pullman.

6–12–1962 The newly formed British Railways Board hold their first meeting ready to take over from the B.T.C. on 1st January 1963 and, with the Minister of Transport's consent, makes appointments to the six new regional boards.

1–1–1963 The Pullman Car Company becomes a wholly-owned subsidiary of the Railways Board, and is to be managed by British Transport Hotels Ltd., along with the restaurant and buffet car fleet; individuality of the Pullman service is to be maintained.

1–1–1963 The assets, rights, and liabilities of

the former British Transport Commission are transferred to the newly formed authorities: British Railways Board, London Transport, British Docks Board, British Waterways Board, and the Transport Holding Company. Dr. Richard Beeching, at the B.T.C. since 1961, becomes the first Railways Board Chairman.

7–1–1963 As part of the Euston–Liverpool–Manchester electrification, some electric services begin on the Crewe–Stafford route of 25 miles, operating initially in steam train timings. During the year, 100 main line electric locomotives and 45 multi-unit train sets for intermediate services are delivered.

10–1–1963 The centenary date of the opening of the world's first underground railway, the Metropolitan from Paddington to Farringdon in London.

27–3–1963 British Rail's Reshaping Report is published. It sets out to determine the extent to which the present pattern of the railway's services is consistent with the characteristics of railways as a means of transport, namely the high cost of their specialised system and the low cost per unit moved if traffic is carried in bulk. The train, and not the vehicle, should be treated as the unit of movement.

8–4–1963 The first London Transport train fitted with automatic driving equipment enters experimental passenger service on the District Line.

–5–1963 Work begins on the major replacement of the superstructure and strengthening of the existing piers of Grosvenor Road railway bridge. It carries all the trains from Victoria on nine electrified tracks over the River Thames. The work, which will take about four years to complete, will include a tenth track. Throughout reconstruction, at least seven tracks will be kept open for trains.

8–8–1963 The "Great Train Robbery" of the travelling Post Office train near Cheddington, Buckinghamshire, travelling overnight from Glasgow to Euston. The train is stopped at 3.15 a.m. by a false red signal lighted from a battery, and a masked gang armed with coshes get away with over £2½ million in used bank notes belonging to every major bank in Britain. Driver J. Mills, aged 57, is coshed and handcuffed to his second man D. Whitby, aged 26, on the diesel engine. Both are Crewe men. By the end of October, eighteen suspects were charged concerning the robbery.

5–1–1964 London Transport begin experiments with electronic ticket barrier control; when the ticket goes

The body of Sir Winston Churchill and mourners were carried in this special train from London to Handborough in 1965, for the burial at Bladon Church. The Battle of Britain class locomotive No. 34051 is the Winston Churchill. (*Photo: British Rail*)

through the slots, the barrier is opened. The first is installed at Stamford Brook station.

20–3–1964 By an Order made today, the Minister of Transport prescribes the commencing capital debt of the Railways Board as £1,562·1 million, of which £857·1 million is interest-bearing and £750 million is suspended. Repayments and interest rates are defined by subsequent Orders.

14–5–1964 H.R.H. Prince Philip, Duke of Edinburgh, formally opens the new engineering laboratories at Derby which provide facilities unique in Europe. They are of special value for large-scale research into the dynamic and fatigue behaviour of structures and the riding behaviour of vehicles on rails. The Duke also visits the locomotive works.

15–6–1964 XP64, an eight-coach prototype train, is put into service on the *Talisman*, London–Edinburgh, as the beginning of a twelve-months trial on various routes of a new conception for passenger carriages. The train features wider folding doors, forced air heating and ventilation, double-glazed windows, sound-proofing, and specially designed seats.

27–9–1964 Two-tier articulated car carriers ("Cartics") are demonstrated at Marylebone station yard in London to leading car manufacturers and distributors. Cars are loaded and unloaded rapidly by being driven on to both levels of the train of wagons at the same time, without the need for lifting appliances.

Each unit of four wagons can carry 24/34 cars, depending on size. Five or more units can form a train to carry upwards of 120 cars in one load. The first services begin in 1965 and later come into extensive use for the car industry.

1–10–1964 The new high-speed Tokaido line opens in Japan on the route of 320 miles between Tokio and Osaka, with trains running at about 128 m.p.h. The electrified line is in the Stephenson gauge of 4 ft. 8½ in., but the Japanese National Railways are in the 3 ft. 6 in. gauge. The railway is equipped with the most modern devices and installations.

30–11–1964 Some electric services begin between Crewe and Rugby in the London Midland Region. Most of the services on this route are electrically hauled from 4th January 1965.

5–12–1964 One of the worst fires in the history of Britain's railways breaks out in the early hours of Saturday at Bishopsgate Goods Depot in London. Two Customs men lose their lives. The depot, consisting of a three-storey warehouse, office and sidings, is 120 years old.

31–12–1964 The Tilbury–Gravesend vehicle ferry across the Thames Estuary is discontinued, made superfluous by the new Purfleet–Dartford tunnel. The railways were obliged by Parliament to maintain the ferry for at least a year following the opening of the tunnel.

30–1–1965 The body of Sir Winston Churchill and family mourners are conveyed in a special train from London (Waterloo) to Handborough for burial at Bladon Church near Blenheim Palace. The train is hauled by a Battle of Britain class locomotive 34051 already named *Winston Churchill.*

16–2–1965 "The Development of the Major Railway Trunk Routes" is published by the British Railways Board. It specifies some 3,000 miles as the major trunk lines to be developed for both passenger and freight traffic.

11–6–1965 The last regular booked steam passenger train leaves Paddington, except for some special workings; the last ran on Saturday 27th November.

14–6–1965 The *Flying Scotsman* is accelerated to cover the London–Edinburgh journey of 393 miles in 355 minutes, averaging 66·42 m.p.h., its fastest time ever for this run; it is raised to 67·30 m.p.h. from 18th April 1966.

14–6–1965 All British Rail's regional timetables are issued on an annual basis, replacing the previous summer and winter timetables, and 24-hour timings are used throughout.

15–11–1965 The first Freightliner service begins between London (York Way) and Glasgow (Gushetfaulds). Using specially designed, air-braked trains to run in units of low, flat wagons carrying light-weight containers, Freightliners became one of the most successful freight services ever introduced.

22–11–1965 Some electric multi-units are introduced between Euston and Bletchley, and some main line trains: the first to Rugby is the 7.25 a.m. from Euston, and the first main line is the 8.35 a.m. to Liverpool.

1965 During the year, "British Railways" becomes known as "British Rail" for other than legal and statutory requirements; and the corporate image is promoted, dealing with every kind of visual image. This includes "Inter-City" and the new British Rail double arrow symbol.

18–4–1966 In the new timetables, 151 trains every weekday average over 70 m.p.h., compared with 54 trains from 14th June 1965.

18–4–1966 Full electric service is introduced between Euston, Crewe, Liverpool and Manchester, the highlight of this important project. Pullmans run both to Liverpool and Manchester.

5–7–1966 British Rail's "Seaspeed" hovercraft service opens between Southampton and Cowes.

8–7–1966 The Prime Ministers of both Britain and France announce that it has been decided the Channel Tunnel should be built, subject to project details being acceptable to both sides. On 28th October, the British Minister of Transport and the French Minister of Equipment set 1975 as the target year for completion. (In the early 1970s, estimated completion date is set at 1980 or beyond.)

–12–1966 The Freight Sundries Division is formed.

1–1–1967 The Eastern and North Eastern Regions are combined to form a new Eastern Region with headquarters at York, to bring substantial operational advantages and reductions in staff.

21–2–1967 The first 100-ton bogie tank wagon is completed for the conveyance of Shell Oil products.

6–3–1967 The Euston electrification is extended to the Birmingham area and to Stoke-on-Trent. An hourly service is introduced between Euston and Birmingham, reducing the journey time to 95 minutes, averaging 71 m.p.h.

20–3–1967 The only remaining line on the Isle of Wight, the 8½ miles between Ryde Pierhead and Shanklin, is re-opened after electrification.

31–3–1967 The Railway Technical Centre at Derby is opened by the Minister of Transport. The Centre is established as the new headquarters of

Birmingham New Street station as rebuilt in the 1960s as part of the programme for the main line electrification from Euston, completed to Birmingham in 1967.

railway technical and scientific activities.

5–6–1967 The Glasgow suburban electrification is extended to Gourock and Wemyss Bay.

10–7–1967 Through electric trains begin between Waterloo, Southampton and Bournemouth, with the completion of electrification from Brookwood to Bournemouth. A maximum speed of 90 m.p.h. is allowed. This year, the whole of the Southern Region timetable is reorganised; it had remained largely unchanged for about 30 years.

1–1–1968 British Rail begin to use the metric system for technical projects as part of a programme for the change-over.

18–3–1968 The container service between Harwich-Parkeston Quay and Zeebrugge is introduced, using British Rail container ships for cellular loading, and wide-span transporter cranes for handling between dock and ship.

13–5–1968 An Advanced Passenger Train (APT), with a unique body-tilting suspension to take curves at high speeds on existing track, and offering new standards of travel, is predicted in the Railways Board's annual report published today.

25–6–1968 British Transport Hotels open the Old Course hotel at St. Andrews. This, with the internationally-renowned Gleneagles and Turnberry hotels, gives Scotland a golfing hotel system that is second to none in the world.

4–8–1968 The last scheduled steam train runs on British Railways, except for summer-only services on the 12-mile narrow-gauge Vale of Rheidol line, between Aberystwyth and Devil's Bridge. Steam has been totally eliminated as foreseen in the 1955 Modernisation Plan. (A special "Farewell to Steam" train is run specially in the London Midland Region on Sunday, 11th August.)

1–8–1968 British Rail's first cross-Channel hovercraft service opens between Dover and Boulogne; the SR N4, which will carry over 250 passengers and 30 cars, is named *Princess Margaret*, and Her Royal Highness made the inaugural journey the previous day. SR N4 crosses the Channel in little over 30 minutes at equivalent land speeds of 60 to 70 m.p.h. The *Princess Anne* was later added to this pioneering service, in which British Rail Hovercraft Ltd., which includes the Solent service, trades under the name Seaspeed.

8–9–1968 British Rail's Selective Prices Manual No. 1 comes into force for the passenger fares, for the use of station staff and travel agents. It lists fares in the various categories between stations throughout the system. Ordinary fares are based on commercial and marketing criteria replacing the fixed amount per mile which had been in use for well over a century.

14–10–1968 The new Euston station is formally opened by Queen Elizabeth II.

25–10–1968 The Transport Act 1968 receives the Royal Assent. Its main provisions, which bring substantial and far-reaching changes in the structure of nationalised transport, come into force on 1st January 1969. Three new bodies are created: the National Freight Corporation (NFC), the National Bus Company (NBC), and the Scottish Transport Group. The N.F.C., with rail and road interests, including British Road Services and Pickfords Ltd., takes a 51 per cent share of British Rail's Freightliners, and the whole of the "Sundries" Division, renamed National Carriers Ltd. The N.B.C. will take a half share in British Transport Advertising Ltd. Provision is also made for the financial and capital reconstruction of the railways, and for a Channel Tunnel Council. The five Regional Boards continue to function, but as non-Statutory bodies as part of the Railways Board management structure.

Robert Stephenson's Britannia Bridge of 1850 across the Menai Straits was set alight by youths in 1970 and re-opened in 1972. This artist's impression shows a proposed roadway above the railway track as an additional link with the mainland. (*Photo: Husband & Co.*)

7–11–1968 Hudson House, the new Eastern Region headquarters, is opened by the Lord Mayor of York. It is to honour George Hudson, the "Railway King", for his contribution in "mania" days, who before his fall from grace, was himself a Lord Mayor of York.

7–3–1969 The Victoria Line of London Transport is formally opened throughout by Queen Elizabeth II, who takes a ride. Automatic trains are introduced, with the motorman remaining in the driving cab.

1–4–1969 A car rental service to link with Inter-City travel at about 70 main stations begins. A contract is signed with Godfrey Davis for "Rail-Drive" and a further contract for five years is signed on 28th June 1973 for what has grown into a sound business.

5–5–1969 The Lea Valley line of 9 miles is inaugurated for electric traction, using the 25 kV AC system.

June 1969 Three new power signalboxes with colour-light signalling come into use at Trent, Derby and Saltley, Birmingham, to control 242 route miles and replace 180 mechanical signalboxes, in the London Midland Region.

27–10–1969 An Agreement is signed in Washington by the Railways Board chairman and the U.S.A. Secretary of Transportation for access to British Rail's Advanced Passenger Train technology, which later earns substantial dollar royalties. The *Flying Scotsman*, which includes a British Rail exhibition coach, is at that time on a five-weeks tour of the USA.

12–11–1969 The Railways Board receive from Prince Philip, Duke of Edinburgh, a Royal Society of Arts Award for "design management". The Citation acknowledges that the design work has been "a model of conviction and co-ordination, the results of which are to be seen most dramatically on the main Inter-City services."

1–1–1970 British Rail Engineering Ltd. begins trading as a wholly-owned subsidiary of British Rail, to develop the 14 main railway workshops. This includes manufacturing for concerns other than British Rail, both at home and overseas, of locomotives, rolling stock, containers and heavy plant. A steady flow of substantial orders builds up.

23–5–1970 The Britannia Bridge, Robert Stephenson's enclosed wrought iron structure across the Menai Straits opened in 1850, is set alight by youths. Seriously damaged, the timber-lined bridge is immediately closed to all trains as girders and superstructure are found to be weakened. Restoration costs are estimated at about £3 million, but train diversion greatly increases the total loss. The rebuilding design included additional provision for a

The prototype High Speed Train (HST) which broke the World's speed record for diesel traction in 1973.

three-lane roadway along the top, and the bridge was re-opened on 30th January 1972.

August 1970 Two train indicator boards, each nearly 40 yards long and considered to be the largest of their kind in the world, are brought into use at London (Victoria) station at a cost of £100,000. Both give identical information, using 30 panels, about train arrivals and departures for the 17 platforms. The boards are operated by punched cards fed into machines in the station control centre. The equipment was installed by General Signal & Time Systems Ltd. of London.

6–9–1970 A minimum "earning level" of £16 a week is introduced for railwaymen, to improve take-home pay of lower paid workers.

1971 During the year, the case for investment in railways is the theme of a British Rail corporate national advertising campaign, using the slogan: "British Rail: a Great British Investment". At a time when the quality of life is much in the public mind, the campaign emphasises the environmental advantages of railways compared with other forms of inland transport.

1–1–1971 "Golden Rail" holidays are introduced, to include rail journey, reserved seats, transport across London, Manchester and Glasgow, and to and from the hotel, and hotel accommodation in a wide price range, with a choice of 24 leading resorts all round the year. By 1974 there were 44 resorts and bookings have shown dramatic increases.

14–2–1971 British Rail changes to the decimal system of currency, one day ahead of most of Britain, to be ready to serve early Monday morning customers.

29–3–1971 An exhibition train, "Come to Britain by Ship and Train", leaves for Europe via the Dover–Dunkerque train ferry, returning on 8th December after it has been visited by 120,000 people in 18 cities in five countries.

–5–1971 The Government announce their decision to establish a national railway museum at York, to be run by the Science Museum, and state that the railways' historical records would remain in London, eventually at a new Public Records office at Kew. Negotiations take place during the year with Swindon Corporation concerning the future of the Great Western Railway Museum there.

12–7–1971 Fully air-conditioned coaches are introduced on regular Inter-City services: for the first time without a supplementary fee. Starting on the

London–York–Newcastle services, they later run on the London–Edinburgh and Hull–Leeds routes. This type of coach, which incorporates double-glazed windows, better sound insulation and other improvements, has now been adopted as standard for future Inter-City trains.

–8–1971 Brunel House, part of the Railway Technical Centre at Derby, is opened.

–8–1971 Government authority is given for British Railways to electrify the Great Northern Suburban lines which extend from King's Cross and Moorgate to Royston, via Welwyn Garden City and via Hertford, a total of 70 route miles consisting of 225 track miles. Completion of the £35 million project, including construction work on the 14 track miles of tunnel, was planned for 1977.

28–2–1972 The "Union Shop" (closed shop) Agreement becomes void. It had been introduced to the railways for the first time by an Agreement signed in 1970. During 1972, a new minimum basic rate of £20 a week is introduced.

4–3–1972 Snow Hill, the former Great Western Railway station in Birmingham is closed.

30–4–1972 The *Brighton Belle* all-Pullman luxury train serving the London–Brighton route makes its last farewell journey, and the coaches are offered to the public for sale.

1–5–1972 Bristol Parkway opens, a new Inter-City station "in a car park", with free parking for 600 cars. A similar station is opened at Alfreton & Mansfield, on 7th May 1973, with free parking for over 200 cars. At both places, extra train services were arranged to meet the growing demand.

4–7–1973 Pullmans run on the Western Region for the last time.

16–5–1973 British Rail announce the introduction of a new and handier size ticket, $5\frac{1}{2}$ in. by $2\frac{1}{2}$ in., at some 250 to 300 main line stations – "easier to locate in pocket, wallet or hand bag". The paper ticket replaces the traditional card and is issued from a special cash register to speed transactions and facilitate records and statistics.

6–6–1973 The prototype High Speed Train (HST) becomes the fastest train to run in Britain when it reaches 131 m.p.h. on a test run between Darlington and York. The previous British record of 126 m.p.h., set in 1938 by the L.N.E.R. *Mallard*, still stands as the world record for a steam locomotive.

On 11th June, the train maintains 141 m.p.h. for more than one mile between Thirsk and Tollerton. This breaks the 133 m.p.h. world record for diesel trains which was established by a German train in 1939. A few days later, the H.S.T. reaches 143 m.p.h., and provides evidence of a braking capacity that is superior to anything on British Railways.

15–6–1973 A prototype commuter train begins 250,000 miles of public service in the London area of the Southern Region. It is known as P.E.P. – Prototype Electro-Pneumatic. Many new features are incorporated. Technical and operating performance will be monitored and proposed modifications studied before large-scale production begins for new trains on inner suburban services of all regions.

23–6–1973 Electric haulage between Crewe and Preston begins as a preliminary stage in the electrification of the line to Glasgow.

30–9–1973 The Total Operations Processing System (TOPS) comes into use at Stage 1 in the Exeter-Plymouth area, a computer system for controlling all wagon and locomotive movements. The main computer in London will be connected to some 200 important freight centres. All areas were scheduled for completion by 1975.

1–10–1973 "Travellers-Fare", the new brand name for British Rail station and train catering, is launched to coincide with a stage of large-scale catering modernisation.

11–10–1973 The A.P.T.-E. (Advanced Passenger Train – Experimental) for the first time reaches 125 m.p.h. on a test run on the special high-speed section of the line between Edwalton (Notts.) and Melton Junction, with power to spare. In July 1972, the train made its maiden voyage on the Derby–Duffield line at a modest 50 m.p.h. Gas turbine power is used, but the future of this motive force depends on its development by the manufacturers. The first A.P.T. to run in public service will use electric traction.

17–11–1973 An Anglo-French Agreement is signed concerning Phase 2 of the Channel Tunnel project; it provides for testing equipment, trial borings, and boring a service tunnel for about 2 miles on the English and French sides. The service tunnel would run between the two main borings, and would be primarily for telecommunications and ventilation equipment.

11–2–1974 The first rail bank to be open to the public from 8 a.m. to 8 p.m. six days a week starts business, which includes foreign exchange, at London (Liverpool Street) station. A Contract has been signed between British Rail and the First National Finance Corporation (FNCF) for some 40 rail banks to be opened at stations within a few years.

22–4–1974 A 12-year contract is announced between British Rail and the British Steel Corporation to carry up to 6,000,000 tons a year of imported iron ore from Immingham to Scunthorpe – 19 miles – in the heaviest trains ever run in Britain. Two coupled diesel locomotives will haul up to 1,575 tons of ore at maximum speeds of 60 m.p.h., in a service of some 13 trains a day, equivalent to about 1,000 lorry-loads. The movement represents the heaviest single flow of freight yet undertaken between two points by British Rail. Over 100 wagons were specially built for this service in railway workshops at Derby and Shildon. British Rail invested £3,500,000 on a modernised marshalling yard, new bridges, track and signalling on South Humberside.

25–4–1974 The chairman of the British Railways Board, Richard Marsh, signs in Washington a two-year contract worth 500,000 dollars, for the sale of British Rail research data to the United States Department of Transportation's Federal Railroad Administration. The chairman and senior railway engineers tour in the U.S.A. to interest American railway companies in British Rail's latest high-speed locomotives and rolling stock.

6–5–1974 The first single-volume timetable for all regions is published by British Rail. A small supplement shows times of European services for ships, hovercraft, and some airlines.

Electrification is completed between Crewe and Glasgow, providing for the first time electric services throughout between London and Glasgow. The project took only four years to carry out and cost some £74,000,000. The fastest train, the *Royal Scot*, completes the 401-mile journey in 5 hours, averaging 80 m.p.h., with a maximum speed of 100 m.p.h.

17–6–1974 The Independent Commission on Transport publishes a 360-page report, a major proposition being the creation of a fully integrated national transport policy, and states: "The Commission feels bound to conclude that present transport policies far from letting people choose what they want, are forcing them into a new way of life which, in spite of its many attractions, is in many ways needlessly ugly, brutal and inefficient. Above all, it is unjust. Those who chiefly suffer its deficiencies are the old, the young, the infirm, and the poor . . ."

The APT-E (Advanced Passenger Train – Experimental) reached 125 m.p.h. on a test run in 1973.

The Commission calculates that transport now consumes nearly one-fifth of the nation's total output.

18–6–1974 London Bridge station, in south-east London, and its associated services, is to be rebuilt at a cost of some £5,500,000, the Government announce.

16–7–1974 A unique signalling scheme is announced by British Rail which, for the first time, will allow trains to run at high speeds in either direction on both line of double track. Two routes are concerned in the major project: Didcot–Bristol via Bath, and Swindon–Bristol via Badminton, a total of 95 route miles. They will be electronically controlled from power signalboxes at Reading, Swindon and Bristol. Completion was scheduled for 1976.

31–7–1974 The Railways Act 1974 is passed, the fifth main statute concerned with the nationalised railways. It ends subsidies for individual "social" lines, the "grant aided" scheme, introduces for the first time subsidies for passenger services generally, and provides for investment assistance to railway customers for installing private sidings and specified related facilities for freight.

The Inverness–Kyle of Lochalsh line of 82 miles and the Cambrian Coast line between Pwllheli and Machynlleth line of 58 miles, two routes of notable scenic beauty, whose heavy losses threatened their closure to passengers, are reprieved. The Minister of Transport states in Parliament that the two lines will remain open "in the public interest."

5–8–1974 London (Cannon Street) station is closed for five weeks for major alterations to track layout in the area, and extensive alterations to Southern Region commuter trains are temporarily made.

12–8–1974 A £25,000,000 project is announced by British Rail for the East Coast main line. It includes a new power signalbox at Doncaster to control 84 miles of main route, flyovers at Newark and Doncaster, and extensive track and signalling improvements. Among the 51 signalboxes to be replaced are many manually operated ones from the 19th century. By 1978, three power signalboxes – Doncaster, Peterborough and King's Cross – will control 185 miles between London and Chaloners Whin Junction, some 3 miles south of York station. Improved track will lift speed limits:

Doncaster	60 to 105 m.p.h.
Retford	80 to 115 m.p.h.
Newark	80 to 125 m.p.h.

A twelve-coach train hauled by a 100-m.p.h. electric locomotive on the newly electrified route to Glasgow from London in 1974, seen in Lake District country. (*Photo: British Rail*)

The largest station redevelopment ever undertaken in Britain is announced in a proposal for Liverpool Street station, with Broad Street station also involved. A completely new station is planned for Liverpool Street for all foreseeable needs. The Great Eastern railway hotel will be demolished after a replacement hotel is built on the Broad Street station site. Offices will be constructed above and alongside the new station, a new bus station erected, and inter-change with the London Underground improved. The project would take some ten years to complete while services continue to run, and the cost is estimated at £100/£120 million.

18–11–1974 British Rail announce that over 1,000 miles of line are now "approved" for steam running, including one new section for 1975 between Shrewsbury and Chester. Privately owned steam locomotives considered for running now total 22, including such famous engines as *Flying Scotsman*, *King George V*, *Sir Nigel Gresley*, and *Pendennis Castle*.

16–1–1975 A British Rail team at the Derby Technical Centre, it is announced, has demonstrated what is claimed to be the most advanced form of magnetic levitation in the world. With this system, the vehicles, propelled by electric linear motors, ride on a cushion of air, as an alternative to the traditional wheel-to-rail suspension.

28–2–1975 The worst accident on London's underground railways occurs in which 42 people are killed and about 70 injured when a morning rush-hour train from Drayton Park runs into a dead-end tunnel at Moorgate station.

–7–1975 The first stage of a 3½-mile extension of London Transport's Piccadilly line from Hounslow West to London Airport is scheduled to open to Hatton Cross. The second stage, to the new Heathrow Central station built under the Airport, is expected to be opened by 1978.

Summer 1975 A prototype High Speed Train (HST) is due for service on Western Region main lines between Paddington, Bristol and South Wales. The train consists of two power cars – one at each end, five of the latest Mark III passenger coaches and two catering vehicles.

27–9–1975 The 150th anniversary of the opening of the world's first proper steam locomotive railway, the Stockton & Darlington Railway, built by George Stephenson in 1825, is celebrated with a wide range of continuing activities in various parts of Britain which began in the spring.

Chapter 2

The Pioneers

Long before steam locomotives arrived, tramroads or wagon ways of timber, stone or iron were in use, the vehicles being hauled by horses or men. This private line is seen at Prior Park near Bath. (*Photo: Victoria & Albert Museum*)

THE BIRTH OF STEAM POWER

HISTORY now accepts that the first railway in the world, consisting of a steam locomotive hauling wagons of goods and carriages containing passengers, in the form of a train, along a track of iron rails, was the Stockton & Darlington Railway which was officially opened on Tuesday, 27th September 1825. A new era had begun.

Steam was the power that made railways possible at that time. All the other equipment and appurtenances were harnessed to this central conception. The power of steam, however, has been known since the century that started with the birth of Christ, and not so long after Caesar had invaded Britain. And behind the development of steam power, as in other spheres, is the restless ambition of the human spirit. Struggling for survival in a challenging environment, man has ever striven to improve his way of life, to travel faster and farther and to carry ever-increasing loads: on land, beneath the ground, on water, in the air and above the stratosphere. Each generation throws up new men of genius with inspired ideas, opening up new frontiers of knowledge and achievement. Endowed with a driving competitiveness, man expresses this basic characteristic in every activity; consider the Roman gladiator, the inventor, the philosopher, modern man at his bench or desk, or on the sportsground, or even the child in school.

A handful of men, of inventive genius and vision, in every era and from every stratum of society, have created innovations that have changed and enriched the pattern and quality of life for the populace.

Such men are to be found in the saga of events that finally led to the invention and perfection of the steam locomotive.

Long before mechanical power was thought about, the earliest methods of moving heavy articles were by gravity, by rolling large timbers and stone on the log of a rounded tree trunk or thick branch, and by the use of domesticated animals. And at some unknown period now lost in the antiquity of conjecture, but probably in Egypt before the Pyramids were built, man evolved his oldest mechancial device: the wheel. It could have taken many centuries before two wheels were attached to a wooden axle, and timbers placed upon two axles, to form a trolley or simple wagon. Smoothing the route by removing rough stones would soon be seen as a way of easing the movement of the wheels on the ground.

The earliest recorded device for using steam power to create mechanical movement is traced to Hero of Alexandria *circa* AD 100, who was in

Egypt during the Greek occupation. His knowledge of geometry showed that he was an accomplished mathematician. Some of his works, which still survive in Greek, describe various contrivances: syphons, "Hero's Fountain", "coin in the slot machines", a water organ, a fire engine, and a system for using the force of steam. His steam device, called the *Pnéumatica*, was a simple idea. Steam from a boiling cauldron was directed through two pipes which were angled to form pivots on which a hollow globe was mounted. The steam that filled the globe escaped through two other pipes, the ends of which were angled parallel with the outside of the globe, into the atmosphere. The mild "jets" of escaping steam caused the globe to rotate. It was not unlike the action of a catherine wheel, but in very slow motion. It may be assumed that Hero's invention aroused the interest of scholars, philosophers, dreamers and travellers down the centuries; and that at some stages, other inventors were inspired to take his ideas another step forward.

In the 13th century, Roger Bacon (1214?–1294), a Somerset-born philosopher with scientific leanings and a scholar of both Oxford and Paris, wrote: "One day we shall endow chariots with incredible speed without the aid of any animal."

Something more practical was proposed by Sir Isaac Newton (1642–1727), renowned for his scientific investigations into the forces of gravity. In 1680, he outlined a scheme for a spherical generator, supported on wheels, and fitted with a passenger seat in front and a jet pipe behind. The apparatus would be

> "mounted on little wheels, so as to move easily on a horizontal plane, and if the hole or jet pipe be opened, the vapour will rush out violently one way, and the wheels and the ball at the same time will be carried to the contrary."

Erasmus Darwin (1731–1802), a country doctor and renowned poet, was inspired by what he termed a "fiery chariot". But he had a busy medical practice and his interests were mainly theoretical. In 1791, he published a short poem about steam power that was illuminated by the prophetic lines:

> "Soon shall thy arm, unconquered steam! afar
> Drag the slow barge, or drive the rapid car;
> Or on wide-waving wings expanded bear
> The flying chariot through the field of air."

It needs to be said that the poet had advantages, for he belonged to the Lunar Society (so-called because members met mostly at night), along with James Watt, Matthew Boulton, and other engineers already working on stationary steam engines.

But before Watt's time, Thomas Savery of Devon (1650?–1715), an English military engineer, on 25th July 1698 took out Patent No. 356 for a steam pump. Steam from a boiler was fed into a reservoir containing water; and with the aid of a one-way outlet valve from the reservoir, the water level fell and rose to create a pump action, in a sequence of continuous movement. Also before Watt, Thomas Newcomen (1663–1729) of Dartmouth, Devon, from about 1698 developed the first known piston-operated steam engine: one of the most important single steps towards a "travelling engine." By 1712, the Newcomen engine was doing practical work.

Totally unrelated experiments were conducted in steam power by Baron von Kempelen of Pressburg, in what is now Czechoslovakia, in 1748. Kempelen tried out a steam reactor turbine to operate on similar lines to the simple waterwheel.

James Watt (1736–1819), in his earlier days an instrument-maker in Glasgow, entered the steam engine arena in his twenties. Fascinated by Newcomen's engine, Watt, with his considerable mechanical skill, set about improving it. In the Newcomen, the power was produced by the pressure of the atmosphere forcing down the piston in the cylinder, on a vacuum being produced within it by condensation of the contained steam by means of cold-water injection. The hydraulic action was similar to a suction pump. It was described by a writer of the day as a "clumsy and apparently a very painful process, accompanied by an extraordinary amount of wheezing, sighing, creaking, and bumping. When the pump descended, there was heard a plunge, a heavy sigh, and a loud bump: then, as it rose, and the sucker began to act, there was heard a creak, a wheeze, another bump, and then a rush of water as it was lifted and poured out." Despite its crudity, Newcomen's "atmospheric fire engine pump", with some improvements, continued in commercial use long after much better engines had been introduced.

When Watt was only 23, a student friend at Glasgow University produced a rough sketch of a steam carriage. Watt was then building up his business as a mathematical instrument maker; but he found time to construct a model which, however, failed to meet his expectations, and he dropped the idea. Later, he set to work on an improved steam engine and had completed it in 1765. Four years later still, he took out a patent for his "new method of lessening the consumption of steam and fuel in a fire engine" – a stationary steam engine, not a fire-fighting machine.

One of the major problems of the times in the coal mines was flooding, creating a demand for efficient pumping engines, to replace the large teams of horses used for raising water. Watt went into partnership with another engineer, Matthew Boulton (1728–1809), who had a small factory at Soho, Birmingham, and in 1775 Watt extended his patent for another 25 years. By the end of the century, some 500 had been made and sold, including some overseas, and were mainly of the rotative type.

Most steam engines were massive and cumbersome, many with large timber beams and enormous flywheels up to above 12 ft. in diameter.

Watt had been urged on many occasions, from his earliest days in steam engines, to build a locomotive. His friend Dr. Small of Birmingham wrote and pressed him to turn his attention to a locomotive, adding, "I hope soon to travel in a fiery chariot of your invention." That was in 1769. In his comprehensive patent of 24th August 1784, he did include in his specification details for a locomotive. William Murdock of Ayrshire (1754–1839), one of the mechanics at the Soho factory, in 1786 built a model about a foot high of a steam locomotive. Watt's reaction was that Murdock should mind the business in hand and leave others to "throw away their time and money in hunting shadows." First, he was not convinced that a "travelling engine" was a practical proposition, and second, he was busy making and selling his highly successful stationary steam engines. At least, the locomotive engineers of the future would have a good start. Their problem would be to construct a track strong enough to bear the weight and the speed.

MAKING TRACKS

At the same time that steam power was evolving, new ways were being sought of making better tramways, wagon ways and rail roads, especially as feeders from mines and quarries to canals, rivers, and the coast, for the conveyance of the minerals in wagons. The two lines of development – steam power and track – ran in parallel, but one day they would converge.

Even in ancient Roman times, a simple method of diminishing the friction and avoiding obstructions that impeded the free movement of wheels of vehicles on the roads they traversed, was found by laying down flat blocks of stone. And it has been discovered that the stone streets of the long-buried city of Pompeii still bear the marks of Roman chariot wheels. Both stone and timber roads for wagons came into greater use with the development of the mining and iron industries. Wooden wagon-ways were laid in and around mines in the 16th century in Germany, Alsace and Roumania; and in Britain in the 17th century, they were used in collieries at Wollaton in Nottinghamshire, and in Shropshire, Durham and Northumberland.

Wagons were inclined to slip off the wooden ways to sink axle-deep into the surrounding mud so a refinement was added in the form of a wooden flange, L-shaped in profile, to prevent this. In the latter part of the 18th century, wooden wagon ways were laid in the coal mining districts of Wales, Cumberland and Scotland. On some of the ways, planks of timber were laid lengthways, either embedded in the ground or laid on short cross-timbers, called "sleepers"; though more timber was needed per length of way, a more stable base was achieved.

Track improvements were developed by a Mr. Beaumont from the south of England. Around 1630, he ventured on horse-back and stage coach to the colliery districts in the north-east, taking with him some £30,000 in the hopes of doing business. At that time, coal was carried from the mines in panniers or bags on horses' backs, and in horse-drawn carts along ways consisting of flagstones, to boats moored at the staithes. Within a few years, Beaumont had improved many wagon ways, but he was financially ruined by his enterprise, and returned home to the south on horse-back. The results of his work meant that horses could pull more wagons hooked together, and move at a better speed.

The first iron rails laid on wooden sleepers were known as early as 1738. The line at Whitehaven was called a "plate-way", from the plate-like form in which the iron plates had been cast: hence the term "platelayer", still in use today, for railway track maintenance men. Plate-way rails were cast experimentally in 1767 at Coalbrookdale Iron Works in Shropshire, and they became more common. A track of this type was laid in 1776 to make a coal line at the Duke of Norfolk's colliery near Sheffield, and it was described as a cast iron tramway. For some obscure reason, the men at the colliery fiercely resented the new track; they tore up the metals and timbers and started a local riot. At the centre of their fury was John Curr, the man who had laid the line; and, terror-stricken, he fled to a nearby wood and remained in hiding for three days and nights.

A unique and promising innovation was applied by William Jessop when he constructed a line at Loughborough in 1789. While some plate-ways had a raised edge to guide the wheels along the track, Jessop introduced wagon wheels with a cast iron flange for the same purpose: the guiding flange was transferred from rail to wheel: the idea was quickly followed elsewhere and today remains fundamentally unchanged.

Yet another variation on the theme was earning favour in the Newcastle-on-Tyne area: wooden rails were made with a rounded top surface; and wagon wheels were cast with concave rims, pulley-wheel fashion, to run smoothly along the rails. They were noted by a French traveller named Saint-Fond, on his visit to Newcastle in 1791; and his writings were published under the title: "Travels in England, Scotland, and the Hebrides". Back home, the Frenchman urged his fellow-countrymen in colliery districts to follow the English example of carrying coal to the ports; he described the tracks as superior to anything he had seen on his travels.

A plate-way was laid for coal haulage from Tranent to Cockenzie, in Scotland, in 1745. It was in the period 1745–1775 that the plate-way established itself. The smoother the surface on which the wheels ran, the greater the load that could be hauled with the same power. Instead of horse, mule or donkey (or manpower) pulling only one wagon at a time, several wagons could be more effectively joined to each other. The investment in a better line of way was amply justified by moving more coal or other minerals in less time at lower costs; and the "train" began to prove its value. As the Industrial Revolution gathered momentum, so too did the activity on the expanding wagon-ways.

Ideas beget ideas and business begets more business. Colliery and ironworks owners, and other promoters of wagon-ways, had to obtain permission or "leave" from owners of land or fields for their lines of "way" to run through them, and the legal term "way leave" gained currency. The landowners sought payment in return, usually in the form of periodical rentals which, in the many industrial areas of Britain, earned large and regular sums.

THE FIRST STEAM LOCOMOTIVES

As trade and industry developed apace, more business was transacted between the various industrial areas of Britain: the south, south Wales, and Midlands, the north-east, the north-west and Scotland. Better transport of coal, quarry stone, slate, ore, tin, other minerals and manufactured goods was desperately needed.

Sails, effective on the water, were tried out on land. Simon Stevinius of Flanders invented a sailing coach at the end of the 16th century; and in the next century Sir Humphrey Mackworth, a mining engineer of Neath in South Wales, experimented with sails on wagons. But the caprice of wind power proved beyond workable control.

Conveyance of goods by road was costly and slow. Vehicles were rude and rough, and as heavy as they were clumsy. "Even if the roads were tolerable," writes John Francis, "it was difficult to move on them; but if bad, the vehicles were either swallowed in bogs, or fell into dykes; sometimes, indeed, they sunk into the miry road so deep, that there was little chance of escape until the warm weather and hot sun made their release easy.

"Markets were inaccessible for months together, and the fruits of the earth rotted in one place . . . " Long after coals came from Newcastle, "London was contented with wood or turf, owing to the impossibility of transmission . . . It was easier to send merchandise from the capital to Portugal, than to convey it from Norwich to London." In Scotland, "coal, manure, and grain could only be carried on the backs of cattle. If waggons were ever used, eight horses were necessary to draw two tons." Thus cost and time added considerably to the price of the goods.

Tolls were as heavy as the roads were bad, but had to be paid to the magnate whose land the roads traversed. Along the rough country roads, horses "dragged their hearts out" pulling the broad-wheeled wagons of Pickfords and other carriers. Teams of 20 to 40 heavily-laden pack horses lumbering along were a common enough sight.

So much for goods. But how did people travel? Dr. Lardner, a railway chronicler, presents a word picture of human isolation: "For a succession of ages, the little intercourse that was maintained between the various parts of Great Britain was effected almost exclusively by rude footpaths, traversed by pedestrians, or at best by horses. Hills were surmounted, valleys crossed, and rivers forded . . . in the same manner as the savage and the settler of the backwoods of America or the slopes of the Rocky Mountains communicate with each other."

By the 18th century the stage coach was part of the common scene, having come into use two centuries earlier. Francis writes: "Nor was it until 1565, according to Stowe, that the first Coach – built by the Earl of Rutland – formed a new era." Letters were regularly despatched by horse, however, "as fresh saddle-horses and guides were to be had at certain convenient distances."

An early 18th century advertisement throws some light on stage coach travel; custom which the railways would one day take over:

York Four Days – Stage Coach
begins on Friday the 12th of April, 1706

All that are desirous to pass from London to York, or from York to London, or any other place on that Road; let them Repair to the Black Swan in Coney Street in York;

At which both places, they may be received in a Stage Coach every Monday, Wednesday, and Friday, which performs the whole journey in four days (if God permits), and sets forth at Five in the Morning, And returns from York to Stamford in two days, and from Stamford, by Huntingdon, to London in two days more. And the like Stages on their return; Allowing each Passenger 14 lb. weight, and all above, 3d. a Pound.

Performed by { Benjamin Kingman, Henry Harrison, Walter Baynes.

Also this gives Notice, that a Newcastle Stage Coach sets out from York Every Monday and Friday, and from Newcastle every Monday and Friday.

Passengers were faced at that time with a marathon, despite the frequent change of horses, of two weeks from London to Edinburgh; but before the end of the century, as better roads were built, it was down to about four days.

It was mainly the conveyance of goods, not passengers, that prompted businessmen and engineers to turn their minds to an improvement on the horse. Watt had shown the way. Had he cocked an ear to some of his advisers, he might well have turned the course of railway history at an earlier stage; but he didn't.

After Watt, many inventors did do more than dream about a "travelling engine": Joseph Cugnot, Oliver Evans, William Symington, Matthew Murray, John Blenkinsop, Richard Trevithick, William Hedley, Timothy Hackworth, George and Robert Stephenson being the most notable. Watt had shown how to convert steam power through cylinders, pistons, and connecting rods, to rotate wheels. Now it was up to them.

Nicholas Joseph Cugnot (1725–1804) built a simple steam engine on three wheels in 1769. The French mechanic, who became a military officer, thought it might pull cannon to replace horses on the battlefield. He built a second, improved version and ran it in the streets of Paris on several occasions; it moved at little more than two miles an hour. Regrettably, it crashed into a wall and was prohibited from further use.

In Britain, a number of steam carriages to carry passengers were built experimentally in the early part of the 19th century. The boiler chimney was placed at the rear end, to keep steam and smoke away from passengers. This kind of steam carriage, to run on roads, evolved in two directions: towards the railway engine, and in large numbers towards the steam powered road car. An American, Oliver Evans from Philadelphia, built a steam carriage of this kind in 1804. It ran along the market street, but was not found practicable, and was later converted to a stationary engine to drive a grinding mill.

One of the most inventive locomotive engineers was a flamboyant and quick-tempered Cornishman, Richard Trevithick (1771–1833), from Illogan near Redruth. He stood 6 ft. 2 in. tall, and had earned a reputation in the West Country as a wrestler. His father acted as purser at several mines, and the young Richard spent much time around the workings, in the engine rooms and picking up information about pumping engines and mining machinery. Many Boulton and Watt steam engines were in use in the area. He became a pupil with William Murdock, the Boulton and Watt engineer who had built a model steam locomotive.

Trevithick joined his engineer cousin, Andrew Vivian, in business and they built their own stationary steam engines at Cambourne. They took out a patent in 1802 at Trevithick's instigation, for an improved steam engine and "the application thereof for driving carriages and for other purposes." The machine he now built was more efficient than any engine before it, and proved that a "travelling engine" was workable. With a watching crowd, he ran his vehicle successfully along the road, then repaired to an inn to drink to its future. It was Christmas-time. He celebrated rather well, forgetting for a while about his steam coach outside. Sadly, it caught fire and was destroyed, along with the shed in which it had been housed for the night.

Undaunted, he built another: this time to combine the steam horse with the iron way. After building a stationary steam engine at Pen-y-darran ironworks near Myrthyr Tydvil in South Wales, he built a railway locomotive – "the first ever constructed," reports Samuel Smiles, the most prolific railway historian of that century. It included many mechanical improvements, and was tested on the Pen-y-darran wagon way on 15th February 1804. A few days later it pulled a train of five wagons carrying ten tons of iron and 70 people for a distance of nine miles, and reaching a speed of about five miles an hour. It proved conclusively that a smooth wheel could grip a smooth rail with sufficient adhesion to draw a train. The plateway had a guiding flange, but the crude track proved too weak for the weight. There were many plateways in the ironworks and collieries of South Wales where the steam locomotive clearly had a future, once the track was perfected. The defect lay not in the engine, but in the track.

Trevithick's experiments gained wide public attention when, in 1808, he exhibited in London his new locomotive and a carriage which ran round a circular enclosed tramway. In the event, he was not taken very seriously, so he closed his exhibition in a furious temper. But at least one spectator was impressed, for he wrote to a friend: "My ride with Trevithick in the year 1808 in an open carriage propelled by the steam engine of which the enclosed is a print, then a waste piece, now Torrington Square." This was near the present Euston station. The print referred to, illustrating the locomotive, contained the caption:

TREVITHICK'S PORTABLE
STEAM ENGINE
Catch me who can
Mechanical Power Subduing Animal Speed

Another admirer among scientific gentlemen who inspected the equipment in detail was Sir Humphrey Davy, who wrote later to a friend in Cornwall: "I shall soon hope to hear that the roads of England are the haunts of Captain Trevithick's dragons – a characteristic name."

To get the exhibition engine to London, "it was successfully run by road from Cambourne to Plymouth, a distance of about ninety miles and shipped to London," writes a chronicler, "where it shortly after arrived in safety, and excited considerable curiosity."

Reports by observers of Trevithick's experiments were published from time to time, and widely read in Britain and overseas by engineers and businessmen. Samuel Smiles wrote: Trevithick "may be fairly regarded as the inventor of the railway locomotive if any single individual be entitled to that appellation . . . a person of extraordinary mechanical skill, but of marvellous ill fortune."

Ill fortune lay in the man himself. He set to work on so many inventions, but then left them to take care of themselves. His mind was always full of new projects which led him astray in search of new things. He failed to persevere in the one thing he had given to Britain – the steam locomotive. But others were to pick up where he left off.

GEORGE STEPHENSON COMES ON THE SCENE

Improvements in wagon-ways and tramroads by the use of iron rails on which flanged wheels of wagons could run, elevated them to the status of "rail-ways", even though still horse-drawn, or gravity-operated: loaded wagons attached to cables going down an incline of a short line and then the empty wagons being drawn up or hauled by cable worked from a stationary steam engine.

The very first Act of Parliament for any public railway in Britain was passed in 1801. It authorised the Surrey Iron Railway Company which opened in 1803: horse-drawn and for goods only. It ran initially for six miles between Wandsworth on the River Thames and Croydon, and was later to be extended. It was hardly a "railway", for the track consisted of cast iron plates about three feet long, secured by a square-headed spike at each end to stone blocks or "sleepers". Mules and donkeys supplemented the horse power. Freight consisted mainly of stone, lime and coal, transported at a penny to threepence per ton mile.

Fare-paying passengers were first conveyed by railway on 25th March 1807: a horse-drawn service on the Oystermouth Railway Company's line between Swansea and Oystermouth. It had been incorporated on 29th June 1804 and opened for goods in 1806. For many years, it was known as the Swansea & Mumbles Railway. Another horse-drawn line, for goods only, was opened on 6th July 1812 between Kilmarnock and Troon, 9¾ miles, to carry coal from the Duke of Portland's colliery to Troon harbour. This was the year of Napoleon's retreat from Moscow . . .

Steam power for railways engaged the attention of John Blenkinsop (1783–1831); but distrusting

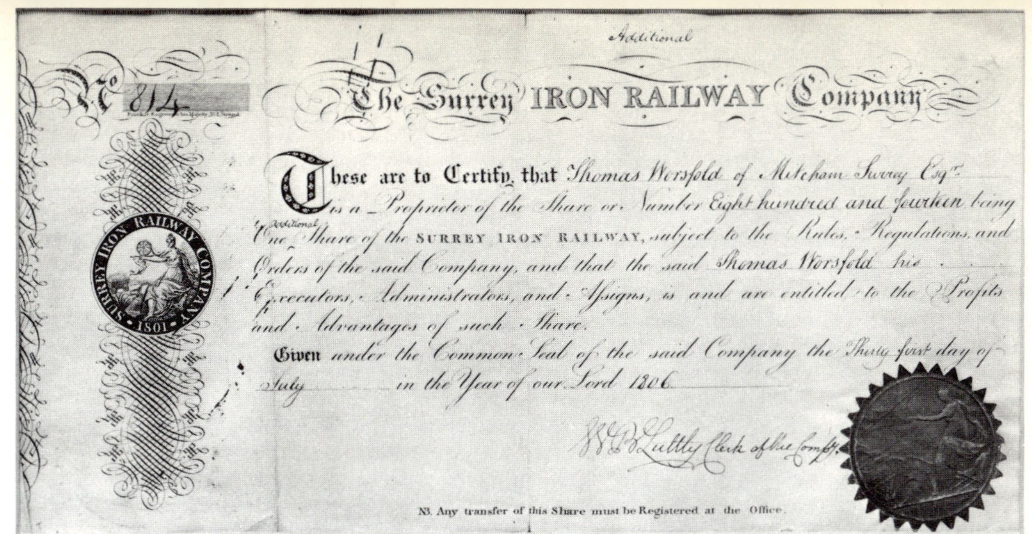

No 814

Additional

The Surrey IRON RAILWAY Company

SURREY IRON RAILWAY COMPANY 1801

These are to Certify, that Thomas Worsfold of Mitcham Surrey Esq[r] is a Proprietor of the Share or Number Eight hundred and fourteen being One Additional Share of the SURREY IRON RAILWAY, subject to the Rules, Regulations, and Orders of the said Company, and that the said Thomas Worsfold his Executors, Administrators, and Assigns, is and are entitled to the Profits and Advantages of such Share.

Given under the Common Seal of the said Company the Thirty first day of July in the Year of our Lord 1806.

NB. Any transfer of this Share must be Registered at the Office.

A Surrey Iron Railway share certificate dated 1806 and numbered 814. The horse-drawn railway was built to a gauge of 4 ft. (*Photo: Science Museum*)

the reliability of adhesion, he built an engine in 1812 with a cogged driving wheel. This meshed with a toothed rail, putting it in the rack-and-pinion class: a driving system still used on mountain railways. This locomotive, and similar ones he built, carried coal from the Middleton Colliery – where he was an inspector – for about 4 miles to Leeds; but it had obvious speed limitations. The rails were of cast iron. This was the first occasion when steam locomotives ran in regular use on a commercial basis.

William Hedley (1779–1843) built his famous *Puffing Billy* (still preserved in the Science Museum in London) in 1813, without driving-wheel cogs. His engine pulled coal some 5 miles from Wylam Colliery near Newcastle to Leamington-on-Tyne. Adhesion between a smooth rail and a smooth driving wheel, proved by Trevithick and confirmed by Hedley, had now come to stay; and the little engine itself stayed in active service for some 50 years, an astonishing working life.

By the time that George Stephenson (1781–1848) had arrived on the scene, the steam locomotive had also appeared. But it was still a poor thing that was crying out for its incredible potential to be thoroughly exploited. Stephenson was determined to do just that. And though he invented a miners' safety lamp, tinkered with clocks, and improved rails and their supporting "chairs", it was the steam locomotive which he now tackled in earnest and on the grand scale. The natural genius of this poorly-educated Geordie lad eventually brought him fame as the world's greatest railway engineer and designer.

His cottage home stood near Wylam Colliery several miles from Newcastle-on-Tyne. As a boy he had watched coal wagons being dragged along the wooden railway by horses. His first job as a farm hand included keeping the cows out of the way of the railway wagons. During leisure hours, he and a friend amused themselves by making models of stationary engines from clay, pieces of cork and wood. Next came a job at Black Callerton colliery, operating the colliery gin and horses, and bringing him into close contact with stationary steam engines. At fifteen he was promoted to fireman of steam pumps, feeding the engine with fuel, doing minor repairs and correcting mechanical faults. His natural mechanical gifts earned him the reputation of being a "good engine doctor".

Stephenson was no scholar. Compulsory education still lay in the future, and private tuition was only for the privileged few. At the age of seventeen he set himself the task of learning properly to read and write, evening study in which he was helped by a local school teacher. He was anxious to "read books and things" about the engineers of the day, among whom he was so soon to shine.

He had been particularly fortunate in 1805 when he was still only twenty-four, for Richard Trevithick, ten years his senior, had brought one of his own early locomotives to try out in Wylam Colliery on Tyneside. Stephenson was captivated. His interest therefore quickened, he was inspired to work out improvements on his own account.

During the next several years, he tried to build

steam engines himself; and in 1812 at the age of 31 (his son, Robert, was nine) he was appointed engine wright at Killingworth Colliery. Here he widened his experience and made a number of improvements to the steam engines around the colliery. More than ever, he saw the need for a more efficient steam locomotive. This need he intended to meet. Gladly he profited from the work of his predecessors, whose successes and failures were alike instructive. There was one feature that Stephenson had noticed about all the steam engines, either stationary or moving. It was that, once having done its job in the cylinders, the exhaust steam was wasted into the air. It seemed to him just plain commonsense to put that wasted power to work; and this he did by directing it through the smoke box and out through the chimney with the smoke, thus drawing the fire by the draught and creating greater heat: steam blast.

Others had thought of this before him, though he was not necessarily to know. Backed financially by Lord Ravensworth, a Killingworth Colliery partner (who was called a fool for wasting his money), George Stephenson built what he described as his first "travelling engine" named the *Blücher*, complete with steam blast. Stimulated combustion produced greater steam energy from the boiler, more than doubling the power of the locomotive itself. Tools were sparse, and so were men with mechanical skills in this new medium; he had to train them. A works mechanic and a colliery blacksmith did wonders within their limitations.

On 25th July 1814, *Blücher* was set upon the rails of Killingworth Railway. It drew eight loaded wagons of some 30 tons at about 4 miles an hour: not as yet a dazzling speed, but it was a date to be noted in engineers' diaries. Influential onlookers were impressed, and Stephenson's reputation was enhanced. After praising this engine, Smiles writes: "*Blücher* was nevertheless a somewhat cumbrous and clumsy machine. The parts were huddled together." In his second locomotive, Stephenson changed the entire construction and mechanics, with improved gearing and springs. These he patented on 28th February 1815.

His achievements were noted by colliery owners, merchants and industrialists who had specifically been cogitating about the faster and cheaper movement of coal and other minerals between two busy towns in Durham about twelve miles apart – Stockton and Darlington. A canal had been considered in 1810, or possibly a railway, to which, of course, canal owners were totally opposed. Competition could be catastrophic. Landlords, too, feared that the railways would ruin their property: sparks from fireboxes would set fire to their summer crops, lineside buildings would be set alight, and the noise of the engines frighten their cattle and result in still-born calves.

After a long series of battles and discussions, a Quaker named Edward Pease (1767–1858) backed the idea; a Parliamentary Bill, firmly rejected in 1820, managed to pass both Houses of Parliament in 1821, authorising the purchase of the land needed, and the raising of £100,000 working capital. In his vigorous campaigning, Pease had written to a newspaper declaring that railways "may be regarded as very little inferior to canals." Pease and his associates were still thinking only of a horse-drawn tramway. When Stephenson heard of the Act, he visited Pease; and later the directors of the Stockton & Darlington Company agreed to his appointment as engineer. "Geordie the engine wright" with a thick local-lad accent became "George Stephenson, Esquire, Engineer." It took a long time for the new engineer to persuade his masters that his Killingworth engine was as powerful as fifty horses, but finally he won; the Act, which had not specified locomotives, was suitably amended.

Stephenson assembled a team of hand-picked men, and surveyed the route. The first rail of the Stockton & Darlington Railway was laid, with much ceremony, near Stockton on 23rd May 1822, 12 years after the first exploratory meeting. Controversy still raged as the line was constructed. On 18th November 1824, the editor of the *Tyne Mercury* wrote: "What person would ever think of *paying anything* to be conveyed . . . in something like a coal wagon, upon a dreary wagon-way, and to be dragged for the greater part of the distance by a ROARING STEAM ENGINE!". This and other onslaughts failed to deter Stephenson.

As surveying progressed, something had to be decided firmly: the gauge – the distance between the insides of the two rails. Stephenson settled for the width used for common carts and wagons that ran on the common roads, which was similar to many horse-drawn tram-roads: a practical working arrangement. So the Stephenson gauge of 4 ft. 8½ ins. was born. For the rails themselves, wrought iron instead of cast was chosen for its greater strength.

Then came locomotives. Stephenson was convinced that a special locomotive works should be erected; he put up £1,000 he had earned for his miners' safety lamp, and Pease and others joined in. A piece of land in Forth Street, Newcastle-on-Tyne, was purchased, and work began the next year. Stephenson's son and understudy had joined his father and the works were called Robert Stephenson & Co., a nucleus that grew into a large business. Stephenson was commissioned to build three locomotives for the new railway. *Locomotion* No. 1 was the first, and is still preserved at Darlington.

(Various Wylam railroad steam locomotives inspired Mackenzie in 1825 in his *History of Northumberland* to describe them: "A stranger is struck with surprise and astonishment on seeing a locomotive engine moving majestically along the road at the rate of four or five miles an hour, drawing along from ten to fourteen loaded waggons, weighing about 21½ tons; and his surprise is increased on witnessing the extraordinary facility with which the engine is managed. This invention is a noble triumph of science.").

THE WORLD'S FIRST RAILWAY OPENS

Stephenson had been appointed engineer to the Stockton & Darlington Railway from the start, and the line took over three years to build. At last came the great occasion when the railway was officially opened, on Tuesday, 27th September 1825; the first railway in the world, complete with steam locomotive to pull wagons of goods and carriages of passengers along iron rails, and at the fastest-ever speed. Stephenson was right: *Locomotion* could certainly do the work of 50 horses. But even then, the regular conveyance of passengers had not been seriously considered.

In Darlington, a general holiday was declared. People came from miles around: from Durham, Newcastle, and Auckland. Men rode in on horseback, and people crowded in gigs, carts and other vehicles. As though for a royal event, crowds assembled at Darlington and Stockton, and all along the route to watch the great train go by. Anxious proprietors whose money was at stake had gathered at six in the morning, and the directors printed a programme of starting and passing times for the train, and a detailed list of the "procession of waggons." Spectators kept their distance from the panting, sparking engine, terrified that it might blow up, as indeed over the years many did.

For some time, the line was to be worked by steam locomotive, stationary engine with cables, and horses. Stephenson's biographer, Smiles, records that on this famous day: "A train of waggons laden with coals and merchandise was drawn up the western incline by the fixed engine, a length of 1,960 yards, in seven and a half minutes, then lowered down the incline on the eastern side of the hill, 880 yards, in five minutes.

"At the foot of the incline the procession of vehicles was formed, consisting of *Locomotion* No. 1 driven by George Stephenson himself; after it six waggons loaded with coals and flour, then a covered coach containing directors and proprietors, next twenty-one coal waggons fitted up for passengers (with which they were crammed), and lastly six more waggons loaded with coals. Strange to say, a man on a horse, carrying a flag, with the motto of the Company inscribed on it, *Periculum privatum utilatas publica*, headed the procession!" (Motto: Through private danger to the public good.)

Excited onlookers ran alongside the train. Gentlemen on horseback galloped across open fields to keep pace with it. Stephenson, eager to try out the speed of his locomotive, shouted and waved to the horseman with the flag ahead to ride out of the way. He then "put on speed" and rolled along the rails at about 12 miles an hour, and reaching 15 in places. Competing horse-riders and runners on foot were soon outpaced, and the journey of 12 miles from Darlington to Stockton was completed in about three hours. The train echoed to the sound of music from a local band of musicians who were travelling aboard. A great crowd welcomed the train on arrival at Stockton, and the directors with their special guests walked through the streets to the town hall for a celebratory dinner party, and to drink a toast to "The Stockton & Darlington Railway." Today was gala day. Tomorrow, there was a serious job to be started.

But interest was now more than local; steam power had been talked about and written about since Watt's day. Newspapers and technical journals told the world about every stage of progress, and the world took notice. On 1st October, before the line was quite ready, the *Newcastle Courant* applauded the venture and foresaw great prospects. The railway "will open the London market to the collieries . . of Durham, as well as facilitate the obtaining of fuel to the country along its line and the northern parts of Yorkshire . . .

"In contemplating the events of the day, either

in a national point of view, or as the efforts of a company of individuals furnishing a speedy, efficacious, and certain means of traffic to a wide and extended district, it alike excites the deepest interest and admiration; and the immense train of carriages covered with people, forming a load from eighty to ninety tons, gliding as it were smoothly and majestically along the Rail-Way through files of spectators, at such an astonishing rate of speed, left an impression on those who witnessed it that will never be forgotten."

Of the public opening, an eye-witness wrote: "The scene on the morning of the procession sets description at defiance. The welkin rang with loud huzzas, while the happy faces of some, the vacant stares of others, and the alarm depicted on the countenances of not a few, gave variety to the picture." He described the violent jolting of the train. Not all had gone quite smoothly. At one stage, a wagon became derailed and the train stopped to re-rail it. Then engine trouble caused another halt. Nervous passengers panicked and leapt awkwardly out of the wagons. When the train was ready to start again, Timothy Hackworth (1786–1850), then locomotive foreman and a skilled locomotive designer, shouted, "Every man to take his own convey", which, broadly translated, meant: "Take your seats, please!"

Another eye-witness recorded: "Nothing could exceed the beauty and grandeur of the scene. Throughout the whole distance, the fields and lanes were covered with elegantly dressed females and all other descriptions of spectators. The bridges under which the procession darted through with astonishing rapidity, lined with spectators cheering and waving their hats, had a grand effect."

George Stephenson's day of triumph was marred only by the absence of his 22-year-old son Robert, who had assisted him on the grand project. Young Robert had sailed the previous year for South America, where he would stay for some three years. He was to take charge of a mine engineering project in Colombia, but the move was mainly dictated by considerations of health. Despite this disappointment, the day had not only vidicated George's claims, but had even opened his eyes to new possibilities. The procession, attaining speeds of up to 15 miles per hour, was the fastest ever seen on earth, and far outstripped even its sponsor's wildest hopes. He was astonished by the numbers of people who vied for places in his coal-wagons – augury of good business for the future.

The coach which he had built in his Newcastle works, the *Experiment* (the first of several to bear the name) gave the directors a reasonably comfortable ride on the opening day. By today's standards a somewhat primitive vehicle, it was said to resemble a showman's caravan. Seats ran along each side of the interior, and a timber table was fixed in the centre. After the official opening, the *Experiment* went into service, horse-drawn between Stockton and Darlington, completing one journey daily each way. It covered the 12 miles in about two hours.

It was soon replaced by better passenger vehicles: the bodies of second-hand stage coaches which were mounted on underframes with flanged railway wheels. For some years they continued to be horse-drawn. Regular passenger business soon built up. First class passengers paid more to travel inside the coaches; second class had to make do with open vehicles with bench seats, little better than goods trucks.

Great industrial towns were created by the coming of the railway. One of the first was Middlesbrough, about 5 miles from Stockton. In 1825, only a few farms and houses occupied the site. Edward Pease and his Quaker friends bought land, built docks and made a new seaport on the River Tees to ship coal brought in by a new extension of the line. Behind these outworks the town itself sprang up – houses, schools, shops, churches, banks and a customs house, as well as giant shipbuilding yards and iron-smelting factories. Local newspapers forecast that Middlesbrough "would soon become a place of great trade and opulance." Within ten years, the population had ground to about 6,000.

This pattern was to be repeated in rapid succession in many other places. A new form of transport, new towns, new industries; but it is not certain that Stephenson realised fully that he had brought to birth a new breed of men – the engine drivers themselves, who were to become the elite among railwaymen.

His next important venture was to create fresh prosperity in the towns of Lancashire.

THE LIVERPOOL & MANCHESTER RAILWAY

When businessmen in the two great cities of Liverpool and Manchester first began to talk of a railway, formidable nation-wide opposition was mounted by landowners and canal companies "determined to wage war to the knife against all railways," both in public and in Parliament. Surveyor and coal owner William James, from West Bromwich, who had already laid several private tramways, was, however, a railway supporter. After seeing Stephenson's pioneering locomotives, he reported: "Here is an engine that will, before long, effect a complete revolution in society . . . It is the greatest wonder of the age, and the forerunner, as I firmly believe, of the most important changes in the internal communications of the kingdom." On James' recommendation, Stephenson was appointed engineer to the projected line in 1824, while still building his first.

As the debate raged in Parliament, violent views were given voice. Cows would be prevented from grazing and hens from laying eggs. Poisoned air from locomotives would kill the birds in the air. Houses near the line would be set on fire from engine sparks. Horses would become extinct. Engine boilers would explode and blow the passengers to pieces. One spokesman, supporting the Bill before Parliament in 1825, argued: "The horses have not started (been startled,) nor the cows ceased to give milk, nor have ladies miscarried . . . " In that year, Stephenson made his first appearance before a House of Commons Committee, and later recalled: "I began to wish for a hole to creep out at. I could not find words to satisfy myself or the Committee . . . was cross-examined by eight or ten barristers, purposely, as far as possible to bewilder me. One member asked me if I was a foreigner, and another hinted that I was mad . . . but I was determined not to be put down." The Hon. Edward Stanley (later Earl of Derby and Prime Minister) called upon the House to "prevent this mad and extravagant speculation." But the Bill became an Act the following year, and the work began.

Potential for the line was excellent, for the canals and roads linking the two cities were overburdened with traffic, canals froze in the winter, tolls were costly, the roads bad and road haulage expensive. On the new line, 63 bridges were built, under or over the railway, for crossing roads and streams. An enormous cutting at Oliver Mount, Liverpool, was hewn from solid rock for about two miles, in some parts at 100 ft. below ground level. Chat Moss, a vast area of bog, necessitated a costly and dangerous track-laying operation. The most notable piece of masonry was Sankey Viaduct, which spanned Sankey brook and canal. Opposition from landowners forced the building of a tunnel 1½ miles long under the town of Liverpool; it avoided Lord Sefton's estate entirely, and the line affected only a few fields belonging to Lord Derby.

Though Stephenson was the engineer, it did not follow that his locomotives would be used. That is why the directors planned a competition at Rainhill – the "Rainhill Trials" – held on 6th to 14th October 1829, with many spectators present, to find the best machine. Several were offered, but only four accepted:

Novelty – Braithwaite and Ericsson
Sanspareil – Timothy Hackworth
Rocket – Robert Stephenson & Co.
Perseverance – Burstall

Unable to make much progress, *Perseverance*

The viaduct over the Sankey Canal and valley, Stephenson's finest piece of masonry on the Liverpool & Manchester Railway. (Photo: Victoria & Albert Museum)

Third class passengers crowded in open wagons on the Liverpool & Manchester Railway where it crosses the Bridgewater Canal, as seen in the early 1830s. (Photo: Victoria & Albert Museum)

was withdrawn at an early stage; both the *Novelty* and the *Sanspareil* developed serious faults which a few days of delay could not put right. Performance of the *Rocket* far outstripped the others, and won the prize of £500. One of the judges was John Rastrick who later built locomotives in the Midlands and railways in the south.

The winning engine was built by George and Robert Stephenson, helped by Henry Booth, at their own works. It completed the allotted journey with "thirteen tons of waggons" at an average speed of 12½ miles an hour, and on one trip reaching 25 miles an hour. Running alone without vehicles, it amazed spectators by attaining 29 miles an hour.

Technically, apart from steam blast, the *Rocket* owed much of its success to its multi-tube boiler which vastly increased the water-heating surfaces for greater steam power. It weighed about 4 tons. Seven more Stephenson locomotives were ordered to be ready for the public opening.

The great event took place on Wednesday, 15th September 1830, with even greater public excitement than the first line had attracted.

Seldom if ever has a railway line been worked by such a distinguished array of engine drivers:

Northumbrian	George Stephenson
Phoenix	Robert Stephenson (aged 27)
North Star	Robert Stephenson (George's brother)
Dart	Thomas Gooch (George's assistant and brother of Daniel who later joined the Great Western)
Rocket	Joseph Locke
Comet	William Allcard (resident engineers of the railway
Arrow	Frederick Swanwick (George's assistant)
Meteor	Anthony Harding

The Prime Minister, the Duke of Wellington (1769–1852) was there, accompanied by his Secretary of State (and a later Prime Minister) Sir Robert Peel (1788–1850). They were joined by William Huskisson (1770–1830), a Member of Parliament who had vigorously supported railways both in and out of Parliament, for whom a tragic reward was in store.

On Monday, 20th September, *The Albion* reported: "The event . . . attracted the greatest number of men of eminence in the political and scientific world that ever assembled together in this town . . . Precisely at ten o'clock, the Duke of Wellington drove up to the door of the station in the Marquis of Salisbury's carriage, drawn by four horses." Another writer stated: "Liverpool was never so full of strangers . . . All the inns in the town were crowded to overflowing, and carriages stood in the streets at night, for want of room in the stable yards . . . Never was there such an assemblage of rank, wealth, beauty and fashion in this neighbourhood."

But rank and wealth on this illustrious journey were to be shattered by tragedy, throwing a dark shadow over the rest of the day's proceedings. The scene was Parkside, about 17 miles from Liverpool. The *Northumbrian* engine, with the Duke of Wellington's carriage, drew up on one line, so that trains on the other might pass in review before him and his party.

"Mr. Huskisson had alighted from his carriage," writes Smiles, "and was standing on the opposite road, along which the *Rocket* was observed rapidly coming up. At this moment, the Duke of Wellington, between whom he and Mr. Huskisson some coolness had existed, made a sign of recognition, and held out his hand. A hurried but friendly grasp was given; and before it was loosened, there was a general cry from the bystanders of 'Get in, get in!' Flurried and confused, Mr. Huskisson endeavoured to get round the open door of the carriage, which projected over the opposite rail, but in so doing he was struck down by the *Rocket*, and falling with his leg doubled across the rail, the limb was instantly crushed. His first words, on being raised were, 'I have met my death', which unhappily proved true, for he expired that same evening in the parsonage at Eccles."

"LOVELY AND WONDERFUL BEYOND ALL WORDS"

It is, to say the least, intriguing for railway history to be indebted to a bright young light from show business. Fanny Kemble (1809–1893), one of the most prominent actresses of the 19th century, had other – hidden – talents as a writer. Her prolific and facile pen filled several volumes of reminiscences, compiled throughout her long and exciting life. In her stage career she had played many dramatic parts, and was a niece of Sarah Siddons. She married a wealthy American, and while in Georgia campaigned for the emancipation of the slaves.

Fanny gained notoriety for herself and publicity for the world's second most important railway; she became the first lady to ride aboard a steam locomotive just a few weeks before the new Liverpool & Manchester Railway's official opening. Fanny was playing in a Liverpool theatre at the time, and was only 21. On 26th August 1830, she wrote vividly from Liverpool to a friend about her ride on a steam locomotive on the new line in company with George Stephenson himself.

"My dear H.," she begins, "A common sheet of paper is enough for love, but a foolscap extra can alone contain a railroad and my ecstasies . . . We were introduced to the little engine which was to drag us along the railways. She (for they make these curious little fire-horses all mares) consisted of a boiler, a stove, a small platform, a bench, and behind the bench a barrel, containing enough water to prevent her being thirsty for 15 miles . . .

"The reins, bit, and bridle of this wonderful beast is a small steel handle, which applies or withdraws the steam from the legs or pistons, so that a child might manage it. The coals (*it was, in fact, almost certainly coke*), which are its oats, were under the bench . . . This snorting little animal, which I felt inclined to pat, was then harnessed to our carriages, and Mr. Stephenson having taken me on the bench of the engine with him, we started at about ten miles an hour . . .

"You can't imagine," Fanny continues, "how strange it seemed to be journeying on thus, without any visible cause of progress other than the magical machine, with the flying white breath and rhythmical unvarying pace, between these rocky walls, which are already clothed with moss, and ferns and grasses; and, when I reflected that these great masses of stone had been cut asunder to allow our passage thus far below the surface of the earth, I felt as if no fairy tale was ever half so wonderful as what I saw. It was lovely and wonderful beyond all words . . .

"He explained to me the whole construction of the steam engine, and said he could soon make a famous engineer of me, which, considering the wonderful things he has achieved, I dare not say is impossible."

Miss Kemble describes the engine taking water and returning "at its most utmost speed, thirty-five miles an hour . . . When I closed my eyes, this sensation of flying was quite delightful, and strange beyond description."

She then turns her attention to Stephenson: "Now for a word or two about the master of these marvels, with whom I am horribly in love. He is a man of from fifty to fifty-five years (*he was actually forty-nine*); his face is fine though careworn, and bears an expression of deep thoughtfulness; his mode of explaining his ideas is peculiar and very original, striking, and forcible; and although his accent indicates strongly his north country birth, his language has not the slightest touch of vulgarity or coarseness. He has certainly turned my head."

One of the best descriptions of the new Liverpool & Manchester Railway comes from James Scott Walker (1793–1850), writer, traveller and pen friend of Sir Walter Scott. As a personal acquaintance of George Stephenson, he was privileged to watch the building of the railway at close quarters. He published a booklet entitled *An Accurate Description of the Liverpool and Manchester Rail-Way*, a facsimile reprint of which is still available. He writes, "The opposition was not without foundation, the nature of a Rail-Way not being yet understood . . .

"The passenger, having seated himself in one of the Rail-Way coaches, chaises, cars, barouches, or 'indescribables' . . . is immediately whirled, by manual agency, through the little tunnel, and if it be the first time in his life he has been plunged under land, he will feel a sensation analagous to that experienced on his first plunge under water, from which, however, he will, in like manner recover, with a glow of animation which will inspire him with confidence to prosecute the journey he has commenced . . . He may be puzzled by the puissance of the fire and steam, of the present application of which Euclid never dreamt in his philosophy . . .

"Arrived at the area behind Edge-hill, his machine, and many others, are yoked to a charger snorting steam and fire . . . the passengers all being seated, the engineer opens the valves, the hissing of the steam is suppressed. The engine moves, and is heard as if to pant, not from exhaustion, but impatience of restraint, the blazing cinders fall behind it, and the train of carriages are dragged along with a sudden and agreeable velocity, becoming, as it were, the tail of a comet.

"The spectators are soon left behind, the Turkish archway is passed, and the first view is obtained of an extent of the open Rail-Way."

Scott Walker describes it as "the greatest national triumph of the age . . . which for speed, elegance, and economy is altogether novel and astonishing." Finally, a prophetic note: "Never has the dominion of mind more fully exhibited its sovereignty over the world of matter than in this instance, and the consummation furnishes an example of successful enterprise which will not only give rise to similar undertakings in other parts of the country, but, it is not visionary to assume, may beneficially influence the future destinies of mankind throughout the civilized world." By the time he died, his prophesy had come true.

In a timetable published in 1835 by the Liverpool & Manchester Railway, departure times from both cities were still printed in full instead of in figures:

SEVEN o'Clock .... 1st Class Train
Quarter-past Seven o'Clock .... 2nd Class Train
TEN o'Clock .... 1st Class Train
Half-past Ten o'Clock .... 2nd Class Train
Twelve o'Clock .... 2nd Class Train
TWO o'Clock .... 1st Class Train
Three o'Clock .... 2nd Class Train
FIVE o'Clock .... 1st Class Train
Half-past Five o'Clock .... 2nd Class Train

(There were some additions on specified days. Times for first class trains were shown in capitals to add to their distinction.)

(FARES)

By First Class Train, Coaches,
Four Inside ...... 6s. 6d.
Ditto Six Inside .... 5s. 6d.
By Second Class Train,
Glass Coaches .... 5s. 6d.
Ditto Open Carriages .... 4s. 0d.
Charges for the conveyance of
Four-Wheeled Carriages...... 20s. each
Ditto Two-Wheeled Ditto 15s. each
Horses –
For One Horse 10s. – Two Horses 18s. –
Three Horses 22s.
(20s. = £1)

"Open Carriages" were little more than goods wagons with bench seats. Horse-drawn private road carriages were conveyed on flat railway wagons.

What the Stockton & Darlington Railway had proved, the Liverpool & Manchester brilliantly confirmed; and the world would never be the same again.

OVERSEAS INTEREST

Both the Stephensons were inundated with commissions to build more railways in Britain; invitations also came from overseas, and both father and son spent much time in Europe, between their railway construction projects in Britain. Industrial transport needs in Europe were just as pressing as those in Britain. The first steam locomotive railways in France opened in 1832; and in the 1840s, the Stephensons received an order for nine locomotives for the line from Marseilles to Avignon; one was named *L'Aigle Peirot*. Marc Seguin in 1829 had built the first steam engine to run on a French railway at Lyon, on a line which opened with horses in 1832. Enclosed fans driven by the tender wheels forced a draught through pipes to the locomotive furnace for greater heat.

Belgium and Germany were next for a railway, in 1835; and in that year, King Leopold of Belgium invited both the Stephensons to advise Belgian engineers about the first routes. They supplied two locomotives: the *Stephenson* and

La Fleché. In that year, Robert Stephenson built a locomotive for the first German railways at Nuremburg, and it was named *Adler* (Eagle). George Stephenson was called to Spain in 1845 for consultation concerning their proposed railways, and three years later the first line was opened from Barcelona to Mataro. The Spanish, despite his advice, built in a gauge of 5 ft. 6 ins. This still remains today, necessitating costly interchange facilities with the rest of Europe, which had adopted the Stephenson gauge as standard. A German engineer named Emil Kessler built a locomotive for the new Northern line in Switzerland; it had much in common with the Stephenson locomotives. Robert also visited Switzerland in the early 1850s to advise on tunnelling through the Alps: a daunting prospect about which he was far from sanguine. Norway was next on his travelling programme, where he was called to advise engineers on their first railway, a 42-mile length between Eidsvoll and Christiania (renamed Oslo in 1925). This railway was financed partly by British capital. He was a railway adviser in both Denmark and Sweden.

Following the reputation he gained in building tubular railway bridges, one across the Menai Straits and the other over the River Conway, he was commissioned to build three more. One was across the River St. Lawrence at Montreal, Canada, and two crossed the River Nile in Egypt.

Sir John Rennie (1794–1875), son of the celebrated canals and docks engineer, in 1852 went to Sweden where he laid out a system of new railways. Other British engineers, and contractors with gangs of navvies, took part in building new railways in several countries overseas. By 1850, principal railways in Europe had cut across frontiers, linking lines in France, Germany, Austria and Switzerland.

Robert Stephenson and his erstwhile partner, Timothy Hackworth, also supplied the first locomotives for the first steam line in Russia, opened between St. Petersburg (now Leningrad) and Pavlovsk in 1837. Rail gauge was then 6 ft.; but on the advice of an American engineer, a gauge of 5 ft. was decided on for their first major railway construction. This line, the Moscow & St. Petersburg Railway, which opened in 1851, took eight years to build. It was practically straight and level for its entire length of some 400 miles. In its day, it was one of the most outstanding railways in the world. Its gauge became the standard for Russia.

About the time of the Stephensons, another father and son named Cherepanov built two steam locomotives for an industrial line in the Urals, and the Russian engineers continued to develop their own locomotives. It may be reasonably supposed that the Russians already knew about the stationary steam engines developed by James Watt, and also that the Stephenson locomotives quickened the progress of their railways.

It was co-incidental that as the Railway Age dawned, masses of people from Britain and Europe were flooding into America, the "New World", to seek a new life. Industry was developing fast, and transport only slowly. Oliver Evans had built a steam carriage in America as early as 1804; but enough Americans had visited, or read about, Britain to know how the railways were developing. Foster, Rastrick & Company of Stourbridge, Worcestershire, sent a locomotive *Stourbridge Lion* to America in 1829 for their first railways, followed soon after by two more, the *Delaware* and the *Hudson*. About that time, Robert Stephenson sent one of his, the *John Bull*, a name that could hardly be more English. Matthias Baldwin (1795–1866), who had worked on stationary steam engines, studied it closely, made a similar model, secured his first orders from the new Philadelphia, Germantown & Norriston Railroad, and soon set up his own locomotive building works in Philadelphia. His business rapidly expanded, and by 1839 he had built 136 locomotives. In time, Baldwins Locomotive Works grew to be one of the largest of its kind in the world.

Two other locomotives were built by Stephensons in 1836, designed for the 5 ft. 6 ins. gauge New Orleans Railway; some financial problem prevented their export, so they were adapted for the new Great Western Railway in Britain.

Canada's first railway opened at Montreal in 1836 and the Stephensons supplied a locomotive called *Dorchester* for the new lines. Robert Stephenson's visit as a young man to South and North America for over three years must also have helped to spread the gospel about the railways of England.

Even without the Stephensons, travelling steam engines had been the subject of experiment in several overseas countries; and they would surely have been developed somewhere at a later date. But it is safe to say that having established the new form of transport in Britain, and done so much to pioneer railways in other countries, the Stephensons literally presented steam locomotive railways to the world.

Chapter 3

The Railway Mania

Manchester Victoria station of the Manchester & Leeds Railway in 1843. (*By courtesy of the Science Museum*)

BUILT as a mineral line, the Stockton & Darlington Railway earned a bonus from the unexpected number of passengers wishing to travel. The Liverpool & Manchester Railway proved beyond question what the Stockton & Darlington had indicated: that the railways with steam locomotion were here to stay. Although the L & M had planned to carry a few passengers, the sprinkling grew to an avalanche, and the line was simply swamped with people. Both goods and passengers far exceeded their expectations. Writing later, W. C. Chambers, who became a railway company chairman, gives some figures:

"Believing that the greater part of their business and of their revenue would be derived from the transport of heavy goods, they had set down £20,000 a year only as the estimated return from passenger traffic; and scarcely a week had passed before they became aware of the fact, as agreeable as it was unexpected, that passengers brought the greatest return. The whole number conveyed from the time of opening to the end of the year – three months and a half – was more than 71,000."

As a spectator of the line, the author of *The Fairchild Family* wrote: "The Monsters, being very civil monsters, not only relaxed their energies in passing the stands, but actually backed to give us time to see more of them, for there were several engines, and each had its line of carriages."

A doubtful comment came from Thomas Creevey (1768–1838), the writer, in a vivid thumb-nail sketch: "The loco-motive Monster, carrying some eighty tons of goods, and navigated by a tail of smoke and sulphur, coming through every man's ground between Manchester and Liverpool." Though later won over, the Duke of Wellington expressed his characteristic antipathy towards railways when he said publicly. "They encourage the lower classes to travel about" – a splendidly Wellingtonian pronouncement!

STEPHENSON: THE MAN OF THE MOMENT

It was largely a matter of persuasion; but excellent though Stephenson was with mechanical equipment, he found himself at a severe disadvantage when trying to defend his projects at various Parliamentary Committees. He was up against some of the most powerful and ruthless advocates of the day, who showed him no mercy as he struggled to be articulate in his thick Tyneside accent. Of the Proceedings for the Bill for the Liverpool & Manchester Railway, it was reported: "The cross-examination of George Stephenson shows how unprepared he was for the legalistic questioning of the Committee, where his natural frankness was continually used to show that he had not made sufficient surveys, and that he was not competent to undertake such responsibility. This was probably the prime example of Stephenson's disadvantage when his own practical judgement was subject to scientific scrutiny." At a Committee in the House, opposing counsel said that he "spoke like a foreigner", that his evidence was "trash and confusion", and he was stigmatised as an "ignoramus, a fool and a maniac." Sometimes he was temporarily shattered, and said so; but he was never beaten. His vision and dedication were absolute, although some of his friends and financial backers had serious qualms.

Many eminent men of genius have "lived before their time". George Stephenson was not one of them. Everything was right for him – at least, in the fundamentals. After the wars of the early 1800s, Britain was emerging as the richest and most powerful country in the world and her Industrial Revolution was sweeping her ahead of any other country. There was money to invest, men to work and an abundance of iron products. Much of the basic work both on steam power and on "waggon-ways" had preceded him. On top of this, his only son was an incredibly gifted engineer in his own right, to share the burden. He was the man of the moment: the right man in the right place at the right time; and he rolled up his sleeves and got on with it.

The fame of both of Stephenson's lines rapidly spread throughout Britain – now the world's railway laboratory. Colliery and other industrial areas were in equally desperate need of better transport, and would-be promoters carefully studied the success of these two lines. Industrialists could see enormous advantages in their transport efficiency; landowners hoped to make money from the sale and lease of land; and financiers were already rubbing their hands at the prospects of fat profits from new lines. One of the most impressive arguments in favour of railways was that the 31 miles between Liverpool and Manchester could be travelled in about two hours, compared with some 18 hours on the Bridgwater Canal.

Connecting lines were soon built: Bolton to Leigh, Leigh to Kenyon, and branches to Wigan, Runcorn and Warrington. Trade throughout Lancashire increased as a result. While still building the Liverpool & Manchester, George Stephenson's help had been sought to assist with a short line of 6 miles from Canterbury to the minor port of Whitstable; but he delegated the survey work to an assistant John Dixon, and construction to Joseph Locke. An Act had been obtained in 1826, and the line opened in 1830. The Stephensons built a locomotive, the *Invicta*, (still preserved in Canterbury) but the severe gradients of from 1 in 28 to 76 meant that stationary engines with cables had to do most of the work. Eight years after opening, the little railway (soon affectionately dubbed "the Crab and Winkle Railway") was leased to contractors, who sadly became bankrupt within two years. It struggled on, handed over operations to a new and expanding railway (the South Eastern) in 1844, selling outright nine years later.

An Act was secured in 1830 to build a railway of 16 miles between the coalfields of Swannington and the city of Leicester, and the Leicester & Swannington Railway opened two years later. George Stephenson had been asked to be the construction engineer; but being heavily committed, handed this work over to his son, Robert, then aged 27. When the question of rail gauge arose, George Stephenson replied: "Make them the same width. They (the other new railways) may be a long way apart now; depend upon it they will be joined together some day." He was right: this short line was to become the oldest section of a great new railway, the Midland, twelve years later. The construction of the line launched Robert Stephenson into a long and distinguished career as a railway engineer in his own right. It was on this line that the locomotive *Samson* became the first to be fitted with a steam "trumpet" following an accident on a level crossing in 1833.

Grandiose schemes elsewhere had been maturing. One of them, proposed in 1825, was to connect Birmingham with Liverpool and Manchester; and the considerable traffic to Ireland was an attraction – a railway that would carry traffic "by day and night, at all times of the year, in periods of frost and drought, at the rate of at least eight miles an hour."

One committee of promoters hoped to carry passengers at even 12 miles an hour, cautiously adding: "But as no experiments have been made on a large scale, we will not pledge ourselves to this."

Support was not forthcoming, either financial or parliamentary, until the first two pioneering railways had proved their value. A committee of

The magnificent curve of Newcastle Central station, opened in 1850 jointly by the Newcastle & Berwick and the Newcastle & Carlisle railways, and still one of the finest in Britain. (*Photo: Victoria & Albert Museum*)

businessmen formed in 1829 modified the plans for a railway from Warrington, which was to be connected to the Liverpool & Manchester at Newton, and south to Birmingham, and the line was given the title of the Grand Junction Railway. Prospects for traffic between the collieries and other heavy industries of Staffordshire and the Merseyside were ample to justify the investment. George Stephenson surveyed the routes; and by keeping most gradients no steeper than 1 in 330, his usual aim, tunnels would be needed. To reduce the number of tunnels the directors insisted on a change of route, and Stephenson was replaced by his assistant Joseph Locke; the permanent result was that gradients were much heavier.

The Grand Junction, after several rejections, received parliamentary authority for their 78 miles of railway in May 1833, and two years later took over the Warrington-Newton line. The Railway had by then acquired the art of "conciliating the landowners", and a very expensive process it proved. Resistance had been harsh. Canal companies, says Smiles, "had described the locomotive to the farmers as a most frightful machine, emitting a breath as poisonous as the fabled dragon of old." A Colonel Sibthorpe openly declared his hatred of the "infernal railroads," and said that he "would rather meet a highwayman, or see a burglar on his premises, than an engineer!" Though battles in public and in Parliament, and costly negotiations with landowners and vituperation from canal owners had been their lot, the way had been made somewhat easier by the first railways, and the Grand Junction Railway between Warrington and Birmingham opened throughout on 4th July 1837. Its own particular piece of history was that it was the first trunk railway to open in Britain.

THE LONDON & BIRMINGHAM RAILWAY

Another important line being constructed at that time was the London & Birmingham Railway. Such a possibility had been discussed by London and Birmingham businessmen of repute as early as 1825, and firm proposals made by 1830, with a committee in each of the two cities. George Stephenson was invited to survey the routes, and was sorely tempted to take on the work for such an important line. Instead, the responsibility was handed over to his son. One route proposed was via Oxford, and the other – which the Stephensons recommended – was via Watford and Coventry. When the Bill came before Parliament in 1831, nearly a hundred witnesses – some for, some against – were heard in committee. The line was to be 111 miles long, later extended from Camden to Euston to total 112 miles. For the London terminus, sites had been suggested at Marble Arch and near the Strand, before Camden was temporarily accepted.

Publication of the Bill prompted canal interests to issue a pamphlet entitled: *Remarks on the proposed Railway between Birmingham and London* in which canal charges were quoted for the conveyance of goods at 2 miles an hour, the fastest boats with frequent changes of horses completing the journey in 60 hours. But traders were far more attracted to the alluring prospects of much greater speeds and lower charges by a new railway.

Robert Stephenson described a personal clash with Sir Astley Cooper, an eminent surgeon, whose private grounds in Berkhamsted, Hertfordshire, lay on the route of the projected line. Sir Astley was one of many influential and inveterate opponents. Stephenson said, "We found a courtly, fine-looking old gentleman, of very stately manners, who received us kindly and heard all we had to say in favour of the project."

The inflexible surgeon replied: "Your scheme is preposterous in the extreme. It is of so extravagant a character, as to be positively absurd . . . You are proposing to cut up our estates in all directions for the purpose of making an unnecessary road. Do you think for one moment of the destruction of property involved by it? Why, gentlemen, if this sort of thing be permitted to go on, you will in a very few years *destroy the noblesse*!"

Landowners and their servants prevented the surveyors from tramping across the land, so much of the work had to be done at night with lanterns. One clergyman was so alarming in his demonstrations that his property was surveyed while he was in the pulpit. "This was managed," wrote Smiles, "by having a strong force of surveyors in readiness to commence their operations, who entered the clergyman's grounds on one side the moment they saw him fairly off them the other side. By a well-organised and systematic arrangement, each man concluded his allotted task just as the reverend gentleman concluded his sermon; so that, before he left the church, the deed was done, and the sinners had all decamped."

Opposition to the railway's Bill was almost unanimous, and it was thrown out. Wealthy landowners in the House of Lords were the most vociferous. Yet when the Bill was re-presented in 1833, it passed both Houses of Parliament with hardly a murmur. The mystery was solved later by a circular from the railway directors: " . . . the most active and formidable had been conciliated." The noble lords and influential landed proprietors had been "conciliated" by prices for their land of nearly three times the original estimates, the railway had paid out about £750,000 for land instead of the original £250,000. Parliamentary expenses had reached £72,868, working out at about £645 per mile before a single rail was laid.

Cuttings, embankments and tunnels on the route presented Robert Stephenson, still only 30, with his most challenging commission to date. As engineer-in-chief, his salary was £1,500 a year. Contractors with their navvies were appointed to the kind of work in which no-one had much experience; and it was reported that Stephenson walked the whole length between London and Birmingham more than twenty times, through hill and dale.

Inhabitants of Northampton, urged on by the local Press, and excited by men of education and influence, refused to have the line near the town; and a deviation meant the costly work of cutting

Railway architecture symbolised the pride felt by railway directors in their enormous achievements. Philip Hardwick designed the famous Euston Doric Arch in 1836 for the London & Birmingham Railway whose route had been selected by George Stephenson. It was sadly demolished in 1962. (Photo: Victoria & Albert Museum)

the Kilsby tunnel. In later years, Northampton was to clamour for a railway; and the branch laid from Blisworth was known among railwaymen for over a century as the "new line."

Stephenson, now married, who had moved his home temporarily from Newcastle to Haverstock Hill in North London, opened the line from Euston to Boxmoor on 20th July 1837, about a year after the Grand Junction had reached Birmingham. Constructing at the same time from the Birmingham end, the London & Birmingham Railway was opened progressively in stages and completed throughout on 17th September 1838. Great celebrations were organised at the important stages. Taking account of the remarkable engineering and landscaping, it was the most outstanding railway work of that time; it caught the imagination of a contemporary writer: "The London and Birmingham Railway is unquestionably the greatest public work ever executed either in ancient or modern times."

Comfort of travel still had a long way to go. Carriages were in three classes. Second class carriages were "without light, cushions, or divisions"; and the third class "without covering" were little more than open wagons with bench seats. Most passenger trains covered the journey in from 5 to 5½ hours; but third class trains took 8 hours and 45 minutes, an average of about 13 m.p.h. When challenged about low speeds, the directors stated that their "guiding principle was to consult the safety of their passengers."

NEW LINES ACROSS BRITAIN

Since 1830, railways in other parts of Britain had been coming into use. These were often isolated lines designed for a particular flow of traffic. In 1831, three lines opened in Scotland; the first section of the Edinburgh & Dalkeith Railway first used horse and cable traction; and so did the Dundee & Newtyle Railway, and the Garnkirk & Coatbridge Railway. Other early lines in Scotland were the Paisley & Renfrew in 1837, the Dundee & Arbroath in 1838 and the Arbroath & Forfar the following year. Cornwall's first line was the Bodmin & Wadebridge Railway in 1834; and in that year the first railway in Ireland was opened – the Dublin to Kingstown line. A gauge of 4 ft. 8½ ins. was used; but 23 years later it was converted to 5 ft. 3 ins., which has since remained as the standard for Irish railways.

As more lines were opened, opposition lessened. Some enthusiasts even suggested that the canals should be filled in and converted to railways. In fact, some canals actually gained from the general increase in trade and industry which the railways had created. Edward Pease, who had backed Stephenson from Darlington days, had once said: "Let the country make the railroads, and the railroads will make the country." The railways, said Smiles, "came to be regarded as inviting objects of investment to the thrifty, and a safe outlet for the accumulations of inert men of capital. Thus new avenues of iron road were soon in course of formation, branching in all directions, so that the country promised in a wonderfully short space of time to become wrapped in one vast network of iron."

New railways in the 1830s were able to make a new technical advance. Joseph Locke, who had worked for many years with the Stephensons, designed and developed a new type of rail in 1835. Low quality track had been one of the earliest problems for the pioneers to overcome, a difficulty that Trevithick had found so discouraging. George Stephenson had made some improvements, especially with chairs and fittings to take the rails. But Locke's new rail with the top section thickened to similar dimensions as the bottom, provided much greater strength to meet the wear and tear of heavier locomotives and higher speeds. This type of rail, known as "bull head", steadily came into general use, and with modifications remained the standard rail for well over a century.

Locke spent much of his working life in the North and the Midlands; and it was in these highly industrialised areas that the railways made rapid strides. The Leeds & Selby Railway, which opened in 1834, reversed the usual process by carrying passengers only, for nearly three months; then goods were carried as well. The line was an early link for later lines connecting right across the country from Liverpool and Manchester to Hull. Stretching across the narrowest neck of northern England, the Newcastle & Carlisle Railway opened its first section in 1835 between Blaydon and Hexham, taking another four years to complete the line throughout; this was just ten years since the railway was originally authorised.

The outline of a network began to take shape as new lines were built to connect with others. In 1839, the first section of the Midland Counties Railway was opened between Derby and Nottingham, and extended the following year to Leicester, and to Rugby where the London & Birmingham Railway was already in business. Further links were made with the opening in 1839 of the Birmingham & Derby Junction Railway, and the Manchester & Birmingham Railway which opened to Stockport in 1840 and as far south as Crewe in 1842. The station was built on the site of a farm at Monks Coppenhall, taking its name from Crewe Hall, the country seat of Lord Crewe. No-one would claim that the name itself had any literary resonance; but its aura of local prestige was enough for the railway. In the following year Francis Trevithick, son of the famous Richard, founded Crewe Works for the Grand Junction Railway; he later became a locomotive superintendent on the London & North Western Railway. As more lines were built Crewe became a nodal point for lines from London, Manchester, Birmingham, North Wales, Hereford and Stoke-on-Trent, and the small village grew to a large and thriving town.

London businessmen were also considering their first railways, and they had to fight for them as hard as had their counterparts in the North. The first public railway in London opened on 8th February 1836, between Spa Road near London Bridge and Deptford, as part of the London & Greenwich Railway. Long before the project reached Parliament (it was authorised in 1833), the *Quarterly Review* had this to say:

"Can anything be more palpably ridiculous than the prospect held out of locomotives travelling twice as fast as stage coaches? We should as soon expect the people of Woolwich to offer themselves to be fired off upon one of Congreve's rockets as trust themselves to the mercy of such a machine going at such a rate. We will back Old Father Thames against the Greenwich railway for any sum."

A viaduct of arches had to be built for about 4 miles; large revenues from lettings under the arches for the use of trades were expected, but never reached full expectations. In the year of opening the line was extended to London Bridge, and two years later to Greenwich, and the Company maintained its identity, despite pressures from competitors, for 87 years. In 1839, the London & Croydon Railway opened, on a route where there was already a canal, building a station alongside London Bridge and running part-way along the Greenwich line.

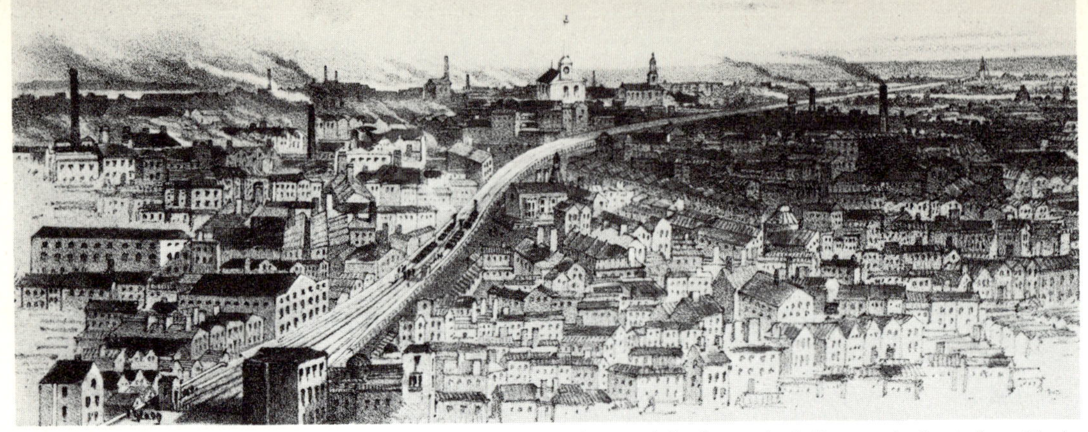

The London & Greenwich Railway opened in 1836, London's first, and the first to be built on a single viaduct. Trains ran on the right-hand rail, a peculiarity that ended in 1901. (*By courtesy of the Science Museum*)

Every new line that opened anywhere in Britain was fêted with the most lavish celebrations. For example, when the Greenwich line opened London Bridge station on 14th December 1836, the railway directors, local dignitaries and the Lord Mayor of London travelled on special trains. At London Bridge, the Scots Fusiliers played the trains away with triumphal brass; and at Deptford, music was provided by the Coldstream Guards. Church bells rang out on the route, and excited onlookers watched from the housetops as the trains steamed by. A celebratory banquet at the Bridge House Tavern rounded off the day.

Five steam locomotives hauled trains every 15 minutes at busier times; and in the first week, £17 was taken in fares, copper checks serving as passenger tickets. In the first full year nearly 1½ million passengers were carried, vindicating the judgment of the pioneers.

To serve the Metropolis, the next project was for a line between London and Southampton. Early railway progress did not deter a company in 1831 from proposing a canal to connect the thriving port of Southampton, with its four tides a day, through to London. Canal men still thought of their waterways as supreme. Another company presented a Bill to Parliament for a railway instead, of 77 miles distance, and received the Royal Assent in 1834. Nine Elms, well south of the centre of London, was chosen as the London terminus, on 7 acres: "a low swampy district, occasionally overflowed by the Thames. Its Osier beds, pollards and windmills and the river gave it a Dutch aspect."

Construction of the London & Southampton Railway began from each end, opening to the public first to Woking on 21st May 1838 and Basingstoke on 11th June 1839; then about that time north to Winchester. Until the railway was opened throughout on 11th May 1840, an enterprising – perhaps even desperate – Mr. Chaplin, owner of 64 coaches and about 1,500 horses, covered the gap of eighteen miles by stage coach to give passengers a through connection.

Just before the route was completed, the directors were eager to build a branch between Southampton and Portsmouth. Jealousy was rife between the two leading ports because of the keen trade rivalry; and Portsmouth would not withdraw their objections until the railway changed its name to the London & South Western Railway. In succeeding years the railway expanded as rapidly and successfully in the South and the West Country as had its northern counterparts, to become one of the leading Victorian railways.

Early London successes prompted promoters to consider railways to the East Kent Coast. Even in the 1820s, soundings had been made; and in 1832 a "gigantic scheme" was planned for a line from Deptford to Dover. It was not only opposed but ridiculed and then rejected. It took another four years for a new company, the South Eastern Railway, to get a Bill through Parliament for a line from Redstone Hill (Redhill) by a circuitous route through Oxted, Tonbridge and Ashford to Dover. Costly tunnels and long cuttings delayed the work. One projected tunnel near the coast and under the Downs that rose 375 ft. above sea level, proved so expensive that the land was "blown up" by a massive gunpowder charge and a cutting made. A Board of Trade Report acknowledged the difficulty of the railway and added a warning that "it would be liable to be overwhelmed by the fall of the cliffs above it or be destroyed by the irruptions of the sea"; but the substantial works of the railway survived.

The South Eastern's line opened on 26th May 1842 to Tonbridge; it was extended to Headcorn in August, Ashford in December, Folkestone on 28th June 1843, and completed to Dover on 7th February 1844. From then on, further expansions began.

London itself was growing fast, and the population between between 1801 and 1841 had doubled from nearly 1 million to about 2 millions. More business was available for the new railways in the conveyance of passengers and the goods they consumed. A railway route to Brighton, the leading watering place on the south coast, had attracted several groups of promoters, the power struggle culminating in 1835 with six separate schemes. Only two of them – one backed by Stephenson and the other by Rennie – reached the Parliamentary Committee stage. Both were rejected. In the following year, Rennie's scheme obtained the necessary powers.

The railway's original name showed an ambitious programme – the Surrey, Sussex, Hants, Wilts and Somerset Railway Company – but it was finally named the London & Brighton Railway. A viaduct had to be built across the Ouse Valley, and five tunnels, the longest of which was the Clayton, of over a mile and a quarter. A writer of the times reported that the tunnels were "whitewashed well throughout, and plentifully lighted with gas . . . to the driver of utmost moment, enabling him to see the road throughout as well almost as in broad day." The line commenced at a junction with the Croydon Railway; the first part to be opened was from Brighton to Shoreham in May 1840, and the remainder in stages in the following year. The London & Brighton Railway was amalgamated with the Croydon Company on 27th July 1846, and the new company was called the London Brighton & South Coast Railway. The year before, the 5-mile section between Shoreham and Worthing had been opened, as part of its expansion programme.

Agricultural East Anglia was somewhat late in acquiring railways; and many schemes were projected both in London and in the country. Railways for the Eastern Counties were considered in 1826, only a year after Stephenson's first line; another project was made in 1831 for a London & Essex Railroad. Nothing came of them. Then the Eastern Counties Railway was formed, to run a line from London through Chelmsford, Colchester, and Ipswich to Norwich and Yarmouth, "a grand line of 126 miles", and an Act was passed in 1836. One writer said of it: "Thus was started a railway which has already excited more attention, caused more correspondence, created more litigation, and been more productive of ill-feeling at public meetings than any other undertaking in the country."

Shareholders refused to pay their instalments (railway shares were often obtained by instalments), and a heavy Government loan had to be sought. Three years after authority to build, the line had only reached Romford. The line was extended to Colchester and ceremoniously opened in February 1843, directors and shareholders travelling on the inaugural run; but heavy rains had made the line unsafe, the banks at Brentwood slipped, and railway arches at the London end were found to be defective. It took about seven years to complete the 51 miles from Devonshire Street, Shoreditch, to Colchester. Complaints from passengers and the press were frequent and furious; and William Makepeace Thackeray (1811–1863), the novelist, wrote: "Even a journey on the Eastern Counties must have an end at last . . . "

The biggest blunder the directors made was to build the first part of their railway in a 5 ft. gauge; and in 1844 it was converted in about two months to the standard gauge, trains running on single lines until this was completed. The directors had wanted a broad gauge of 7 ft.; but the railway's engineer, Braithwaite, who had spent many years with the Stephensons on Tyneside, dissuaded them – yet surprisingly settled for a 5 ft. gauge.

At one stage, the Company's finances were in such a state that creditors held their rolling stock as security; but the ill-fated line survived to extend its routes, including a 56-mile section from Bishop's Stortford to Brandon in 1845.

During this decade, railways were rapidly springing up throughout the country: The Great Eastern, Great Northern, the Newcastle & Darlington Junction, the Birmingham & Gloucester, the Manchester & Leeds, the Bristol & Exeter; established railways were extending or taking over smaller companies, and new lines were opened in Scotland, including the Edinburgh & Glasgow in 1842, and in Ireland.

THE START OF THE GREAT WESTERN RAILWAY

Another railway of outstanding achievement in these pioneering days was the Great Western Railway. Committees were active in 1832 both in

Vauxhall station in 1841, Birmingham terminus of the Grand Junction Railway to Warrington. The company was absorbed in the London & North Western Railway formed in 1846. (*By courtesy of the Science Museum*)

London and in Bristol to build a railway between the two cities; and the following year the Company issued its first prospectus. At the same time, the directors appointed a young man of 27 as its engineer. Isambard Kingdom Brunel (1806–1859) was the son of a distinguished French engineer, Sir Marc, who had spent much time in Britain and America on unusual engineering projects.

Brunel entered his father's office at seventeen, and three years later was appointed resident engineer for the building of a tunnel under the River Thames at Rotherhithe. He suffered a number of hardships and setbacks, including one incident when the tunnel became seriously flooded and he nearly lost his life. During his career he erected buildings, constructed bridges, designed three famous ships and made a name for himself by a diversity of achievement. But at 27 he was fascinated by railways, and the world was before him.

In the years 1833–35, Brunel and the directors faced the accepted opposition that bedevilled railway constructors. Concern about canals, rivers, stage-coaches, farms and estates of the landed gentry were all reasons for protest. Some people complained that the railway would be too close to their land; others, that it was too far away. On top of this, the strongest and most well-organised opposition came from a rival railway, the London & Southampton. This Company argued that their line to Basingstoke and a new line to Bath and Bristol would be the best routes for the port. Debates raged in the House of Lords for 40 days. Opposing counsel claimed that the River Thames would stagnate for lack of traffic, and that drainage would be impaired. London's bad characters would travel to Eton and ruin its College; and, worse still, scholars would be likely to travel to London and be tempted into degrading dissipation.

Both inside and outside Parliament, alarm was spread about the tunnels, particularly the one planned in Wiltshire, the Box Tunnel. Aggravating the natural public fear, Dr. Buckland, a geologist, warned that vibration from the trains could bring the tunnel roof crashing down. His theory was later disproved by the Government's Inspector-General of Railways, who pronounced the tunnel secure. Threats, protests and frightening forebodings were all overcome, and the battle for the Great Western Railway was won. Parliamentary approval was secured in 1835, and work began before the year was out.

Brunel kept lengthy journals and at that time he noted: "The Railway is now in progress. I am engineer to the finest work in England. A handsome salary of £2,000 a year, on excellent terms with my directors, and all going smoothly." His first serious blunder was in his choice of highly unsatisfactory locomotives.

Brunel was not an original builder of locomotives and had to buy them elsewhere. Two came from the Vulcan Foundry – the *Premier* and *Vulcan*; and two from Hawthornes of Newcastle – the *Hurricane* and *Thunderer*. Before the first section of the new line was publicly opened, George Gibbs, one of the directors, reported in 1838 after a test run on the *Thunderer*: "The engine ran beautifully smooth and for some of the way we cleared sixty miles an hour," a fantastic

Above: Metropolitan Railway 4–4–0T No. 23, built in 1866 by Beyer Peacock to Fowler's basic design. Preserved today at Syon Park. (Photo: John Adams, Esq.) Below: Great Northern Railway No. 1, Patrick Stirling's masterpiece of 1870. The renowned Stirling Singles with 8 ft. 1 in. driving wheels hauled expresses between King's Cross and the North. (Photo: By courtesy of J. M. Jarvis, Esq.)

A signal post on an early Great Western Railway broad gauge line. (*Photo: British Rail*)

sight in those days. But the mixed bag of unsatisfactory engines left the railway in an anxious state. Better engines were now urgently needed.

A year earlier, Brunel had engaged as his chief locomotive assistant a talented mechanical engineer named Daniel Gooch (1816–89) who had worked for the Stephensons. His brother, Thomas Gooch, was Stephenson's assistant. At Newcastle, Daniel had helped design two locomotives intended for America: the *North Star* and *Morning Star*, with 5 ft. 6 ins. gauge; but the deal fell through. Fascinated by a wide gauge railway, Gooch persuaded Brunel to take the two engines after conversion by the Stephensons to 7 ft. gauge. When *North Star* arrived, it was the only locomotive the GWR possessed that was really reliable. Without Gooch and the two Stephenson engines, and a number of others supplied over the years, the new railway would have been in an impossible position.

At 21, Gooch became the right-hand man to the 31-year-old Brunel and between them they built up this great railway. In later years, Gooch created a series of outstanding locomotives for his Company, and their derivation from Stephensons' little engine the *North Star* was acknowledged to be unmistakable.

Despite the youthful optimism, Brunel was to suffer severe setbacks in his most distinguished career, and to die at a comparatively early age, discouraged and worn out. One of his major disappointments concerned the gauge of his railway. He had persuaded the directors to accept a wide gauge of 7 ft., despite the fact that nearly all other railways were 4 ft. 8½ ins. He was determined that the Great Western should be a "giant's road", and that his trains should travel twice as fast as others, and that riding would be smoother. Because of the layout of the countryside, except in the extreme west, Brunel was able to build his line without too many heavy gradients.

The Great Western Railway was opened from Paddington to Maidenhead via Slough on 4th June 1838 – the first train hauled by Stephenson's *North Star* – and extended to Twyford on 1st July 1839 and to Reading on 30th March the following year; the section between Bristol and Bath was opened on 31st August. The line throughout from Paddington to Bristol was completed on 30th June 1841, to become one of the most important lines in Britain. Brunel was fêted. By taking his line through Slough, only a few miles from Windsor, he could reasonably hope for Royal patronage.

A ROYAL JOURNEY

The Royal accolade was bestowed on 13th June 1842 when Queen Victoria (1819–1901), travelling from Windsor Castle with her Consort, Prince Albert, made her first railway journey in a luxurious royal saloon supplied by the Great Western Railway; and Brunel rode on the engine footplate to supervise affairs. The Queen was then only 23 years old, and the mother of two young children. The younger was Prince Edward, who later became King Edward VII. Her Majesty was heard to remark upon her new travel experience as being "free from dust and crowd and heat." Writing the following day to her uncle, King Leopold of Belgium, she said of the railway, "I am quite charmed by it."

Railway carriages and locomotives were still crude, and it was natural that the Queen should be criticised for risking her life. Despite public disquiet, she continued to travel by train from time to time, and later a branch line was built from Slough to Windsor. Royal travel did much to popularise railways at a time when there were still many people who would never go near them.

Queen Victoria was responsible for encouraging the Duke of Wellington to travel by train. Smiles records: "It was long before the Duke of Wellington would trust himself behind a locomotive. The fatal accident to Huskisson, which had happened before his eyes, continued to prejudice him strongly against railways, and it was not until the year 1843 that he performed his first trip on the South Western Railway, in attendance upon Her Majesty."

COMPETITION BETWEEN COMPANIES

Competition was rife as both the Great Western and the London & South Western pushed their lines further in the South-West; and the Great Western met competition on another front as it thrust towards the Midlands. Brunel could foresee trouble ahead, as is seen from a letter he wrote in 1844 to his friend Charles Babbage: "Things are in an unhealthy state of fever here, which must end in a reaction; there are railway projects fully equally to £100,000,000 of capital for next year, and all the world is mad. Some will no doubt have cause to be so before the winter is over." And during the winter, he wrote to another friend, one from his youth: "Here the world is railway mad. I am really sick of hearing proposals made. I wish it were at an end. I prefer engineering very much to projecting . . . it would suit my interests and those of my clients perfectly if all railways were stopped for several years to come."

But still more railways were planned. Successful lines had made good profits and some investors were tempted to put their total capital into new lines. Yet hundreds of people lost money or were ruined for life. Unfettered by sound legislation, many schemes went ahead that had not the slightest hope of succeeding. Large amounts were unnecessarily wasted in futile parliamentary and public battles. One idea was for a line from Yarmouth to Swansea. It was given the impressive title of Great Eastern & Great Western Railway. Another was named The Southern Counties Union, Bristol, Bath and Dover Direct. *Punch* drily observed: "It's John O'Groats and Land's End Junction, with branches to Ben Lomond and Battersea!" The previous year, a solicitor had noted in his diary: "I am alarmed at the number of new lines before Parliament and continuing to be brought forward. A panic will come. That is unquestionable, but I think it will be staved off so long as we have fifteen millions in the Bank of England. As soon as a bad harvest comes, then the gold will be withdrawn, accommodation at the bankers' will decrease, instalments continue to be called for, shareholders will not be able to sell, and then for the crash."

Many young engineers and surveyors on the railways were sacked. This grieved Brunel when he wrote: "It is positively shocking to see how many of these young engineers have looked upon their positions as a certainty, have been marrying, and making themselves happy, and now suddenly

Engine house at Swindon, opened by Brunel in 1843 for the Great Western Railway. (Photo: Victoria & Albert Museum)

find themselves in debt and penniless." Railway investment, for the get-rich-quick speculator or the retired professional gentleman, was risk capital in every sense. The fever swept the money markets. This was indeed "Railway Mania".

During the boom years of 1845–48 about 650 Acts of Parliament were passed for new railways, or expansion of railways already in operation, with 272 Acts passing through Parliament in the peak year of 1846 for still more new railways. Many of the projected railways never saw the light of day; and the preparation of Parliamentary Bills, surveyors' plans and architects' drawings wasted massive sums of money subscribed by many people greedy for the quick profits promised from the boom. The enormous legislature clogged parliamentary procedure.

Writing later, Chambers recorded: "With the success of the Liverpool & Manchester Railway began that course of commercial enterprise, unregulated, and often wasteful, which has since assumed such importance. Refraining from all control over railway operations, the Government left speculators to carry lines anywhere or anyhow that Parliament could be persuaded to sanction.

"The result, as is well known, has been in many places a complication of competing lines on no principle of economy or enlightened foresight. Abandoned, as it were, to the audacity of promoters and the mere brute force of capital, schemes good, bad and indifferent, had to fight their way at a cost almost exceeding belief; while at the same time there has been much waste of money in constructing circuitous lines to places which are afterwards, in a great measure, superseded by others more direct."

Samuel Smiles made much stronger accusations: "Parliament, whose previous conduct in connection with railway legislation was so open to reprehension, interposed no check – attempted no remedy. Many of its members were themselves involved in the mania, and as much interested in its continuance as the vulgar herd of money-grubbers.

"The railway prospectuses now issued – unlike the original Liverpool & Manchester, and London & Birmingham schemes – were headed by peers, baronets, landed proprietors, and strings of MPs. Thus, it was found in 1845 that no fewer than 157 Members of Parliament were on the lists of new companies as subscribers for sums ranging from £291,000 downwards! The projectors of new lines even came to boast of their parliamentary strength, and of the number of votes which they could command in 'The House' . . . many utterly ruinous branches and extensions projected during the mania, calculated to benefit the

The first Paddington station, opened in 1838 as the London terminus of the Great Western Railway. In 1854 it was rebuilt and enlarged to Brunel's design on a nearby site much as it is today. (By courtesy of the Victoria & Albert Museum)

Second class travel in early days – sides open to the elements, hard seats, wooden carriages, no lighting or heating, and probably in a jolting train including goods wagons. Such a journey was often frightening, but still better than sitting on a stagecoach for many hours. From a contemporary painting. (*City of Birmingham*)

inhabitants of a few miserable boroughs . . . were authorised in the memorable sessions of 1844 and 1845."

George Stephenson was frequently entreated to lend his name to shady companies. Had he been less scrupulous about the numerous projects for which he was consulted, he might well have accumulated a vast fortune. As it was, he acquired considerable wealth and his son Robert became a millionaire. But according to Smiles, "He held aloof from the headlong folly of the hour; and endeavoured to check it, but in vain . . . he had no desire to accumulate a fortune without labour and without honour. He himself never speculated in shares." A list of new railways opened in the years 1832–48 was published by George Bradshaw, the timetable expert, in his manual dated 1849; some dates vary from other official sources because some lines opened and had to close temporarily to meet problems, some were opened experimentally, and others had an "official" ceremonial opening which may have been before or after the date opened for public traffic:

1832.	Apl.	10.	Dundee & Newtyle opened.
1836.	Dec.	14.	London & Greenwich opened.
1837.	Jul.	6.	Grand Junction opened.
1838.	May	31.	Manchester & Bolton opened.
	Jun.	5.	Great Western partly opened.
	,,	18.	Newcastle & Carlisle opened.
	Sep.	17.	London & Birmingham Railway opened throughout.
	Oct.	20.	Durham Junction opened.
	,,	22.	North Union & Preston opened.
	,,	30.	Sheffield & Rotherham opened.
1839.	Jan.	3.	Arbroath & Forfar opened.
	Jun.	14.	London & Croydon opened.
	Aug.	11.	Birmingham & Derby opened.
1840.	Jan.	8.	Chester & Birkenhead completed.
	Apl.	1.	Dundee, Perth & Aberdeen Junction (16¾ m.) opened.
	May	3.	Preston & Longridge opened.
	,,	11.	South Western opened throughout.

The impressive frontage of Newcastle Central station: an appropriate edifice for Stephenson railway country. Drawn in 1850. (W.P.L.)

	Jun.	20.	Newcastle & North Shields.
	,,	29.	Midland Counties opened.
	,,	30.	York & North Midland opened.
	Jul.	13.	Glasgow & Ayr opened.
	,,	14.	Maryport & Carlisle opened.
	,,	17.	Preston & Wyre opened.
	Sep.	15.	Northern & Eastern partly opened.
	Oct.	9.	Taff Vale partly opened.
	Nov.	13.	Stockton & Hartlepool opened.
1841.	Jan.	2.	London & Blackwell completed.
	,,	4.	Birmingham & Gloucester completed.
	Jun.	26.	Lancaster & Preston Junction opened.
	Sep.	22.	Chester & Birkenhead opened.
	Oct.	1.	Chester & Crewe opened.
1842.	Feb.	5.	Durham & Sunderland opened.
	,,	6.	Edinburgh & Glasgow opened.
1843.	Feb.	7.	Glasgow, Kilmarnock & Ayr opened.
	Mar.	29.	Eastern Counties opened.
	Jun.	22.	Bolton & Preston opened.
1844.	Jan.	5.	Bristol & Gloucester opened.
	Jan.	9.	Dublin & Drogheda completed.
	Feb.	9.	Yarmouth & Norwich opened.
	May	1.	Bricklayers Arms Extn. (S.E.) opened.
	,,	2.	G.W. opened to Exeter.
	,,	4.	Liverpool & Leeds Junction opened.
	Dec.	3.	Warwick & Leamington opened.
1845.	Jul.	27.	Eastern Counties opened to Cambridge and Ely.
	Sep.	13.	Her Majesty's Railway at Gosport opened.
1846.	Apl.	14.	Lancashire & Yorkshire (Ashton Branch) opened.
	May	26.	Exeter to Teignmouth opened.
	Jun.	1.	East Lancashire, Blackburn to Preston, opened.
	,,	15.	Eastern Union opened.
	Aug.	6.	Nottingham & Lincoln opened.
	Sep.	3.	Syston & Melton Mowbray opened.
	,,	28.	East Lancashire, Manchester to Rawtenstall, opened.
	Oct.	3.	Stamford & Peterborough opened.

Oct. 4. Hull & Bridlington opened.
,, 27. Lynn & Downham Branch opened.
Nov. 3. Shrewsbury & Chester opened to Ruabon.
Dec. 1. S. East Margate Branch (3½ m.) opened.
,, 17. Lancaster & Carlisle opened.
1847. Jan. 12. Eastern Counties (Ely to Peterborough, 28¼ m.) opened.
Feb. 10. Wymondham to Dereham (12 m.) opened.
,, 23. Lancaster & Carlisle opened with double line.
Mar. 20. Whitehaven Junction (12 m.) opened.
Apl. 20. Kendal & Windermere opened.
May 10. Croydon & Epsom opened.
,, 24. Dundee & Perth (20¼ m.) opened.
,, 28. Eastern Counties, March to Wisbech, opened.
Jun. 2. Southampton to Dorchester opened.
,, 14. Havant & Portsmouth opened.
Jul. 2. South Eastern (Deal Branch, 8¾ m.) opened.
,, 4. Whitby & Pickering opened.
,, 31. Lowestoft Branch opened.
Aug. 16. Narboro' to Swaffham (5¾ m.) opened.
,, 23. Gravesend & Rochester reopened.
,, 27. Eastern Counties, Cambridge to St. Ives opened.
Aug. 28. Edinburgh & Glasgow, Shieldhill Branch, opened.
Sep. 5. Eastern Union, Hadleigh Branch, opened.
,, 6. Erewash Valley (12¾ m.) opened.
,, 7. Leeds & Bradford, Skipton Branch, opened.
,, 18. Trent Valley opened.
,, 20. Edinburgh & Northern opened to Cupar.
Oct. 2. London & Brighton, Keymer Branch, opened.
,, 26. East Anglian, Downham to Ely, opened.
,, 31. Gloucester & Cheltenham Branch opened.
Dec. 8. London & Brighton, Newhaven Branch, opened.
,, 19. Reading & Hungerford Branch opened.
1848. Feb. 8. Watlington to Wisbech opened.
,, 13. Weybridge to Chertsey opened.
,, 19. Caledonian from Carlisle to Edinburgh opened throughout.
Mar. 3. York & Newcastle (Bedale Branch) opened.
,, 19. Eastern Counties (Woolwich Branch) opened.
,, 30. St. Ives to March (17¾ m.) opened.
Apl. 3. Wakefield, Pontefract & Goole opened.
,, 7. Melton to Peterborough (26 m.) opened.

Celebration at Huntingdon station in 1850. (Photo: W.P.L.)

1848. May 5. South Devon (21¼ m.) opened.
,, 29. L. & N.W. Dunstable Branch opened.
,, 30. Castle Cary to Perth (45½ m.) opened.
Jun. 19. East Lancashire, Blackburn to Accrington, opened.
Jul. 5. Edinburgh & Glasgow, Campsie Branch, opened.
,, 11. Waterloo Bridge Extn., S.W. Rly., opened.
,, 24. Liverpool, Crosby & Southport opened.
Aug. 1. Chester & Holyhead opened throughout.
,, 17. East Lancashire, Stubbins to Accrington, opened.
,, 22. South Western (Richmond to Datchet Branch) opened.
Sep. 4. Edinburgh & North (70 m.) opened.
,, 11. East Anglian, Swaffham to Dereham (12 m.) opened.
Oct. 19. Great Northern, loop line opened.
,, 29. Reading to Basingstoke (G.W.R.) opened.
Nov. 7. Liverpool & Bury opened to Wigan.

It is surprising that the railway fever was allowed to grow to such intensity without serious Government intervention. The first measure to exercise effective control in certain details was introduced by Gladstone, President of the Board of Trade, 24 years before he became Prime Minister, and passed in 1844. Previously, treatment of third class passengers varied from one railway to another. The new Act improved standards. It laid down a maximum fare of a penny a mile ("Parliamentary Tickets") for third class; seats were to be provided in all the vehicles, with protection from the weather. Some passenger vehicles had no seats, and even if there was a covering over the top, the sides were open to the elements in all weathers. At least one train a day with third class carriages had to run on every line and branch each way at a minimum speed of 12 m.p.h. Many railways continued to run fourth class carriages with open sides, at cheaper fares. Railway management and operation was also dealt with in the Act, and gave an option for the Government to purchase any new railway outright after twenty-one years, an option under highly complicated terms that was never taken up.

Angry railway directors and shareholders tried to howl it down with the slogan "The Railway Plunder Bill": but to no avail. Some railways, notably the Great Western which looked with disfavour upon third class passengers, ran their third class trains very early in the morning and

A landslip on the South Devon Railway near Teignmouth in 1852. The ravages of the sea rendered this a costly railway to maintain. (By courtesy of the Science Museum)

The scene at Castle Howard, Yorkshire, as Queen Victoria arrives in a royal carriage in the 1850s. (*Photo: W.P.L.*)

late at night. Even so, travel for third class passengers was better than they had experienced ever before, the poor gaining most of all.

THE BATTLE OF THE GAUGES

Further official intervention that was long overdue came the following year: this time about the rail gauge. Judging by the different gauges built on short isolated railways remotely distant from each other, few projectors had yet visualised a national connected rail network. Each went its own costly way. In addition to the Stephenson gauge of 4 ft. 8½ ins., other gauges in use included 4 ft., 4½ ft., 5 ft., 5½ ft. and, biggest problem of all, 7 ft. These "railway frontiers" created barriers to the inflow of traffic. On 6th August 1845, the Government belatedly but firmly stepped in by setting up a Gauge Commission, and in the following year came down decisively in favour of the Stephenson gauge (which, incidentally, was gaining ground in Continental Europe and America), with the exception of the G.W.R. and associated lines already of 7 ft. gauge. It was a severe personal blow to Brunel, whose railway had to be converted to the Stephenson gauge well before the century was out, and long after he was dead.

At the Gauge Commission, Robert Stephenson was asked whether his father had in fact advocated the 4 ft. 8½ ins. gauge. He replied: "No. It was not *proposed* by my father. It was the original gauge of the railways about Newcastle-on-Tyne, and therefore he *adopted* that gauge."

GEORGE HUDSON

Throughout those tempestuous years of the railway mania, when gigantic sums of money changed hands and fortunes were won and lost, it was almost inevitable that the times would produce the man. George Hudson (1800–71), a farmer's son, was the only man in the history of railways to be acclaimed as the "Railway King". This chubby fellow who sported frizzy side-whiskers started his business life with a drapers' shop in York. At the age of 27 he inherited what was in those days a fortune of £30,000. His influence in the city grew and about 1840 he was attracted by the new railways, particularly the line to Leeds which added to the prosperity of his native city. Shares of the railway were already falling in value and the first chairman was about to retire; Hudson was invited to take his place and he shortly increased the dividends, the proprietors asking no questions. He next leased the Leeds and Selby Railway at 5 per cent., a line that had been losing money: a good bargain for shareholders, who sung his praises. His next success was with the York & North Midland, with an increase in the dividend to 10 per cent.

His rising star brought him a directorship with another railway, the North Midland, which was also in financial straits. This bustling, pushing,

Third class carriage to be seen in the 1850s on West Country railways and a notable improvement on open wagons. (By courtesy of the Science Museum)

persevering character gained for himself more influence in the board room, and he soon pushed the old members from their stools. He worked hard and tirelessly, reorganised the Company and improved its financial standing. Eventually he got what he wanted: the coveted position of chairman.

Though Hudson reached high civic rank as Lord Mayor of York in 1837, and became Member of Parliament for Sunderland in 1845, he was no public speaker; but his dominating and magnetic personality brought him a big following.

During the decade 1840–50, 4,600 route miles of new railways were opened: more than in any other decade in Britain's history; and equal to about two-fifths of the total mileage in use at the present time. But more lines were already being built than were truly necessary, for routes were duplicated by competing companies, and even in small towns two or three stations were built separately by the different railways. After the scramblings and the panics, it was the survival of the fittest; and natural selection, in a business sense, produced a stronger animal.

One of the ways of gaining strength was by the amalgamation of smaller railway companies into larger ones, and the boardroom manoeuvrings and public libelling were merciless. Joining lines together removed cut-throat competition and saved costs. The first rationalisation of real significance joined three strong companies: the North Midland, the Midland Counties, and the Derby & Birmingham Junction Railways to form one of the great giants of Victorian Britain: the Midland Railway, on 10th May 1844. The man who pulled it off was the Railway King himself.

Hudson was no railway engineer, and he wisely left the technicalities to others. Railways attracted him mainly for financial gain and political power, and for some years he revelled luxuriously in both. He hob-nobbed with the wealthy, rubbed shoulders with Government ministers, travelled with Royalty, and was welcomed in London's most exclusive clubs.

Stimulated by his successes, he struck out or supported many new projects, and was elected chairman of another railway, the Newcastle & Darlington. To complete another link in the chain, he and George Stephenson together purchased the Durham Junction Railway for £88,500. "King George" knew a good bargain when he saw one. Smiles observes: "It was an exceedingly fortunate purchase for the Company, to whom it was worth double the money. The act, though not strictly legal, proved successful in the issue and he was much lauded. Thus encouraged, Mr. Hudson proceeded to buy the Brandling Junction line for £500,000 in his own name – an operation at the time regarded as equally favourable, though he was afterwards charged with appropriating 1,600 of the shares created for the purchase, when worth £21 each." The unique feature of this railway – authorised in 1834 and opened in 1839 to connect the Newcastle & Carlisle Railway with Sunderland, Shields and Gateshead – was that it was the project of a single individual, R. W. Brandling; it was rare indeed for a railway to bear the name of the man and not the place.

By the time the Great North of England line

had been completed, George Hudson had secured the entire line of communication from York to Newcastle, a route he opened as the Midland Railway came into being. The adulation which followed Hudson would have intoxicated even a stronger and more self-denying man. Entering the railways at a prosperous time, he made much money for many people, including his friends; and he made vast sums for himself.

He subsequently found himself chairman of nearly 600 miles of railway, stretching from Newcastle to Rugby. He also headed numerous new projects, a means by which paper wealth could be created, as it were, "at pleasure." Over the companies he presided, he held almost the entire administrative power: chairman, board, manager, and all. His admirers, inspired sometimes by gratitude for past favours, but more often by the expectation of favours to come, supported him wholeheartedly in all his measures. They called him the "financial wizard of the age." Sometimes at a railway company meeting, a suspicious shareholder would venture to put a probing question about the accounts; and he would be snubbed from the chair, and hissed and booed from the body of the hall: the King was on his throne. How dare anyone dissent!

Hudson was voted lavish praises, testimonials, and surplus shares alike. His entertainments at Albert Gate were crowded by sycophants, many of whom were titled; and he made his rounds of visits among the peerage like a prince. As an MP, he was valuable to his fellow directors; and Smiles says of him: "In the session of 1845, when he was at the height of his power, it was triumphantly said of him that he walked quietly through Parliament with some 16 railway bills under his arm."

George Stephenson, now nearing the end of his days, became associated with Hudson on many occasions. One was for a Bill for a railway between Newcastle and Berwick. Hard words were exchanged between them, for the straightforward Stephenson resisted any false promises.

Others were beginning to call the Hudson bluff; and soon the artificial prices of shares in the Railway King's empire dropped faster than they had risen, and his dazzling but brief reign began drawing to a close. Smiles gives a summary: "The merchant who had left his business and the doctor who had neglected his patients to gamble in railway stock, had been ruined; the penniless knaves and schemers who had speculated so recklessly and gained so little; the titled and fashionable people, who had bowed themselves so low before the idol of the day, and found themselves deceived and done; the credulous small capitalists, who, dazzled by premiums, had invested their all

One of the many mishaps that occurred in railway pioneering days. On the bridge and banksides hundreds of spectators watch the rescue operations on a wrecked livestock train with dead cattle and sheep strewn around. (*Courtesy, W.P.L.*)

Finchley Road station, north London, still "in the country" on the Hampstead Junction Railway; drawn in 1860.

in railway shares, and now saw themselves stripped of everything – were grievously enraged, and looked about them for a victim.

"In this temper were shareholders, when, at a railway meeting in York, some pertinent questions were put to the Railway King. His replies were not satisfactory, and the questions were pushed home. Mr. Hudson became confused. Angry voices rose in the meeting. A committee of investigation was appointed. The golden calf was found to be of brass, and hurled down; Hudson's own toadies, and sycophants eagerly joining the chorus of popular indignation.

"Similar proceedings shortly after followed at the meetings of other Companies, and the bubbles having by that time burst, the Railway Mania thus came to an ignominious end."

The year was 1849. No longer could the publicly disgraced Hudson mingle with the mighty, talk with Robert Peel or William Gladstone, nor take personal charge of a splendid Royal train. During the year, a Committee of Enquiry investigated his shady dealings and reported that he had "abused the confidence that was placed in him by wielding the power he obtained to forward his own interest", adding that he had "lost his better judgment and moral rectitude when left with the entire control."

At the peak of his career, he had controlled nearly a third of the railways of Britain; the creation of the Midland Railway by amalgamation had been his crowning success. From his earliest essays into railways, his ambition had been to weld together small, unconnected railways into bigger railways: he saw the potential of running passenger and goods trains for much longer distances, for standardising equipment, rolling stock and operating methods, and thereby reducing overhead costs and increasing profitability. He foresaw, finally, a great nationwide railway network, an accomplishment that never reached fruition until the railways became state-owned in 1948; his thinking was years ahead of his time.

Hudson was young enough to have taken amalgamation much further than he did; but he had gained control by gigantic frauds and the manipulation of finances, and it was inevitable that one day these shady tactics would be his own undoing. His power had bred corruption and greed. After being drummed out of the railways he left the country, but was later arrested and imprisoned. His star faded and he died in poverty at the age of 71. In an obituary notice, *The Times* wrote: "He was a man who united largeness of view with wonderful speculative courage, the kind of man who leads the world." Nearly a century afterwards, the lasting contribution he made to railways was marked when a new railway headquarters erected in his home-town of York was named Hudson House.

Soon after the Midland had been formed, other

amalgamations took place thus creating other powerful railway companies; but many small ones maintained their independence for nearly eighty years. In their creation, boardroom battles and public protest had been accompanied by financial sharp practice: but none to match the audacity of George Hudson.

THOSE FIRST FIFTY YEARS

The first half of the 19th century, during the reigns of George IV, William IV and Queen Victoria, saw the beginning of radical social and industrial changes in the lives of the masses. The democratic processes were rapidly speeded up with the coming of the railways; travel brought an intermingling of the classes that had never been known before, and more industrial jobs were created. The horizons of ordinary working people were enormously widened. They wanted to break their chains of poverty and suffering and to gain for themselves a bigger share of the material benefits of an industrialised society, of which they formed the lowest and most deprived stratum. Ironically, the landowners and other wealthy people who had made vast fortunes from the new railways, had unwittingly sowed the seeds of a vigorous democracy which was slowly to rob them of that which they treasured most: their prestige, wealth and power.

The gathering momentum of the Industrial Revolution, of which the railways formed an integral part, had continued to transform Britain from a basically agricultural to a basically industrial country. In 1800, Ireland had been united with England; the war with America of 1812–14 had been followed in 1815 by Wellington's decisive victory over Napoleon at Waterloo, thus ending the French Emperor's ambitions to rule Europe. Slavery, still practiced in America until 1863, had been abolished throughout the British Empire in 1833. But most significant of all for the common man was the first Reform Bill of 1832, which brought Parliamentary reform and the vote for £10 householders at the dawn of an industrial democracy.

Men on the railways worked for long hours. Women, and boys and girls, were still working in the mills and factories for up to 15 hours a day in wretched and unsanitary conditions that broke their health and shortened their lives; discipline was prison-like and children were cruelly treated. At least the Mines Act of 1842 made it illegal to employ women, and girls and boys of under ten years of age down the mines; and the factory inspectors appointed after the Factory Act of 1833 were beginning to improve industrial safety. With the backing of the progressive Whigs (later termed Liberals) and great parliamentarians such as Gladstone (1809–98) and Disraeli (1804–81), the working man's lot was much improved. But social justice still had a long way to go before the Education Act of 1870 introduced elementary education for all, and an Act of the following year made trade unions legal.

A Brunel masterpiece, the Royal Albert Bridge, spanning the River Tamar near Plymouth and built in 1859. It carries only a single line on the Great Western Railway's main route. (By courtesy of the Victoria & Albert Museum)

Chapter 4
The Railway Builders

Blasting rocks at Linslade, near Leighton Buzzard, London & Birmingham Railway. (*By courtesy of the Science Museum*)

OF all those involved in the making of the railways – promoters, investors, directors, parliamentary officers, rolling stock manufacturers, and many more – the pioneers who selected and surveyed the routes and laid the tracks across Britain, who dug tunnels, erected bridges and blasted rock – the builders – have earned their own special place in railway history. The large gangs of men, urged on by their foremen, worked feverishly against time and collapsing finances, in all weathers, in all seasons, night and day, meeting unexpected and dangerous obstacles, and hostile human obstruction, as they drove forward the iron road. Many paid the price of serious injury and death as tunnels collapsed, cuttings caved in, and track was washed away in storm and flood, and many a man suffered injury from a frightened horse or a runaway wagon.

Of the great pioneering builders, three names stand out: George Stephenson and his son Robert, and Isambard Kingdom Brunel. Engineers who worked for them and thus gained valuable experience struck out on their own and tried their fortunes in other territories. The Stephensons built railways mainly in the North and Midlands, in North Wales, and down to Euston; Brunel's lines were principally from London to the West Country, Wales and the South Midlands. Lesser known, but competent engineers applied their skills widely across Britain, even as the three great builders were blazing the trails.

WHISHAW'S IDEAS

A civil engineer named Francis Whishaw called attention to lesser known builders in a book he published in 1842 (second edition). He described in detail 58 separate railways that had been opened up to that time, when the total railways had reached a route length of over 1,500 miles. The volume, entitled *The Railways of Great Britain and Ireland*, was inscribed:

To the Railway Capitalists of the United Kingdom
this volume is respectfully dedicated
by their Obedient Servant
Francis Whishaw

Whishaw had earlier reported on a number of projected railways for Cumberland, Hertfordshire and Cornwall, and had been appointed as engineer to several projects during the mania years. Over a long period he travelled more than 7,000 miles and visited most of the railways of his time, noting in detail everything he observed. His documentation proved invaluable to railway promoters in the formative years. For example, well before the gauges were standardised, he wrote: "If the intended line is to join any other railway, it must of course correspond with the gauge of that line". Remarkably, Whishaw had a preference for a gauge of 5 ft., which he professionally recommended.

With the builders in mind, Whishaw wrote out a complete system for the construction of new lines and called it the "Reciprocating System of Railways". Though included in his book, his system was submitted to the Institution of Civil Engineers, of which he was a member, in March 1839. Having seen much waste in the early railway building, Whishaw intended to bring a simple form and pattern into a hotch-potch of numerous isolated lines.

He lamented: "Had this plan emanated from a Stephenson or a Brunel, it would, no doubt, ere this have been carried into execution." Whishaw, who had probably seen more of the first railways than any other man of his time, knew that his name did not carry the magic of those three great men. He wrote:

"The present expensive mode of constructing railways is quite incompatible with their further extension; and unless an economical and, at the same time, efficient system is introduced, a large mass of the population of the United Kingdom will be for ever debarred of the comforts and conveniences afforded directly to those places which are included in the catalogue of railway cities, towns or districts."

It is easy to understand that the builders of the Bodmin line in Cornwall, for example, were not remotely interested in what was going on at Canterbury, or Edinburgh or Darlington: they had enough problems of their own. They certainly never expected, or perhaps even cared, that one day the little line at Bodmin would run through to Paddington, or that London would be connected with Darlington and Edinburgh. The promoters of each new little railway would be totally immersed in building their new lines to carry a specific traffic.

It fell to George Stephenson to have the vision of the great railways of the future. As his first line, the Stockton & Darlington, neared completion, he was inspecting progress with his assistant, John Dixon, and his son. They called at an inn at Stockton for a meal, and for this rare occasion Stephenson ordered a bottle of wine to toast the success of the railway. John Dixon records the sentiments of the untutored and professionally unqualified George Stephenson, then aged 43, spoken in the thick Geordie accent that was to confound the élite in Parliamentary Committees:

"I venture to tell you, that I think you will live to see the day when railways will supersede almost all other methods of conveyance in this country. Mail coaches will become the great highways for the King and all his subjects.

"The time is coming when it will be cheaper for a working man to travel on a railway than to walk on foot. But what I have said will come to pass as sure as you now hear me. I only wish I may live to see the day."

(And, of course, he did, to the extent of nearly 6,000 miles of railway, which is more than half the length remaining in 1975.)

"I know how slow all human progress is," he continued, "and with what difficulty I have been able to get the locomotive introduced thus far, notwithstanding my more than ten years' successful experiment at Killingworth."

What other railway builder would have made such a confident prediction before his very first line was completed and proved and which, for some years, needed his pioneering steam locomotives to be aided and abetted by cable stationary engines and horses?

His inner confidence came from the strength of his utter conviction in his steam locomotives using the smooth-wheel-to-smooth rail principle, and he soon began building them to a higher power and larger size.

Whishaw's ideas already had the benefit of the pioneering work of the early railway builders; and he divided his Reciprocating System into seven parts: Land and Fencing; Earthworks; Drainage; Tunnels, Viaducts and Bridges; Level Road-Crossings; Permanent Way; and Stations and Depôts.

Unaccountably, he recommended single lines when many railways were already of double lines: "The peculiar feature proposed in the construction of railways, according to the reciprocating plan, is the adoption of a single line of way throughout, whatever may be the expected amount of traffic; by which the original cost . . . would necessarily be reduced to a considerable extent . . ."

He probably felt that the vast sums that were being spent on railways could be their downfall. After praising the stations of the North Midland Railway built by the architect, Mr. Thomson, he questioned the cost: "But although highly estimating the elegantly chaste designs which characterise the architecture of the North Midland stations, we cannot but deplore the growing evil of expending large sums of money on railway appendages. Instead of cottage-buildings, which, for the traffic of most of the intermediate stopping places on this line, would have been amply sufficient, we find the railway literally ornamented with so many beautiful villas, any one of which would grace the sloping lawn of some domain by nature highly favoured." Other railways were similarly criticised for "erecting expensive buildings at every intermediate station".

There was method in the apparent financial madness of the builders. "Handsome villas" were much more tempting than "cottage buildings" to the nobility, the squires and the wealthy with their elegant ladies as, in carriage-and-pair, they swung into the forecourt of a station boasting architectural distinction. Many splendid railway stations have survived to this day as a reminder of the railway age, to be preserved by the State and enjoyed by an appreciative populace. Other builders, notably Brunel, not only erected impressive stations, but embellished tunnel entrances with turrets and castellated walls; and some of the finest bridges and viaducts, with curving arches, figurations in painted wrought iron, and decorated masonry, were built for the railways.

Themselves highly sensitive to the accusations of many people who rued the carving up of established estates, and the tearing up of the countryside in "great gashes of railway track", the builders made an honest attempt to erect edifices that would be a joy to behold, and engaged the best architects and masons to achieve their aim.

When Stephenson plotted the route for his first railway, he had to take the sights with a spirit level, working with his own hands and eyes, and walking every yard of the ground. As he called out the figures, his son would write them down in a notebook. He started early and worked until dusk, dressed in a blue tailed coat, breeches and top-boots. Living frugally, he would take some bread and milk at a nearby cottage, occasionally joining a homely dinner at a neighbouring farmhouse. Smiles wrote: "He was always welcome, for he was full of cheery and homely talk, and, when there were children about the house he had plenty of humorous chat for them as well as for their seniors."

His financial backers supported his decision to work to a gauge of 4 ft. $8\frac{1}{2}$ in.: about the width for carts and wagons on the roads, and wagons on the horse-drawn tramways of that time. In the absence of any scientific or technical criteria, Stephenson used his native commonsense; and the "Stephenson Gauge" or the "English Gauge" was to become the standard for Britain, Continental Europe, America, and many other places overseas.

Stephenson took great pains to lay his first line as near straight and level as the contours of the land would permit, a principle he strove for on the other lines with which he was associated; the steepest gradient was only 1 in 341. Though it was only some twelve miles between Stockton and Darlington, the main lines and branches to collieries eventually totalled 38 miles, to which other branches were added later. Small coal in this rich colliery area was first used as ballast for the track. In addition to many bridges, level crossings and cuttings on which large gangs of men were employed, the line near the sea was embedded with well-puddled and solid clay. Whishaw reported twenty-five years later: "Its stability has already been subjected to repeated tests during many very heavy seas, which have washed over it again and again; but yet it continues to stand well . . ."

A much tougher proposition was the building of the Liverpool & Manchester Railway. George Rennie, a distinguished engineer, had been considered by the directors, but Stephenson was chosen for the job, and he took up residence in Liverpool. Gradients on this line had to be much stiffer than on his first railway, and sixty-three bridges had to be built. One of them – at Rainhill – had to be at a sharply oblique angle, and committing the design to paper baffled Stephenson. One report said that he cut out the shape of it from a turnip plucked from a nearby field.

CROSSING CHAT MOSS

One of the biggest problems was to cross the four miles of Chat Moss, which many said was impossible, and which a civil engineer at a Parliamentary Committee estimated would cost £200,000; Stephenson's actual costs came to less than £28,000. Smiles said of the Moss: "An immense peat-bog of about twelve square miles . . . the result of the growth and decay of ages . . . one year's growth rising over another".

Building retaining walls in rural Camden Town, London, during construction of the London & Birmingham Railway. (*By courtesy of the Science Museum*)

It was impossible to drain and was twenty to thirty feet deep. The line was staked out by using planks of wood; and John Dixon, one of Stephenson's three resident engineers, in July 1826 slipped off a plank when half-way across the Moss and sank up to his knees in the bog. Terrified, the more he struggled the deeper he went. He might have disappeared for ever had not the navvies rushed to his rescue with more planks and dragged him out. It was with difficulty that his fellow-resident engineer, Joseph Locke, persuaded him to see the work through.

The massive job of filling a length across the bog to take the track was not finished until January 1830, when an experimental train conveying passengers and hauled by the *Rocket* passed over safely without sinking.

Sankey Viaduct, which crossed the Sankey brook and canal, was Stephenson's most impressive piece of masonry on this line. Piers of its nine arches of fifty feet span each, were supported on two hundred piles driven into the soil below water level. It was built of brick, with stone dressings and facings, with a simplicity of style, and cost about £45,000. During its construction, one of the directors said: "Now, George, thou must get on with the railways . . . thou must really have it ready by January next," and quoted Napoleon's famous phrase that "nothing is impossible". George replied: "Give me the men, money and materials, and I'll do what Napoleon couldn't do – drive a railroad from Liverpool to Manchester!"

Three tunnels had to be dug under the streets of Liverpool, and an enormous cutting through Olive Mount. Some 500,000 tons of solid rock had to be cut for two miles, and its deepest point was over 100 ft. This rock ravine provided a spectacular sight for travellers. Excavated rock and stone went into bridges and other structures. Whishaw wrote: "The railways which have been executed since the Liverpool & Manchester line have had a larger amount of earthworks per mile; and certainly none have presented, upon the whole, greater difficulties in effecting their removal."

Stephenson's salary as the line's engineer was a princely £1,000 a year at a time when many labourers were getting 3s. (15p) a day. His services were rapidly taken up elsewhere. In 1836, the Grand Junction Railway was being built between Warrington and Birmingham, Stephenson taking the northern part and John Rastrick the southern. Gangs of navvies dug the cuttings and built the embankments. Of the various viaducts built, Ditton, spanning the River Weaver, was probably Stephenson's finest. Piles for the foundations were driven 20 ft. deep, and 20 arches of 60 ft. span straddled the river level.

About the same time, Stephenson was busy with the Manchester & Leeds Railway, another line which the pessimists predicted would never

Robert Stephenson's unique Britannia Bridge spanning the Menai Straits, opened in 1850 to complete the Chester & Holyhead Railway and the first tubular railway bridge. (*By courtesy of the Victoria & Albert Museum*)

succeed. When Summit Tunnel near Littleborough was being built, a slight cave-in was said to have buried the navvies alive. None had been hurt, but the event had been "exaggerated by the lying tongue of rumour". Inspection by the directors proved it safe, and Stephenson said of it, "I don't think there is such another piece of work in the world. It is the greatest work that has yet been done of its kind." Its entire length of nearly 1¾ miles had occupied over 1,000 navvies, 13 stationary engines and about 100 horses for nearly four years.

Cotton, wool, worsted, silk and linen carried between Liverpool and Hull prompted the building of the Manchester & Leeds Railway, a line literally studded with engineering difficulties from end to end. Eight tunnels had to be cut and 116 bridges built. The main viaducts were at Manchester, Gaulxholm, Horsfall and Wakefield.

Both the Stephensons built the North Midland Railway between Derby and Leeds, a distance of 73 miles. It went through Chesterfield, Sheffield, Rotherham, Normanton (connecting with the Manchester & Leeds) and within about 2 miles of Wakefield. No single contractor and his gangs could cope with so long a line, and the works were let to over thirty contractors, each taking half-a-mile to about 4 miles, depending partly on the terrain. For some years, Robert Stephenson was general manager of the Company.

In his later years, Stephenson was entertained by many distinguished people. On returning from church one Sunday with such a group, the party saw in the distance a train flashing along behind its billowing white plume of steam. Smiles takes up the dialogue:

"Now, Buckland," said Stephenson, "I have a poser for you. What is the power that is driving that train?"

"I suppose it is one of your big engines."

"Oh, very likely a canny Newcastle driver. What do you say to the light of the sun?"

"How can that be?" asked Dr. Buckland.

"It is light bottled up in the earth for tens of thousands of years – light, absorbed by plants and vegetables, being necessary for the condensation of carbon during the process of their growth, if it be not carbon in another form – and now, after being buried in the earth for long ages in fields of coal, that latent light is again brought forth and liberated, made to work as in that locomotive, for great human purposes."

Bottled sunshine was a favourite theme of the engineer's, who held that what produced light and heat – coal – had originally been light and heat.

THE FIRST TUBULAR RAILWAY BRIDGE

Volumes would be needed to describe the railways and associated structures the Stephensons built; but none would omit the splendid Britannia Bridge which spanned the Menai Straits, a short distance from Telford's suspension bridge, across to the Isle of Anglesey.

When in 1836, a line was first proposed to run from Crewe to Chester, a distance of 21 miles, George Stephenson urged the promoters to extend it for a total of 106 miles to Holyhead, with a bridge across the Straits; and the coastal route he surveyed from Chester to Holyhead two years later is almost identical with the line as it is today.

Robert Stephenson was appointed as engineer of the line and he designed a bridge of unique structure, the first tubular railway bridge, through which the trains would run entirely enclosed. Three masonry towers were erected: one on either side and one in the middle, the bridge itself being constructed with huge wrought iron plates. Design had to allow for the pressures of high winds as well as for the weight of trains. It was an incredible feat to hoist the heavy sections into position with the crude lifting tackle available.

Alternative schemes and massive protest had followed the usual form until Parliamentary sanction was obtained in 1844. The foundation stone was laid on 10th April 1846 and the bridge opened on 18th March 1850, to complete the Chester & Holyhead Railway. The line had been opened as far as Bangor in 1848. New business came to the little harbour, thus to develop Holyhead into one of the important ports of Britain. Stephenson also built a shorter tubular railway bridge across the River Conway near Llandudno.

In taking stock of the progress of railway building, Smiles wrote: "Such was the growth of the railroad, which, it will be observed, originated in necessity, and was modified according to experience: progress in this, as in all departments of mechanics, having been effected by the exertions of many men; one generation entering upon the labours of that which preceded it, and carrying them onward to farther stages of improvement.

"The invention of the locomotive was in like manner made by successive steps. It was not the invention of one man, but of a succession of men, each working at the proper hour, and according to the needs of that hour; one inventor interpreting only the first word of the problem which his successors were to solve after long and laborious efforts and experiments."

These sentiments were echoed at a public meeting in Newcastle by Robert Stephenson, renowned for his generous spirit: "The locomotive is not the invention of one man, but of a nation of mechanical engineers." His greatest compliments were reserved for his father, whom he literally

Crimple Valley viaduct which carries the Harrogate branch of the York & North Midland Railway across the Leeds–Thirsk main line. Built by Birkinshaw, it was described in 1847 as a "stupendous work . . . of beautiful proportion and great height". (By courtesy of the Victoria & Albert Museum)

worshipped. To Smiles, he said, "It was his thorough training, his example, his character, which made me the man I am." And in an address to the Institution of Civil Engineers in January 1856: "It is my great pride to remember, that whatever may have been done, and however extensive may have been my own connection with railway development, all I know and all I have done is primarily due to the parent whose memory I cherish and revere." To Mr. Lough, the sculptor, the childless Robert said that he had only two real loves: his father and his wife.

Chambers gave another view of the railway builders when he wrote in 1865 that they were "not philosophers, or learned societies, but certain obscure and generally illiterate individuals in the north of England. Railways, in short, are an invention of the coal carriers of Northumberland and Durham; though the perfecting of these undertakings, as we now see them, belongs to others. At first, the contrivance was only a plan of simplifying the transit of coal from the mines to the places of shipment on the Tyne and Wear."

BRUNEL

What sort of man was Brunel? No single phrase can capture his complex character. Short in stature, and not physically robust, he was a giant in drive and ambition which led him to be accepted as one of the greatest railway engineers of the 19th century. His success had been meteoric. He displayed engineering genius and an incredible capacity for hard work. Never was he deflected by his monumental failures, which were far outshone by his brilliant successes.

There was an aura of magic about him, and a personal magnetism that made him one of the great persuaders of the age: an extraordinary personality. What is more, in his appearances before Parliamentary Committees, board meetings, and especially at his first public meeting in Bristol, he had discovered this great power within himself and he used it with the art that conceals art, as would an experienced actor.

In a personal memoir St. George Burke, K.C., wrote about his friendship with Brunel as a young man: "Seldom a day passed without our meeting . . . He could enter into the most boyish pranks and fun, without in the least distracting his attention from the matter of business . . . I believe that a more joyous nature, combined with the highest intellectural faculties, was never created, and I love to think of him in the character of the ever gay and kind-hearted friend of my early years."

Burke occupied chambers at that time facing Brunel's in Parliament Street: "To facilitate our intercourse it occurred to him to carry a string across Parliament Street, from his chambers to mine, to be there connected with a bell, by which he could either call me to the window to receive his telegraphic signals, or, more frequently, to wake me up in the morning when we had occasion to go into the country together, and great was the astonishment of the neighbours at this device, the object of which they were unable to comprehend.

"I believe at that time he scarcely ever went to bed, though I never remember to have seen him tired or out of spirits. He was a very constant smoker, and would take his nap in an armchair, very frequently with a cigar in his mouth; and if we were to start out of town at five or six o'clock in the morning, it was his frequent practice to rouse me out of bed about three, by means of the bell, when I would invariably find him up and dressed, and in great glee at the fun of having curtailed my slumbers by two or three hours more than necessary.

"No-one would have supposed that during the night he had been poring over plans and estimates, and engrossed in serious labours, which to most men would have proved destructive of their energies during the following day; but I never saw him otherwise than full of gaiety, and apparently as ready for work as though he had been sleeping through the night.

"I have never known a man who, possessing courage which to many would appear almost like rashness, was less disposed to trust to chance . . .

"I frequently accompanied him to the West of England, and into Gloucestershire and South Wales, when public meetings were held in support of the measures in which he was engaged, and I had occasion to observe the enormous popularity which he everywhere enjoyed."

It was always Brunel's desire to create railways that were pleasing to the eye: locomotives of splendid lines, decorative carriages and castellated tunnel entrances. His stations and bridges displayed their own intrinsic architectural and engineering beauty. One aspect of the man's character is reflected in his early diary notes: "I often do the most silly, useless things to appear to advantage before those whom I care nothing about . . . My self-conceit and love of glory, or rather approbation, vie with each other which shall govern me. The latter is so strong that even of a dark night, riding home, when I pass some unknown person, who perhaps does not even look at me, I catch myself trying to look big on my little pony."

Also intimately revealing are Brunel's own journal notes. Sitting by the fireside in his Parliament Street office late on 26th December 1835, nearly four months after the Great Western Railway Act had been passed and two and a half years before the first section opened, he was scribbling away: "The Railway now is in progress . . . but what a fight we had – and how near defeat – and what a ruinous defeat it would have been! . . . And it's not this alone but everything I have been engaged in has been successful."

He then lists the work in hand:

Capital	
70,000	Clifton Bridge [Clifton Suspension Bridge, Bristol]
20,000	Bristol Docks – to come – Portishead Pier
2,500,000	G.W. Railway – to come – Oxford Branch
750,000	Chelt^{m} Railway
1,250,000	Bristol & Exeter do. do. – perhaps Plymouth etc.
250,000	Methyr & Cardiff do. Gloster & S. Wales
150,000	Newbury Branch
50,000	Sunderland Docks
100,000	Thames Suspension Bridge
450,000	Bristol & Gloster Railway
5,590,000	

Starting in 1847, Brunel built the imposing Royal Albert Bridge across the River Tamar estuary at Saltash near Plymouth, as part of the main line to Penzance, but for single line only. It was opened by Queen Victoria's Consort, Prince Albert, at an impressive public ceremony on 3rd May 1859, the year of the engineer's death. It consisted of two eliptical spans for a length of 2,200 ft., clearing high water by a hundred feet. Of all the bridges of the Great Western Railway, into which the line was absorbed, it was the most outstanding. Years later, a Great Western engineer described it as Brunel's "crowning glory and a monument worthy of such genius."

In the absence of the good train service that the builders were busily occupied in providing for future generations, the engineers had to get about the country like everybody else – on foot (people really walked in those days), on horse-back, and by stage-coach – a traditional form of travel whose death-knell the railways were already solemnly ringing. Brunel had opened an office at No. 53 Parliament Street to be near the Houses of Parliament, in the austere and towered architectural pile of which he would have to spend many gruelling hours. His travels had been bedevilled by the unreliability of the stage coaches and hired hacks, to exhaust his patience. So he designed and had built his own coach, a black britzska, which was to become a familiar sight to construction gangs and engineers along the lonely lanes of the West Country. He could carry his plans and engineering instruments with him, and a good stock of cigars which he smoked incessantly. His immense cigar box held fifty. The seating could be adapted to a couch so that he could take a few hours' nap in between times. A private coach – a striking one at that – added to his personal prestige; and it earned the nickname of the "Flying Hearse."

STEPHENSON SUPPLIES ENGINES TO BRUNEL

Stephensons' locomotive works at Newcastle had saved the day for Brunel's Great Western Railway. Having already obtained from Newcastle the *North Star* and *Morning Star*, in the autumn of 1839, *Evening Star* and *Dog Star* were added to the sorely tried locomotive department.

Engines built by Stephensons' works at Newcastle were originally for use on the railways they built, but soon they were supplied to other railways, at home and overseas. A large number of the smaller railways could not afford to build their own. Soon after the Stephenson works opened in Newcastle, other engineers set up their own locomotive works, a handful to become important firms building locomotives for Britain and overseas. Some of the engineers had learnt their craft originally with the Stephensons before going into business on their own.

THE FIRST SWINDON WORKS

Two years before the Great Western Railway line between London and Bristol was opened throughout, the Company realised that they would need to build, somewhere on the route, a depot or workshops for the locomotives. Brunel and Gooch were discussing this with Charles Saunders, the Company secretary, in June 1839. Reading seemed a possibility, or perhaps Didcot, the junction for the Oxford branch line. Gooch finally favoured Swindon, the connection with the Cheltenham Railway, as being the most likely place where locomotives would need attention. The reason was that he expected to use engines with small driving wheels on the more heavily graded section between Swindon and Bristol, and fast locomotives with 7 ft. driving wheels on the comparatively long and level galloping route from Swindon to London. Brunel agreed and the directors approved.

A site was taken in the fields below the tiny market town, and soon the buildings were going up. The first important depot and works of the Great Western Railway was opened on 2nd January 1843. In a few years, rows of terrace houses with their tiny backyards and smoking chimneys began to straddle the fields in their geometric pattern, and the history of this great and distinguished railway town, the home of some of Britain's finest locomotives, started its course.

In the 1840s, Brunel was led into one of the greatest errors of his otherwise brilliant career: a railway to run on air pressure without any locomotives – the atmospheric railway. It was a fascinating idea to run a railway without the noise, smells, dirt and smuts of smoky and expensive steam locomotives, and with air as the "free" fuel instead of costly coal and coke. The system caught the imagination of many inventors who, within thirty years or so, registered seventeen patents for various components in this new wonder of the age.

The basic idea was simplicity itself. A cast iron tube of, say, 15 in. diameter, was laid between the rails throughout the line. Running along the top of the tube was a slit which was covered by a flexible leather flap to keep the tube airtight. Inside the tube was a tight-fitting piston, with a rod from it coming up through the flexible flap. The rod was connected at its top to a wagon on the track. By means of pumping engines, air pressure through the tube behind the piston (or a vacuum in front of it) forced it through the tube, hauling the wagon with it; and of course any wagons or carriages attached. As the upright rod moved along the tube slit, it forced open the flexible flap to allow its continuous passage, the flap closing behind it, thereby maintaining the air seal.

As early as 1810, George Medhurst had thought up the idea of an atmospheric railway, but with the train being forced by air pressure *inside* a giant tube of 30 ft. diameter. He took out a patent but the system was never built.

Another version, with a small tube, was put in use in London for sending postal packages through it, but it had only a short life.

An atmospheric railway that worked – for a time – was the London & Croydon; but the line that attracted much attention and led many emminent engineers astray, was the 1½ mile extension of the Dublin & Kingstown Railway between Kingstown and Dalkey. The Samuda Brothers supplied some of their equipment, patented in 1839, for the new line which ran experimentally in 1843 and was officially opened to the public the following year.

Despite numerous breakdowns, speeds of well over 60 m.p.h. were reputed to have been reached, faster than ever previously achieved. It must have been a breath-taking experience.

An official of the Public Works Department of France, Monsieur C. F. Mallet, after inspecting it, recommended the French Railways to adopt it throughout the country. Though his advice was not taken, a short stretch of 5½ miles was built, but was later converted to steam locomotive traction.

George Stephenson described the atmospheric system as "a great humbug"; and Robert said that if the London & Birmingham had used the system, 38 pumping stations would have been needed and he foresaw far too many insuperable obstacles to its permanent acceptance. Hudson condemned it, too. There was also the key problem of points and crossovers.

Nevertheless the Irish experiment fascinated Brunel, who failed to persuade the Newcastle & Carlisle Railway to adopt it, but succeeded in talking the directors of the South Devon Railway to accept it; and he was appointed engineer to build it. Capital for the new line had been subscribed by three railways: the Great Western, Bristol & Exeter, and Bristol & Gloucester.

Brunel had chosen the route for the South Devon, from Exeter to Plymouth, of 52 miles, via Dawlish, Teignmouth, Newton Abbot and Totnes, skirting Dartmoor. With heavy gradients, Brunel had concluded that steam locomotives could not do the work. He had reported on the Irish line to his directors: " . . . the Atmospheric apparatus has succeeded perfectly as an effective means of working trains by stationary power, whether for long or short lines, at higher velocity and with less chance of interruption than is now effected by locomotives."

The work went ahead. "The first portion from Exeter to Teignmouth," reported the *Railway Chronicle*, on 11th April 1846, "is to be opened on 1st May."

Pumping stations were built nearly three miles apart at eight places on the route, including Exeter, Starcross, Dawlish, Teignmouth and Newton Abbot. Installation costs rose far higher than expected, breakdowns were frequent, and pumping engines failed: some having come from Boulton & Watt, and the Rennie Brothers. The leather flaps on the tube wore quickly and in the winter froze as hard as wood. Every device was tried to overcome the continuous mechanical failures. Although speeds of 68 m.p.h. were reached with 28-ton loads, the system rapidly disintegrated throughout its entire length – the beginning of the end; it was abandoned on 10th September 1848 and steam locomotives came on the scene in a rescue operation. The South Devon Atmospheric Railway turned out to be the most costly railway engineering failure of its time, and would have destroyed a stronger man than even Brunel. Other atmospheric lines were also converted to steam.

A large number of influential people – engineers, landowners, investors and leading politicians – had really believed that the system offered a glowing future. Brunel was not the only railway builder to be caught. At the height of the interest in the 1840s, many atmospheric railways were planned in different parts of Britain, but reached no further than the registering of plans or prospectuses and the raising of initial capital. A few official titles are quoted below:

Brighton & Arundel Atmospheric Railway
Direct Epsom & South London Atmospheric Railway
Direct Birmingham Oxford Reading & Brighton Atmospheric Railway
Direct City & South Union Atmospheric Railway
Edinburgh & Leith Atmospheric Railway
London & Northampton Direct Atmospheric Railway
Manchester & Bury Atmospheric Railway
Manchester & Oldham Atmospheric Railway
Metropolitan South Suburban Atmospheric Railway
Pilbrow's Atmospheric Railway
Windsor, Slough & Staines Atmospheric Railway
Windsor, Staines, Brentford & London Atmospheric Railway

With the benefit of hindsight, the atmospheric railway, at first so full of exciting promise, looked like a great mechanical joke. Chambers expressed a sympathetic view: "How frequently do the things jeered at as chimeras in one age become sober realities in another! . . . One, therefore, should not be too ready to laugh at the schemes of the projectors, however seemingly impracticable."

Kent viaduct of the Ulverston & Lancaster Railway, opened in 1857. (W.P.L.)

RIVALS BUT FRIENDS

Two main professional differences stood between Brunel and the two Stephensons: the battle for the gauges, and the occasions when their respective railway districts marched in close proximity. They were destined often to come into collision. Yet Brunel recollected that it was the Stephensons' *Star* locomotives which helped him to start the Great Western Railway; and Robert, his contemporary, several times rallied to his support.

Brunel noted in his journal in May 1846 after spending an evening with Robert: "It is very delightful in the midst of our incessant personal professional contests, carried to the extreme limits of fair opposition, to meet him on a perfectly friendly footing and discuss engineering points." When Robert was about to float the first tube of his bridge across Menai Straits, he called for help and advice from Brunel, who travelled to North Wales to assist.

Robert, who inherited his father's "kindly spirit and benevolent disposition", listened on one occasion to Brunel's complaints about his contractors. Stephenson said: "You hold them too tightly to the letter of your agreement. Treat them fairly and liberally."

"But," said Brunel, "They try to take advantage of me at all points."

"Perhaps you suspect them too much?"

"I suspect all men to be rogues, till I find them to be honest."

"For my part," said Stephenson, "I take all men to be honest till I find them to be rogues."

"Ah, then I feel we shall never agree."

The two of them met in Cairo and dined together on Christmas Day 1858. Brunel, with his wife, a son and his doctor, was in Egypt for his health, then journeyed to Naples and Rome, returning home in May, the year of his death. Stephenson was also in Egypt for health reasons; and it is likely that at the Christmas dinner party, both realised that they might never meet again.

Smiles compared the two rivals: "Both were the sons of distinguished men, and both inherited fame and followed in the footsteps of their fathers. The Stephensons were inventive, practical, and sagacious; the Brunels ingenious, imaginative and daring. The former were thoroughly English in their characteristics as the latter perhaps were as thoroughly French . . . measured by practical and profitable results, the Stephensons were unquestionably the safer men to follow."

Brunel and George Stephenson met at Newcastle in the early 1840s. Stephenson grabbed him by the collar good-naturedly and challenged: "What business have you north of the Tyne?" Brunel was there to recommend the atmospheric system for the projected Newcastle & Berwick Railway. Later at a Parliamentary Committee, Brunel took one side and Robert Stephenson the other. The atmospheric system was rejected and the Stephenson line opened with steam locomotives in 1847.

Cannon Street station and railway bridge across the River Thames, with St. Paul's Cathedral in the background
(*By courtesy of the Victoria & Albert Museum*)

Nine Elms station in 1838, London terminus of the London & Southampton Railway, later named the London & South Western. In 1848, a new and more central terminus was built at Waterloo. In the 1840s, a first class passenger could be accompanied by a liveried servant at a special rate of 13 shillings (65p). (By courtesy of the Victoria & Albert Museum)

TREVITHICK

Man of moods and of volatile temperament, Trevithick lacked the sheer dogged perseverance to take an idea to its potential practicability in the way that characterised the achievements of Stephenson and Brunel. He possessed an exceptional imagination and inventive mechanical skill which, in his tempestuous 62 years, led him along many paths. He dredged the River Thames by steam power, took out new patents for high-pressure steam boilers, and partly built a tunnel under the Thames. With his first successful steam locomotive in 1804, ten years ahead of Stephenson's, he proved the ability of a smooth wheel to grip a smooth rail sufficiently to propel the engine and to haul wagons. His high-pressure boiler with a return flue, a steam jet into the chimney and a coupling device on driving wheels established him as the first man to design and build a railway steam locomotive in its true sense.

The efficiency of his steam pumping engines brought him many orders for pumping water from mines and quarries, mainly at first in his native Cornwall. He obtained orders from overseas, and was persuaded to visit Peru where he sold many more, with the prospect of great wealth. There he became involved in a gold-mining project. When all seemed in his favour, his plans were dashed as a patriotic rising against the Spanish broke out in Peru in the early 1820s.

According to Smiles, Trevithick dejectedly set off for home, and by an astonishing coincidence at Cartagena he ran into Robert Stephenson, who was also homeward bound. Stephenson found him "gaunt and hollow, the picture of privation and misery, and penniless," but already planning another new venture. Stephenson lent him £50 to get home. They sailed together to New York, and on the way the ship ran aground in a storm and the two of them almost lost their lives. They parted company at New York where Trevithick took a ship to Falmouth in his native Cornwall. The year was 1827 and Robert was only 24.

It is easy to imagine that the two engineers for several days must have talked endlessly about the steam locomotive and what was happening with railways in England. The older man may well have said enough to give the young engineer new inspiration to rejoin his father, who was already building his second railway, the Liverpool & Manchester.

Smiles described Trevithick as "a man of original and intuitive genius in invention. Every mechanical arrangement which he undertook to study, issued from his hands transformed and improved. But there he rested. He struck out many inventions, and left them to take care of themselves. His great failing was lack of perseverance. His mind was always full of projects; but his very genius led him astray in search of new things, while his imagination often outran his judgment. Hence his life was but a series of beginnings."

Then comes an interesting comparison of the characters of Richard Trevithick and George Stephenson: "There may have been some moral twist in the engineer's (Trevithick's) character into which we do not seek to pry. But it seems clear that he was wanting in that resolute perseverance, that power of fighting an uphill battle, without which no great enterprise can be conducted to a successful conclusion.

"In this respect the character of Richard Trevithick presents a remarkable contrast to that of George Stephenson, who took up only one of the many great projects which the other had cast aside, and by dint of application, industry and perseverance, carried into effect one of the most remarkable but peaceful revolutions which has ever been accomplished in any age or country."

To end the sad story of one of the most brilliant inventors of his time, Trevithick, about a year before he died in poverty in 1833, had a final fling. He persuaded Halls, the engineers of Dartford in Kent, to allow him to develop yet another invention: a steam vessel driven by water ejected through a tube. Experiments took place in a nearby creek, but were unsatisfactory. Meanwhile, he had stayed at the old coaching inn, The Bull at Dartford, leaving a debt of some £60. He would have had a "pauper's grave" at the expense of the local parish, if Halls and their workmen had not collected money to give the "great inventor" a decent burial; and they followed his remains to Deptford churchyard. An old road near Dartford station still perpetuates his name – Trevithick Drive.

In the blaze of the fame of his followers, the Cornish engineer was almost forgotten; but to him belonged the glory of inventing the first practical railway steam locomotive. Francis (1812–77) one of his six children, followed in his father's footsteps and carved a successful career as a locomotive engineer in one of the great Victorian railways; and, thankfully, he wrote his father's unique life story.

JOHN RASTRICK

A builder whose light has been outshone by brighter stars, but who produced some original work, was John Urpeth Rastrick (1780–1856). A civil engineer who worked with the Stephensons and Brunel and other builders of the time, he was born in Morpeth, a little north of Newcastle, and studied engineering under his father. He constructed railways, designed steam locomotives, supported the idea of railways in parliamentary committees and spoke in favour of a large proportion of the principal lines, and was one of the judges who selected the *Rocket* at the 1829 Rainhill trials. As early as 1814, when George Stephenson was first building locomotives, Rastrick took out Patent No. 3799 for a steam locomotive which he ran experimentally on wagon-ways. He also sold a few locomotives to the first American railways. His engineering firm at Stourbridge, Foster, Rastrick & Co., designed and constructed rolling mills, steam engines and other heavy machinery.

He constructed the line between Stratford-on-Avon and Moreton-in-the-Marsh in the Cotswolds, and built a colliery railway in Staffordshire. With Stephenson in 1830 he surveyed the line which formed the Grand Junction Railway and was engineer to the Manchester & Cheshire Junction Railway in 1835. He teamed up with Sir John Rennie in 1837 and, against several competing projects for different routes, he and Rennie built the direct London–Brighton line. For this railway, he was involved in building the Merstham, Balcombe, and Clayton tunnels; and the splendid Ouse viaduct of thirty-seven arches which London–Brighton travellers know so well today. It was completed in the autumn of 1840. After that, he built extensions to the line which was later named the London, Brighton & South Coast Railway.

He also planned the Direct London & Manchester Railway, but the scheme became defunct in 1851.

Heavy engineering work in Stourbridge, Wolverhampton and other places in the Midlands occupied much of his time as a civil engineer; otherwise, he might well have matured into one of the great railway builders of the age.

JOSEPH LOCKE

Another builder whose name has faded with time is Joseph Locke (1805–60). Born in Barnsley, Yorkshire, he was one of George Stephenson's most able pupils. At 18 he was articled to the master at Newcastle, helped him to build the Liverpool & Manchester Railway, and joined him in compiling a pamphlet arguing the case for the steam locomotive. Working later in his own right, Locke constructed lines on many railways, of which the following are the principal:

Grand Junction 1835–37
London & Southampton 1836–40
Sheffield & Manchester 1838–40
Lancaster & Preston 1837–40

Greenock, Paisley & Glasgow (later including Greenock Docks on the Clyde estuary) 1837–41
Paris & Rouen 1841–43
Rouen & Havre 1843
Barcelona & Mattaro (Spain's first railway) 1847–48
Dutch-Rheinish (first part opened 1856)

Constructed jointly with his partner, John Edward Errington:

Lancaster & Carlisle 1843–46
East Lancashire 1845
Scottish Central 1845
Caledonian 1848
Scottish Midland 1852
Aberdeen 1852
Mantes, Caen & Cherbourg 1852

Locke also built the "Crewe Engine", using a high mathematical accuracy so that principal parts could be used in various locomotives. Like a conjuror, he kept many balls in the air at the same time. In a lifetime of 55 years, travelling extensively in those hazardous days, he did more than most in spreading the gospel of George Stephenson.

SCOTLAND'S PROBLEM

One of the first railways in Scotland was the Kilmarnock & Troon mineral line of $9\frac{3}{4}$ miles, opened with horses in 1812 and built in a gauge of 4 ft. Five years later, the railway ordered one of Stephenson's first Killingworth engines and Stephenson attended in person to supervise operations. But the track proved inadequate and the engine had to be withdrawn until the line was strengthened, and the engine returned to work the line for many years.

According to the report of a Select Committee on Railways up to June 1843, about 200 miles of route had by then been built in Scotland. They had reached Kilmarnock, Troon, Glasgow, Edinburgh, Ayr, Greenock, Monkland, Garnkirk, Coatbridge, Paisley, Dundee, and Arbroath. Builders chose a variety of gauges. The Garnkirk & Glasgow, and the Slamannan Railway were both 4 ft. 6 in., which had looked very much like becoming the standard for Scotland. Incidentally, unlike most railways, the Slamannan was presented with land free of charge on which to build the line. Whishaw wrote: "The names of these

The first sod is cut for a great Victorian railway, a short line with a grandiose title – the Great North of Scotland Railway. Within a few years it would link the thriving towns of Inverness and Aberdeen. This "gathering of the clans" is pictured at Westall, Aberdeenshire, in 1852. (W.P.L.)

Above: Highland Railway 4–6–0 No. 103, designed in 1894 by David Jones, who pioneered this wheel arrangement. Seen here on the Inverness–Kyle of Lochalsh line in 1960. Below: Great Western Railway 2–4–0 No. 1336, originally a Midland & South Western Railway locomotive, at Cirencester with a Gloucester Railway Society special in 1953.
(Photos: By courtesy of J. M. Jarvis, Esq.)

gentlemen are – Robert Jamieson, Esq., of Arden; Robert Haldane, Esq., of Auchingrey; and George Waddell, Esq., of Balquhatson." Several lines were built to the 5 ft. gauge; and the Arbroath–Forfar to 5 ft. 6 in. – the engineer's reason was that Brunel's was too wide and Stephenson's too narrow. At that stage, he had not foreseen a nation-wide network.

As the railways in Scotland pushed farther into the mountains and round the rugged coastlines, they faced severe engineering problems, with heavy gradients, tunnels and formidable rock formations; but with much less industry than in England, problems in obtaining land were fewer. Scottish builders also learnt from the pioneers who had made such rapid progress south of the border. Then, as more links were forged between the north and the south, Scottish lines had be to converted in stages to the standard English gauge.

Builders of the Edinburgh & Glasgow Railway used the English gauge for their line which opened on 21st February 1842 via Linlithgow and Falkirk. It was described by Whishaw as "a grand trunk railway", though only 46 miles in length. He added: "Who can foresee, we say, the great, the wonderful revolution that will take place in the affairs of Scotland by the opening of this line?"

Massive earthworks made the setting for the builders. Never had so much soil been moved before. Experience had earlier been gained during the canal era of roughly 1760 to 1830, with innovators such as James Brindley (1716–72), and from the road-making of Thomas Telford (1757–1834) and John Loudon Macadam (1756–1836).

THE RAILWAY NAVVIES

Promoters dreamed up their magnificent schemes for new railways, men of capital put up the money, directors saw the project through several years of campaigning to get past Parliament, surveyors marked out the routes, engineers took charge of the building of the lines and rolling stock, builders erected the vehicles, but it was the navvies, in contractors' teams, who physically built the railway lines. In doing so, this tough and romantic breed has earned a special place in the history of the railways.

Between 1825 and 1840, the total route mileage built was 1,484; by 1850 it was 6,084, and by 1860 9,069. By 1870 it was 13,563, creeping up at a slower pace to reach the peak of over 20,000 miles by the 1930s. Thus, more than half of the total railway network ever built in Britain had been laid out by the early 1860s; the navvy formed part of the British scene for more than half a century.

On a major line navvies would number in their thousands and horses in their hundreds. Smiles often saw them at their work, and presents his own vivid picture. "They were drawn by the attraction of good wages from all parts of the kingdom; and they were ready for any sort of hard work.

"Many of the labourers employed on the Liverpool lines were Irish; others were from the Northumberland and Durham railways, where they had been accustomed to similar work; and some of the best came from the fen districts of Lincoln and Cambridge, where they had been trained to execute works of excavation and embankment.

"These old practitioners formed a nucleus of skilled manipulation and aptitude, which rendered them of indispensable utility in the immense undertakings of the period. Their expertness in all sorts of earthwork, in embanking, boring, and well-sinking – their practical knowledge of the nature of soils and rocks, the tenacity of clays, and the porosity of certain stratifications – were very great; and, rough looking as they were, many of them were as important in their own department as the contractor or the engineer."

Many had worked on the canals (hence their name, abbreviated from "navigators") where they gained experience with horses, wheel-barrows, winching equipment, and moving enormous masses of earth.

Smiles turns his attention to their appearance and personal habits: "During the railway-making period, the navvies wandered about from one public work to another – apparently belonging to no country and having no home. He usually wore a white felt hat with the brim turned up, a velveteen or jean square-tailed coat, a scarlet plush waistcoat with little black spots, and a bright-coloured ker-chief round his herculean neck, when, as often happened, it was not left entirely bare.

"His corduroy breeches were retained in position by a leathern strap round the waist, and were tied and buttoned at the knee, displaying beneath a solid calf and foot encased in strong high-laced boots.

"Joining together in a 'butty-gang', some 10 or 12 of these men would take a contract to cut out and remove so much 'dirt' – as they denominated earth-cutting – fixing their price according to the

A train is wrecked in Spittal-gate cutting, Great Northern Railway, in 1852 after earth slippage. (*W.P.L.*)

character of the 'stuff', and the distance to which it had to be wheeled and tipped."

The engineer would already have planned the line so that earth moved to make cuttings could be transferred to form raised embankments as required by the lay of the land.

"The contract taken, every man put himself to his mettle; if any was found skulking, or not putting forth his full working power, he was ejected from the gang. Their powers of endurance were extraordinary. In times of emergency they would work for twelve and even sixteen hours, with only short intervals for meals." (An eight-hour working day and a five-day working week were still a long way off.) "The quantity of flesh-meat which they consumed was something enormous; but it was to their bones and muscles what coke is to the locomotive – the means of keeping up the steam. They displayed great pluck, and seemed to disregard peril. Indeed, the most dangerous sort of labour – such as working horse-barrow runs, in which accidents are of constant occurrence – has always been most in request among them, the danger seeming to be one of its chief recommendations.

"Working together, eating, drinking, and sleeping together, and daily exposed to the same influences, these railway labourers soon presented a distinct and well-defined character, strongly marking them from the population of the districts in which they laboured. Reckless alike of their lives as of their earnings, the navvies worked hard and lived hard.

"For their lodging, a hut of turf would content them; and, in their hours of leisure, the meanest public house would serve for their parlour. Unburdened, as they usually were, by domestic ties, unsoftened by family affection, and without much moral or religious training, the navvies came to be distinguished by a sort of savage manners, which contrasted strangely with those of the surrounding population.

"Yet, ignorant and violent though they might be, they were usually good-hearted fellows in the main – frank and open-handed with their comrades, and ready to share their last penny with those in distress."

Large teams were engaged in cutting the Kilsby tunnel, just south of Rugby, on the London & Birmingham Railway being built by Robert Stephenson. Smiles says of those times: "Their pay-nights were often a saturnalia of riot and disorder, dreaded by the inhabitants of the villages along the line of works. The irruption of such men into the quiet hamlet of Kilsby must, indeed, have produced a very startling effect on the recluse inhabitants of the place."

Robert Stephenson used to tell a story about

the clergyman of the parish "waiting upon the foreman of one of the gangs to expostulate with him as to the shocking impropriety of his men working during Sunday. The but (the head navvy) merely hitched up his trowsers, and said, 'Why, Soondays hain't cropt out here yet!' " In short, Smiles wrote, "the navvies were little better than heathens, and the village of Kilsby was not restored to its wonted quiet until the tunnel-works were finished, and the engines and scaffolding removed, leaving only the immense masses of *debris* around the line of shafts which extend along the top of the tunnel."

Gang fights frequently broke out among the navvies in drunken brawls, especially on pay nights, as they invaded the inns of local villages. Sleepy hamlets were disturbed from a pastural tranquility they had enjoyed since Shakespeare's time, and the innocent villagers were often frightened to death. At weekends, the foremen were given the thankless task of trying to keep law and order in the absence of any police force to help.

Apart from the aggressive outbreaks, the navvies worked hard, were loyal to their foreman, did not go on strike, and maintained a comradely loyalty among themselves. In any area which they entered, like an invading army, every available bed was taken, and day-shift men moved into beds that were still warm from the night-workers. Sometimes, a comrade would be fatally injured; and he would be accompanied by his mourning mates to a local church and the burial ground, in silent and respectful ceremony.

Busy scene of railway navvies at work

In terms of physical suffering, one of the worst projects was the Box tunnel, nearly 2 miles long, and one of the biggest excavations yet attempted. Brunel needed the tunnel on the section between Chippenham and Bath to complete the line that was to make his railway name – from Paddington

Many railway builders designed attractive masonries; this is the west portal of Brunel's Box Tunnel, nearly two miles long near Bath on the Great Western Railway main line, and opened in 1841. (*By courtesy of the Victoria & Albert Museum*)

to Bristol. Preliminary work on the shafts, some of them 300 ft. deep, began in September 1836 and a year later contracts were advertised. Detractors had described the proposal as that "Monstrous and extraordinary, most dangerous and impracticable tunnel at Box."

Brunel put his assistant, William Glennie, in charge of construction. A pioneering railway contractor from Herne Bay, Kent, named George Burge, was commissioned to build three-quarters of its length from the western end, and two local contractors for the remainder: a Mr. Lewis of Bath and Mr. Brewer of Box. The main part, which contained marl, clay and a granular limestone called oolite, needed a brick lining; and about a hundred horses and carts took three years to transport about 30,000,000 bricks from a yard near Chippenham. Most of the spoil was hauled in large buckets through the shafts, using horses and mechanical gins. Tons of gunpowder blasted rock for over two years, and thousands of tallow-candles a week lighted the men to their digging.

Severe flooding in November 1837 filled the partly-dug tunnel and rose high up the shafts to the terror of the navvies. A second pumping engine was brought in to shift the water. A year later another in-flow halted work for ten days.

The story is told that as work progressed, Brunel persuaded some of the directors to descend in buckets down a shaft to inspect the work. For these prosperous and pampered gentlemen, muddy buckets, creaking ropes and earthy smells as they swung down into the darkness below must have been an eerie experience to remember.

Construction fell behind the expected opening date in August 1840, and four months later Brunel bolstered the working force to some 4,000 men and 300 horses in one great final drive. After nearly five years of work, Box tunnel, with a heavy track gradient of 1 in 100, was completed in June 1841. It was estimated that during this time about a hundred men died and many were injured: a heavy price to pay. Costs, too, which Brunel had originally estimated at £6,500,000, mounted to well over twice that figure.

And the story of Box – the heartache, frustration, delay, injury, death, and final triumph – is the story of the other great tunnels scooped out of the hills of Britain to make way for the iron road.

Included in the railways were some of the most massive engineering works that had ever been undertaken, and considered as a whole these were a feat of construction never previously equalled nor perhaps surpassed. Engineering skill and daring, mechanical ingenuity, industrial organisation – all far more advanced in Britain than in any other country in the world – combined to bring the railways into existence. But above all, they are a monument to the railway navvies in that "untiring, savage industry". They managed with little earth-moving equipment other than the primitive contraptions of ropes, windlasses, horses and carts, cumbersome wheelbarrows and simple gravity; and nothing more technically advanced than gunpowder for blasting out rock. In fact, it might even be claimed that the railways of Britain were made by pick and shovel.

CONTRACTORS GO BANKRUPT

When contractors were asked to estimate for a specific task in a railway building programme, they were often somewhat out of their depth in this new kind of work. Soil and rock formations, underground springs and flooding, especially in tunnel work, presented some of the unknown hazards they had to face, not to mention the weather. And how many men and horses and winches and barrows would be needed? How many picks and shovels? The engineer wanted a firm price; and if the contractor wanted the job, he would have to provide one.

The health and lives of many good contractors in all parts of Britain were ruined as the iron road straddled the country to satisfy the voracious appetite of Railway Mania. When Robert Stephenson was building the London & Birmingham Railway, he told his old friend Smiles of the heart-breaking vicissitudes: "After the works were let, wages rose, the prices of materials of all kinds rose, and the contractors, many of whom were of comparatively small capital, were thrown on their beam ends.

"Their calculations as to expenses and profits were completely upset. Let me just go over the list. There was Jackson, who took the Primrose Hill contract (in North London) – he failed. Then there was the next length – Nowells; then Copeland and Harding; north of them Townsend, who had the Tring cutting; next Norris, who had Stoke Hammond (near Bletchley); then Soars; then Hughes: I think all of these broke down, or at least were helped through by the directors. Then there was that terrible contract of the Kilsby Tunnel, which broke the Nowells, and killed one of them. The contractors to the north of Kilsby were more fortunate, though some of them pulled through only with the greatest difficulty.

"Of the eighteen contracts in which the line was originally let, only seven were completed by the original contractors. Eleven firms were ruined by their contracts, which were relet to others at advanced prices, or were carried on and finished by the Company.

"The principal cause of increase in the expenses, however, was the enlargement of the stations. It appeared that we had greatly under-estimated the traffic, and it accordingly became necessary to spend more and more money for its accommodation, until I think I am within the mark when I say that the expenditure on this account alone exceeded by eight- or ten-fold the amount of the Parliamentary estimate." Unexpected landslides also threw out schedules and raised the costs.

One of the great railway contractors of the age was Samuel Morton Peto (1809–89). Aided by an erstwhile partner and huge gangs of navvies, he built railways for a large number of companies including the Great Western, Great Eastern, Great Northern, Eastern Counties, London Chatham & Dover, East Lincolnshire, London and South Western, London, Tilbury & Southend, South Eastern, Oxford, Worcester & Wolverhampton, and Hereford, Ross & Gloucester. He also built the Christiania-Eidsvoll Railway in Norway, the Lyons-Avignon in France, and lines in Russia, Algeria, Australia and Canada.

RAILWAYS THAT MIGHT HAVE BEEN

Of the hundreds of potential builders whose railways never saw the light of day, some failed to get their lines registered; others registered their prospectuses but could not obtain parliamentary authority; many were abandoned or simply allowed to lapse. Most were promoted during the mania period. All of them lost much money in preliminaries. Including Ireland, over fifty of them had as the first word of their titles "Great . . ." – tiny though some of them were; and over sixty began with "Direct . . .": at that time, two highly fashionable railway words.

A selection of important towns and cities that might have been connected by "direct" railways is listed below; and had they been built straight through, they would have changed the railway map of Britain:

Bedford	– Exeter
Birmingham	– Aberystwyth
Birmingham	– Southampton
Birmingham	– Brighton
Birmingham	– Boston via Leicester
Bristol	– Dover
Cheltenham	– Harwich via Hertford
Cheltenham	– Dover
Cheltenham	– Brighton
Cheltenham	– Lincoln
Dover	– Yeovil
Gloucester	– Ipswich via Bedford and Cambridge
Hull	– Southampton via Northampton
Hull	– Holyhead
Hull	– Swansea
Leicester	– Harwich
Leicester	– Shrewsbury
Lincoln	– Holyhead via Mansfield

Two projects carried names with a touch of originality: the Grand London & Dublin Approximation Railway, and Cooke's National Railway; both registered their prospectuses but faded from view.

★ ★ ★

From the earliest days and indeed until well into the 20th century, the railways have thrown up many great personalities: talented designers of locomotives, carriages and wagons, track and signalling, distinguished architects, autocratic general managers and dynamic superintendents. But the Stephensons and Brunel stand alone as the greatest of the pioneering railway builders. Their finest creative work was concentrated in about a quarter of a century from 1825 to 1850; and they allowed no problem – financial, Parliamentary, public objection, storms, floods, disaster or death to stand in their way.

These three men, supported by a dozen or so of their close associates and contemporaries, bequeathed to Britain and the world a sum total of railway engineering and technical knowledge that grew far too complicated to be absorbed by any one mind, however brilliant. As more lines came into use, the work of the pioneers was carried forward more and more by specialists in different departments and techniques, with a division of labour right down the line. The builders set the pace, and dedicated railwaymen ever since have devoted their life's work to ensuring that the railways of Britain are still the best in the world.

Chapter 5
Great Victorian Railway Companies

Charing Cross station, London, built by Sir John Hawkshaw and opened in 1864 for South Eastern Railway trains. Outside the station was erected the famous Charing (Eleanor) Cross, regarded as the centre of London. (By courtesy of the Science Museum)

FROM the early pioneering days, through the rapid spread of lines leading to the epidemic of railway mania, and the progress to amalgamations and cautious consolidation, a great railway network came into being. Of the hundreds of separate companies, which settled down eventually into something over 100, consisting variously of from 10 miles to 2- to 3,000, about a dozen finally emerged to establish themselves as the great Victorian railway companies. Each one became a household word, to be known far beyond the lines on which they ran. Some were known from the very first line they opened; others acquired new names as they amalgamated to build up their power and influence.

The railways as a whole were prosperous, and the country knew that much of the nation's prosperity had come with the advent of railways. Companies evolved their own clearly identifiable images by style, design, architecture, colours, coats-of-arms and printed public material, in fierce competition not only for the passengers and the goods but for investment and shares. Generations came and went, but the biggest names remained big, and it seemed then that they would reign for ever. The development of all the railways is reflected in the following table:

1825–35	the pioneering period
1836–44	a boom period for the lines first developed
1845–47	the peak of mania, its spread and collapse
1848–49	many amalgamations take place, following the lead set by the Midland Railway in 1844
1850–54	the railways are proving themselves and speculation gradually gives way to caution
1855–59	a notable expansion in branch lines
1860–64	a period of numerous separate railway companies as many more new lines open
1865–69	a minor boom develops but is followed by some serious financial collapses
1870–79	restrained expansion continues and about 2,000 route miles are added to the network
1880–89	a peak period of stable business and greater public acceptance
1890–99	a period of "light" railways with nar-

row gauge rails for routes on which potential traffic is also light

1900– the great age of railways still continues, with little awareness of the first threat to their monopoly beginning to appear on the distant horizon

* * *

In selecting 14 companies for brief description, the author has arranged the sequence in four groups – beginning with the largest – which constituted the main line railway companies which emerged on 1st January 1923 after amalgamation: the London Midland & Scottish Railway; the London & North Eastern Railway; the Great Western Railway; and the Southern Railway.

THE LONDON & NORTH WESTERN RAILWAY

Self-styled "The Premier Line", and frequently advertised as "The largest Joint Stock Corporation in the World", the London & North Western Railway made its debut on 16th July 1846. It was formed by the amalgamation of three other railways: the London & Birmingham, Manchester & Birmingham, and the Grand Junction. As the Grand Junction had taken over the Liverpool & Manchester the year before, this provided the new company with trunk routes between its London terminus at Euston and the two leading northwest cities. The Grand Junction had earlier taken over other smaller railways, including the Warrington & Newton (in 1834), the Chester & Crewe (1840), and the Kenyon & Leigh Junction and the Bolton & Leigh (1845). Among the railways taken over by the London & Birmingham were lines serving Warwick, Leamington, Bedford, Dunstable and Aylesbury.

One of the factors that pushed the three constituent companies into the L.N.W. amalgamation was Brunel's plan to drive his line to Oxford northward to Birmingham and Leamington – "united we stand". The Great Western later gained its objective, and eventually reached Chester and Birkenhead.

At its formation, the Company began with some 350 miles of route, and operated several smaller railways: a common practice among the leading companies. More amalgamations followed quickly, including the Buckinghamshire Railway, Huddersfield & Manchester Railway and Canal, and Leeds, Dewsbury & Manchester. The Chester & Holyhead sought a deal, for traffic was light. It was not until the Great Western was planning to build to North Wales that the North Western thought the time was ripe; a threat on its western flank could be dangerous, and the merger took place in 1858. The lucrative traffic for Ireland justified the move and later the North Western owned two short lines in Ireland to handle its business.

Railways in South Wales and South Staffordshire extended the services; more joint line ventures matured, including three shared with its adversary the Great Western: the Shrewsbury & Welshpool, Shrewsbury & Hereford, and Birkenhead Railway. Rivalry concerning joint lines often flared and clashes created odd situations. In Wolverhampton the North Western, determined to stop a competitor's train from reaching Birmingham, not only blocked the line with two engines but pulled up some of the track. The North Western had been warned in advance: "We shall stand no humbug . . . We shall run to Birmingham tomorrow by force." The story had leaked out and a crowd gathered to see the fun, but the

A great railway builder, Brunel (centre), the "little giant" who strove for architectural and engineering beauty in all his works. (Photo: (British Rail)

obstruction remained. The Mayor attended and brought about a temporary peace; but the case reached the courts, although subsequent amalgamations made the dispute void.

Over the years the North Western penetrated many areas served by its competitors, and healthy rivalry promoted higher speeds and improved services of all kinds. Its trains reached far beyond the main-line territory and joint lines extended to Peterborough, Nottingham, Newark, Swansea and Blackpool.

Strangely enough, the Company did not have a good reputation with its locomotives; they were not particularly fast, and trains frequently had to be double-headed. From the 1840s, Edward Bury's engines were notably small and under-powered. Yet there had been several distinguished and original locomotive engineers. A remarkable engine was built at Crewe by Francis Trevithick (son of the famous Richard) in 1847, the *Cornwall*, later improved and rebuilt. Its unique visual feature consisted of a pair of driving wheels of 8 ft. 6 in. diameter, higher than the ceiling of a modern suburban house; the boiler rested ingeniously under the high driving axle. It hauled expresses on the Liverpool and Manchester line until the turn of the century.

Of the successive locomotive engineers, James Ramsbottom (1814–97) introduced many new ideas. In 1862 he concentrated the locomotive building and heavy repair work at Crewe, which grew to one of the most comprehensive railway works in the world. The Company's other works was at Wolverton, whose engineers were not at all pleased with Ramsbottom's preference for Crewe. One of his best series was the 2–2–2 *Lady of the Lake* class with outside cylinders and 7 ft. 6 in. driving wheels. These graceful engines did excellent work for many years.

Ramsbottom introduced water troughs in 1860, a system which was adopted widely on main lines of other companies, well over 50 being installed. A scoop lowered from the tender scooped water from a trough laid between the rails as the train was running at speed. Filling the tender in this way avoided the delays of filling up at water columns.

He was succeeded by F. W. Webb (1835–1906), who experimented with a "compound" system in 1878, since when "Webb's Compound" has slipped into railway engineering language. It was designed to use the steam exhausted from one cylinder to enter another cylinder, at which moment pressure was lower but still potent. The steam was thus used twice. Other railways introduced their own versions of compound engines, but engineers could rarely agree about overall and relative merits.

Other well-known classes of locomotives from the L. & N.W. stable included the *Ironic*, *Sir Gilbert Claughton*, *Dreadnought*, *Teutonic*, *Greater Britain*, *Adriatic*, *Precedent*, and *Jumbo*. Jumbo 2–4–0s were some of the best engines ever built in Britain at that time. From the 1850s, Euston–Rugby–Birmingham trains for many years were hauled by the 2–2–2 *Bloomers*.

By the time he retired in 1903, Webb had built over 2,500 locomotives, and was Crewe's most outstanding personality. He had organised, standardised and developed his department to high standards of efficiency. Crewe engines were black; when alternative colours had been discussed, Webb is reputed to have said, "I don't care what the colour is, as long as it is black."

Some handsome stations were built by the L. & N.W., and what is regarded as the first passenger station in the world formed part of its system; the station in Liverpool Road, Manchester, erected by George Stephenson, was a two-storey building, and is being preserved for the nation.

Throughout most of the Company's lifetime, Euston station, its London terminus, fronted by the luxurious Euston Hotel and the grand and remarkable pillared Doric Arch, formed an eloquent symbol of its Victorian power and prestige. Built by Philip Hardwicke, this striking edifice in Bramley Fall stone was described by a writer at the time: "A propylaeum or arch gateway of pure free Doric. Its length is 300 ft., it cost £35,000 . . . Its columns are higher than any other building in London."

Within the station was Hardwicke's son's highly decorative Great Hall, fashioned like the main hall of a splendid English palace. The divided, balustraded staircase led to a balcony running high along the walls; it led also to the Company's boardroom and the shareholder's meeting room, furnished in Victorian splendour. Near the foot of the stairs stood a huge statue – erected in 1852 – of George Stephenson, looking down thoughtfully on the scurrying passengers bound for Birmingham or Rugby. The stairs were well worn by the feet of the Company's mighty men.

Euston station started modestly as a shed for four tracks; two of them were earmarked for the Great Western, a plan which was abandoned. On its very first day, 13th July 1937, the little station was "christened" as the return train from

Berkhamstead of fourteen four-wheeled carriages carrying a special party of 150 people, ran hard into the buffers. For the first seven years, trains were hauled to Camden by a cable 3 in. thick, usually ascribed to the steep gradient of 1 in 70, thought to be too heavy for locomotives. It was also said that the engines would frighten horses in nearby streets. More trains meant a bigger station, eventually extended to fifteen platforms. This splendid array of Victoriana had to be demolished to make way for the "New Euston" in the 1960s, and Stephenson's statue was put into store.

At the end of its independent career of nearly 77 years, the L.N.W. finished up with 2,149 route miles of railway, slightly exceeded by the Midland, but vastly exceeded by the Great Western. Its trains penetrated as far as Swansea, Hereford, Leeds, Peterborough, Oxford, Cambridge, Nottingham, Newark and Blackpool, well beyond its own main territory.

As a predominantly passenger line, the L.N.W. had move locomotives and more passenger carriages than its contemporaries, but fewer freight wagons than either the Great Western or the Midland. It also owned 17 ships, and shared ownership of four more with the Lancashire & Yorkshire Railway, which was the company with the largest fleet of railway ships. On total mileage, and rolling stock fleets, the L.N.W. ranked with the Midland and the Great Western as one of the three great Victorian railways; and as a largely Stephenson line, many railway historians have awarded it the accolade – "the greatest". Robert Stephenson was closely associated with the Railway until his death.

Some may still remember the livery, the black locomotives relieved by lines in yellow, pale blue and vermilion; purple lake carriages with white upper panels and lined in yellow, and the grey wagons: all to be lost in the "grouping".

THE MIDLAND

When George Hudson created the Midland Railway in 1844, under Act of Parliament, by the amalgamation of three other strong railways, and became its first chairman, a cohesive railway of 180 miles connected some of the wealthiest industrial areas of the Midlands. They all centred on Derby as the headquarters. The Midland Counties Railway ran from Derby to Nottingham and Leicester, reaching the London & Birmingham by a branch to Rugby; the North Midland ran to Leeds; and the Birmingham & Derby Junction ensured connections to Euston. Three more railways were added in 1846: the Leicester & Swannington to become the oldest section of the Midland; the Birmingham & Gloucester with its heavy gradient of 1 in 37·5 of over 2 miles – the Lickey Incline, Bromsgrove – which for many years needed a "bank" engine, produced by Sir Henry Fowler in 1919, of ten coupled wheels at the rear of trains; and the Bristol & Gloucester of 7 ft. Brunel gauge.

Hudson, the "amalgamator", fell from grace in 1849, but the expansionist pattern he had set continued: Leeds & Bradford, 1851; Skipton & Morecambe, 1852. After that, rarely two years went by without an amalgamation, a joint line, running powers or new lines, culminating in 1912 with an important line, the London, Tilbury & Southend Railway. This line had opened in 1854 and was built jointly by the Eastern Counties and the London & Blackwall.

Among the scores of railways taken over were the Furness & Midland (1863), Cheshire Lines Committee – jointly (1865), Sheffield & Midland Junction – jointly (1869), Manchester, Buxton, Matlock & Midlands Junction and the Morecambe Railway & Harbour (1871), Halesowen & Bromsgrove Branch (1872), Hereford, Hay & Brecon (1874), Wolverhampton & Walsall (1876), Bedford & Northampton (1885), Dore & Chinley with the second longest tunnel (1888), Midland & Great Northern Joint Committee reaching into Norfolk (1893), Kettering, Thrapston & Huntingdon (1897), and Tottenham & Hampstead Junction (1902). A Parliamentary Bill of 1853, to amalgamate with the London & North Western and subsequently with the Great Northern had been rejected as against the public interest.

Most of these railways had begun independently, with their own Acts of Parliament, before joining the Midland; many were too financially frail to continue standing on their own feet. At some of the larger towns, more stations were built by competing lines than could possibly be justified indefinitely, storing up problems for later railway managers. The same applied to goods stations, marshalling yards, locomotive and engineering depots and their administrative offices. This was true of all the main railways.

As the Midland progressed, its biggest single lack was its own main line to London and it had to depend on its mortal enemies, the London & North Western and the Great Northern, to get its passengers and goods into and out of the Metropolis. In the late 1850s and 1860s the Midland found themselves in an impossible and ludicrous position. In one day alone, Midland coal trains delayed in the L.N.W. sidings at Rugby would have stretched end to end for about 5 miles. Working its way steadily south, the Midland built a line from Leicester through Market Harborough and Kettering to Bedford, and from 1858 their trains could run from nearby Hitchin on Great Northern lines to King's Cross. It was noted in 1862 that many thousands of Midland passengers were seriously delayed into King's Cross. It was natural that the two Midland competitors, one on either flank, should put their own passengers and goods first, despite the heavy dues paid for the privilege; but it spurred the Midland on to London, a notion first brought up in 1845 in the delirious heat of mania.

A four-track main line from Bedford was projected, and finally built by way of Luton and St. Albans to St. Pancras. This would shake up its two competitors who had made life so difficult. William Henry Barlow (1812–1902), the Midland's consulting engineer, built the train shed – carrying the largest single-span roof in Britain – with thousands of men, hundreds of horses, stationary and locomotive steam engines, wooden scaffolding and the simplest of implements.

Its frontage consisted of the Midland hotel, towered and turreted in a lavish and flamboyant Gothic style that was to dwarf the Great Northern's yellow brick structure just across the road at King's Cross. Sir Gilbert Scott (1811–78), who came in for devastating and hurtful criticism later from the architectural profession, was the designer. Another floor would have been added to the hotel, which was lavishly furnished and fitted in the Victorian mode, but the money ran out. The cathedral-like front was to be expected from a man who had built a number of churches and cathedrals in his distinguished career. The original structure of the whole of the station and buildings can still be seen, the hotel since converted to railway offices.

Sir James Allport (1811–92), the Midland general manager, and one of the greatest in the Victorian period, had been a main driving force behind the new line and station, which had been bitterly opposed by competitors. It was authorised in 1863, and opened to the public at a celebration on 1st October 1868.

At about the same time, the Midland had its eye on Manchester; this meant crossing the mountains of the Peak District, piercing the hills with many tunnels and taking the line a thousand feet above sea level. It opened to New Mills in 1867, reaching Manchester London Road on Manchester, Sheffield & Lincolnshire metals. It was 1902 before the Midland had its own line to Manchester Central. Midland trains also ran regularly to Bournemouth.

Another ambition was achieved when its line opened from Settle to Carlisle in 1875, first for goods traffic. From 1876, Midland trains ran to Glasgow on the Glasgow & South Western route and to Edinburgh on the North British. Three routes then linked London with Scotland: the East Coast, West Coast and Midland, the Midland being the slowest.

The massive neo-Gothic façade of St. Pancras Hotel fronting St. Pancras station and dwarfing King's Cross, seen on the right. Lavishly furnished, it could sleep 500 guests. First class sitting rooms were each provided with an Erard piano. (*Photo: British Rail*)

St. Albans City station was opened in 1868 when the Midland Railway first reached London. The station was completely rebuilt in 1973 when the gas lighting was replaced by electricity. (*Photo: British Rail*)

Its main locomotive, carriage and wagon works were built at Derby, its headquarters. At first, locomotives came from outside firms, including 50 *Jenny Lind* 2–2–2 type with 6 ft. driving wheels. In 1851 the locomotive engineer, Kirtley, began to build Midland engines. In later years, some 4–4–0s constructed under Johnson formed the basis of main line engines for the London, Midland & Scottish Railway in the 1920s.

As the Midland approached the end of its career, ranking as one of the greatest railways, it owned about 50 per cent more goods wagons than either the London & North Western or the Great Western. Its passenger locomotives were painted in "Derby Red", lined in black and yellow; goods engines were black, coaches "Midland Lake", and goods wagons light grey. The Company also owned five ships, and short lines in Ireland. As the grouping approached, a new battle was to be fought – should the power of the new London, Midland & Scottish Railway be located at Derby or Euston?

LANCASHIRE & YORKSHIRE

Leases, agreements, and joint lines characterised the brief history leading to the incorporation of the Lancashire & Yorkshire Railway (the "Lanky") in 1847, on the crest of the mania wave. Principal components were the Manchester & Leeds (surveyed by George Stephenson), Wakefield, Pontefract & Goole, and the West Riding Union. A lease was taken on the Sheffield, Barnsley, Wakefield & Goole in 1850 and takeover completed in 1858. Next year the East Lancashire was absorbed, itself having already amalgamated the Blackburn & Preston, Bolton & Preston, and the Liverpool, Ormskirk & Preston lines.

Essentially an east-west railway, the Lanky stretched from Liverpool and Southport to Goole near the Humber port. Running powers and joint lines took its trains to Blackpool, Fleetwood, Leeds, York and Hull. Cotton, wool, coal and heavy industries ensured a busy line, serving such densely populated centres as Manchester, Bolton, Burnley, Rochdale, Bradford, Huddersfield, and Wakefield. A joint line – the North Union – was partly used by L.N.W. trains to and from Scotland and the Lake District.

At one stage in its career, the Lanky went through a degenerated period when the meticulous Victorian attention to detail found on other lines was sadly lacking. A local railway serving in general mill and factory workers, miners, men from heavy engineering and their families, its standards fell. Early "Victorian Villa" stations became inadequate, carriages filthy, engines decrepit, rolling stock neglected, and timekeeping – even in those leisurely years – disastrous. Weak management and staff indiscipline led to an indifferent attitude.

It took years of public ridicule and scorn to put the railway on its mettle, and the needled management steadily climbed back into public esteem. Restaurant and corridor coaches were introduced on expresses for Manchester, Southport, Bradford and Leeds, and carriages ran to further destinations on neighbouring main lines. A good reputation was earned by the Liverpool–Newcastle Express.

Lanky routes crossed the main lines of leading English Railways – the London & North Western, Midland, North Eastern, Great Northern and Great Eastern – to give the railway country-wide connecting services. Manchester formed the centre and headquarters of this active railway which, on average, had a station every 2 miles.

So close to the Pennines, gradients were steep and numerous, and the branch from Rochdale to Bacup reached an altitude of nearly 1,000 ft. At Huddersfield, the graceful Lockwood Viaduct was a notable engineering achievement, and the Aspen Valley was spanned by an unusual trestle bridge in timber.

As the railway was predominantly for short-distance trains, two out of five of its locomotive fleet were eventually tank engines. A large number were of the 0–6–2 type introduced in 1879, and the 2–4–2s were designed in 1899 and built for another 20 years for passenger trains. These were followed in 1908 with 4–6–0 express engines, later versions being adopted as standard expresses on the London Midland & Scottish Railway after the 1923 grouping. The Lanky was also early in the field among the leading railways with electrification, opening the Liverpool and Southport line services in 1904.

Of all the great Victorian railways, the Lancashire & Yorkshire built up the largest fleet of ships to total 23, and shared four more and Fleetwood Docks with the L.N.W. for services to Belfast. L. & Y. steamers also served Drogheda in Southern Ireland, Goole, Hull and the Continent.

Before losing its identity in the grouping, the railway owned the fourth longest route mileage, and a greater proportion of locomotives, carriages and wagons per mile of route than most of its contemporaries. Its black locomotives were lined in white and red (sometimes yellow); carriages were purple, their upper panels in buff with yellow lines; wagons were in a dark grey.

THE NORTH EASTERN

York was as important in the north-east as Derby, Crewe and Birmingham were in the Midlands, and as Liverpool and Manchester were in the north-west; and the city has remained a key railway centre, with Hudson House the headquarters. York became the headquarters of the new North Eastern Railway when the Company was incorporated by amalgamations in 1854 during the decade of rapid expansion. It was made up of three railways: York, Newcastle & Berwick (by far the largest), York & North Midland built by George Stephenson, and Leeds Northern. The Newcastle & Berwick had been a promotion of George Hudson's, and T. E. Harrison, general manager of the Y.N. & B. the driving force behind the new amalgamation.

Another important route was added in 1862, the Newcastle & Carlisle, belting the narrow waist across northern England, and connecting east and west coast main routes. The following year, the world's oldest public railway, the Stockton & Darlington, entered the fold. With the Company went its engineer, William Bouch, brother of Thomas Bouch who built the ill-fated Tay Bridge. Soon, the North Eastern owned nearly all the railways in Northumberland, Durham and the East Riding of Yorkshire, embracing such good solid territories as Sunderland, the Hartlepools, Whitby, Scarborough, Selby and Hull, and reaching the Lake District. The Company also owned docks at Hull and Hartlepool, and interests in ships using Hull.

North Eastern lines climbed some of the highest summits in England, strode across moor, pike and fell, skirted rugged sea-lashed coasts where lines were sometimes washed away, and straddled swift rivers rushing through picturesque dales down to the North Sea. Some of the bridges, such as Newcastle and Durham, were famous round the world. Robert Stephenson had built the Company's Royal Border Bridge astride the River Tweed that formed the English–Scottish border at Berwick, a grandly impressive structure of 28 arches on their piers rising from below the river bed, and stretching to a length of 2,160 ft. It was fittingly opened by the young Queen Victoria in 1850. Robert also built the unique High Level Bridge at Gateshead in 1849; it carried three railway tracks on the upper deck and a public roadway below. The North Eastern had acquired these bridges in amalgamations.

Ranking fourth of the great railway systems, the North Eastern was also the largest of those provincial railways still without their own lines to London. It was a rich industrial area: the very cradle of our railways, and forever associated with the great names in railway history. Even Brunel, while still in his twenties, had visited Sunderland to promote his Monkwearmouth Dock scheme; and some years later in Newcastle, he had proposed an atmospheric railway to Berwick, losing the argument to Stephenson and steam.

Mineral traffic was the Company's bread and butter, and it finished up with more goods wagons than any of its great contemporaries. Some of the fastest expresses in Britain roared along NE metals to win speed records that made railway history. Among its architecturally impressive stations stood Newcastle Central with its unique diamond crossings, Leeds, gracefully curved York, and Darlington where Stephenson's *Locomotion No.* 1 of 1825 is proudly displayed to today's Inter-City travellers.

Inter-railway competition produced better locomotives, and locomotive engineers often moved from one railway to another, even from Brighton to Glasgow, each job offering its own challenge and spreading the best techniques. The North Eastern was among the first to abandon "singles" (one pair of driving wheels), and from about 1864 engines with coupled driving wheels hauled the expresses. Two years later, the NE introduced Britain's first goods engines with six coupled wheels and compound cylinders; 171 were built in six years for heavy mineral trains. In 1899 and 1900, the Company built ten 4–6–0 express engines, also the first to be seen in England.

Because the Company encouraged design freedom at its works at Gateshead, Darlington, York and Leeds, the locomotive stud grew to be a mixed bag, but with commendable pride in the job. Some supreme engines in several individual standards emerged from the mixed assembly, to give a performance that was majestic, dominating and powerful. Under Fletcher, Johnson, McDonnell and their successors, the bulk consisted of 2–4–0s, 2–2–2s, 0–6–0 goods engines, and the well-known "Whitby Bogies" and "Ginx's Babies" of the 4–4–0 wheel arrangement. Livery settled down to a bright green, lined in black, white, and later, gold; safety valves had polished casings and some engines had brass chimney caps. Carriages were painted in crimson lake with yellow lines, and goods wagons in grey.

In the closing years of the century, the North Eastern took its share of the glory in the "Races to the North" against its formidable competitors of the West Coast Route.

THE GREAT NORTHERN

Stage coaches had been rattling up the Great North Road, once familiar to the Romans, for nearly two centuries by the time railway pioneers planned a railway from London to York. Starting in 1835, schemes and counter-schemes had cost promoters fortunes before a single rail was laid. Only one line from the north ran into London – the London & Birmingham, later part of the LNW. That line was Objector Number One. The Midland under Hudson were fearful of losing much business, and so were Eastern Counties lines. Other objectors and their reasons were numerous. The Parliamentary battle for the Great Northern was the most intense in pioneering railway history, costing the London and York Committee a quarter of a million pounds and the Direct Northern Company £90,000.

The wildest mania scheme had never before proposed a Bill for a network of 327 miles of railway including 186 miles of main line in one lot. Surveyors found a route with no gradient steeper than 1 in 200, except that leaving London, and remarkably free from severe curves; the main line was built for speed and was to be the scene of world records. Starting from Maiden Lane near King's Cross, it was opened in 1850 to Werrington Junction near Peterborough and two years later to Doncaster, ushering in a new railway era. In 1853 a new station was opened at King's Cross, built by Lewis Cubitt in yellow brick in the style of the Tsar's riding school in Moscow, and was acknowledged to be the largest and finest in London.

A second line to London meant that the Euston people could not have things all their own way. Competition flourished, but revenues did not always benefit. When reduced fares were offered for steamer services down the coast from Hull for the Great Exhibition of 1851, the railways followed suit. Fares from Yorkshire, for example, were reduced to 15s. (75p), then 10s., then 5s. Nobody could make a profit out of that. Conceivably, it could tempt people to the railways for the first time. Finally, the GN agent in Leeds announced that whatever fares other railways charged, the GN would go sixpence lower. This was typical of the experimental, thrusting new railways. Bitter feuding went right down the line from boardroom director to station porter.

Another, more subtle and cunning ploy was for

an agent of one railway to buy shares in another, then to attend shareholders' meetings to subvert the directors' plans for joint lines, extensions or other competitive measures.

A long and complicated episode in 1852 concerned GN running powers into Nottingham; and when a GN engine irregularly hauled a train into the station, the Midland placed an engine behind it, and virtually imprisoned the GN engine for seven months until the dispute was settled. Variations on an obstructive theme were common strategies.

Mr. Denison, already a veteran, was the GN chairman from its formation in 1850 until he retired in 1864 at the age of 77. Under his dominant and driving personality the railway rapidly expanded, to link with Dunstable, Grimsby, Skegness, Nottingham, Derby, Lincoln, and Doncaster where its workshops were built; running powers and joint lines took GN trains as far as Manchester, Liverpool, Southport and Chester. Joint ownership of the Midland & Great Northern Joint line brought Lowestoft, Cromer and Yarmouth within its reach; other agreements took in Leicester, Stafford and Uttoxeter. All the leading railways penetrated deeply into each others' territories. As the century progressed, nearly a third of all the mileage used by GN trains consisted of joint lines, which must have created a monumental administrative and accounting procedure. Of the seven English-based railways with the longest route mileage, the GN was the only one with neither ships nor docks.

Only one viaduct of note had to be erected by the GN on its comparatively level lines. It was built on the main line at Welwyn in Hertfordshire, consisted of 40 arches and was 1,560 ft. long; at one point it was about 100 ft. above the ground.

GN locomotives were supreme. Engines were first bought from outside firms until locomotive superintendents took over. In 1853 Archibald Sturrock, a former Great Western engineer, built large express engines with 7 ft. singles. Following him in 1866 was the renowned Patrick Stirling from the Glasgow & South Western, who set a new pattern of 2–2–2 engines with 8 ft. wheels. Stirling stayed with the GN for thirty years, bringing notable innovations in locomotive practice and performance. Next came H. A. Ivatt, who built his first engines with 8 ft. 6 in. singles; but the day of coupled driving wheels had finally arrived, and he produced his first 4–4–2 Atlantic types with a steam pressure of 175 lb. psi. Another great locomotive engineer, Nigel Gresley, took over in 1911 and took coupling a stage further with his 2–6–0 and 2–8–0 classes.

Royal Blue with black and red lines, touches of blue and polished brass was the livery for passenger engines, and black for goods. Carriages were in varnished teak, changed to crimson lake during World War One; wagons were painted grey.

THE GREAT EASTERN

From the 1830s, numerous projects had been advanced for short and isolated railways in the

Junction of three railways at King's Cross – the Midland, Great Northern and Metropolitan as illustrated in 1868.

eastern counties and from London to Essex and East Anglia. The Eastern Counties Railway secured an Act of Parliament in 1836 to construct a line from London to Norwich, at that time the longest main line so far planned. It opened to Romford in 1839 and was extended to Colchester in 1843, but then the money ran out. The Directors had wanted a 7 ft. gauge, but Braithwaite, the line's engineer, persuaded them to use 5 ft., which had to be converted to standard in 1844. When the Norwich & Brandon Railway opened in 1845, a through route connected Norwich with London. That was the year George Hudson, chairman of the Midland, was appointed chairman of the Eastern Counties. During his three years of office, he paid dividends out of capital instead of from revenue, a fool's trick which put the Company in financial straits in 1848. Furious creditors held rolling stock against the heavy debts.

Other lines at that period included the Northern, Eastern, and Eastern & Hadleigh Junction; three other companies served Ely, Dereham and Lynn which, in 1847, joined to form the East Anglian Railway. Other short lines were taken over by the Eastern Counties Railway which transferred its locomotive works from Romford to Stratford in East London. John Gooch, brother of Daniel of the Great Western, took charge, to build engines instead of buying them all from private firms.

A larger amalgamation, found so successful elsewhere, was obviously desirable for the several railways serving such scattered and rural communities, which had no major port or industrial centre, other than the London area. In this setting, the Great Eastern Railway came into existence in 1862 by joining the Eastern Counties, East Anglian, Newmarket, Eastern Union, and Norfolk Railways – none of them flourishing concerns. Few had suffered the public abuse and ridicule which the Eastern Counties had faced, however.

Now a stronger Company, the G.E. expanded, in time, to link London, Cambridge, Peterborough, Huntingdon, most coastal places in Norfolk, and Essex, and Southend-on-Sea, fed by a web of cross-country lines. Joint lines took G.E. trains to Doncaster and York. Fish trains from Yarmouth and Lowestoft and goods trains from the London docks and East London industries added to the busy passenger traffic to make a well diversified railway.

The G.E. eventually owned 11 ships, some of them serving Holland and other continental ports from Harwich. They were the largest and best serving the continent. Ports at Harwich, Felixstowe and King's Lynn owed much of their prosperity to the Company. Harwich, Parkeston Quay had been completed in 1882, and was named after the G.E. chairman.

From the time that Liverpool Street station opened in 1875 as the city terminus, the punctuality and reliability of the passenger services could match any other railway. Earlier the chairman, Lord Cranborn (who became the great Marquis of Salisbury) had dragged the ailing railway from the doldrums into a respectable and reputable concern. Two other outstanding chairmen were Parkes, with a keen eye for administrative detail; and Lord Claud Hamilton, who followed him in 1893, to promote the prosperity of the Company and the good will of the staff.

No locomotive engineer stayed with the Company long enough for marked continuity until James Holden from the Great Western arrived in 1885, staying until 1908. He concentrated on a handful of good locomotives: 4–4–0s for expresses and 0–6–0 tanks for suburban trains. His historic innovation was the introduction of 60 oil-burning engines, one of which was the classic *Claud Hamilton*. Though successful, rising oil prices created by the arrival of the first motor vehicles forced their abandonment. Holden's son succeeded him for four years, then Hill took over until 1923.

Prestige was gained from the frequent Royal trains to Wolferton station for Sandringham, and the presence of the University of Cambridge. Well before the First World War, the well-known and popular *Hook of Holland Continental* (still running) and the *Norfolk Coast* expresses had joined the ranks of Britain's crack trains. Another development was to run G.E. trains into Fenchurch Street and St. Pancras stations, bringing entry into central London at three key places.

In 1908, it was proposed to amalgamate the three "greats" – Great Eastern, Great Northern and Great Central as the Great Northern, Central & Eastern Railway; but Parliament turned it down.

G.E. passenger locomotives were in a livery of royal blue, characterised by red, gleaming brass and polished fittings, changing to war-time grey. Carriages were in varnished teak, and wagons in a dark brick red.

THE GREAT CENTRAL

Three features distinguished the Great Central Railway, which was created in 1897. It was formed by the amalgamation of a number of railways dating back for more than half a century; it was the last company to build a main line into London; and it was the last important railway company to be formed. By that time, all the best routes from the north to London had been snapped up.

Sheffield was its home ground. In 1837, a line between Sheffield and Manchester was projected by the Sheffield, Ashton-under-Lyne & Manchester Railway, sharing Manchester London Road station with the Manchester & Birmingham Railway, which later was a strong rival. Crossing the Pennines entailed heavy engineering works, including Dinting Viaduct and a tunnel at Woodhead about 1,000 ft. above sea level. Charles Vignoles, the first engineer, found too many obstacles and handed over to George Stephenson's protégé Joseph Locke. The single bore tunnel, just over 3 miles long and then the longest in Britain, was opened in 1845 to give a through line; seven years later a second bore was made, to give a double track throughout, but the railway never recovered fully from the financial outlay. Some branch lines were also opened. About that time, two other railways were being built: the Great Grimsby & Sheffield Junction, and the Sheffield & Lincolnshire Junction. Even before they were ready, the Company took them over, together with the Great Grimsby Dock Company.

In 1847, the new group was called the Manchester, Sheffield & Lincolnshire Railway, usually known as the Sheffield Company. Two years later, joint ownership with the L.N.W. of the Manchester South Junction & Altrincham was carried through.

In this formative period, finances dwindled so seriously that angry shareholders formed a committee to investigate. One result was that a great railway manager, James Allport, took over as chairman in 1850, staying for three years. For over a quarter of a century the Sheffield Company, sandwiched between powerful neighbours, struggled for its existence; its lines were often heavily congested by the through traffic of competing lines whose traffic it had to carry under joint agreements.

Edward Watkin, fresh from Euston, took over the chairmanship in 1864, a natural leader with a fighting spirit who injected new life into the railway. He initiated several joint operating schemes of benefit to the Company. In Cheshire, a number of new lines were promoted for which a partnership with the G.N. was formed in 1861. The Midland joined as a third partner in 1866/7, and the jointly owned company was named the Cheshire Lines Committee. The Sheffield Company's tendency to play one of its many associate railways against another earned the nickname "The Railway Flirt".

Under Watkin the line spread far and wide, largely through joint arrangements, for he was also chairman of the Metropolitan, East London, South Eastern and the Channel Tunnel Company. His unfulfilled ambition was to run trains from his native Manchester direct to Paris through a Channel tunnel. Much more practical was a line to London, which would improve the Company's business. An Act in 1893 authorised a new line of 92 miles from Annesley through Nottingham, Leicester, Rugby and Woodford to Quainton Road, using Metropolitan lines to St. John's Wood, and a new short line to a new London station and a goods depot at Marylebone. In 1897, anticipating great things to come, the Company changed its name from the Manchester, Sheffield & Lincolnshire Railway to the Great Central Railway. An excellent track was built, including a fair amount of tunnelling and bridging, and stations were designed with island platforms; but it passed through too few large centres of industry for any dramatic success.

Coal trains ran to Marylebone in 1898, and a full service for passengers and goods in 1899. Opposite the station a splendid Victorian hotel was opened, complete with wide staircases, huge banqueting rooms, a "winter garden", and outside, a covered forecourt for the horse-carriages of the gentry.

Superb carriages were introduced, with corridors and electric lighting. In 1900 a useful connection with the Great Western was made on a line to Banbury. Expansion included the absorption of the Wrexham, Mold & Connah's Quay Railway in 1905, and the Lancashire, Derbyshire & East Coast Railway two years later. A large marshalling yard was built at Wath in industrial Yorkshire. Shipping, too, was developed, steamers from Grimsby serving Hamburg, Amsterdam and Rotterdam. Grimsby as a port and Cleethorpes as a resort flourished because of the railway. Grimsby fish produced good revenue.

Excellent train services ran in conjunction with other companies to serve important routes: Liverpool–Parkeston Quay, Liverpool–Yarmouth, Halifax–Ilfracombe, Newcastle–Cardiff, Newcastle–Bournemouth, Scarborough–Southampton and Manchester–Dover.

Some sound locomotives were produced, including 4–4–2 and 4–6–0 types and a four-cylinder version of the Sir Sam Fay 4–6–0s around 1917; and the 2–8–0s were later developed for use on the other railways. Good management and hard work under Fay (1902–22) produced a more rosy outlook, only to be darkened by the outbreak of the 1914 war.

Dark green locomotives, relieved by colourful accessories, headed the passenger trains of varnished teak; goods engines were black and wagons grey.

THE GREAT WESTERN

Of all the important Victorian railways, the one that tends to spring most readily to mind is the Great Western Railway. Three principal features account for this: as a name, it had by far the longest life – 1833–1947 (the next being the Midland, 1844–1922); the railway itself achieved some outstanding successes; and it was closely identified with one man of great genius, Brunel. In fact, Brunel and the Great Western Railway became synonymous. While the L. & N.W. was known as the aristocrat, the G.W.R. was described as "the fine old English Gentleman of Britain's Victorian Railways". Certainly, some of the finest scenery in Britain was put within easy reach of Great Western passengers.

Its first spectacular success, and Brunel's finest railway achievement, was the completion of the 7 ft. gauge line from Paddington to Bristol in 1841, three years after the first section had opened to Maidenhead, the Act being obtained in 1835. (The name itself dated from 1833.) Unlike many others, the G.W.R. did not start as an amalgamation. But in addition to opening many more lines, the Company undertook more amalgamations and joint agreements in its lifetime than any other company.

Starting with a line to Oxford in 1844, the Gloucester and Swindon line was soon opened, joining up with the Bristol and Exeter, and the West Cornwall, and running from Gloucester into South Wales. Using the wide gauge of 7 ft., Brunel and the G.W.R. resisted attempts by other companies in the vicinity to infiltrate the Stephenson gauge which, however, was used on the Birmingham & Gloucester Railway.

Joint agreements were made with the Shrewsbury & Birmingham and the Shrewsbury & Chester, both railways being absorbed in 1854. In 1852 a mixed gauge line, to take both wide and standard gauge rolling stock, was opened from Oxford to Birmingham. The West Midland Railway, already a merger of four smaller lines, was taken over in 1863, stretching to Stratford-on-Avon, Worcester, Wolverhampton, Hereford, Abergavenny and Newport. Some of these railways had been persuaded by the G.W.R. in hard

Marlow station on the Great Western Railway branch line from Maidenhead; from a photograph of the 1870s. (*By courtesy of British Rail*)

bargaining to build in wide gauge, in return for operational concessions. The Bristol & Exeter had remained independent until it joined the G.W.R. in 1876. In that year, the South Devon and the Cornwall railways took G.W.R. trains to Plymouth and Penzance.

A long detour to South Wales was avoided with the opening of the Severn Tunnel; at 4 miles 628 yd., the longest railway tunnel in Britain and the longest under-water tunnel in the world. (It has since been exceeded only by the London Underground.) As in other similar works, the Severn Tunnel, which took 14 years to build, had its tragedies; it also leaked heavily and continuously from the river above and needed pumping engines to cope. The G.W.R. turned the seepage to good account by selling millions of gallons of water a week for industrial use.

Meantime, amalgamations hardly ceased, so that by the time of the grouping the G.W.R. owned far more route mileage than any other company, was second only to the L. & N.W. in numbers of locomotives and passenger carriages, the third largest owner of goods wagons, and the owner of 11 ships. Spreading far from its main territory, the G.W.R. ran its trains to Crewe, Chester, North Wales, Manchester, Merseyside and Weymouth, and owned some lines in Ireland.

One of the most curious stories in the G.W.R. saga is that the locomotive to pull the first train out of Paddington, then a temporary structure in a field, was built by Brunel's life-long competitors the Stephensons in their Newcastle works. It happened this way. Brunel was not a locomotive man, and a year before the line opened in 1838 he bought from different manufacturers about 20 engines, virtually oddities and freaks, each with a dramatic name, including the *Thunderer*, *Hurricane*, *Snake*, *Viper*, *Premier*, *Vulcan* and *Ajax*. During the year (1837) a 20-year-old mechanical engineer named Daniel Gooch, who had been trained at the Stephenson Newcastle factory, applied to Brunel, then aged 31, for a job. They met in the Liverpool & Manchester Railway office in Manchester, and on the spot the young man was appointed assistant locomotive superintendent.

On joining the G.W.R., Gooch was appalled by the array of engines and persuaded Brunel to purchase the *North Star* from Stephensons, and soon after, the *Morning Star*; both had to be adapted by Stephensons to the wide gauge. Crude though they were, they set the G.W.R. off to a good start; and Gooch made considerable design and technical improvements on them, laying the foundation for an outstanding array of renowned G.W.R. engines that were to break world speed records.

If the G.W.R. had not had the benefit of Stephenson's pioneering *Stars*, its history could well have taken a different turn. But which way? Supposing the talented Gooch had remained with the Stephensons? But it was at Newcastle, when working on a wide gauge engine for another railway, that he was bitten by the wide gauge bug, and he hitched his destiny to the leading exponent of wide railways. Fortified by the Stephenson training, Gooch built his first engines in Swindon works in 1846, the *Great Western* class of 2–2–2s with 100 lb. steam pressure, followed by 4–2–2s with driving wheels of up to 8 ft.; among them were the *Iron Duke* and *Firefly* with speeds of well over 50 m.p.h. That was the year that the Gauge Commission came down in favour of Stephenson's gauge as the standard, and Brunel's wide gauge was doomed.

Even his early tracks were of a non-standard design. Beech piles were driven into the ground every 15 ft., on which 30 ft. timber sleepers, with periodic ties to maintain the gauge, were laid lengthways under the rails, instead of crossways like a ladder; these, too, had to be changed.

A programme for converting wide gauge to standard began in 1868 and a large number of engines, carriages and wagons had to be scrapped. Completion took until 1892, and the last broad gauge train, the *Cornishman*, left Paddington for Penzance on 20th May as the cheering of the crowds echoed in the lofty roof. It was the end of a battle-scarred era.

It was during the changeover period that the failing finances lurched the Company into a crisis so serious that bankruptcy seemed imminent, the worst shake-up in its history. G.W.R. stock had fallen to 38½. Gooch had resigned in 1864 to undertake an Anglo-American cable-laying project, for which he received public distinction. He was sent for urgently, and returned in 1865 (as Sir Daniel) to be chairman of the Company. Over the years, his organising ability and financial skill gradually put the Company back on a sound footing, and he remained as chairman until his death in 1889, a service almost unique in railway history. By that time, G.W.R. stock was being quoted at over 160.

Another great personality of the G.W.R. was George Jackson Churchward, regarded in his day as a genius with steam locomotives. He followed

Converting a section of Great Western Railway broad gauge track to standard gauge, ending the era of the "Battle of the Gauges" 33 years after the death of Brunel, creator of the broad gauge. (Photo by courtesy of British Rail)

William Dean and from 1902 brought in 4–6–0s for expresses on non-stop runs. They proved their value particularly on the heavy gradients beyond Bristol, the most powerful types in service before the First World War. From Swindon in 1908 came Britain's first Pacific 4–6–2, the *Great Bear* of 225 lb. pressure for the London–Bristol run. It was later converted to 4–6–0 for wider availability. By introducing many new designs and techniques, Churchward rapidly took Swindon and the G.W.R. years ahead of other railways, and built up a fleet of high-quality trains with buffets and corridors. From the same stable came the *King* and *Castle* locomotives, to head some of the best trains in the country.

Paddington station, a superb structure designed by Brunel and opened in 1854, was the first large station to be equipped with electric light. In the new century, the G.W.R. were among the first railways to run road motor coaches. It also made history by introducing audible cab signalling which developed into automatic train control for improved safety, many years ahead of any of its contemporaries.

Around the system were many country stations in local stone that captured the atmosphere of this great railway; and at the key city of Bristol, a frontage in fine old stone in an impressive sweep along the station forecourt was worthy of the place where the G.W.R. had virtually been born.

Livery went through various stages, the best remembered being green for locomotives, lined in orange and black, with carriages in chocolate with cream upper panels, and dark red and grey wagons.

THE LONDON & SOUTH WESTERN

When an Act was obtained for a railway between London and Southampton in 1834, the Company followed the common practice of naming it from its geographical extremities. The first section of the London & Southampton Railway was opened in 1838 and completed throughout within two years under its engineer, Joseph Locke. By the time a branch had been opened from Bishopstoke (now Eastleigh) to Gosport near Portsmouth in 1842, the name had been changed to the London & South Western Railway.

Railway mania was already spreading to the south, and the Company was soon on the extension and amalgamation rampage. A line acquired in 1845 had been built only a year earlier. With an eye on heading west to Bath and Bristol, the L. & S. had built their first railway from London westerly to Basingstoke. Firm propositions further west incensed the Great Western, which had now reached Bristol. Relations between the two Companies became strained and they remained fierce rivals throughout their independent existence. Meantime, the L. & S.W. opened branches to Guildford and Windsor. A curious situation arose when the Company in 1847 bought the tiny Bodmin & Wadebridge in remote Cornwall, first opened in 1834. Totally isolated, it was not physically linked to any other railway until 1888 (GWR) and to the parent company in 1895.

In 1847 the Southampton–Dorchester line was acquired, and ten years later powers secured to work trains over the Great Western mixed gauge line to the popular Georgian resort of Weymouth.

As in the Midlands and the North, physical violence between rivals often erupted. When a dispute broke out with the Brighton Company, the Brighton people blocked Havant Junction to stop L. & S.W. trains. A special L. & S.W. train brought a gang of platelayers from London and a noisy battle ensued. Amid the abuse, lines were torn up by one party and relaid by the other; engines were chained to rails and then released. It was described as an "exciting but disgraceful affair" which had to be taken to the law courts.

Still the L. & S.W. pushed ahead. The Basingstoke–Salisbury line was completed in 1857 and three years later the Salisbury & Yeovil Railway was opened, operated by the L. & S.W. and acquired in 1878. By 1890, its trains were running direct from Waterloo to Plymouth through entrenched G.W.R. territory. Further expansion came from joint ownership with the Midland Railway of the Somerset & Dorset Joint Line which ran from near Poole to Bridgwater and Bath, and the Company reached Bournemouth. Other lines were built or acquired, including the pretty Barnstaple–Ilfracombe line.

One of the Company's best and most profitable acquisitions was Southampton Docks, with its four tides a day, purchased in 1892. It was the idea of the general manager, Charles Scotter, a docks expert who came from the Manchester Sheffield & Lincolnshire Railway.

Basically, the L. & S.W. was a passenger line. In addition to good residential, business and holiday travel, large numbers of people travelled to and from the various race courses on the line, military centres at Aldershot and Salisbury Plain, and naval bases at Portsmouth, Devonport and Portland. Osborne House, the Royal residence on the Isle of Wight, reached by the Royal Yacht, ensured frequent Royal patronage; and the Company (not the only one!) called their railway "The Royal Road". Steady business also came from perishables – milk, fruit and flowers. The Company ran its own steamers to Cherbourg, Le Havre, St. Malo and the Channel Islands, and shared some Isle of Wight ferries with the Brighton Company.

L. & S.W. trains lacked the lustre of the glamorous expresses of the East and West Coast routes, but services were sound and punctuality excellent; this was partly because the lines did not have to be shared with so many freight trains. Luxury Pullman cars were introduced on Bournemouth and West of England expresses well before the end of the century. The Company also pioneered the London suburban electrified services in 1915, and was the first railway in Britain to adopt automatic signalling.

A succession of talented locomotive engineers, such as John Gooch, Joseph Beattie, followed by his son George, Adams, Dugald Drummond (who opened Eastleigh Works) and Urie, worked for the L. & S.W. during their distinguished careers. Urie, who had arrived in 1912, concentrated in a businesslike fashion on building simple sturdy engines for consistent hard work and reliable services. Drummond had produced a four-cylinder 4–6–0 type in 1905, then the largest engine in Britain; these locomotives did some of their best work on the heavy gradients west of Salisbury.

Some outstanding chairmen and general managers had put the L. & S.W. on its feet and established its reputation. Herbert Walker, who came from the L. & N.W. in 1911, earned a knighthood for his services, and became the first general manager of the Southern Railway in the 1923 grouping. Some splendid stations had been built, and under his direction Waterloo was completely redesigned and rebuilt and the signalling modernised; it was opened by Queen Mary in 1922.

Passenger locomotive livery was in light green, lined in chocolate, black and white; goods engines were dark green. Carriages were brown with salmon pink upper panels, changed in 1921 to green, lined in orange. Wagons were in dark brown.

THE LONDON BRIGHTON & SOUTH COAST

Promoters could hardly resist a line from London to Brighton, with the attractions of Regency fashion and splendour, and the scenic beauty of the Surrey hills down to "Sussex by the Sea". After rival contenders had battled through several years of preparatory strain, the London & Brighton Railway Company opened its first modest line between Brighton and Shoreham in 1840. With incredible speed under the two great masters, Sir John Rennie and John Rastrick, the line was opened throughout only 16 months later. Stage coach proprietors on this established and Royal route could see that their great days were numbered.

In that exciting period of amalgamations, the L.B. & S.C. had come into being by joining with the seven-years-old London & Croydon Railway in 1846. In the absence of heavy industry, the line would be mainly for passengers. In 1853 the directors recommended amalgamation with the L. & S.W. and the South Eastern; but in the face of a stern and repressive Parliament and a public anxiety about monopoly, it came to nought. Territory was extended by building new lines and acquiring railways built by other companies. Powers were obtained by another company, the West End of London & Crystal Palace Railway, to build a line from Crystal Palace to Norwood, a junction to the L.B. & S.C., opening to Wandsworth within three years and to Battersea in 1858. That year, the L.B. & S.C. took a lease on the line and acquired it the following year.

The Brighton Company took a half share in a new company, the Victoria Station & Pimlico Railway, authorised in 1858 to link with the Crystal Palace line and to build a new station "near Victoria Street, Pimlico". A bridge across the River Thames was also required. Victoria station gave the Brighton Company its desperately needed terminus in the West End.

Steady expansion fanned out the railway's territory roughly to a triangular shape, the apex in London with terminals at Victoria and London Bridge, down to Brighton with branches off to various places including Guildford and Tunbridge Wells, and stretching along the south coast from Portsmouth to St. Leonards with running powers on to Hastings.

Backing from the Brighton Company helped to develop the port of Newhaven and from 1867 the Company ran steamers jointly with a French company to Dieppe, connecting to Paris. The Company's own steamers that year also ran from Littlehampton to St. Malo, and three years later to Jersey and Honfleur near Le Havre.

The Brighton Company was among the leaders in introducing Pullman cars in 1888 – the Brighton Pullman Limited, later known as the Southern Belle, maturing to the famous Brighton Belle.

Of the many locomotive engineers, W. Stroudley was the most illustrious innovator. Coming from the Highland Railway in 1870, he found about 70 different types of engines, many decrepit, unreliable and poor timekeepers. He began condensing into fewer classes, and quickly produced his first modern 0–6–0 types, earning a reputation for constructing small but powerful engines. His 0–4–2 Gladstones appeared when the "Grand Old Man" was Prime Minister, a type which continued in service for half a century; and his strong little Terriers weighing only 24½ tons were seen all over the system.

Stroudley the individualist achieved excellent engine performance by treating his drivers as individuals; each driver had his own engine and took a personal pride in its performance and appearance. As every steam man knows, each engine had its own foibles and needed nursing to get the best out of it. Stroudley also used a sparkingly green livery to encourage drivers to clean and polish. Many other railways also used the one-man engine system.

His successor, D. Earle Marsh, formerly at Doncaster, from 1908 onwards built 4–4–2 passenger tank engines of 74 tons and 4–6–2 tanks of 86 tons. The day of the large engine had arrived. The Company's last locomotive superintendent, R. J. Billinton, made his name with the Baltics – express 2–6–0 tank engines for mixed traffic, the biggest and most powerful express tanks then seen in Britain.

Before grouping, locomotive livery was in umber, lined in yellow and black; goods engines were black with red lining. Carriages were in umber, lined in yellow, and wagons grey.

THE SOUTH EASTERN & CHATHAM

From the days of Roman invasion, Dover, the nearest harbour to the Continent, had maintained its strategic importance. By the time railway pioneers cast their eyes on the route to London, stage coaches had been rumbling along that great highway, the London–Dover road, for nearly two centuries.

Railways connecting all parts of Kent were built in bits and pieces, one company working the trains of another, sharing stations and Thames bridges, joint working arrangements and amalgamations – all of which combined to unfold a highly complicated early history.

Limited mainly to Kent, two principal railways survived to rule the roost as the iron road criss-crossed the county in a complex pattern: the South Eastern Railway and the London Chatham & Dover Railway. These implacable rivals, crossing each other's paths at numerous places, clashed as violently as any two other railways in the kingdom, as their first lines struggled through the mania years. A truce, if not a peace, was signed when the two merged before Queen Victoria's reign was ended.

The South Eastern

An Act of 1836 gave powers to the South Eastern to build a line from Redhill to Dover, reaching Folkestone in 1843 and Dover in 1844. Expansion year by year took the railway to Gravesend, Rochester, Maidstone, Tunbridge Wells, Tonbridge, Ashford, Canterbury, Ramsgate, Margate, Deal and St. Leonards. A line was opened to Charing Cross station in 1864 and to Cannon Street two years later. Lines, stations and bridges over the River Thames in London were the most costly investments.

The tiny Canterbury & Whitstable line, built by Stephenson in 1830, was leased to the S.E.R. in 1844 and taken over in 1853.

Much of the Company's track was of poor standard; but a masterpiece of line built by William Cubitt between Redhill and Ashford through the Weald of Kent was practically straight and level, one of the few stretches in Britain.

Locomotive standards were poor, too. The S.E.R. depended on outside firms to supply their engines, and it was not until talented locomotive engineers were engaged that a well-organised and professional department was assembled. When James Stirling, brother of the famous Patrick, arrived from the Glasgow & South Western in 1878, he began to bring the stud up to date. Among the excellent engines he produced were the 4–4–0s with domeless boiler which performed well on expresses for many years.

A few expresses, such as the American Car Train and the Folkestone Vestibuled Limited, added a touch of prestige to an otherwise shabby lot of old carriages serving the suburbs, rural areas and minor seaside resorts, which attracted a regular stream of vociferous complaints.

The London Chatham & Dover

Holding such a good initial lead, it is surprising that the S.E.R. had not been enterprising enough to probe further into Kent than it did. That is why a Chatham company set up the East Kent Railway from its Act of 1853 for a line from Strood to Canterbury via Chatham and Faversham. With an eye on expansion, the Company changed its name in 1859 to the London Chatham & Dover Railway. Seven years later this line was opened throughout, and another year saw the line in Dover Harbour at one extremity and St. Mary Cray near Orpington at the other. The Company reached the West End by sharing the Brighton

Mainline signal-box at Waterloo, London, as rebuilt by the London & South Western Railway in 1892. A shelf of block telegraph signalling instruments is seen about eye level. (*By courtesy of the Science Museum*)

Railway's station at Victoria, then continuing its own main line to Beckenham Junction in 1862. Other lines were opened from Faversham to Margate and Ramsgate, and from Sittingbourne to Sheerness.

Such fast development drove the Company into serious financial trouble in 1864 and a "receiver" was appointed. Plant, rolling stock and movable equipment were assigned to creditors as security. An ugly situation had to be resolved by a special Act of Parliament and measures authorised to see the Railway through its crisis. An able chairman and managing director named Forbes mustered his team and they managed to save the Company.

Further expansion went ahead in the 1880s; a line was completed in stages to connect Swanley, Sevenoaks, Maidstone and Ashfield, a joint section with the S.E.R. was opened between Deal and Dover, and a short spur built to Gravesend.

During the decades of recovery from financial strain all the trains, except boat trains and a few expresses, were notoriously poor; and rickety four-wheeled carriages were still clattering along the metals until the end of the century.

From the Company's earliest days, the locomotive stock had been a poor collection of second-hand engines and some hired from other railways such as the Great Northern. A few good engines were obtained from outside firms. Sir William Cubitt, formerly engineer to the S.E.R., brought some order out of the chaos, but departed in 1860 for other engineering fields. At the Battersea Works, Martley built some useful 2–4–0s, and Kirtley introduced many tank engines and some express 4–4–0s; but they were never brilliant performers.

As the century ended, and the independence of the Company was lost, this spirited railway was beginning to see the fruits of an admirable enterprise.

The new Company – South Eastern & Chatham

Peace had to come sometime; but it was a disturbed peace as the two mortal enemies, the S.E.R. and the L.C. & D.R., came together for the first time. A joint management called the South Eastern & Chatham Railway, created by the Act of 1899, officially took charge from 1st January of that year.

A vast improvement programme was planned. Stations needed renovating, deplorable track had to be made sound, tunnels needed relining and bridges strengthening, and locomotives needed standardising into fewer classes.

Both the constituent companies had built up a fleet of ships giving through services to the Continent, the S.E. & C.R. having thirteen on their books at the time of grouping. These old steamers were among the forerunners of the splendid Sealink fleet of the 20th century.

The Great Victorian Era had ended, and the reorganised Railway was built up in the new century, to hand over a good system when the Southern Railway took charge in 1923.

Livery of the mixed collection of locomotives had been standardised to a Brunswick green, lined with yellow; carriages were in dark maroon also with yellow lining; and wagons dark grey.

THE GREAT RAILWAYS OF SCOTLAND

Of the numerous railways in Scotland, five remained the leaders for many years and acquired their own distinctive personalities before being finally swallowed by two of the "big four" in 1923. Like their English counterparts, most of them began as small local railways and developed through amalgamation.

Scotland's railways were cradled in the rich areas stretching from the Firths of the Forth and Clyde and in the Ayr and Lanark districts. Despite the lessons taught by the South, the Scottish lines remained strictly local for something like 20 years before serious thought was given to trunk and connecting lines: hence the wasteful variety of gauges that were built.

When English railways sought powers to build lines across the border, they were resisted with the ferocity normally provoked by an invading army. It was a period of massive pamphleteering and public and Parliamentary campaigning, involving great cost before any particular line was even built.

George Stephenson became involved in the first Scottish railways early in his career. About five years after the first railway was opened in Scotland, the Troon & Kilmarnock of 1812, the Duke of Portland ordered one of Stephenson's first two Killingworth engines and invited the engineer to visit the line. This remained the only steam locomotive to work on Scottish railways for 14 years, and it gave service there until 1848, the year of Stephenson's death.

Massive campaigning for steam locomotives in Scotland was conducted by Charles Maclaren (1782–1866), who established the renowned newspaper *The Scotsman* in 1817, and of which he remained the editor until 1845. A year before the

Stockton & Darlington opened in 1825, Maclaren devoted the front page of four issues to the possibilities of railways. Maclaren earned a reputation as a "moral and mechanical philosopher". Because of his propaganda, nobody of note in Scotland could plead ignorance of what the steam locomotive was doing in England.

Another Scottish paper, the *Glasgow Herald*, lent its influence in an article on 5th November 1824:

"Although the locomotive engine is a late invention and not generally understood, it seems to be nearly perfect in construction, and it is efficient almost beyond belief in operation. The power employed is only that of eight horses and in compass it does not much exceed the size of a single horse. A cart of coals (tender) is more than sufficient to supply the engine for twelve hours so that beyond the original cost there are very few attendant expenses."

The newspaper summary is converted to an equation:

one steam locomotive one train of wagons plus one man plus one boy	=	ten canal boats plus ten horses plus twenty men

* * *

THE NORTH BRITISH

Formed of smaller lines, the embryo North British Railway was created by Act of Parliament in 1846, the year it opened its first important line between Edinburgh and Berwick-on-Tweed. Until the line from the south reached Berwick, passengers had to travel by stage coach to Gateshead, a few miles north of Newcastle, then by through express via York, Normanton, and Rugby to Euston; this was four years before the Great Northern Railway opened at Maiden Lane near King's Cross, and the Aberdeen Railway was completed giving connections via Perth to London. The Royal Border Bridge at Berwick, built during 1849–50, completed the East Coast route, strengthening the hold in Scotland of the North British.

Expansion around this nucleus grew, the line to Carlisle opening in 1862; and in that year too came amalgamation with the Edinburgh, Perth & Dundee Railway. Another important addition was the absorption in 1865 of the Edinburgh & Glasgow Railway, originally opened in 1842. Main spheres of activity were centred round the Berwick, Glasgow and Fife lines, but the Firths of Forth and Tay meant ferries for passengers and wagons of freight. It took many years of negotiation before the Tay bridge was constructed.

The North British had four main express routes: two to England via Berwick and via Carlisle, one to Glasgow, and one to Aberdeen; but gradients on the Carlisle and Aberdeen lines were too heavy to allow consistently high speeds.

A bridge across the Firth of Forth was the outstanding feat of the North British, reducing the distance between Edinburgh and Dundee by about one third and giving faster and more direct services farther north to Aberdeen. There was also heavy coal traffic to be carried southwards from the coalfields of Fifeshire. Before the bridge was built, passengers and merchandise had to cross the Firth by ferry. Not a prosperous railway, the North British found itself unable to bear the cost alone, and the three companies who were interested in the route together formed a new company for construction. As planning was going ahead, the Tay Bridge, opened in 1878, blew down and a loaded passenger train crossing over it dropped into the stormy Firth, with heavy loss of life, only 19 months after its completion. It was rebuilt in 1887. After that, the Board of Trade insisted on a much stronger bridge for the Forth than had at first been visualised.

This most notable bridge in Britain opened to the public on 4th March 1890 to carry trains on the East Coast route from London (King's Cross). It was constructed on the cantilever principle with two main spans, with a total length, including the approaches, of about a mile and a half. Some 54,000 tons of steel was used and the cost was £3 million. It still has to be painted in a continuous rota for its maintenance.

A year before the Forth Bridge opened, a proposal was made for an amalgamation between the North British and the Glasgow & South Western Railway; but it suffered the fate of many similar propositions, and fell through.

The North British residential line met the West Highland Railway at the end of its residential line at Helensburgh. It passed through Arrochar near the "Bonnie Banks of Loch Lomond" and on to Fort William, near the head of Loch Linnhe, and to Banavie, opened in 1894. Seven years later it reached Mallaig to connect with ferries to the Isle of Skye. Much of the route passed through desolate but picturesque country with hardly a village in sight. The railway was amalgamated with the North British in 1908 following many years of close working. N.B. lines spread beyond the border to Morpeth, Hexham and Reedsmouth, eventually owning well over 100 miles of railway in England.

The railway's superb station and headquarters nestled in the deep ravine, banked by the world-famed gardens of Princes Street, beneath the frowning heights and dark outline of Edinburgh Castle. As well as good passenger business, the railway carried much fish, and more coal than any other Scottish railway. On its Aberdeen–Berwick route, it served most of the docks and owned several, and the Clyde was served by its paddle steamers.

Splendid locomotives were developed, notably the 4–4–0 type with solid bogie wheels, dome over the firebox and inside cylinders. Locomotive and rolling stock livery changed with succeeding locomotive engineers, anxious to imprint their own individuality. The later standard was bronze-green lined in red and yellow for the passenger engines, crimson lake lined in yellow for carriages, and grey for goods wagons. Engine building and heavy repairs were concentrated at Cowlairs works of the former Edinburgh Railways, and other works in the group closed. Of the succession of engineers, the man who left his indelible stamp on the quality of the locomotive stud later in the 19th century was Dugald Drummond, who came from the Brighton railway.

Among its subsidiaries, the N.B. could claim the Monkland & Kirkintilloch line, originally opened in 1826, and one of Scotland's first railways.

THE CALEDONIAN

Scotland's second largest railway in its lifetime created a happy family atmosphere, and many of its stations were gay with colourful patches of garden. It also built up a handsome fleet of sturdy locomotives to cope with the heavy gradients. The Caledonian completed its first line throughout in 1848; a main line, it ran from Edinburgh to Carlisle via Carstairs and Lockerbie, with a fork from Carstairs to Glasgow where Buchanan Street became its terminus, Central station being added in 1879. With its English counterparts, it completed through connections on the West Coast route between Edinburgh and London (Euston). Good business came from the industrial lowlands and sturdy growth around Glasgow and to Gourock, the site of its first locomotive works.

Acquisitions and extensions followed: in 1865, the Scottish Central Railway serving Perth, Dundee, Alloa and Callander; the next year, the Scottish North Eastern Railway connecting Aberdeen with Montrose, and giving a route south to Perth via Stanley. Four years later, the Cleland and Mid-Calder line was opened, the second but shorter route between Glasgow and Edinburgh, to enter into strong competition with the North British, which had earlier acquired the first railway on this route. When the Wemyss Bay–Port Glasgow Railway opened in 1865, it fell to the Caledonian to operate it, assuming ownership in 1893. When the short line was built from Greenock to Gourock, it meant cutting the longest railway tunnel in Scotland – the Moncrieff. The line opened in 1889. Another small railway operated by the Caledonian from 1890 was the new Lanarkshire & Ayrshire Railway, but the Company maintained its independence for 33 years, despite overtures.

Another line operated by the Caledonian, but remaining aloof from takeover, was the Callander & Oban, enabling the operating company to reach still farther north. When a western coast line was built from Connel Ferry near Oban, completed in 1880, the company built a cantilever bridge at the ferry which was second in dimensions only to the Forth Bridge of the North British.

In this period of amalgamations and expansion, complicated arrangements included special running powers over other lines, leasing agreements, lines operated jointly by two or more companies, and the sharing of important terminus stations. The Portpatrick & Wigtownshire Joint Committee railway was owned by four separate companies: the Caledonian, Glasgow & South Western, London & North Western, and Midland. Operating the joint line was left to the two Scottish companies in alternate three-year periods. Though the locomotives were changed each period, the enginemen were not, because they "knew the road", and they worked alternately for the "Cale" and the G. & S.W.

Queen Victoria had added to the Cale prestige when she travelled from Balmoral to London in the autumn of 1848. She was then aged 29. Credit was earned by the several officials concerned, for inclement weather had made the return in the Royal Yacht unwise and only short notice was given. On the way, the Royal party stayed overnight at Perth and Crewe. Many similar journeys followed due to the annual visits of the Court to Balmoral, on either the East or West Coast route. Strangely enough, after the death of

Prince Albert, at the age of 42 in 1861, the Queen never travelled by the East Coast route again.

The Cale had had things all its own way on the Edinburgh–Aberdeen route, until it received a hard competitive knock when, in 1890, the North British opened the Forth Bridge. Nevertheless the Company excelled on the Glasgow–Aberdeen run, especially with its well known and stylish *Grampian Express*. The Cale was also years ahead of its competitors with more comfortable bogie coaches, while East Coast trains still rattled along via York with six-wheelers. In train braking, the Cale also pioneered the air brake (which came into wide use in the 20th century) while many other railways used the vacuum system.

Locke had conducted the original survey for the Cale, and was the railway's first engineer; he had been engineer to the Grand Junction and other English railways and had learnt much from the Stephensons. Some splendid locomotives were built, including "singles" with driving wheels of 7 and 8 ft. diameter, earning a fine reputation for speed. Good power was needed to climb Beattock Summit, which rose to 1,114 ft. above sea level. The highest railway in Scotland, indeed in the British Isles, was built for the Leadhills–Wanlockhead branch reaching 1,498 ft. Impressive viaducts were erected at Creagan and at Glenury, and a swing bridge at Alloa.

Extensions of the Cale took it to Carlisle and Brayton in England, and to Edinburgh, Glasgow and the Clyde area, Oban, Ballachulish and Aberdeen, with several branches and jointly-owned lines through some of Scotland's most beautiful heather-clad mountains. Docks were also owned, and a fleet of steamers which plied on the Clyde and Loch Lomond.

The fast locomotives were striking in light ultramarine blue lined in white and black; carriages were in crimson lake with white upper panels, and goods wagons brick red. Finishing its distinguished career after three-quarters of a century, the Caledonian still commands affectionate memory as one of Scotland's great Victorian railways.

GLASGOW & SOUTH WESTERN

It was after the dust of railway mania had settled that the Glasgow & South Western Railway was formed. In 1850, two railways were amalgamated for the purpose: the Glasgow, Paisley, Kilmarnock & Ayr, and the Glasgow, Dumfries & Carlisle. It absorbed the historic Kilmarnock & Troon which had started with horses in 1812, until George Stephenson's Killingworth engine arrived. The G.P.K. & A.R. had opened throughout in 1840 as the first serious attempt to the south-west of Glasgow to develop railway communications, taking over the Paisley & Renfrew Railway six years later. Other lines were also built to present a strong competitive front against its neighbour, the Caledonian, especially between Carlisle and Glasgow. The G. & S.W. line between these two key places was longer, but gradients much easier than on the Cale, which had to contend with Beattock. Ballochmyle Viaduct was built, forming the largest stone arch in the world, and the Templand Viaduct, near Old Cummock, consisted of 19 spans: both remarkable engineering feats at that time.

Expansion of the G. & S.W. included the takeover of the Dumfries & Castle Douglas Railway in 1865, which had been opened five years previously. A new branch had been built to Kirkcudbright. Connections were made to Stranraer and Portpatrick on the railway in which, with the Cale, the G. & S.W. owned a half-share from 1885. Other amalgamations widened the horizons, giving two ways into Stranraer: one from Glasgow and one from Carlisle. In 1872, the Stranraer & Larne Steamboat Company established a daily steamboat service over this shortest route to the "Emerald Isle", connecting with express trains to and from Glasgow and London.

Further developments took the services to Prince's Pier, Greenock, to Barrhead, and in 1876 across the Clyde to an impressive new terminus at St. Enoch. When the Midland reached Carlisle from the south, through services began between London (St. Pancras) and St. Enoch. Before the West Coast lines had been completed, passengers and goods were conveyed from a port such as Liverpool by ship to Clyde waters. New English–Scottish through traffic was generated, giving a greater impetus to Scottish trade and industry, and opening up some of the magnificent scenery of the Scottish Highlands and West Coast islands.

Close relations with the Midland offered amalgamation possibilities – a logical step; but Scottish nationalism was still too powerful and the battles between English soldiers and the clansmen too recent (by Celtic standards) to allow such "English infiltration".

Of the several engineers who developed the G. & S.W. locomotive stud, Patrick Stirling was the man who introduced some of the best engines of the day, and the "Stirling" 2–2–2s with large driving wheels of over 6 ft. diameter for higher speeds, have earned a permanent place in locomotive history.

A medium green, lined in white and black, was the standard livery; green wheels and crimson lake frames and outside cylinders added to a striking exterior finish. Carriages were in a matching crimson lake and goods wagons were in grey.

Known locally as the "Sou' West", the G. & S.W. carved a special niche for itself in Glasgow, on the Clyde reaches, the Ayrshire coast and into the romantic Burns country. A special corner of G. & S.W. folklore was Gretna Green station, to which countless lovelorn couples from the South sped by express train to plight their troth at the romantic village smithy. Intermingling of passengers from north and south of the border helped both English and Scots to understand each others' speech and customs, and to promote the commerce that ever followed in the wake of the developing railways.

THE HIGHLAND

Perhaps it was the very remoteness of north Scotland that blessed the Highland Railway with more than a touch of romance. Its wild and rugged territory, bleak and formidable in the winter, with only a scanty population of clansmen and crofters who were a law unto themselves, combined with limited local technical resources and capital to delay the railways for some two decades after they began to serve industrial centres.

Nevertheless the railway engineers invaded and conquered the challenging Grampians, Aviemore and the Cairngorms, to reach the very tip of Scotland. Produce traffic to the only towns of any size – the Highland capital of Inverness, and Aberdeen – offered sound reasons for railways; and there were hopes of reaching Glasgow and Edinburgh by way of Perth.

The Highland Railway was formed in 1865 by the amalgamation of two other lines (both already composed of smaller lines): the Inverness & Aberdeen Junction, opened in 1858, and the Inverness & Perth Junction, opened in 1863. Playing a lesser role than its larger Scottish contemporaries, the Highland developed its railway modestly by amalgamations and extensions. To the north it reached Thurso and Wick, and Stanley Junction to the south, where its trains ran on Caledonian metals to Perth; and to the west as far as the Kyle of Lochalsh, one of the most picturesque routes in Scotland, connecting with ferries to the Isle of Skye.

Good tourist business came in the summer and shooting in the autumn; but in the winter, trains were sometimes completely buried in snow for days on end and entire communities, which depended on the railways, were isolated. It is not surprising that of the five main railways in Scotland, the Highland – consisting mainly of single lines – had the smallest number of locomotives, carriages and wagons per mile of track owned. A notable locomotive development was the Highland's introduction in 1894 of the first British 4–6–0 type, the six coupled wheels being designed for heavy freight traffic up steep gradients.

Standard livery for locomotives was olive green, enlivened by a sparkle of red on the buffer beams and coupling rods. Ordinary carriages were green, and saloons and sleeping cars were in varnished teak.

In the 1923 amalgamations, the second smallest of the Scottish "big five" was to become the remotest part of the biggest of the "big four".

GREAT NORTH OF SCOTLAND

A line from the comparatively rich city of Aberdeen to isolated Inverness, with a number of branches, was the objective of the Great North of Scotland Railway Company which was formed in 1846. Eight years later it had opened as far as Huntly, about halfway along the route, and it extended some 12 miles towards Inverness as far as Keith in the next two years.

The chairman had said, "While the works are unusually light, our traffic prospects are unusually good." Expansion came from the takeover of the Alford Valley and other lines in 1875. The Aberdeen line gave access to Ballater, the station for Balmoral Castle which nestled among mountains rising to 3,000 ft. Other lines connected Aberdeen with Peterhead, Fraserburgh, Banff, Elgin, and Lossiemouth on the Moray coast.

Capital for development was scarce, and pressure from rivals intense. Shortsightedly, the North British obstructed the free movement of through traffic of competitors. One favoured tactic was to time its trains deliberately to miss connections from the South. An enlightened chairman later discarded such practices and sought peaceful coexistence.

No striking originality could be claimed for the locomotive fleet, except the introduction of a Stephenson Company's 4–4–0 type bogie engine with tender in 1866, seven years after Robert's death.

Many lines were of single track only, but

tourists found it the best route for the Grampians. Good business arose from the Royal presence, and the railway ran the prestigious *Queen's Messenger Express* to Ballater. Goods traffic included fish from the tiny northern harbours, rich agricultural produce from the north-east, and services for paper mills, granite quarries, and the distilleries of the world-famous "Scotch". Amalgamation with the Highland had often been proposed, but in 1907 was discarded in favour of closer working arrangements.

The Great North's best piece of engineering was the graceful bow-string Spey Bridge with flanking girders, which spanned the Spey about 10 miles east of Lossiemouth. In 1915 the Company rebuilt Aberdeen joint station to a splendid architectural magnificence, for serving also Caledonian expresses from the South.

Two years later, locomotive livery was changed from a bright green to black with red and yellow lines; carriages were in a purple lake with the upper panels in cream lined in red and yellow, and goods wagons in a dark grey.

Some idea of the relative sizes of the five leading railways in Scotland, at the time they were absorbed in 1923 into either the London Midland & Scottish Railway or the London & North Eastern Railway, can be gained from the following table (parent company in parentheses):

Railway Company	*Route Miles*	*Loco-motives*	*Passenger Vehicles*	*Freight Vehicles*
North British (LNE)	1,378	1,107	3,701	59,972
Caledonian (LMS)	1,115	1,067	3,022	53,326
Glasgow & South Western (LMS)	494	529	1,605	20,681
Highland (LMS)	506	173	799	2,830
Great North of Scotland (LNE)	335	122	773	3,777

A comparison of route miles with rolling stock throws some light on the relative density of train operation.

* * *

Queen Victoria's saloon, used on the Great Western Railway and photographed as rebuilt in 1887. (Photo by courtesy of the Science Museum)

Frith's famous painting of Paddington station, Great Western Railway, in 1862 depicting all the pathos of railway travel to far away places. (*Royal Holloway College, Egham*)

Chapter 6

The Champagne Years

TRAVEL FOR THE POOR

AFTER the early struggles of the pioneers, the battles in Parliament and in public to gain acceptance for the concept of railways, the feverish period of building tracks the length and breadth of Britain, the crazy mania years and financial crashes, followed by consolidation of all the great works, the railways in the second half of the tempestuous 19th century entered a Golden Age.

For the masses, they offered cheap travel to far-off and exciting new places; for the wealthy, a luxury in long distance travel at high speeds that had never been known before. New industries and great wealth were being created by fast and frequent rail transport throughout the land; new towns sprang up, the seaside resorts entered a new phase of opportunity, and the prosperity of Britain as the centre of a great Empire gave it greater world prestige. Together, the railways became the greatest dock owners in the world, and railway ships – there were over 150 in the fleets at the time of the grouping in 1923 – increased rapidly the volume of passenger and goods trade with Ireland and the Continent.

All the main industries – coal, iron and steel, shipbuilding, cotton, wool, pottery, agricultural products – found new markets. Coal could now be carried cheaply to London and other centres at much lower costs. Quicker transport for agricultural goods meant much less waste from deterioration, and more people could enjoy fresh fruit and vegetables.

Though some railways carried mainly goods or mainly passengers, the passenger business far exceeded expectations. For railways on the whole, revenue from passengers and goods was roughly equal, the proportions varying as industries prospered or slumped.

From the beginning, comfort for first class passengers offered a notable improvement over the stage coaches which trains were replacing. Early first class carriages were virtually two or three stage coach bodies mounted on to railway wagon bases; and the guards initially sat perched on seats on the tops of the vehicles as in stage coach days, complete with lusty post-horn, facing all weathers and breathing the fumes of the tunnels. Rails at the tops of the vehicles were provided for securing roof-top luggage. Many rich people had their personal carriages conveyed on flat railway wagons, horses being arranged at either end; sometimes the horses would be conveyed in horse boxes on the same train as the carriages.

Wagons for third class passengers were at first no more than cleaned-out coal trucks, and later simply wagons with doors at the side and bench seats. Others had no seating, and poor families with their bundles of personal belongings clung to rails on the wagon sides, as the train rattled and bumped and swayed for hours along the rough tracks. To save them standing ankle deep in rain water, the added fineness of holes drilled in the wagon floors ensured a simple drainage. A luxury for the poor came with the addition of a roof, but these still left the sides open to the elements.

In the year of its opening, the London & Birmingham Railway announced:

First Class Coaches carry six passengers inside, and each seat is numbered

Second Class Coaches carry eight passengers inside, and are covered, but without lining, cushions, or divisions, and the seats are not numbered

Third Class Passengers carry four passengers on each side and are without covering

About the same time, the new London & Southampton Railway announced:

"The Directors being desirous of accommodating the poorer classes by third class Carriages without the inconvenience experienced on other Lines by abandonment of the Second Class vehicles in fine weather, had adopted the plan of attaching such Carriages on the goods trains only, with travel at lower speed than the ordinary passengers."

The jerking and jolting of wagon-loads of people in a loose-coupled buffer-clanging goods train open to the sky leaves the imagination reeling. Some totally covered wagons were lighted only by skylights and ventilated by slits at the side, aptly described by *Punch*, that public watchdog of the railway passenger, as "little better than locomotive sheep-pens."

At first the Great Western did not deign to carry third class passengers, and the management delivered themselves, in truly feudal terms, of the opinion that "Doubtless the very lowest order of passengers would eventually be conveyed, by very slow trains once a day, in inferior accommodation, at a very low price, and probably at night." A year later, the Company bent to public pressure and announced: "Goods train passengers will be conveyed in uncovered trucks by goods train only."

Despite these hardships, records compiled in 1842 for over 40 principal railways revealed that over a third of all the passengers carried were third class, a proportion totally unexpected. Figures in the table have been rounded off:

Class	*Number*	*Percentage*	*Average fare per mile*
First	3,700,000	18½	2¾d.
Second	9,200,000	46	1¾d.
Third	7,100,000	35½	1 1/7d.

(Stage coach fares were around 3½d. inside and 2½d. outside).

That tireless Liberal reformer, William Ewart Gladstone (1809–98), who became Prime Minister four times, put an end to some of the nonsense about the "poorer classes" with his Act of 1844, the first Parliamentary measure to exercise effective control over the railways. It laid down a maximum fare of a penny a mile for third class

The inscription on this sombre-looking Victorian luxury coach of the South Eastern Railway reads "Carriage used by the late Duke of Wellington". (By courtesy of the Science Museum)

passengers; seats were to be provided in every vehicle, with protection from the weather; and at least one train a day must run with third class carriages at a minimum speed of 12 miles an hour. Such trains were known for years afterwards as "Parliamentary Trains". The Act also dealt with management and operation, and gave an option for the Government to purchase (under specific conditions) any new railway after 21 years, a policy not invoked for more than a century. Angry directors and shareholders derisively referred to it as the "Railway Plunder Bill". Showing its scorn, the Great Western ran its third class trains very early in the morning and late at night. One of them, from London to the West Country, left Paddington at six in the morning. "Railway servants" ridiculed it as the "Plymouth Cheap". Of all the sections of the community benefiting from the Act, the poor gained most of all.

The plethora of legislation, before and after the 1844 Act, grew so vast and complicated that in 1888 the Companies' Clauses Consolidation Act was passed to bring together and simplify the thousands of statutory clauses.

Literate Victorians gained greatly from the service of mails by the railways, as indeed George Stephenson had foreseen even before his first line had opened. Stage coach mails took days and weeks for even the shortest journey. The cost was prohibitive, too, as much as 1*s*. 4*d*. for a letter from London to Edinburgh. Then, after a long campaign, a former school master, Sir Rowland Hill (1795–1879), in 1840 introduced his "penny post" for letters. In that year, the first adhesive postage stamps were introduced, Queen Victoria's head being printed in black. A new hobby was created, and today philatelists will pay a huge sum for a "penny black". (Incidentally, Rowland Hill in 1843–46 became first a director and then chairman of the Brighton Railway, where he introduced excursion trains.)

Letters and postal packages earned large revenues for the railways. Increasing literacy, wider railway services and cheaper postal rates are reflected in the following figures:

Year	*Number of letters dispatched*
1838	76,000,000
1864	642,000,000

AND TRAVEL FOR LIVESTOCK

Another interesting change came about as the railways developed. There was a time when droves of cows, sheep and pigs were to be seen on the roads of Britain as they were driven for long distances to the nearest cattle market. They held up pack horses, horse-drawn wagons and stage coaches (which continued long after the arrival of the first railways) and damaged road-side property. (Often a "cow on the line" held up trains). It took three days and nights to drive a herd, for example, from the rich farming pastures of Buckinghamshire to London. Many animals became injured, sometimes fatally; most lost considerable weight and consequently market price. "Livestock traffic" grew to be big business for the railways and remained so for well over a century, and special cattle trucks and other vehicles were built. Stops on the journey were arranged for food and water, and it was a welcome "perk" for railway porters to milk the cows, while giving the desperate animals much-wanted relief.

THE BOOKING OFFICE

When early Victorians went to the station to catch a train, they impatiently joined the queue as the station clerk laboriously entered the details in a book and issued a form (ticket) with the essential travel details: hence the terms "booking clerk" and "booking office". On some railways, the form bore a printed message:

> "This Ticket is given subject to there being room on arrival of the Train, the precise hour of which will not be positively guaranteed. No smoking allowed. No gratuities to be given by passengers."

A bright young booking clerk named Thomas Edmundson (1792–1851) of the Newcastle & Carlisle Railway, irked by this cumbersome system, invented a small card ticket, the racking to contain them (he was formerly a cabinet maker), and a hand printing press to stamp the date. He was soon snapped up by the Manchester & Leeds railway at a higher salary. But he was too bright to stay long, and began his own railway ticket printing business to supply a number of railways. One of his machines is preserved in the Science Museum. Later, the larger railway companies set up their own ticket printing works. Because most railway station staff were illiterate, some railways designed tickets in different shapes and colours identified with specific stations.

A nice little side-line was worked by station masters as the century progressed, particularly in the north-east and Tyneside colliery areas. They took orders, on behalf of the collieries, from local people on a commission basis; some station masters earned more from their coal commissions than from their railway masters, and a few left the railways to start their own businesses as coal merchants.

BRADSHAW

Each railway company published its own timetable, in earlier days usually approximate times which were on the hour or half-hour. As each new railway opened a flood of railway guide books appeared, produced by various publishers. In addition to times, the story and a description of the railways were included, and details of towns, villages and country mansions to be seen from the trains. Some printed the services of horse-drawn coaches and omnibuses connected with the trains, and maps of the lines. One published by Baily & Co. of Cornhill, London, in 1838, bore the title: *The Iron Road Book and Railway Companion.*

Timetables of this kind proliferated as the novelty of railways caught on, but were often out of date by the time they were printed. George Bradshaw (1801–53), a Lancashire engraver and printer and an ardent Quaker, was already making a name for himself with his maps and guides of canals. The most reliable date of the first "Bradshaw" seems to be 10th October 1839, by which time some 1,400 miles of railway were in use. Bradshaw did the job more efficiently than anyone else; soon his monthly guides were a regular feature, continuing to appear for well over a century, and earning a place in the Oxford Dictionary:

> Bradshaw, Railway Guide, a timetable of all passenger trains running in Great Britain. (Originally issued in 1839 by George Bradshaw, printer).

He had the greatest difficulty in obtaining the information from the railways in time for print, and train times were frequently altered at short notice or trains simply cancelled. His dedication pushed most of his competitors out of the running in this lucrative business. As a devoted Quaker, he still found time throughout his life for much charitable work among the poor.

Bradshaw received a massive correspondence: people pointing out mistakes, seeking further information, suggesting alterations, or making compliments. For some unaccountable reason, parsons were always great enthusiasts of Bradshaw, and indeed of steam railways as a whole. In 1845 the Reverend Edmund, writing from Lincoln to *The Times*, said: "We owe much to Bradshaw. It is compact, well arranged and, with a little trouble to master its details, very easy to comprehend." He followed the compliment with a suggestion to improve.

BRADSHAW'S

RAILWAY GUIDE;

CONTAINING

A CORRECT ACCOUNT OF THE HOURS OF ARRIVAL AND DEPARTURE OF THE TRAINS ON EVERY RAILWAY IN GREAT BRITAIN;

A MAP OF ENGLAND,

WITH THE RAILWAYS COMPLETED AND IN PROGRESS,

HACKNEY COACH FARES, &c.

FOR DECEMBER, 18

MANCHESTER:

PRINTED & PUBLISHED BY BRADSHAW & BLACKLOCK, 27, BROWN-ST.

AND SOLD BY

W. J. ADAMS, 170, FLEET STREET, LONDON,

AND MAY BE HAD THROUGH ALL BOOKSELLERS AND NEWSMEN.

Title page of Bradshaw's first Guide of 1841, two years after his original timetables. Seasoned Victorian travellers never consulted a timetable; it was more fashionable to consult "Bradshaw".

Bradshaw wrote letters of an exquisite Victorian charm, adding a delicate touch of salesmanship. Here is an example:

> "Respected Friend, Herewith thou hast a copy of our Railway Companion which we have pleasure to state has had unprecedented sales and beg thine acceptance of it . . .
>
> "Should any of the Gentlemen in the Establishment feel disposed to have a few dozen for sale at any of thy stations, we should have much pleasure in supplying them at 25 per cent off the selling price.
>
> "I am, Respectfully, Sir,
>
> "Your Obedient Servant."

A writer of the times remarked: "I cannot imagine Mr. Bradshaw ever missing a train. His face is that of a lover of order, accuracy and punctuality." Another observed that Bradshaw looked as though he never caught a train, but always travelled on top of a stage coach!

NO "RIGHT" TIME

Early Victorian travellers could not enjoy the

luxury of punctual train departures, for there was no such thing as universal time. Two clocks on one station could be five minutes apart, and this confusion was a common railway joke. This mattered little until the railways, originally separate, began to join with each other.

Local time was the vogue. Railway companies used the local time of the location of their head office or most important station, which might be fifteen minutes different from another line. Glasgow local time, for example, was seventeen minutes later than that in London. London railways used the mean time of the Royal Greenwich Observatory which had been founded by Charles II in 1675 "to improve knowledge of the position of celestial bodies as an aid to navigation." Connections from one railway to another, especially on cross-country routes, were missed and hours lost. On 14th September 1838, three days before the line was completed, the London & Birming-

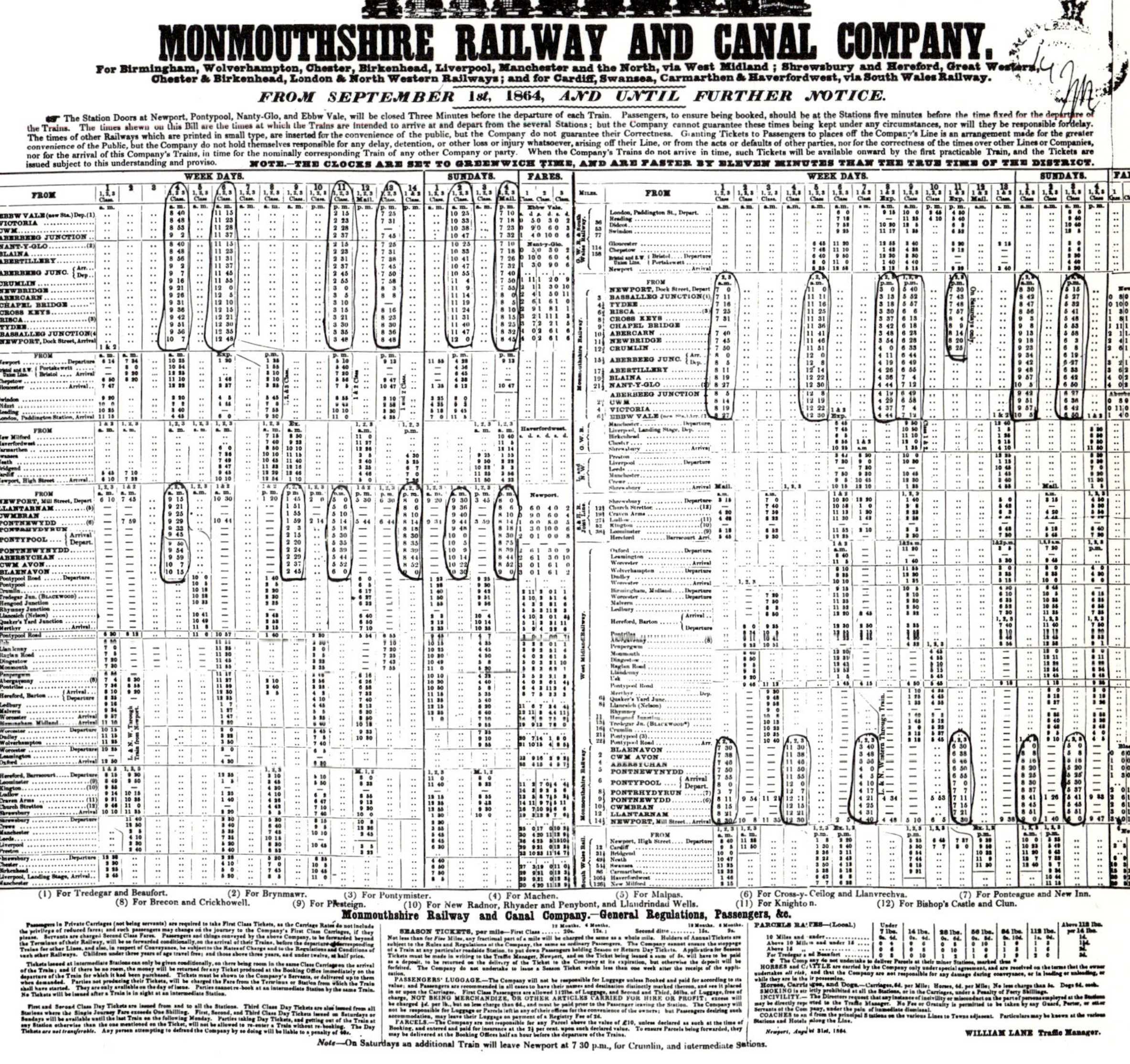

MONMOUTHSHIRE RAILWAY AND CANAL COMPANY.

For Birmingham, Wolverhampton, Chester, Birkenhead, Liverpool, Manchester and the North, via West Midland; Shrewsbury and Hereford, Great Western, Chester & Birkenhead, London & North Western Railways; and for Cardiff, Swansea, Carmarthen & Haverfordwest, via South Wales Railway.

FROM SEPTEMBER 1st, 1864, AND UNTIL FURTHER NOTICE.

The Station Doors at Newport, Pontypool, Nanty-Glo, and Ebbw Vale, will be closed Three Minutes before the departure of each Train. Passengers, to ensure being booked, should be at the Stations five minutes before the time fixed for the departure of the Trains. The times shewn on this Bill are the times at which the Trains are intended to arrive at and depart from the several Stations; but the Company cannot guarantee these times being kept under any circumstances, nor will they be responsible for delay. The times of other Railways which are printed in small type, are inserted for the convenience of the public, but the Company do not guarantee their Correctness. Granting Tickets to Passengers to places off the Company's Line is an arrangement made for the greater convenience of the Public, but the Company do not hold themselves responsible for any delay, detention, or other loss or injury whatsoever, arising off their Line, or from the acts or defaults of other parties, nor for the correctness of the times over other Lines or Companies, nor for the arrival of this Company's Trains, in time for the nominally corresponding Train of any other Company or party. When the Company's Trains do not arrive in time, such Tickets will be available onward by the first practicable Train, and the Tickets are issued subject to this understanding and proviso. NOTE.—THE CLOCKS ARE SET TO GREENWICH TIME, AND ARE FASTER BY ELEVEN MINUTES THAN THE TRUE TIME OF THE DISTRICT.

(1) For Tredegar and Beaufort. (2) For Brynmawr. (3) For Pontymister. (4) For Machen. (5) For Malpas. (6) For Cross-y-Ceilog and Llanvrechva. (7) For Ponteague and New Inn. (8) For Brecon and Crickhowell. (9) For Presteign. (10) For New Radnor, Rhyader and Penybont, and Llandrindod Wells. (11) For Knighton. (12) For Bishop's Castle and Clun.

Monmouthshire Railway and Canal Company.—General Regulations, Passengers, &c.

Newport, August 31st, 1864. WILLIAM LANE Traffic Manager.

Note—On Saturdays an additional Train will leave Newport at 7 30 p.m., for Crumlin, and intermediate Stations.

A page from the Monmouthshire Railway & Canal Company's timetables of 1864. (By courtesy of British Rail)

ham Railway ordered the station master at Euston to work to Post Office time, and the Birmingham station master "the mean true time at Birmingham;" and instructed that all trains should depart three minutes after the published times.

To secure more uniformity in railway times, the Liverpool & Manchester Railway petitioned Parliament in June 1844 for the adoption of a universal time; and in October 1847 the Midland Railway, then only three years old, recommended other railways to adopt Greenwich time as soon as it could be arranged through the General Post Office. Most railways were still altering their timetables every month to meet the rapid increase in new connecting railways and in the numbers of trains running.

For years, angry passengers were frequently left stranded at far-distant junctions, and neighbouring railway companies wrangled with each other about the "correct" time. But the law supported local time. About that time, a defendant facing a legal dispute in which his case depended on his use of Greenwich time, was defeated: the court ruled in favour of local time. In America, where railways were beginning to cross vast tracts, time variations verged on the chaotic. An international conference held at Washington proposed zonal times based on Greenwich; it gained scanty support.

Campaigning by Britain's railways continued for many years as more new lines were built; time was their life-blood. No group of enterprises needed a universal time so desperately as the expanding railways. The weight of industry and commerce was added. Trying to keep their own house in order, the Great Western Railway instituted their own "standard time" in 1852; this was made possible because they had erected telegraph wires along the routes from Paddington to Swindon, Gloucester, Bristol, Exeter, Plymouth, Birkenhead and South Wales. As early as 1841, the Great Western had adopted London time, with the following variations:

Reading – four minutes later
Chippenham – eight minutes later
Bristol and Bath – fourteen minutes later

The local time variations were taken mainly from local sundials.

After about 40 years of persistent railway campaigning, a sensible arrangement, long overdue, came into force in 1880 when the Statutes (Definition of Time) Act was passed, and for the first time in history Greenwich Mean Time became the legal time throughout Britain.

Campaigning on the international scale began as more services connected with Europe; but it was not until 1912 that a conference held in Paris proposed Greenwich Mean Time as the basis for international time, with wireless telegraphy as the medium. In subsequent years, G.M.T. came to be accepted in most civilised countries in the world, using zonal key areas in multiples of half an hour.

After the 1880 Act the railways disseminated a daily time signal, over the years developing a network of electric telegraph instruments which were installed in main stations and signalboxes. Telegraph poles alongside the tracks carried the wires, and at a later stage wires for telephones.

THOMAS COOK'S FIRST EXCURSION

Very soon after their formation, the bigger railway companies began to arrange excursion trains at reduced fares to places of special interest. Even before Rowland Hill introduced excursions on the Brighton line in the 1840s, the Midland Counties Railway which linked Derby, Nottingham and Leicester, on 24th August 1840 carried 2,400 passengers from Nottingham to Leicester for an exhibition in one excursion train composed of the crudest wagons. One report said that four engines pulled the 65 "carriages".

This may well have stimulated the interest of Thomas Cook (1808–92) in party travel, for on 5th July 1841 he booked his first excursion train from Leicester to Loughborough. The 12-mile journey, for which he charged a shilling a head, was arranged for members of the public to attend a temperance meeting at Loughborough. It was recorded that 570 passengers, standing cheek by jowl in open wagons, endured the clattering and bumpy journeys.

Thomas was a wood turner by trade, and temperance society work was his spare time activity. He was secretary of the Market Harborough Temperance Society in the days when drunkenness was a serious social scourge. The success of Cook's first train excursion led him to arrange others, and he began developing party travel by train for pleasure and culture. Later, his son joined him and the business expanded rapidly to become in time a world-wide travel agency – Thomas Cook & Son – and a household name. Cook had run his first trip at the age of 33, only 16 years after George Stephenson had opened the first railway, the Stockton & Darlington.

Every kind of public function or sporting occasion brought more passengers to the railways, and the railways were quick to organise "specials" for the many events. One of these was the boat race. The first took place on the River Thames at Henley-on-Thames in 1829, before the local railways had arrived; it had resulted from a challenge from Cambridge University to Oxford. The next race took place just west of London in 1836, and in time the contest became one of the most important annual sporting events. It attracted fashionably dressed Victorian gentlemen garbed in frock coats and top hats, accompanied by their ladies in picture hats and flouncing dresses; and their encouraging shouts were as uninhibited as those of the poorer elements in cloth caps, who had travelled third class on cheap day excursions, and who mixed freely with the élite on the crowded river banks. "Boat Race Fever" reached its height later in the century; and railway companies serving London planned their extra services months in advance.

Racecourses around the country were another fruitful source of extra revenue, both for passengers and for horses in horse-boxes. Race-goers started travelling by train to watch the Derby at Epsom as early as 1838. Enormous crowds were attracted by an announcement in *The Times* that special trains would run on 29th May from Nine Elms, the new terminus of the partly completed London & Southampton Railway, to Kingston (now Surbiton), then the nearest station to Epsom racecourse. Some 5,000 people turned up at Nine Elms station, and such was the mood of the many disappointed that they had to be dealt with by the police.

Unhappily, for many years race trains attracted seedy touts and crooked tipsters and bookmakers. Bullying card-sharpers in enclosed railway compartments fleeced the innocent, especially with the famous three-card trick, "Find the Lady", and their brutal demeanour terrified the passengers.

When the Crystal Palace, centre-piece of the Great Exhibition of 1851 (in which Brunel had had a hand and which had attracted over 6,000,000 visitors in six months) was moved from Hyde Park to Sydenham a few years later, the London, Brighton & South Coast built a new line from London Bridge. A special return fare of 1*s*. 6*d*. (7½p) included admission to the Palace and amusement gardens, which kept the line busy. Crystal Palace became a fashionable place for a day out, especially for middle-class Victorian families. It was finally destroyed by fire in 1936.

Better-off people found a new pleasure in visiting towns and cities by train for shopping expeditions, an example of the increasing trade which railways brought. London offered the best attractions, and in the 1840s Bond Street was a happy spending ground for the rich. Bond Street shops then included ten boot and shoe makers, 17 milliners, 22 tailors, ten perfumeries, a dozen booksellers, numerous bakers, butchers, confectioners, fruiterers and venison dealers. For the more active there was a club for pugilists, and Dr. Culverwell's Bathing Establishment, which boasted salt water from Brighton, a resort popularised by Royalty.

COALS FROM NEWCASTLE – AND ELSEWHERE

The luxury of coal fires was brought by the growing railways to more people in the large towns and cities that were remote from the coalfields. Prices also fell. Coastwise shipping from Tyneside to London had long been the route for Newcastle coal. Figures for London produced by the Registrar of the Coal Exchange showed the effect of railways: (rounded off)

Year	*Tons carried by railway*	*Customer price per ton*
1827	nil	28*s*. 6*d*.
1847	19,000	20*s*. 10*d*.
1857	1,207,000	18*s*. 8*d*.
1867	3,300,000	20*s*. 8*d*.

A similar pattern was found in other towns, and in foodstuffs and a great variety of products in common use.

SHIFTING POPULATIONS

In choosing a place to live, city workers were strongly influenced by the development of suburban and local railways. During the 40 years to 1841, the population of London had increased from nearly 1,000,000 to nearly 2,000,000, rising to just under 3,000,000 by 1861. Within the same 60 years, the population of Britain rose from roughly 16,000,000 to 29,000,000. Londoners who could afford it moved out of the crowded and unhealthy Metropolis to healthier and more pleasant surroundings in which to bring up their families. To a lesser extent, the same pattern was followed in cities such as Birmingham, Liverpool, Manchester, Cardiff, Glasgow and Edinburgh.

To encourage the building of villas from, say, 10 to 20 miles from the terminus, some companies provided personal tickets free of charge, for a number of years up to five, related to the value or rental of a passenger's house. Small outlying villages grew into large communities and towns which, in turn, created new businesses in the new areas.

At a later stage, when trains were faster and more frequent, some Companies issued "residential" tickets at much below the usual charges. Towns on the coast, for example, from Margate in Kent to Brighton and Portsmouth, grew rapidly and property values increased as faster train services were introduced. The very existence of the railways was responsible for vast population movements, helping to bring a better way of life, and earning greater railway revenues, both for passengers and goods.

But what of the earnings of railwaymen? The standard 10-hour day often stretched into 15 and 18 hours with no overtime pay. An experienced express train driver of the 1860s was still earning little over £2 a week, and the following table shows the current rates paid by the Great Western Railway in 1867:

		Daily wages
Driver:	1st year	5*s*. 6*d*. (27½p)
	2nd	6*s*. 0*d*. (30p)
	3rd	6*s*. 6*d*. (32½p)
	4th	7*s*. 0*d*. (35p)
Fireman:	1st year	3*s*. 6*d*. (17½p)
	2nd	3*s*. 9*d*. (19p)
	3rd	4*s*. 0*d*. (20p)
Shunters and turners		5*s*. 0*d*. (25p)

The fashionable and phenomenal habit of the British of converging regularly on the seaside in large numbers was a unique by-product of the railways, whose first objective had been to carry coal, other minerals and general goods. In the course of the Victorian period, hundreds of tiny places dotted around the 6,000 miles of infinitely varied coatline grew into prosperous resorts of great wealth and reputation.

Scarborough is credited with being Britain's first seaside resort, dating from the early 18th century, when personages of note began to "take the waters" there. Long before the railways King George III had popularised Weymouth, while his son, the Prince of Wales, had patronised Brighton, and his daughter, Southend. Later, Victoria and Albert had chosen the Isle of Wight. And where Royalty went, the aristocracy, the gentry and the middle classes surely followed.

Wealthy Victorians took the waters at inland watering places such as Bath, Cheltenham, Droitwich, Harrogate, Tunbridge Wells, Matlock, and Leamington for the supposed healing powers of the waters, to bathe in or to drink. The spas were the domains of wealthy invalids and upper-class hypochondriacs seeking a "cure" from windiness, gout, apoplexy and impotence. The waters were also taken at a number of seaside resorts; but from the mid-1850s, as the masses moved in, the aristocracy began to retreat.

Town and city dwellers, escaping from the miserable surroundings and smoky atmosphere, sped wide-eyed through the countryside by steam train to the edge of the land, to see the sea for the first time, to listen to the lapping waves, and to gaze at ships small and large sailing off into the sunset. They returned to their slave labour conditions in better heart, with something new to talk about. And of course, they discovered something else: everybody didn't speak in the same accent; the Cockney probably thought the Yorkshireman or the Scot was speaking in a foreign language!

The mass exodus by train to the coast, which has never ceased, was itself a remarkable and permanent contribution to the finances of the expanding railways, and changed the social patterns of the country. New businesses were started by the far-sighted. Hotels and play-houses were built. Large Victorian houses, many still in service, were converted to take in visiting boarders. Property prices soared. Eating places blossomed forth, from the plebeian whelk stall to the plushy restaurant served by waiters in tails, luxurious in a setting of red velvet upholstery and glittering chandeliers.

Local builders and traders flourished, as did those in the entertainment business. The country fair, with its variety of gaudy side-shows and grinding music from steam organs decorated by animated figurines, set up shop to add gaiety to the scene. Hard-earned wages were tempted from the pockets of wide-eyed families. The naughty postcard made its debut, a harmless vulgarity that had survived the computer age.

With its windows discreetly curtained, the bathing machine arrived, in which the modest could undress in privacy, at a small charge. A horse or donkey trundled this Victorian contraption back and forth with the changing tides. Family fun was always assured as the ladies emerged in their frilly voluminous bathing costumes, and the men in skin-tight costumes, with a tiny "modesty" skirt, and limbs hidden to knees and elbows. A contemporary rhymester wrote:

"The ladies dressed in flannel cases
Show nothing but their handsome faces."

Mixed bathing – men and women in the water together – was strictly forbidden in many of the "posh" resorts such as St. Leonards-on-Sea at least until towards the end of the century. The very term "mixed bathing" had a daring implication to staid Victorian minds; and even in the 1930s, it was not "the done thing" at many town swimming baths, except on occasions specified by the town councillors.

As the resorts grew more popular, new attractions were created: deck chairs for the beach, curio and gift shops, and sticks of pink rock lettered all through with the name of the resort. A later novelty in a cast iron fixture was called "What the Butler Saw". By putting a penny in the slot and turning a handle, the daring Victorian male could peep in secret at a dozen pictures – naughty scenes of a keyhole nature – of handsome hussies clad in camisole and corsets lounging in a luxurious Victorian boudoir. And there was the breathless adventure of sailing in a tiny boat on a choppy sea that threatened to engulf the scared holiday-makers who had been tempted by an old salt bellowing: "Any more for the Skylark?"

Punch-and-Judy shows on the sands fascinated the children, and the whole family was entertained by the music and dancing of gaily costumed pierrots and pierettes, itinerant minstrels and strolling players cavorting in the pavilions of piers that straddled out to sea. The seaside pier, which started its life in most cases as a jetty for packets and pleasure craft, came into its own as an attraction. Men could fish well out to sea and children could peep through the cracks of the "deck" at the surging waters below. Brighton pier – the Old Chain Pier – was reputed to be the first of its kind, built in 1823 and blown down in 1896. Southend, built seven years later and extended in 1898 to one mile 600 yards to become the world's longest, also had its own railway. From 1856, when the railways first reached Southend, the resort made dramatic progress.

Later in the century, too, photography arrived and indoor and outdoor studios were opened at the resorts, at which holiday visitors could have their photographs taken against exotic backdrops, to show their friends at home. Photography for the amateur came into its own from 1888, when Kodak and other manufacturers mass-produced their first roll-film cameras; at first, the camera and exposed film had to be returned to the firm for processing.

In the latter half of the century, boom time came to such resorts as Brighton, Blackpool, Scarborough, Southend, and areas such as Kent, Sussex, Cornwall, Devon, Norfolk and resorts in Scotland and Wales. But except for the larger places, it was a highly seasonal business; and the railways had to keep large fleets of locomotives and carriages which then often stood idle in the out-of-season months. This was partly offset by the increase in goods traffic brought by the resorts' business.

One thing was certain: the increased travel for poorer people widened their horizons, gave them a brief insight into the good life, and enabled them to mix with social classes usually outside

A Victorian gentleman traveller's portmanteau and dressing case, advertised as "essential for comfortable travel". The bottles contain a few "noggins" and gents' toiletry. (Keith Heckler)

their daily experience; with a subtle inevitability, these influences oiled the engines of the emerging democratic processes in an Age of Reform that was to shatter Victorian complacency. There was no turning back the clock.

Railway bosses were quick to notice these changes and one of them once remarked that the great mass of people must necessarily remain in humble employment and that class distinction must continue. This calls to mind a lyric of Sir W. S. Gilbert (1833–1911) in a Gilbert & Sullivan operetta:

"When everyone's somebodee
Then no-one's anybody!"

Meantime, the masses needed to be fed. Railways south of the Thames developed largely as passenger lines, and except mainly for fruit, vegetables, milk and hops, brought little sustenance to feed the millions in London and surrounding districts. Grain, flour, potatoes, wheat, barley and fish were brought by railways from the eastern counties of England and Scotland; cattle and sheep for beef and mutton came from the grazing counties in the west and north-west and from the Scottish Highlands – all of which broadened the diet of the populace.

SMITH'S BOOKSTALLS

People who travelled to and from work and who could read took reading material with them. William Henry Smith (1825–91), who was born in London, had early ambitions of making the Church his career, but abandoned the idea and instead joined his father's newsagency in the Strand, London. By the age of twenty-one he was made a partner in the business. Striking out on his own account, he opened a few bookstalls on railway stations and in 1851 secured the exclusive rights to operate bookstalls on the London & North Western Railway stations.

At a time when other railway stalls were notorious for their unsavoury publications, young Smith made his name by selling a high standard of literature. He became known as the "North Western Missionary". In 1862, he secured for his company exclusive rights to sell books, periodicals and newspapers on all the important railways in England. He entered Parliament as a Liberal in 1868; under Benjamin Disraeli he rose to high office, and later joined the Cabinet.

Smith's bookstalls carried their share of railway literature of all kinds, that came to be so fashionable. The very word "railway" was as up-to-date then as "moonshot" was in another period. Humorists, satirists and cartoonists made great play with every foible and fault they could find; and delighted the literate who could afford magazines. Even the comic papers found the railways fair game. In trying to define the most useless thing in the world, a writer named Samuel Butler described it as "the last six inches of a line of railway; there is no part of the road so ugly, so little travelled over, or so useless generally, but it is the end at any rate of a very long thing." Rarely a week went by without *Punch* hitting out amusingly – at incompetent railway managements or commiserating sadly with frustrated passengers.

Waxing romantic, a Quaker friend of Bradshaw wrote: "I love to see one of these huge creatures, with sinews of brass and muscles of iron, strut forth from its smoky stable, and saluting the long train of cars with a dozen sonorous puffs from his iron nostrils, fall back gently into harness. There he stands, champing and foaming upon the iron track, his great heart a furnace of glowing coals; his lymphatic blood is boiling in his veins; the strength of a thousand horses is nerving his sinews; he pants to be gone."

And of the engine driver: "There is a little sober-eyed, tobacco-chewing man in the saddle, who holds him with one finger, and can take away his breath in a moment, should he grow restive or vicious. I am always deeply interested in this man; for, begrimed as he may be with coal, diluted with oil and steam, I regard him as the genius of this whole machinery, as the physical mind of that huge steam horse."

Descriptive writers, armed with steel-nibbed dip-pens, found irresistible the numerous openings of new lines and stations: every one was a gala day of dazzling spectacle which onlookers would remember for the rest of their lives. Bunting, banners and flags; cheering crowds and hosts of excited but half-starved urchins; the rhythmic oom-pah-pah of the raucous brass band; the flamboyant arrival of the local nobility in carriage-and-pair, galloping up to the station; anxious railway directors and officials muttering to each other as the train was prepared. And then the train itself, loaded to the brim with directors and guests, the local mayor, important businessmen and shareholders hoping to make a fortune, and perhaps a Member of Parliament who had his own political axe to sharpen. For the exquisite detail of these great historical moments, much is owed to the writers of the day.

Contemporary painters equally recorded the people and the places: whether a portrait of

Modern railway station advertising of 1874 which brought revenue to the railway companies and sales to business houses. Merchandise offered to the travelling masses included Whelpton's purifying pills, burglar-proof safes, Brinsmead pianos, Ede's patent eye liquid, gem jewellery, Crosby's balsamic cough elixir, Goodall's baking powder and Lamplough's pyretic saline for biliousness. (*Photo: London Transport*)

Stephenson or Brunel, or a busy scene at a station. When Frith's famous painting showing travel conditions in Paddington station in 1862 was publicly exhibited, over 21,000 people paid admission fees to see it within seven weeks. The original painting, over eight feet wide, brought Frith fees of £5,250 when many railwaymen were earning £1 a week; today it hangs in the Royal Holloway College at Egham in Surrey.

The continuous progress of the railways, including every technical feature, was faithfully recorded in a proliferation of railway magazines. Many came and vanished; but the *Railway Gazette* and its pioneering antecedents, which first appeared ten years before mania days, still survives as *Railway Gazette International*. One or two other excellent railway magazines started later, and have stayed the course.

ADVERTISEMENTS

When advertisers observed the crowds at stations they saw the value of displays of posters in prominent places; the railways also realised they had a new source of unexpected income. Main stations were eventually so plastered with advertisements that some people found them an eyesore. Unfettered by a Trades Descriptions Act or an Advertising Standards Authority, many advertisers in Victorian times were ruthless charlatans who offered remedies for desperate diseases. A complaint published in 1847 stated: "Unprincipled individuals, for the sake of gaining a trifle more profit, vend the most spurious compounds under the same names, some under implied sanction of Royalty and Government Departments, with similar attempts at deception, while they copy the labels, advertisements, and testimonials (substituting fictitious names and addresses for the real) of the original preparations."

To the credit of the railways, in later years they commissioned some of the best scenic painters of the day to paint views for posters of popular inland and coastal resorts to tempt people to travel there by train.

THE END OF THE STAGE COACH

The new railways had dealt a body-blow at the canals, and the network of inland waterways for the transport of raw materials and produce, built up by such great engineers as Telford, Rennie and Brindley, suffered an immediate setback. Even so, some canal companies either bought out or built their own railways, and a few of the major waterways benefited from the general increase in trade generated by the railways.

For the stage coaches the story was different. Faster and more comfortable trains covering greater distances finally eclipsed an adventurous part of the British scene which had enlivened the highways for two centuries. Some desperate coach proprietors clung on, running "feeder" services to main stations. One of them traded on passengers' fears of railway tunnels, running stages between stations on either side of the unnerving abyss. One Coghlan ran his coaches for 35 miles between Denbigh Hall, near Bletchley, and Rugby, until the line from Euston was completed; he named one coach *The Railway* and the other *The Rocket*. But these were measures of desperation; rail travel was more than twice as fast and half the price, and the competition was overwhelming.

An old Coaching Bill of 1835 gives some interesting journey times. "Safe and Fast Coaches" ran from the Inn and Coach Office at the Old Bell, Holborn, London; to Dover – the *Defiance*, departing at 6.30 p.m. for a night journey; to Gloucester – the *Prince*, in eight hours, and connecting to all parts of South and North Wales; to Stamford – the *Regent*, giving connections to places further north.

Older people, in particular, were sad to see the last of the stage coach and its steaming chestnuts, calling at a post to be welcomed by the ruddy-faced innkeeper serving brimming tankards of English ale. Imagine the ladies in their bonnets, crinolines and bustles, courteously handed down from their seats by frock-coated gentlemen in tall hats . . . A hurried change of horses, the sound of post-horn and cracking whip, the burly driver settles the many capes of his coat around his shoulders, and the coach grinds off into the distance in a cloud of dust . . .

To what extent was the romance clouded by the sheer misery of a long stage coach journey? Samuel Smiles, that seasoned traveller by train and stage, who died at the ripe old age of 91 in 1904, published his impressions in 1868:

"Many deplored the inevitable downfall of the old stage coach system. There was to be an end of that delightful variety of incident usually attendant on a journey by road.

"The rapid scamper across a fine country on the outside of the four-horse *Express* or *Highflyer*, the seat on the box beside Jehu (coach driver), or the equally coveted place near the facetious guard behind. The journey amid open green fields, through smiling villages and fine old towns, where the stage stopped to change horses and the passengers to dine – was all very delightful in its way; and many regretted that this old-fashioned and pleasant style of travelling was about to pass away.

"But it had its dark side also. Anyone who remembers the journey by stage from London to Manchester or York, will associate it with recollections and sensations of not unmixed delight. To be perched for twenty hours, exposed to all weathers, on the outside of a coach, trying in vain to find a soft seat – sitting now with the face to the wind, rain, or sun, and now with the back – without any shelter such as the commonest penny-a-mile parliamentary train now daily provides – was a miserable undertaking, looked forward to with horror by many whose business required them to travel frequently between the provinces and the Metropolis.

"Nor were the inside passengers more agreeably accommodated. To be closely packed in a little, inconvenient, straight-backed vehicle, where the cramped limbs could not be in the least extended, nor the wearied frame indulge in any change of posture, was felt by many to be a terrible thing.

"Then there were the constantly recurring demands, not always couched in the politest terms, for an allowance to the driver every two or three stages, and to the guard every six or eight, and if the gratuity did not equal their expectations, growling and open abuse were not unusual. These *désagrémens*, together with the exactions practised on travellers by inn-keepers, seriously detracted from the romance of stage coach travelling, and there was a general disposition on the part of the public to change the system for a better."

Before the railways arrived, coaches took four days from London to Edinburgh; but after the few first lines had opened and competition begun – about 48 hours.

THE FIRST QUALITY TRAINS

Having demolished stage coach competition, the leading railways tried to demolish each other's revenue, in a period of inter-railway rivalry that persisted well into the next century. Competition was such that each endeavoured to surpass the other in speed, comfort, safety, station and train amenity, long distance connections and fare reductions. Joint agreements, joint operation and amalgamations were all attempted to avoid competitive elements where possible, but large-scale amalgamations were resisted by the Government as being against the public interest.

In this setting, outstanding improvements took place, mainly in the last thirty years of the century, to establish firmly the Golden Age of Railways. Several of the large companies scored pioneering "firsts" that were later adopted by all. These were mainly in the realm of passenger trains; at the same time, improved goods trains, served by large goods depots and marshalling yards, became deeply entrenched in the nation's industrial and commercial life as the principal carriers of every kind of commodity. When coupled with railway-owned ships and docks for the export of goods, the iron road reigned supreme.

In competing for passenger traffic, the Midland Railway in 1872 caused a furore in board rooms elsewhere by carrying third class passengers on all their trains. This was heresy! Never before had the "poorer classes" been allowed to travel on expresses. But the Midland were convinced that this was the way to encourage the travel habit. That year, the Great Eastern Railway followed suit. Both increased their carryings.

Encouraged by the results, three years later the Midland rubbed salt into the wounds by abolishing second class accommodation completely and having all their third class carriages upholstered. Directors of rival companies were apoplectic and voiced publicly their strong disapproval, eating humble pie very soon afterwards and being forced to follow suit.

Another lead was set by the Midland in 1874 when they introduced Pullman luxury carriages. Mr. (later Sir) James Allport, the general manager, following a visit to America, imported 18 Pullman carriages from George Mortimer Pullman (1831–1897), who had originated luxury vehicles for long distance travel in America. A contract for 15 years was signed. The vehicles were shipped in sections and re-assembled at the Derby Works. Midland Pullmans ran on the London (St. Pancras)–Bedford–Bradford route and also served Liverpool, Edinburgh and Glasgow. Further Pullman contracts were made in succeeding years with the London Brighton & South Coast, London & South Western, Great Northern, Great Eastern, and South Eastern & Chatham.

Midland Pullmans were in a livery of rich chocolate brown, with gold lining and decorations. Interiors were lavishly furnished, curtained and carpeted in the comfort and style of a Victorian "best parlour" and lit by paraffin lamps. Instead of running on four or six wheels, they were mounted on two bogies, each with four wheels; coupled with heavy structure, the Pullmans rode more steadily and smoothly than any previous vehicle on Britain's railways. So enamoured were the Midland that in 1875 they began to introduce their own first and third class carriages fitted with bogies.

A widely travelled railway chairman named

The parlour of a Midland Railway Pullman car, introduced in the 1870s. It had a celestory roof, large windows, a carpet on the floor and good oil lighting. (*By courtesy of the Science Museum*)

William Chambers, who had seen bogie carriages in America about ten years earlier, wrote: "The wheels of the cars being attached to a swivel or *boggie* framework, these vehicles can turn round corners with the ease and security of a gentleman's carriage . . . most ingenious." But he added: "The Railway system of the United States can in no shape be brought into comparison with that of the United Kingdom . . . "

TO BED ON THE TRAIN

The first regular sleeping-car services in Britain were introduced by Scotland's largest railway, the North British, in 1873, first class only. They ran on alternate nights each way on the East Coast route from Glasgow to Edinburgh to King's Cross, followed three months later by a similar service in a sleeping car provided by the Great Northern Railway. Each of the two compartments connected by a short corridor, contained three seats which pulled out to form berths. A luggage-locker, as well as a special compartment for those essentials to all Victorian expeditions, the servants, was also provided. Interiors were elaborately fitted out in crimson velvet, with ebony panels and cornices and fittings of silver plate. Passengers had to bring their own bedding, except for a small hard pillow which the railways supplied. The North British vehicles were 30 ft. long, less than half the length of modern passenger carriages.

Queen Victoria, a regular patron of the railways, being received on this occasion at Chester in 1852. (*W.P.L.*)

Before the year was out, a slightly different sleeping car was introduced on the West Coast route between Euston and Glasgow. This kind of saloon was exclusively for the wealthy. Servants and luggage travelled elsewhere on the train. Not far behind, the Great Western ran their first sleepers in 1877. Sleeping carriages of the 1870s were the first to provide lavatories, primitive though they were.

Crude sleeping compartments had been tried out much earlier. In 1838, a year after opening, the London & Birmingham and the Grand Junction railways ran a "bed carriage", mainly intended for the old and infirm. The seat backs were hinged up at night and a pair of poles with webbing and a cushion were placed across the space between each pair of seats so that passengers could lie down. This was a comfort furnished by the guard for a tip and installed in any first class compartment on request. An example still exists in the special coach built for the Dowager Queen Adelaide, William IV's widow, in 1842, which is now in the Railway Museum. Queen Adelaide's coach resembled three joined stage coaches; her coat of arms, beautifully hand-painted on a bodywork background of deep claret was emblazoned on the sides. The handles of the coach were gold-plated; interior furnishings were sumptious, as befitted a Royal personage, but the four-wheeled vehicle must have rattled and rocked through the night allowing only fitful slumbers to the restless occupant. Two sputtering oil pot lamps provided the lighting.

In 1875, the London Chatham & Dover Railway put a "boudoir carriage" on its Continental service between London and Dover, intended for honeymoon couples on the outward journey and seasick passengers on return: a forerunner of the modern night ferries. The first sleeping carriages fitted with bogies and side corridors appeared in 1878 when the Highland Railway built three of these vehicles for the Inverness–Glasgow route.

The prototype of the first class sleeping car as it is known today was built in 1894 by the North Eastern Railway. It contained four single-berth compartments, two double compartments with lower berths only, a smoking compartment which could be made up as a double for the grouse season, and an attendant's pantry with a gas cooker. Then in 1900 the railway works at York produced the first 12-wheeled sleepers with much improved riding qualities. They contained five single-berth, two double-berth, and smoking and attendants' compartments. For the first time, each compartment had its own pedestal wash basin with table top. The form of the standard British sleeping car had at last been set.

While new comforts were being devised to tempt the passengers, the time came in 1875 to celebrate the jubilee of Stephenson's first railway, the Stockton & Darlington; and the North Eastern staged a memorable public show at Darlington. Another historical project was complete two years later with the opening of the last section of 7 ft. gauge track of $4\frac{1}{4}$ miles from the main Great Western wide gauge line at St. Erth to St. Ives, an attractive stretch that survived the vicissitudes of the massive branch line closures of the 1960s.

COMFORT ON THE TRAINS

Soon after the Midland introduced their first Pullmans, they began to serve refreshments aboard; but only those seated in the car could enjoy this novel amenity. Five years later, the Great Northern introduced the first proper dining car, then known as a "hotel car". It was a converted Pullman and it ran between King's Cross and Leeds.

Another luxury in train travel came with the corridor trains, first introduced by the Great Western in 1892. At first, connections between the coaches were kept locked and the guard held the keys. When the corridors were opened throughout, it must have been fascinating to walk along an express for the first time, to struggle through the rattling and shaking "bellows" connections from one carriage to the next, and to peer inquisitively into the compartments at other passengers and their assortment of belongings. As corridors became more popular, the experience must have been heightened for third class passengers now able to steal a side-long glance at the well-dressed occupants lolling luxuriously in carpeted and curtained compartments marked forbiddingly "First Class". In any case, it was good to stretch the legs on a long journey.

For a while, corridors on some of their best trains gave the Great Western the edge on their competitors, but lines from London to the North gradually followed suit. South of London, the lead was set in 1900 by the London & South Western Railway.

Toilets on corridor trains of all railways gradually became common practice, to the relief of travellers making long journeys. Corridors also meant that people in any part of the train could take a meal or refreshments, and the booked stops at main stations for a quick snack and a drink were cut out and enabled more express trains to run non-stop.

For half a century, travel in draughty four-wheelers in the depth of winter, with ice on the windows, had been a misery, especially for the elderly and children. They needed to wrap up in coats and blankets to make the ordeal bearable.

Long before railway snowploughs, railwaymen had to dig trains out of deep snow with shovels, as in this scene of "The Great Snow Storm in Northumberland" near Acklington in Northumberland in 1861. (W.P.L.)

As early as 1855, the Great Western provided hot-water foot-warmers, but only for their beloved first class passengers. In 1870, second class passengers could enjoy this luxury; and succumbing three years later to competitive pressures, foot-warmers were allowed for the "poorer classes", or, as a Great Western official document put it in its autocratic Victorian language: "The favour of their use was conceded to third class travellers." The Great Northern supplied footstools filled with hot water, which soon cooled off; heat was retained a little longer in some foot-warmers containing acetate of soda, which required an occasional shake to activate the contents. The charge for footwarmers on some railways was sixpence.

As far back as 1856, a patent had been registered for steam-heating apparatus for trains; but it was a long time before a system had been perfected that would force steam from the engines through flexible pipes to radiators in the carriages, and for most of the 19th century, passengers had to make do with the foot-warmers.

Train lighting had also passed through many progressive changes. Total darkness in pioneering days was broken first by tallow candles, then by oil lamps. Oil through pipes was fed to a shallow glass globe containing a wick, to give only a feeble glimmer. The lamp-lighter walked along the roofs of the carriages when lighting-up time arrived. Later, oil was vaporised and the gas stored in cylinders under the carriages; and when the "gas mantle" was invented, train lighting was adequate for reading in comfort. Ordinary coal gas was also used, stored in a container in the guard's van. Gas-lighted carriages remained in service on old stock well into the 1930s.

Electric lighting for trains was used experimentally for the first time in 1881 on the London Brighton & South Coast Railway, introduced by the locomotive engineer, William Stroudley, who had come from the Highland Railway in 1870. It was tried out in Pullman cars on the London–Brighton service, batteries supplying the power. Other railways began to use electric lighting, development including dynamoes rotated by belts from the carriage axles.

Throughout the 19th century railway development, station lighting was by oil or gas, oil remaining in use at numerous small stations until well into the 20th century. As each new technical innovation appeared, railway companies were quick to assess its use in their services. Electric lighting was just one of a great number.

Quickly following Swan's and Edison's invention of a practicable light bulb in 1878/79, Paddington station became one of the first large public buildings to be electrically lit. In November 1880, the Great Western directors authorised the Anglo-American Brush Electric Company to install 34 electric lamps and all the wiring and fittings. By Christmas the lights were switched on, to the wonder and admiration of the passengers, most of whom had never seen electric lights before.

Sir Daniel Gooch, the Great Western chairman, who had been trained in his youth by George Stephenson, must have been conscious of this great historic step forward when he made a sober note in his diary dated 27th January: "We lighted Paddington station with Bush electric light at Christmas. It is a good light, but we have not yet got it into working. I have no doubt all the difficulties will be overcome." From then on, stations were variously lighted by the three systems, gas light still continuing at some stations in the 1970s. Railways used their own electricity generating stations in the absence of power supplies.

Gas for home lighting was first used experimentally in 1792 and came into increasing use from about 1800, and the famous Gas Light & Coke Company reigned long as a household name. (The first permanent gas street lighting was seen in 1809.) Hailed in its day as the "greatest invention of artificial light" and a boon to mankind, gas, after Edison, slowly fell into disrepute as a smelly, sputtering and explosively dangerous element, an element that survived, however, as an economical form of heating. (Incidentally, the man who invented lighting from coal gas in the form of a bright flame in 1795 was William Murdock, whom his employer, James Watt, had chided for wasting his time building a model "travelling engine"!)

SUBURBAN OVERCROWDING

Though luxury travel was to be found on a few expresses, "a scandal" was how the Press described some of the overcrowding of trains on the London suburban lines in the 1880s. A Board of Trade inspector, Major Mandarin, was asked to make a report: "Whatever may be done, I do not think that overcrowding can be altogether avoided. Bad weather, the unpunctuality of even one train, the unwillingness of passengers to wait, if only for five minutes, the fact that a large proportion of workmen commence work at about the

Fleet Street, Ludgate Circus and St. Paul's are the setting for this artist's drawing of London's crowded streets, a situation which justified Charles Pearson's plea for railways under the ground.

same hour, and the curious anxiety to get into the front carriages, or into those nearest the exits, which is observed on nearly all the lines, are causes of overcrowding, which the Companies could never entirely overcome, without resorting to steps which would cause great discontent, and still greater inconvenience."

The morning and evening peaks, as people went to work and returned home, were already a serious problem for suburban railways, one that has never been completely overcome. Liverpool Street station was one of the worst in London and its "workman's traffic" in the mornings reached a peak at about half-past six, for the start of a twelve- or fourteen-hour working day. Overcrowding was severe for all main railway stations on bank holidays.

Shareholders of the South Eastern & Chatham made a fuss when the directors authorised cheap workmen's fares between Victoria and Blackfriars; but they were told that railway construction had demolished property and turned the working man from his home; it was therefore a "graceful concession on the part of the Company" to issue these cheap tickets. . .

RAILWAYS UNDER THE GROUND

Victorian travellers who had to cross London from one main line terminus to another, as well as city people, enjoyed a greater convenience as lines were built under the heavily congested streets. The first line from Paddington to Farringdon Street via Euston and King's Cross was on the cut-and-cover principle. Huge trenches were dug, rails laid, and the street made good again overhead. It was opened on 10th January 1863. The steam locomotives were built by the Great Western Railway and the line was in mixed gauge

The entrance to Clerkenwell tunnel in London as sketched in 1868. (*W.P.L.*)

to take the two main sizes of rolling stock. More lines were built; but the fume problems of steam led to the development of electric traction, and the first "real" tube underground, the City & South London, was opened on 18th December 1890, the world's first city underground electric railway. As more lines were built, connections were made with all the main-line stations in London.

SAFETY COMES FIRST

Accidents continued to occur in the years since Stephenson's *Rocket* killed Huskisson on the day the Liverpool & Manchester Railway was opened. The fear of mishap cast a dark shadow and for numerous Victorians spoiled the delights of train travel. Some swore they would never enter a train as, a century later, certain people shied away from air travel long after the giant Jumbo Jet had mastered the skies.

Bitter disputes frequently arose between railway managements and Board of Trade officers about the haphazard methods for operating many lines, brought to a head by each fatal disaster. The Press and public continuously complained about faulty braking, poorly maintained track and carriages, and rudimentary signalling, particularly on the smaller railways. Public alarm reached a peak after a collision in June 1889 at Armagh on the Great North of Ireland Railway, when eighty people were killed: the highest number since official accident records began in 1840. Soon after, the Government acted.

The Regulation of Railways Act, passed on 30th August 1889, forced all railways to come into line on a number of safety measures that the more forward-looking railways were already observing. It required them:

(a) to adopt the block system on all or any of their railways open for the public conveyance of passengers;

(b) to provide for the interlocking of points and signals on or in connexion with all or any of such railways;

(c) to provide for and use on all their trains carrying passengers continuous brakes complying with the following regulations, namely:

(i) the brake must be instantaneous in

action and capable of being applied by the engine drivers and guards;

(ii) the brake must be self-applying in the event of any failure in the continuity of its action;

(iii) the brake must be capable of being applied to every vehicle of the train, whether carrying passengers or not;

(iv) The brake must be in regular use in daily working;

(v) The materials of the brake must be of a durable character, and easily maintained and kept in working order.

The "block" system meant that each section of line between two signalboxes must be considered blocked, until the signalman was satisfied the line ahead was clear. It replaced the "time interval" system which, too often, had resulted in a delayed train being struck in the rear by a following one.

Interlocking prevented a signalman pulling a signal lever to the clear position before the points for the route concerned were first fitting correctly. At a later stage in signalling equipment, electric interlocking was introduced, contacts proving the points were correctly set.

Train braking was operated either by vacuum or air (Westinghouse system) pressure, flexible pipes running from the engine, right through the train to the guardsvan. If the couplings between the carriages broke, as sometimes happened, the pipe would also break, to break the vacuum or release the air pressure, which would automatically apply the brakes to both portions of the divided train.

These regulations, which still apply today, created new standards of train safety throughout the railway systems.

THE COMMUNICATION CORD

In keeping with the reserved temperament of the British, the privacy of the railway compartment had considerable disadvantages when passengers, isolated and helpless, were threatened with outrage; young females were molested and passengers robbed. The Press and public called for some system of summoning the guard and stopping the train; but the railways feared trains would be stopped for trivial reasons and the safety of trains on the line impaired. A personal whim or imaginary fear could seriously disrupt the lines.

Public outcry reached a crescendo after a passenger was murdered on the North London Railway in November 1864. An enquiry was held by the Board of Trade which recommended an improved system of passenger communication. At about that time, a system common on some railways consisted of a rope running along the out-

This rail disaster on the Chester & Holyhead Railway in 1868 was sketched by the artist only ninety minutes after the accident. (*W.P.L.*)

side of the train; when it was pulled by a passenger, it rang a bell on the engine to attract the driver, and another in the rear van to attract the guard. In 1875 William Stroudley, engineer of the London Brighton & South Coast Railway, introduced the first electrical passenger communication, a notable improvement on the outside rope and bell.

Brutal attacks became so common that the Government stepped in to enforce the installation of a proper passenger emergency system connected to the train braking. A regulation was finally incorporated in the 1889 Act which also required continuous braking throughout all trains carrying passengers.

Later refinements included small discs at the ends of carriage roofs, so that the guard could quickly identify the carriage where assistance might be needed; the discs were turned when the communication cord (usually a small-link chain) was pulled, the cord hanging down loosely in the compartment in which it had been pulled. Pulling the cord made only a partial application of the brakes (vacuum or air pressure), indicated by falling pressures in the gauges in guardsvans and on engines, thus enabling the driver to continue into a nearby station, or to clear a tunnel or long viaduct or other inconvenient stretch of line.

RACES TO THE NORTH

The flush of new comforts that enabled Victorians to travel in style was prompted partly by the need to recover from the industrial and agricultural depression of the late 1870s, as well as by inter-railway competition. Following comfort came speed, and a period of rivalry that made world railway history. Speeds on Britain's railways were the highest in the world, thanks to some outstanding engines designed and built by the larger companies. The slice of cake the leading contenders sought was the long-distance business between London and Scotland: the East Coast route from King's Cross, G.N.R., and the West Coast from Euston, L. & N.W.R.: two dedicated rivals.

In July and August 1888 a number of fast runs were made, but with trains under the usual weights. The fastest train on the East Coast covered the distance of 392½ miles to Edinburgh in 447 minutes, and the West Coast 400 miles in slightly longer time, but both averaging over

GREAT NORTHERN RAILWAY.

Circular No. 6293a.

SPECIAL 1, 2, 3 CLASS DAY EXPRESS

KING'S CROSS TO EDINBURGH.

On and after Monday, 13th August, the 10.0 a.m. down Special Express King's Cross to Edinburgh will run as below, and this working will be continued, on Week-days, throughout August.

		A.M.
King's Cross	**dep.**	**10 0**
Hatfield...	pass	10 22
Hitchin...	,,	10 37
Huntingdon	,,	11 5
Peterboro'	,,	11 23
Grantham	**arr.**	**11 55**
,, ...	**dep.**	**12 0**
Newark	pass	12 17
Retford...	,,	12 36
Doncaster	,,	12 54
Selby......	,,	1 14
York	**arr.**	**1 30**

This train will convey passengers for Edinburgh.

Tickets to be examined and the York tickets collected at Grantham.

The number of vehicles will be restricted to eight. No vehicle to be attached or detached at Grantham.

CIRCULAR 6275a IS CANCELLED.

FRANCIS P. COCKSHOTT,
Superintendent of the line.

King's Cross,
August, 1888.

A page from the Great Northern Railway timetable of 1888 showing a journey from London to York in 3½ hours.

Above: A preserved Great Northern Railway saddle tank locomotive on a Stephenson Locomotive Society special in 1962. Below: North Eastern tank engine hauling a train from Pickering to Whitby at the end of the steam era. (*Photos: By courtesy of J. M. Jarvis, Esq.*)

fifty miles an hour. At little over 6½ hours between the two capitals, it was a landmark in speed, and the timetables for both routes were afterwards tightened, with material improvements on the main line and connecting services.

The historic Race to the North on 22nd August 1895 was the race to Aberdeen. The fastest time was made over the tracks of the two railways forming the West Coast route: the L. & N.W. and the Caledonian. The distance of 540 miles was covered in 8 hrs. 32 mins. at an average of 63·3 m.p.h., including three stops and climbing

EUSTON TO ABERDEEN
8 P.M. EXPRESS, 22ND AUGUST 1895
RUNNING TIMES EUSTON TO CARLISLE

Timing Station	Time of passing	Station to Station			Start to stop av.	
		Time	Dist.	Speed		
	h. m. s.	min. sec.	miles	m.p.h.		Driver
Euston (*dep.*)	8 0 0					R. Walker
Watford (*pass*)	8 17 0	17 0	17·3	61·0		
Tring	8 30 30	13 30	14·2	63·1		Load 3–4½
Bletchley	8 43 0	12 30	15·0	72·0		
Rugby	9 17 0	34 0	36·0	63·5	64·3	7 ft. Comp.
Nuneaton	9 30 30	13 30	14·6	64·9	m.p.h.	Pass. Eng.
Tamworth	9 41 30	11 0	13·0	70·9		*Adriatic*
Stafford	10 4 0	22 30	23·4	62·4		from London
Crewe (*arr.*)	10 27 30	33 30	24·6	62·8		to Crewe
Crewe (*dep.*)	10 29 30					
Warrington (*pass*)	10 51 25	21 55	24·1	66·0		Driver
Wigan	11 1 35	10 10	11·5	67·9		B. Robinson
Preston	11 15 15	13 40	15·5	68·0		
Lancaster	11 34 5	18 50	20·6	65·7		6 ft. 6 in.
Carnforth	11 39 42	5 37	6·5	69·6	67·2	4-wheel
Oxenholme	11 51 10	11 28	12·8	67·0	m.p.h.	coupled
Tebay	12 4 0	12 50	13·1	61·2		Pass. Eng.
Shap Summit	12 10 0	6 00	5·8	58·0		*Hardwicke*
Penrith	12 21 0	11 0	13·3	72·5		Crewe to
Carlisle (*arr.*)	12 35 30	14 30	18·0	74·4		Carlisle
			299·25			
	RUNNING TIMES CARLISLE TO ABERDEEN					
Carlisle (*dep.*)	12 38 0					
Beattock (*pass*)	1 17 30	39 30	39·75	60·3		
Beattock Summit	1 31 0	13 30	10·0	44·4		
Carstairs	1 52 0	21 0	23·75	67·8	60·5	Driver
Law Junction	2 2 30	10 30	10·5	60·0	m.p.h.	A. Crooks
Holytown	2 7 30	5 0	5·75	69·0		
Larbert	2 27 0	19 30	20·0	61·5		Engine No. 90
Stirling	2 34 30	7 30	8·0	64·0		
Perth (*arr.*)	3 7 30	33 0	33·0	60·0		
Perth (*dep.*)	3 9 30					
Forfar (*pass*)	3 39 0	29 30	32·5	66·1		
Kinnaber Junction	3 57 0	18 0	19·25	64·2		
Drumlithie	4 9 30	12 30	15·5	74·4	65·4	Driver
Stonehaven	4 16 30	7 0	6·75	57·8	m.p.h.	J. Souttar
Aberdeen						
Ticket Station (*arr.*)	4 30 0	15 30	16·0	61·9		Engine No. 17
Ticket Station (*dep.*)	4 31 0					
Aberdeen (*arr.*)	4 32 0					

Totals . . . 512 mins. 540 miles

Winning run of the Great Race to Aberdeen – 1895 – *and a world record for steam*

the Shap and Beattock summits, with a train of only 70 tons. This created a new world record.

On the East Coast route, the best time was made on 21st August when the distance of 523½ miles was completed in 8 hrs. 38 mins., averaging just over 60 m.p.h. On the G.N.R. and N.E.R. as far as Edinburgh, the average speed was 62·3 m.p.h., the train of 120 tons making three stops. Much public attention was attracted to these high-speed events, bringing still greater prestige to the several railway companies taking part.

In the following year, history was made south of the Thames when a special train ran from London to Paris, connecting with a cross-channel ship, in 6½ hours. Though it was a specially organised run, the time was ten minutes faster than the regular timings of the crack express the *Golden Arrow* some 40 years later.

Fast trains had been foreseen by the promoters of the Manchester & Leeds Railway. One of the pamphlets read: "We shall, one of these days, hear of a man breakfasting in London, dining in Manchester, supping at Leeds or York, and sleeping in Edinburgh! Then, may the ardent and anxious lover, the object of whose idolatory is in a distant part of the Kingdom, 'fly on the wings of love', not in imagination only, but find himself really and corporally in the presence of his mistress, by the potent agency of a railway and locomotive engine, with a rapidity that almost outstrips his ardour; thus realising the poetical extravaganza:

Ye Gods! annihilate Time and Space
To make two lovers happy."

The line opened in 1841.

END OF VICTORIANA

As the end of Queen Victoria's great reign drew to a close, the railways of Britain could look back on three-quarters-of-a-century of incredible history. Bursts of speed had reached 80 and 90 miles an hour; a high standard of safety had been secured, and the best trains were highly comfortable and matched any in the world. Some of them bore names, and acquired their own distinctive personalities. Scores of magnificent stations with every amenity had been built as architectural gems in their own right, and models of engineering ingenuity. Some of the most luxurious hotels in the country had been built by the railways, and were patronised by Royalty, the nobility and gentry; the Midland hotels were regarded as among the best social centres in Britain.

Every kind of trade, industry and commerce had progressed from the steadily improving services the railways provided; and steady employment was found for large numbers of men, most of whom spent a working lifetime on the iron road, sons following fathers for generations. The Industrial Revolution had set Britain on the pinnacle of technical and industrial standing, both at home and abroad; and the Age of Reform had brought a new level of social justice and a better life for working people, side by side with railway progress.

A typical 19th century Tudor-style cottage station at Fenny Stratford near Bletchley on the Oxford-Cambridge line of the London & North Western Railway. (*Roger Palmer*)

Chapter 7

Railways in the 20th Century

City of Truro, *4–4–0 No. 3440, Great Western Railway, the first steam locomotive to establish a 100 m.p.h.-plus speed record*

THE upheavals in the railways that the new century brought were totally unforeseen, and were totally different from those of the previous era. Necessity being the mother of invention, the changing needs of transport down the ages have always offered scope for the inventive mind to work within the limits of technical knowledge and materials contemporarily available. Inventors within the railway framework have had a field day, and the process still continues in new areas; but the invention that was to have the biggest single impact on the railway monopoly was the internal combustion engine, first on the ground and then in the air. Railway history was also fundamentally altered, in a different way, by the experience of two world wars.

The dramatic developments in the story of the railways in the first half of the 20th century can be seen against the brief historical table below:

- 1900–14 expansion continues and some lines are electrified; the railways introduce their first road motor services
- 1914–18 The railways at war
- 1919–22 post-war rehabilitation, leading to the grouping of the numerous railways into four main line companies
- 1923–39 adjustment as individual companies are absorbed into their respective groups; the motor vehicle arrives in rapidly growing numbers to end the railway monopoly; internal airlines begin to develop
- 1939–45 the railways again at war
- 1946–47 post-war rehabilitation, leading to State ownership.

As the new century dawned, the railway network had grown to 18,665 route miles, and in the next 30 years less than 2,000 miles would be added, to reach the peak length of about 20,500 in the 1930s. Underground railways in London continued to spread, changing over steadily to electric traction; and in 1905, the last steam train ran on the Inner Circle.

THE FIRST ELECTRIC RAILWAYS

Electrification seemed to many people to be the right traction for future railways, and a slow process of change began in Brighton. In 1883, Britain's first electric railway was a short holiday jaunt in narrow gauge along the sea front, built by a Brighton man named Magnus Volk, whose son and biographer, Conrad, is now in his nineties. Volk's Electric Railway, still fascinating young seaside visitors, was taken over by Brighton Corporation in 1940.

In the same year as Volk's, but eight weeks later, a short line was opened at Giant's Causeway in Northern Ireland, the first railway in the world to run on hydro-electric power. The Mersey Railway, first opened between Liverpool and Birkenhead in 1886, was converted to electric power in 1903. In 1893 the first section of the Liverpool Overhead Railway was opened, the first elevated electric railway in the world. It was closed in 1956.

Next came the Tyneside electrification on the North Eastern Railway, the first section between Newcastle and Benton opening in 1904. Services were electrified that same year between Liverpool and Southport on the Lancashire & Yorkshire Railway, later extended to Ormskirk. At first, both steam and electric trains were in use. In 1908 the Midland Railway electrified the Lancaster–Morecambe–Heysham line. In practically every case, electric trains by their speed and cleanliness attracted many more passengers and justified the heavy capital investment.

During the following year, the London Brighton & South Coast Railway electrified the South London line, using overhead power wires, between Victoria and London Bridge, considered to be the oldest part of the present-day "Southern Electric". But large-scale electrification in the south did not start in earnest until the lines from London to Brighton and Worthing were converted from steam in 1933. An unusual example was found in 1913 when 19 miles of line were electrified between Middlesbrough and Shildon for the conveyance of coal traffic.

Electrification continued during the early years of the 1914–18 war and by 1916 was in operation on the Broad Street to Richmond line. At the same time, new comfortable carriages replaced the antiquated four-wheelers with their cramped wooden seats which had earned for the line such a bad reputation. In the years 1915–16, the London & South Western Railway electrified short stretches of route, including the Waterloo–East Putney line completed in October 1915. Instead of overhead wires, an electrified rail carrying direct current was adopted, a system the Company's engineer, Herbert Jones, had brought from America.

Years of planning and vast capital went into the electrification of the London & North Western Railway line between Euston and Watford: 17 miles of intense commuter business which included such large suburban areas as Wembley and Harrow. Part was opened in 1917, the lines being completed to Watford and Croxley Green in 1922, and to Rickmansworth five years afterwards. Electric trains from Broad Street and the Bakerloo underground trains also used the route. In 1931 the Manchester South Junction & Altrincham Railway was converted, a line jointly owned by the London Midland & Scottish and London & North Eastern railways. Large-scale electrification had to wait until after the Second World War.

Electric power was also introduced into railway signalling; the London & South Western Railway installed automatic signalling as early as 1902 between Andover and Grateley. The most common signalling practice had been the use of semaphore signal arms mounted on posts and worked by wires through pulleys from a signalbox fitted with a row of levers for signals and points. Points were operated largely by rodding connections. Oil lamps lighted the signals at night. In later years, a long-burning type of oil was used, and the signal lamps remained lighted day and night, and would burn usually for about a week. A large number of oil-lighted signals operated from the old type manual signalboxes are still in use.

Another development was the electric telegraph, so that messages could be telegraphed from one signalbox to the next, indications being made by instruments with magnetic needles, and the sounding of bells in codes. Equipment varied, and so did methods, between one railway company and another, but a measure of standardisation accumulated through the inter-railway committees organised by the Railway Clearing House.

Perhaps the most important single development was the "track circuit," which began to appear about the turn of the century. A low voltage current was fed from line-side batteries into the rails; when vehicle wheels ran over a "section" of line, the circuit was "shortened", which, in turn, operated an instrument in the signalbox to show "line occupied" or similar message. All the signalling apparatus was designed to "fail safe", so that if equipment failed or a signalman made an error, signals and instruments would show "danger", "line blocked", or similar indication, whether a train were present or not.

Throughout the first quarter of the century, signalling made rapid strides to cope with higher speeds and more intensive use of tracks. Electric "colour-light" signals were gradually introduced on the busiest lines, beamed in a powerful ray to the driver's eye level, and far more easily seen in dense fog and heavy falling snow. A later refinement was for the passage of trains over track circuits to operate the electric signals, but with the signalman maintaining control; points were fitted with electrical contacts so that the signal reading through them could not be placed to clear, either manually or electrically, until the points were proved to be fitting tightly.

It was just one more stage to the electrical operation of miniature signal levers, or tiny switches, in the signalboxes, for working points and signals in a power installation (all-electric signalbox). On the walls, large panels contained miniature bulbs that were automatically lighted as trains passed over the track-circuited rails: this system formed the basis for modern railway signalling.

AUTOMATIC SIGNALLING

Signalling history was made by the Great Western Railway in 1906 when equipment was installed in locomotive driving cabs and on the track, to indicate to the driver the position of the signals on the line. It was first tested on the Henley branch line, and two years later installed on the four-track route between Reading and Slough, completed to Paddington in 1912.

Four bright young men at Paddington had created the Great Western's pioneering system: R. H. Nicholls, who became superintendent of the line; E. A. Bowden, a signalling expert and the first lecturer at the G.W.R. signalling classes; C. M. Jacobs, later signal engineer, and R. J. Insell, who became his assistant. Their original idea had been to make the line safer during fog, so their colleagues dubbed them "The Fog-signalmen". Their experiments succeeded by sheer persistence, and they were all rewarded by handsome promotion.

Developed as Automatic Train Control (ATC), the operation involved actual contact between the equipment under the locomotive and that on the track. Progressively, the system was introduced on all G.W.R. lines, increasing the safety of trains. Sound though the system was, many years elapsed before other railways adopted this kind of signalling.

Basically, three signals controlled the working of trains: the distant or warning signal with a yellow semaphore arm and a yellow light which tells the driver whether he should be prepared to stop at the next signal – the home signal – with a red arm and red light; and the starting signal, which is the same. The home signal is usually placed on the approach side of a station or junction, and the starting signal at the front end of the station. The distant signal is usually over a thousand yards in rear of the home signal, and is the key to safe working. The length of line between one set of signals and another is known as a "section"; telegraph instruments, and telephones when they came into wider use, were the means of communication between one signalbox and the next. Although later technical developments altered the details, the principles have remained basically the same. In those days, there was much variation in detail between one company and another.

Two slip coaches released from an express from Paddington approaching Slough on the Great Western Railway in 1905. The guard brakes the vehicles into Slough station as the express continues at speed. Slip coaches were first used in 1840, the last remaining on the Great Western in 1960. (Photo: British Rail)

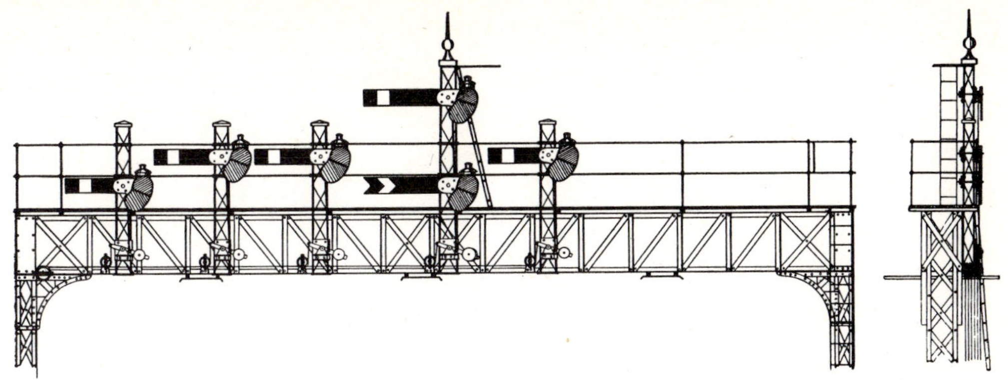

A signal gantry in the early 1900s. The swallow-tailed semaphore arm is a "distant" signal interlocked with a stop signal a mile further ahead. All are lit by oil lamps.

"CITY OF TRURO"

Improved signalling was essential for safe and efficient operations at higher speeds; but the early part of the 20th century was not particularly notable for speed records, except for one outstanding performance in 1904 when the Great Western broke through the 100 m.p.h. barrier. The *City of Truro*, when heading the *Ocean Mail*, was the first steam locomotive in the world to pull a train at over 100 m.p.h. From Plymouth to Bristol, a maximum of 102 m.p.h. was recorded, but when the records were checked afterwards there was some doubt about the precise speed. The *Duke of Connaught* engine completed the journey from Bristol to London, also reaching high speeds. In speeding up this service, the Great Western were competing against the London & South Western for traffic from trans-Atlantic liners which called at Plymouth.

ROAD COMPETITION THREATENS

Early in the century, one of the first forms of competition faced by the suburban railways in London and other large towns came from the electric tramcar, which was powered through overhead wires or by a contact rail just below ground level. Within a few years, trams were running in towns all round Britain – in Lancashire and Yorkshire, the Midlands, the West Country, Wales, Scotland and Ireland, but most of all throughout London and the suburbs. By about 1908, more Londoners were travelling by tram than by suburban train. The story was much the same elsewhere. For example, electric trams serving Arnold Bennett's "five towns" – Longton, Stoke-on-Trent, Hanley, Burslem and Tunstall, unlike the railway, ran through the main shopping centres of the Potteries towns of Wedgwood and Royal Doulton fame; they lured passengers away from one of the North Staffordshire Railway's busiest routes between Longton and Kidsgrove via the Hanley loop line.

Trams also replaced horse-drawn omnibuses and steam road carriages, and appeared to be a permanent answer to urban transport problems; but the vehicle was restricted to its track. As more motor vehicles came on the streets, the tram got in the way, and by depositing its passengers in the middle of the road it was sure to make enemies.

As streets became more congested, trolley buses replaced many trams, exploiting the greater versatility of the motor vehicle but still making use of the heavy capital investment in overhead wires and power depots.

Meanwhile, inventors in their tiny workshops were busy with the motor vehicle which, for the railways, would be a far greater competitor. A primitive German Daimler omnibus was tried on the roads of Britain in 1899, followed by a Thornycroft steam operated coach in 1902. The General Omnibus Company had its first petrol-electric vehicle in 1903, followed by a steamer the next year: all of rather an experimental nature. Until 1896, all mechanically-propelled road vehicles were required to be preceded by a man on foot carrying a red flag. This was a result of the Locomotive Acts, known as the Red Flag Acts, originally formulated to protect the railways from competition.

It was 1888 when a Karl Benz three-wheel

Horse omnibus of the London & North Western Railway for conveying passengers across London between Euston and Waterloo, photographed in 1905. (*Photo: British Rail*)

A Midland Railway Maudslay motor bus of c. *1905 at Rothwell, Northants. Notwithstanding the speed limit of 12 m.p.h. inscribed on the side of the vehicle, the solid tyres bestowed a very bumpy ride.*

Brass bells, known as swingers, flyers or terrets from the headbands of the bridles of railway horses. On special occasions plumes of coloured feathers completed the decoration. (*Photo: Herbert Hinchley*)

Railway horse brasses, spanning some thirty years, carefully mounted by a collector. (*Photo: Herbert Hinchley*)

motor vehicle was first imported from Europe, and by 1900 the contraption displayed distinct possibilities for carrying passengers. To the railways, it was still something of a novelty; they never dreamed it would hit them as hard as they had hit the canals and stage coaches in the railway mania days.

The Great Western Railway was the first to see the light, and was the first railway to operate a permanent motor bus service (instead of a light railway as originally planned). Starting in 1903, it ran as a feeder service to the main line between Helston and the Lizard in Cornwall. This was quickly followed by similar services elsewhere including Penzance–Newlyn–Marazion, Slough and Beaconsfield, Modbury and Yealmpton, Saltash and Callington, Wolverhampton and Bridgnorth. Sir Felix Pole, a former general manager of the Great Western Railway, wrote: "The Great Western was the pioneer Road Motor Transport Company. Long before motor vehicles reached London, the Great Western fleet had reached considerable dimensions." He quotes the following figures:

	G.W.R. Number of motor buses
31st December 1904	34
31st December 1905	72
31st December 1906	80

By June 1907, the buses had run more than 1,600,000 miles. In the period before the First World War, other larger railways built up their own fleets of motor vehicles, but did not yet see them as a serious threat when operated by specialist competitors. But within a few years, rivalry and competition would have to yield to the overriding priorities of what the politicians were to describe naively as "a war to end all wars".

The latest in motor cars (c.*1903*) *with bulb horn, pneumatic tyres, tiller steering, chain drive and acetylene lamps. Used by London & North Western Railway inspectors on their London rounds.* (*Photo: British Rail*)

THE FIRST WORLD WAR – AND THE RAILWAYS

As early as 1911 Britain was seriously concerned about the possibilities of a European war in which she might become involved. The fatal shooting of Archduke Franz Ferdinand, heir to the Hapsburg throne, and his wife Sophia, on 28th June 1914 was the dramatic fuse that set Europe alight. Britain had certain defence commitments which prompted her to declare war against Germany on 4th August. A railway executive committee, consisting mainly of leading general managers, had been formed in readiness for such an emergency; and by midnight, the Government took control of the railways, under the authority of the Regulation of the Forces Act passed in 1871. For four terrible years of slaughter the railways and their men were to share the sacrifices of the nation and her allies until victory was won.

The war was a shattering blow to the railways, for technical progress was making great strides; services were good and Britain's railways stood high in the esteem of the country and of the world. Yet the end of a great railway era was near.

One of the first war-time jobs for the railways was to transport troops, Territorials and equipment from numerous parts of Britain to Southampton, the port of embarkation for the British Expeditionary Force. By the end of August, 670 troop trains had been run. Lord Kitchener, then Secretary for War, in making a speech to the House of Lords, added: "The Railway Companies, in the all-important matter of the transport facilities, have more than justified the complete confidence reposed in them by the War Office, all grades of the railway services having laboured with untiring energy and patience."

Railway services were severely reduced as large numbers of men were called up for military service or joined Government departments; thousands of girls and women took on railway jobs. In addition to vast quantities of war materials by freight, coal for the Navy, which had previously been transported by ship, had to go by rail. At one stage, over 100 trains a week were carrying more than 40,000 tons of coal from the South Wales coalfields to Grangemouth Docks on the Firth of Forth, the principal naval coaling station.

Munitions and other war equipment were manufactured in the main railway rolling stock works, and special hospital trains were assembled. As a temporary war-time expedient, Charing Cross was used for ambulance trains conveying war wounded, and Victoria for servicemen on leave and for military mails. During the emergency 6,500,000 journeys were made by men travelling in 15,000 "leave" trains at Charing Cross and 10,000,000 mailbags were handled at Victoria. At Waterloo, some 8,000,000 soldiers and sailors used the free buffet service in the years 1915–20, and a plaque was affixed in a subway there as a reminder to future travellers in peacetime.

Frequently, locomotives hauled freight trains far in excess of the official maximum loading which is specified for each class of engine, something a driver or guard would never allow in peace time. Among the amazing performances was that of a train of over 400 tons, hauled from Gloucester to Birmingham by a class 2 4–4–0 Midland engine whose official maximum freight load was only 180 tons. With a long train of loose coupled wagons, only skilful driving could have avoided a "break-loose" from a snatch or extra sharp braking. It was also a reflection of the high standard of engine maintenance for which the Midland Railway was noted. Throughout the war years, maintenance of all railway equipment was generally severely neglected, and rolling stock building programmes curtailed; to recover from such arrears took the railways several years.

In 1917, a tribute was paid by Sir William Robertson, then Chief of the General Staff: "During the last five or six weeks we have expended no less than 200,000 tons of munitions in France alone, and we took out some 50,000 tons of stone for making and mending roads. All these things meant a tremendous amount of railway work. And in this connection, I would like to acknowledge the most valuable services rendered to the Army by the railway managers and the railway employees who have gone out to do that work for us in France. No word of praise is too high for the skill and determination these men have shown." (Sir William's son Brian, the late Lord Robertson, became head of British Railways in 1953 as chairman of the British Transport Commission, retiring from that appointment in 1961).

When it was all over, more praise was showered on the railways. One Government report said: " . . . The success that has attended the operation of the railways throughout the war, which has been superior to that witnessed in any other of the belligerent countries, affords conclusive proof of the adequacy of the arrangements which had been

A Midland Railway locomotive driver and fireman in the uniform of about 1910. (Photo: British Rail)

made in advance, and of the capacity of those who had been concerned with their execution.

"There has been little dislocation, notwithstanding that, in addition to a very large Government traffic, the volume of civilian traffic both of passengers and goods, has been heavier than in pre-war days, that large numbers of the staff have been inexperienced, and that considerable demands have been made upon the railways for rolling stock and materials for use with the armies abroad."

The burden of war fell unevenly upon the different railway companies. Some were virtually in the front line of defence. With the military bases of both Salisbury and Aldershot, and Southampton docks as a terminal, the London & South Western Railway bore a heavy share. So, in the vulnerable south-east corner of England, did the South Eastern & Chatham. At the far end of Britain the Highland Railway, much of it single line, was called upon to meet the heavy military demands of two key bases of the Grand Fleet at Scapa Flow and Cromarty Firth.

Railways were involved prominently in the war right up to the end, and the Armistice itself was signed in a railway dining car in the Compiègne Forest in Northern France on 11th November 1918. The Peace Treaty was signed on 28th June 1919 at the Palace of Versailles some 15 miles to the south-west of Paris. (France was forced to sign her humiliating Armistice of 1940 in that same preserved carriage – a suitable symbol of the futility of Europe's hopes for lasting peace after the catastrophic sacrifices of 1914–18.)

POST-WAR UNREST

In almost indecent haste, a general election was called on 14th December 1918 by the victorious war-time premier, David Lloyd George, who took office once again. At that time, when hatred for the vanquished Germans was at a peak, political propaganda brandished such evocative slogans as "Hang the Kaiser"; make the Germans pay for the war "until the lemon pips squeak;" and "Let us make Britain a land fit for heroes to live in". Capitulating to the campaigning of Mrs. Emmeline Pankhurst (1858–1928) and her followers, the Government granted the vote to women over thirty; during the war, women's labour had been needed and they had learned how to do the jobs of men.

Political unrest, poverty and post-war unemployment formed the national mood as the railways tried to get back on their feet, and the second serious railway strike (the first took place in 1911) was called in 1919. Railwaymen won substantial wage increases and an eight-hour day.

During the misery of the early 1920s, millions of ordinary people began to find relief and laughter when for 6*d.* (2½p) they could enjoy an evening at the bioscope (cinema); watching the silent films in the darkness, they would go into near hysterics at the absurd antics of Charlie Chaplin, Buster Keaton and Harold Lloyd on the silver screen upon which it seemed to be perpetually raining. For the railways, the new habit of cinema-going brought additional suburban business, and the distribution of packages of film throughout the country by passenger train.

While the fortunes of the railway companies hung in the balance, the new station at Waterloo, planned many years earlier, was finally completed. It was opened by King George V and Queen Mary on 21st March 1922. With its 21 platforms, massive signalbox, a private telephone exchange linked with numerous suburban stations and signalboxes, and 240 synchronised clocks served by a master clock and fed by batteries, it embodied all the latest railway station improvements, to become one of the finest in London.

From parliamentary powers obtained in 1899 and 1900, the London & South Western Railway had extended the property by 6½ acres, considered at the time as reckless and wasteful. A church and seven streets had been demolished, and alternative homes found for at least 1,750 people. Twenty-two years later, the investment paid off.

THE GROUP AMALGAMATIONS

From 1919, the Government was seriously considering the future of the railways. Several leading politicians favoured State ownership; in an official statement, Winston Churchill said that the Government policy was for nationalisation, which the railway companies vigorously opposed. In the event, the Government itself decided on compulsory amalgamation into four main groups. In the past, the railway companies themselves had initiated amalgamation; now, it was by Government edict.

More Government influence was brought to bear when the Ministry of Transport was created in 1919 by a special Act of Parliament, and transport functions, including the railway inspectorate, were formally transferred from the Board of Trade. Then in 1921 the Railways Act was passed, requiring the formation of the four main line railway companies; they began operations in their new role on 1st January 1923. Three joint lines continued to function: Cheshire Lines Committee, Midland & Great North Joint, and the Somerset & Dorset. Of the 120 railways absorbed into the four main groups, the larger ones were termed "constituent companies" and the smaller "subsidiary companies":

London Midland & Scottish

This group consisted of eight constituent and 27 subsidiary companies. The constituents were:

London & North Western	Furness
Midland	Caledonian
Lancashire & Yorkshire	Glasgow & South Western
North Staffordshire	Highland

London & North Eastern

This group consisted of seven constituent and 26 subsidiary companies. The constituents were:

North Eastern	Hull & Barnsley
Great Northern	North British
Great Eastern	Great North of Scotland
Great Central	

Great Western

This group consisted of seven constituent and 26 subsidiary companies. The constituents were:

Great Western	Cardiff
Barry	Alexandra (Newport & South Wales) Docks & Railways
Cambrian	
Rhymney	
Taff Vale	

Southern

This group consisted of five constituent and 14 subsidiary companies. The constituents were:

London & South Western
London Brighton & South Coast
South Eastern
London Chatham & Dover
South Eastern & Chatham

The Great Western was successful in maintaining its original historic name. New group names gave some idea of the territory covered but many lines of one company penetrated into the geographical areas of the others, evidence of the hard bargaining that had taken place in railway board rooms and government offices. No indication was given in the name of the L. & N.E.R. that its lines reached the north of Scotland.

Some conception of the respective sizes of the new companies, including joint lines, can be gained from their estimated route mileages given in round figures below:

L.M.S.R.	7,500
L.N.E.R.	6,700
G.W.R.	3,800
S.R.	2,200

The list which follows gives the names of the 120 separate companies amalgamated. Companies with the longest names often had the shortest railway. To browse through them is to capture a glimpse of the magic and history of the tiny lines that grew into great and influential companies with strong personalities of their own. Small railways such as the Plymouth & Dartmoor, Furness, North Staffordshire, Highland, Wick & Lybster, Yorkshire Dales, Kilsyth & Bonnybridge, Isle of Wight, Taff Vale, and West Somerset were to lose their identities in the anonymity of the mighty groups; but for a long time, railwaymen from directors to porters still called their own particular railway by the old name they had grown to love. No railway could possibly be as good as their old line.

Before finally losing their treasured identities, some of the companies promoted selected administrative and technical staff, even low-grade clerks, with the intention of exerting a stronger influence within the new group. In the board rooms, there was much "jockeying for position" and many directors and senior officers were paid off. There were battles, too, for the location of the new head offices. The Midland scored a great scoop by the selection of Derby as a main headquarters, with some offices at the L. & N.W. Euston station, and outposts in Manchester, Glasgow, Crewe, and South Wales. Between the Midland and the North Western the battle did not abate, and within a few years there was a steady drift to Euston, which rose to a great exodus culminating in the opening of the ten-floor Euston House by the Prince of Wales (Duke of Windsor) in February 1934. Similar problems bedevilled the other three groups.

LIST OF RAILWAY COMPANIES AMALGAMATED

L.M.S.

Arbroath and Forfar Railway Company
Brechin and Edzell District Railway Company
Caledonian Railway Company
Callander and Oban Railway Company
Cathcart District Railway Company
Charnwood Forest Railway Company
Cleator and Workington Junction Railway Company
Cockermouth, Keswick and Penrith Railway Company
Dearne Valley Railway Company
Dornoch Light Railway Company
Dundee and Newtyle Railway Company
Furness Railway Company
Glasgow and South Western Railway Company
Harborne Railway Company
Highland Railway Company
Killin Railway Company
Knott End Railway Company
Lanarkshire and Ayrshire Railway Company
Lancashire and Yorkshire Railway Company
Leek and Manifold Valley Light Railway Company
London and North Western Railway Company
Maryport and Carlisle Railway Company
Midland Railway Company
Mold and Denbigh Junction Railway Company
North and South Western Junction Railway Company
North London Railway Company
North Staffordshire Railway Company
Portpatrick and Wigtownshire Joint Committee
Shropshire Union Railways and Canal Company
Solway Junction Railway Company
Stratford-upon-Avon and Midland Junction Railway Company
Tottenham and Forest Gate Railway Company
Wick and Lybster Light Railway Company
Wirral Railway Company
Yorkshire Dales Railway (Skipton to Grassington) Company

L.N.E.R.

Brackenhill Light Railway Company
Colne Valley and Halstead Railway Company
East and West Yorkshire Union Railways Company
East Lincolnshire Railway Company
Edinburgh and Bathgate Railway Company
Forcett Railway Company
Forth and Clyde Junction Railway Company
Gifford and Garvald Railway Company
Great Central Railway Company
Great Eastern Railway Company
Great North of England, Clarence and Hartlepool Junction Railway Company
Great North of Scotland Railway Company
Great Northern Railway Company
Horncastle Railway Company
Hull and Barnsley Railway Company
Humber Commercial Railway and Dock Company
Kilsyth and Bonnybridge Railway Company
Lauder Light Railway Company
London and Blackwall Company
Mansfield Railway Company
Mid-Suffolk Light Railway Company
Newburgh and North Fife Railway Company
North British Railway Company
North Eastern Railway Company
North Lindsay Light Railway Company
Nottingham and Grantham Railway and Canal Company
Nottingham Joint Station Committee
Nottingham Suburban Railway Company
Seaforth and Sefton Junction Railway Company
Sheffield District Railway Company
South Yorkshire Junction Railway Company
Stamford and Essendine Railway Company
West Riding Railway Committee

S.R.

Bridgwater Railway Company
Brighton and Dyke Railway Company
Freshwater, Yarmouth and Newport (Isle of Wight) Railway Company

Halings Railways Company
Isle of Wight Central Railway Company
Isle of Wight Railway Company
Lee-on-Solent Railway Company
London and Greenwich Railway Company
London and South Western Railway Company
London, Brighton and South Coast Railway Company
London, Chatham and Dover Railway Company
Mid Kent Railway (Bromley to St. Mary Cray) Company
North Cornwall Railway Company
Plymouth and Dartmoor Railway Company
Plymouth, Devonport and South Western Junction Railway Company
Sidmouth Railway Company
South Eastern and Chatham Railway Companies Managing Committee
South Eastern Railway Company
Victoria Station and Pimlico Railway Company

G.W.R.
Alexandra (Newport and South Wales) Docks and Railway Company
Barry Railway Company
Brecon and Merthyr Tydfil Junction Railway Company
Burry Port and Gwendreath Valley Railway Company
Cambrian Railway Company
Cardiff Railway Company
Cleobury Mortimer and Ditton Priors Light Railway Company
Didcot, Newbury and Southampton Railway Company
Exeter Railway Company
Forest of Dean Central Railway Company
Great Western Railway Company
Gwendreath Valleys Railway Company
Lampeter, Aberayron and New Quay Light Railway Company
Liskeard and Looe Railway Company
Llanelly and Mynydd Mawr Railway Company
Mawddy Railway Company
Midland and South Western Junction Railway Company
Neath and Brecon Railway Company
Penarth Extension Railway Company
Penarth Harbour Dock and Railway Company
Port Talbot Railway and Docks Company
Princetown Railway Company
Rhondda and Swansea Bay Railway Company
Rhymney Railway Company
Ross and Monmouth Railway Company
South Wales Mineral Railway Company
Taff Vale Railway Company
Teign Valley Railway Company
Vale of Glamorgan Railway Company
Van Railway Company
Welshpool and Llanfair Light Railway Company
West Somerset Railway Company
Wrexham and Ellesmere Railway Company

It is easy to imagine the conglomeration of engines, carriages, wagons, signals and every kind of equipment and operating practice which the four group companies inherited in 1923. If the old railway companies were anything at all, they were aggressively independent. In the new climate, standardisation was the key word. But it was not easy. Engines and rolling stock built for the Midland, for example, during the past few years were quite different from those of the North Western, though both were now in the L.M. & S.R. network, and would have a working life of 30 or even 40 years. Little could be done about the recently built rolling stock; but all the main companies began to standardise in every possible way within their own territories, with the obvious advantages of economy and efficiency, and to build larger and more powerful locomotives. Wagon sizes were increased for better payloads and carriages lengthened.

An enormous internal reorganisation was needed to standardise all the rates, fares, charges and printed material that went with them. Another problem of standardisation that had to be faced, and which has had scant public attention, concerned the loading gauge. Profile of the loading gauge is basically the space through which the highest and widest vehicles on the track can pass, plus a safety margin. Bridges, tunnels, station buildings and other structures that cannot be moved, are the main limiting factors. Brunel, the Stephensons, Rastrick, Locke and the others certainly did not confer about the dimensions of their bridges and tunnels. It would have saved trouble if they had. Early engineers of individual railways, excepting perhaps George Stephenson, hardly thought of a nationally connected network; they had enough troubles of their own. But when the expanding railways operated their vehicles on other companies' lines, the loading gauge naturally attracted more attention. After the amalgamation, the four companies began to build rolling stock that could be used on the greatest number of their own and other lines. Until new stock was built, vehicles had to be restricted to certain routes, and printed booklets

A chef in the kitchen of a restaurant car early in the century. Eventually British Railways operated almost as many restaurant and buffet cars services as the whole of Western Europe. (*W.P.L.*)

were supplied to staff at every level containing full details.

Passenger rolling stock was eventually confirmed at a height of about 12½ ft. above rail level, and 9¼ ft. in width; dimensions that make an interesting comparison with the rail gauge of 4 ft. 8½ ins. (With the same rail gauge, in America the height is about 15½ ft.; in Russia, 17½ ft. on a 5 ft. gauge; and in South Africa, 13½ ft. high and 10 ft. wide on a 3½ ft. gauge.)

ROAD COMPETITION – A REALITY

Perhaps railway managers were too absorbed in making their new systems work to realise fully the enormous technical progress that had been made by the motor vehicle under the pressures of war; and though the horse still remained supreme and had been seen in thousands on the battlefields of Europe hauling cannon, guns, men and materials, each year more motor lorries appeared. During hostilities, some 80,000 servicemen had had experience with motor transport for the first time, both in driving and maintenance. After the war the Government disposed of about 60,000 vehicles at very low prices. They were snapped up by ex-servicemen who used their war gratuities and personal savings to start one-lorry haulage businesses; traders bought them to carry their own goods, and road haulage companies with fleets of vehicles went into the transport business.

Unhindered by the restrictive statutory measures that faced the railways, the new hauliers quickly captured a growing volume of former railway business. Most of the vehicles still had solid tyre wheels, but the pneumatic tyre, invented as early as 1888 by a Scottish veterinary surgeon named John Dunlop (1840–1921) and used first for bicycles, advanced the progress of lorries, buses and cars to new levels of speed and efficiency. Petrol in the 1920s was 1*s*. 6*d*. (7½p) a gallon.

Throughout the war the Government had refused to allow the railways to increase their goods rates, despite rising operating costs. In 1920, with Government approval, they raised these rates by an average of some 120 per cent, which increase sent traders scurrying to the private haulier, or direct to the motor vehicle dealer. All the railways became seriously disturbed by the visible inroads made into their goods and passenger business by the motor vehicle. The following table (figures rounded off) shows the dramatic increase in road traffic:

Year	*Private cars*	*Goods vehicles*
1904	9,000	4,000
1914	132,000	82,000
1919	110,000	62,000
1920	187,000	101,000
1921	243,000	128,000
1922	315,000	151,000

Within a decade the transport scene had changed out of all recognition as the road hauliers consolidated their newly-seized gains.

INDUSTRIAL UNREST AND THE TRADE UNIONS

Higher wage costs because of the additional staff required to meet the eight-hour day were eating into the economies which the new groups were hoping to make in their new organisations. Industrial unrest resulted in numerous strikes throughout industry. They continued after Lloyd George had resigned in 1922, culminating in one of the worst strikes in Britain's history – the general strike of 4th May 1926. Most of the railways shut down, skeleton services being operated by volunteers. On visiting his main line terminus Felix Pole, general manager of the Great Western, added in his report: "Paddington station was dead."

The strike officially ended on 10th May, but the men drifted back slowly. Coal deliveries, vital to the railways, were delayed for months afterwards. During the strike, an official statement was issued: "His Majesty's Government have no power to compel employers to take back every man who has been on strike." Railway business fell off so much that many men were not allowed back to work for months. Some railwaymen who refused to strike were "sent to Coventry" by their mates for a year or more.

Railway managements stubbornly and desperately opposed the railway trade unions, even though local departmental committees and sectional councils, composed of representatives of both sides, had been set up since 1922.

HOUSES FOR RAILWAYMEN

Despite their antipathy to trade unionism, some of the old railway companies were benevolent employers; but a firmer discipline evolved under the new groups. Even so, they built numerous houses for their staff, and rows of terrace houses were a common sight in railway towns. Staff housing societies were formed by the companies, who advanced up to 90 per cent of the cost of purchase, and arranged mortgage rates of about 4½ or 5 per cent for railwaymen who wished to buy. Otherwise, low rentals were arranged. Within a few years in the 1920s, the Great Western alone had advanced over £1,000,000 for staff purchases, and had invested large capital sums for the purpose, with the authority of an Act of Parliament.

Industrial unrest notwithstanding, competition from the road motor vehicle was tackled by the railways on three fronts: they invested in their own lorries and buses, improved railway services, and campaigned for fairer competitive conditions. In 1930 the Road Transport Act was passed. One section prevented coach operators from running a new coach service without first applying to the appropriate authority and allowing the railway companies to oppose the applications in the new traffic courts. Sometimes they won, sometimes they lost. Restrictions were imposed on the operation of road haulage vehicles in the Road and Rail Traffic Act of 1933 when A, B and C licences came into use, limiting carriers to specific work, and allowing the railways to make objections in the courts. The railways continued in their campaign for a "square deal" in other spheres, notably rates, and "common carrier" obligations where they insisted they stood at an unfair disadvantage. But road conveyance of passengers and goods had many natural advantages which traders and travellers insisted on exploiting.

In that period, the railways secured substantial financial holdings in such groups as the British Electric Traction, Thomas Tilling and the Scottish Motor Traction companies, presumably on the principal "if you can't beat 'em, join 'em."

During the years of depression in the 1920s and early 1930s, with one to two million unemployed, and endless queues forming at local authority soup kitchens for bare sustenance, railway porters and labourers were earning about £2 a week; at least railwaymen had some security, but the poorer ones often had to sell their uniforms to buy food. The world slump in trade hit Britain the hardest around 1931 during the premiership of Ramsay MacDonald, the Labour Party leader; and in 1931 the unemployed rose to about 2,500,000. So the times were not particularly propitious for dazzling railway performance.

Early in 1929, letters in newspapers complaining about the railways were frequent, sparked off by an article in *The Times* on 1st December:

"It is not easy to find a reason, other than inertia, for failure of most of our railways to improve the speed of passenger trains in the last quarter of a century . . . What the Great Western Railway can do many times a day all through the

A motor omnibus fitted with adjustable wheels to travel by rail or road, seen in 1931 at Redbourne, Harpenden and Hemel Hempstead Branch, Hertfordshire: a branch line experiment to cut costs. (Photo: British Rail)

A famous train, the Royal Scot, *northbound from Euston to Glasgow, steaming through Lune Gorge in Lake District country in 1936. It is headed by 4–6–2 No. 6203 L.M.S. This regular morning train was inaugurated, but unnamed, in 1848 by the London & North Western Railway.* (*Photo: British Rail*)

year should be possible on some of the other lines."

In 1929, because of the harsh economic situation and falling railway revenues, railwaymen, from porters to directors, had to accept a temporary reduction in wages of 2½ per cent. The railway companies had sought 5 per cent, to which the trade unions would not agree.

NAMED TRAINS

Even before the depression, the railways had started to give individual names to some of their best trains on main routes, and the term "crack express" gained currency. One of them, the L.M.S.R. *Royal Scot*, leaving Euston for Glasgow at 10 a.m., first ran on 15th February 1848 when the West Coast route was completed, though it was not officially named, complete with train boards, until 1927. It still runs today, but with a new departure time.

Its great competitor for the Scottish business was the L.N.E.R. *Flying Scotsman* from King's Cross to Edinburgh, which first ran as a through train in June 1862, its title becoming official much later. The Company also named their prime service from Liverpool Street to Harwich Parkeston Quay for the Hook of Holland boat service the *Hook Continental* which its predecessors, the Great Eastern Railway, instituted in 1904.

On the Great Western Railway, the most famous train was the *Cheltenham Spa Express*, popularly known as the *Cheltenham Flyer*, its official title dating from 1923. In 1929, it was timed to cover the 77·3 miles from Swindon to Paddington in 70 minutes, then the fastest scheduled run in the world. Its best recorded run, averaging 81·7 m.p.h., was made on 6th June 1932.

Best known train on the Southern Railway was the *Brighton Belle* on the Victoria–Brighton line. It started life on 5th February 1908 as the *Southern Belle* of the London Brighton & South Coast Railway, first operating as an electric train on 1st January 1933. Highly popular among showbusiness people, it made its last nostalgic journey on 30th April 1972.

The other best known train on the Southern Railway was the *Golden Arrow*, linking with British Railways ships sailing between Dover and Calais and providing a fast service between

London and Paris. Connection was made at Calais with the French version, the *Fleche d'Or*. For many years the train, its specially designed platform entrance, and a cocktail bar of the same name, formed part of the Continental scene at Victoria station. It departed every day, including Sundays, at 10 a.m.

Employees of the Southern Railway were invited in a competition to find a name for the 11 a.m. express from Waterloo serving Devon and Cornwall, the winning name being *Atlantic Coast Express*. The train, which made its inaugural run on 19th July 1926, was commonly known among railwaymen as *The Ace*.

Scores of other top-flight trains were given individual names conferring prestige and glamour; and with the growing use by the railways of the new techniques in public relations and publicity, each naming ceremony was planned to create the widest possible public interest.

Only a handful of trains carry individual names today; and the 1920s and 1930s stand out as a "period piece" in the railway saga, before being overwhelmed by war-time austerity operations.

A collection of other historic named trains follows:

Aberdonian
Brighton Limited
Cambrian Coast Express
City Limited
Comet
Cornish Riviera
Coronation
Coronation Scot
Devonian
Eastbourne Sunday Limited
Eastern Belle Pullman
Elizabethan
Flying Welshman
Folkestone Car Train
Further North Express
Granite City
Granville Express
Hebridean
Irish Mail
Irishman
John o' Groat
Lakes Express
Lancastrian
Lewisman
Mancunian
Manxman
Master Cutler
Mid-Day Scot
Norfolk Coast Express
Norfolkman
Northern Belle
North Star
Ocean Mail
Orcadian
Palatine
Peak Express
Queen of Scots
Red Dragon
Scandinavian
Scarborough Flyer
Sheffield Pullman
Silver Jubilee
South Devon
South Yorkshireman
Sunny South Express
Thames-Clyde Express
Thames-Forth Express
Thanet Belle
Torbay Pullman
Tynesider
Ulster Express
West Riding
White Rose
Yorkshireman

HIGHER SPEEDS

Trying though the conditions were during the 1920s and 1930s, the railway companies never ceased in their efforts to make Britain's railways the best in the world. In 1924, train ferries were introduced on the Harwich–Zeebrugge route, and 12 years later on the Dover–Dunkirk route to convey specially designed sleeping cars direct between London and Paris. The first all-steel trains went into service in 1928: the two *Queen of Scots* Pullmans on the L.N.E.R. London–Edinburgh–Glasgow route. The run between King's Cross and Edinburgh was the longest non-stop journey in the world. Keeping pace with modern thinking, sleeping cars for third class passengers were introduced for the first time in 1928 on three railways: the London Midland & Scottish, London & North Eastern, and Great Western.

Streamlined trains came on the scene, the first being run by the L. & N.E.R. on the London–Newcastle route in 1935. Called the *Silver Jubilee* (King George V had reigned for 25 years), the train on a trial run averaged 100 m.p.h. for 43 miles, reaching 112½ m.p.h. at two places. Not to be out-done, the L.M. & S.R. in 1937 put on a streamlined express, the *Coronation Scot* between London and Glasgow, a trial run reaching 114 m.p.h. approaching Crewe.

The greatest triumph was a speed of 126 m.p.h. in 1938, achieved near Peterborough by the London & North Eastern 4–6–2 locomotive *Mallard*, which is still preserved. The train of seven coaches weighed 240 tons. It created a record for speed for a steam train in Britain, and almost certainly in the world. By then, about a hundred trains were running at start-to-stop speeds of 60 miles an hour or more.

Higher speeds were being steadily built up for both passenger and freight trains on all the main lines, made possible by technical improvements to locomotives and rolling stock, tracks, signalling, area traffic control centres, and general scientific research. The design and upholstery of third class carriages was of a good standard, certainly much higher than those on Continental railways where wooden seats were common, even on long distance trains. Services in the London suburban area were being improved by more electrification, resulting from a Government credit scheme of £35,000,000 announced in 1935, and later increased to £45,000,000.

Freight rolling stock was improved, goods depots were rebuilt and marshalling yards extended. Sorting sidings at Toton, near Nottingham, were mechanised on the "down" side in 1939, the "up" side having to wait until 1952. More power signalling was introduced in the 1930s, notably at Paddington (368 levers), Bristol (720 levers) and Cardiff (527 levers). One of the first power boxes, with 38 levers, had been put into operation at Didcot as early as 1903. Motors for operating rail junction points came into increasing use.

Even *The Times* could not now reasonably claim that the railway companies were not trying. In fact, Britain's most influential newspaper on at least a dozen occasions during 1934 reported fully the plans and progress of Railway Air Services Ltd., as main line railways combined to join the competition for inland air travel which was already hitting train services. Aviation progress had been rapid following the pioneer work, during the First World War, of the Royal Flying Corps (R.F.C., R.A.F. from 1918), and the great flights of Charles Lindbergh, Jim Mollison and his wife Amy Johnson, and J. N. Boothman, who had won the Schneider Trophy for Britain in 1931. Railway aircraft flew to the West Country, the Channel Islands, Scotland, Northern Ireland and Eire, and Railway Air Services Ltd. was beginning to make its mark; but its future was to be short.

THE SECOND WORLD WAR

The approaching war-clouds were clearer on the horizon in the late 1930s than they had been twenty-five years previously, and at least this time there was some opportunity for the railways to prepare. In 1937 the general managers of the railway companies approached the Ministry of Transport for contingency discussions; but the Government did not clearly state its intentions until September 1938, when the fate of Czechoslovakia hung in the balance. An Order was signed on 24th September 1938 by which the Minister of Transport appointed a Railway Executive Committee to co-ordinate and direct the railways and London Transport: in effect, State control. Sir Ralph Wedgwood, former chief general manager, L.N.E.R., was the first R.E.C. chairman.

In the early hours of 1st September 1939 Germany invaded Poland; on the 3rd Prime Minister Neville Chamberlain, his policy of appeasement in ruins, announced the declaration of war by Britain and France against Hitler's Germany.

Several months previously, detailed plans had been made for mass civilian evacuation from London. A railway publication described the important role played by the railways and London Transport which started in July and ended on

Pride of the L.M.S., a Royal Scot type 4–6–0, The Northamptonshire Regiment, *built in 1927. (Photo: British Rail)*

The passenger aircraft Neptune, *a de Havilland D.H.86B, operated by Railway Air Services Ltd., a company formed by the railways in 1934 to set up their own internal airline business; photographed at Croydon. (Photo: British Rail)*

8th September: "Despite all the other demands made on them at that time, 2,345 extra trains were run during the period to carry women and children to safety in the North, the Midlands and the West Country. Of these extra trains, nearly a fifth conveyed over 750,000 'official' and 'semi-official' evacuees, including mothers, children, the aged, infirm and invalids. The remaining trains were provided for the hundreds of thousands of people who left London of their own accord.

"Over and above this movement, extensive feeder services had to be organised both to London and within the Metropolitan area. These called for a further 424 trains, the bulk of which were operated by London Transport, and the running of 4,797 special buses and 363 trams. And while all this was going on, the railways brought into London from various parts of the country, 65,800 Anderson and Morrison shelters." The shelters were mainly for erection in peoples' back gardens. Railwaymen of all grades worked long hours and at weekends to see this job through, as indeed they did throughout the war years.

Ambulance Trains

The day before Neville Chamberlain declared war, orders came to the railways to go ahead in fitting out the first 12 ambulance trains, as part of a possible fleet of 34 for which designs had been prepared several months earlier: eight for use in Britain and four overseas. They were handed over to the military authorities. Home trains included accommodation for resident doctors and nurses; ward cars for stretcher, sitting and mental cases; a kitchen car, and space for medical stores. All told, 925 vehicles were converted for ambulance trains, in workshops at Swindon, Derby, Wolverton, Doncaster, York, Eastleigh and Lancing. Early in the war years, nearly 150 carriages were lost in France. Between 6th June 1944 – D-Day – and 8th May 1945 – V.E. Day, the date of victory in Europe – ambulance trains made over 1,800 journeys in Britain. Large numbers of other vehicles and locomotives were shipped to Europe from time to time as the war progressed.

As war began, passenger services were severely curtailed, including seat reservations, sleeping cars, restaurant cars, and reduced fares. In 1941, first class travel in the London area was abolished. Later, to discourage non-essential travel, a campaign was launched with the slogan: "Is Your Journey Really Necessary?" a contrast to pre-war posters such as "Come to Scarborough – It's So Bracing!"

War Time Financing

For the period of Government control of the railway companies, highly complicated financial arrangements were made, naturally of great interest to the shareholders. Simplified, they meant that the Government would guarantee a net revenue of £40,000,000 a year. The figure had been calculated from the net revenue of 1935/6/7, omitting the poor financial year of 1938. In the event, revenues soared, and the allocation of costs and revenues had to be left until the end of hostilities.

Worsening the war-time transport conditions, the four main line companies had to release large numbers of their staff for national service, as shown in the table:

	men	*women*	*total*
His Majesty's Forces	98,603	3,129	101,732
Full time Civil Defence	1,181	397	1,578
Mercantile Marine (Merchant Navy)	439		439
Coal mining	861		861
Essential industries	4,222	680	4,902
	105,306	4,206	109,512

Most of the large railway workshops, in which engines, carriages, wagons and other heavy equipment were built and overhauled, were turned over to a proportion of war-time equipment manufacture, and shift working increased. Articles produced included tanks, boats, aircraft components, midget submarine superstructures, and periscope parts. At some workshops, nearly a third of the work consisted of war equipment. At Eastleigh, Hants, 1,475 conversion sets were made for converting Blenheim bombers into fighters; Derby handled ten pairs of aeroplane wings a week for a variety of aircraft such as Typhoons, Tempests and Rocs. Components were produced at Wolverton, Doncaster, York, and Cowlairs (Glasgow). Repair and parts work was handled for Hampden bombers, Lancasters and Whitleys; and about 150 Spitfires were repaired at the Barassie wagon shop in Scotland. Nearly 60,000 high explosive bombs – 250 lb. to 4,000 lb. – were produced in Great Western workshops at Swindon, Worcester, Tyseley, Oswestry, Caerphilly and Newton Abbot. These works, and others at Slough, Swansea, Neath and Danygraig manufactured about 250,000 bomb components.

The number of special trains worked by the railway companies on behalf of the Government, September 1939 to 11th August 1945, was as follows:

passenger	258,624
freight	279,935
total	538,559

The heaviest year was 1944, when the special trains totalled 178,362.

Air Raid Precautions

A Government system for warning the public that enemy aircraft were approaching was set up through the Post Office and disseminated by the railways on their own internal telephone networks. Railway lights had to be extinguished and trains slowed down or stopped. The table shows the number of "red" warnings received in two severely hit areas:

	Central London area	*Folkestone district*
1939	3	1
1940	414	530
1941	156	864
1942	25	606
1943	95	475
1944	511	162
1945	23	5
	1,227	2,643

Aberdeen and Forfar were the last places to receive warnings – on 30th April 1945 – two days before the system was ended.

In the early part of the war, everyone carried a gas mask in the firm expectation of enemy gas attacks which happily never came; larger ones provided for babies were pumped by their mothers, whether at home or in a pram in the street. Railwaymen carried masks day and night with other necessary equipment, such as electric torch or oil-filled handlamp, whistle and rule book.

The Home Guard

When Britain was threatened by invasion in 1940, the Government appealed to all fit men to form the Local Defence Volunteer Corps (L.D.V.). About 99,000 men from the railways and London Transport immediately joined; this figure rose to some 120,000 when the Corps was later renamed the Home Guard, and L.D.V. armlets were exchanged for khaki uniforms. Many were veterans of the First World War and served well as instructors for raw recruits. Railway properties guarded included vulnerable areas such as stations, bridges, tunnels, junctions, engine sheds and other places which could be sabotaged. Thirty-seven railway Home Guard men received honours: C.B.E., O.B.E., M.B.E., B.E.M. and two George Medals; 23 men lost their lives through enemy action while on Home Guard duty.

Railwaymen also took up fire-watching duties, following the Fire Prevention (Business Premises) Orders of January and September 1941, which made employees in industry responsible for fire-watching and fire-fighting as an additional support to the National Fire Service. Over 300,000 railway men and women took their share in off-duty time, and were well equipped by training and apparatus to meet any emergency.

Austerity Locomotives

To help the depleted locomotive stock, a War Department engine, WD 2–8–0, was designed in conjunction with the North British Locomotive Company using "auterity" techniques to simplify maintenance and the exchange of components. They began to be turned out by the North British and the Vulcan Foundry in 1943; 450 were lent to the railways before being shipped overseas from October 1944. Upwards of 500 more did service on the L.N.E.R. tracks before being transferred to War Department depots. A 2–10–0 was ordered by the Ministry of Supply, designed for hauling slow, heavy trains over difficult routes. A hundred of them "ran in" on both L.N.E.R. and L.M.S.R. routes. The Americans also built 2–8–0 locomotives for U.S.A. army use on European railways, but arranged for 398 of them to be used in Britain in 1943 until they were needed overseas; they came into Britain at Cardiff, Birkenhead, Manchester, Hull, Glasgow and London Docks. British railwaymen found them an interesting comparison with their own, for they exposed to view – as did European engines – piping, running gear and stays; and they had bar-type frames and a high running board so that the sand boxes on top of the boiler barrel could be easily reached.

When victory was in sight, Winston Churchill, the Prime Minister, wrote to the Railway Executive Committee:

"I should like to take the opportunity of expressing to the railway managements and to every railway employee the Nation's thanks for the highly efficient manner in which they have met every demand made upon them during the last four years of our desperate struggle with Nazi Germany.

"Throughout the period of the heavy German air raids on this country, the arteries of the Nation – the railways – with their extensive dock undertakings, were subjected to intensive attacks. Yet the grim determination, unwavering courage, and constant resourcefulness of the railwaymen of all ranks have enabled the results of the damage to be overcome very speedily, and communications restored without delay. Thus, in spite of every enemy effort, the traffic has been kept moving, and the great flow of munitions proceeds.

"Results such as the railways have achieved are only won by blood and sweat, and on behalf of the Nation I express gratitude to every railwayman who has participated in this great transport effort which is contributing so largely towards final victory."

Damage by Enemy Action

At strategic centres emergency repair trains were fitted out, ready to rush to any scene of damage from enemy action; they could carry up to 90 men with tools and equipment. Thousands of incidents were recorded throughout the railways. A few examples are given: at Twerton near Bath, the line was hit in nine places in two air raids on successive nights. A high explosive bomb struck a bridge at East Acton which carried the Central London Railway and two goods lines. On 20th December 1940, a large bomb destroyed part of the viaduct which carried two steam and two electric lines into Exchange station at Liverpool. Five bombs fell on St. Pancras station on 10th May 1941, a 1,000-pounder penetrating the foundations and exploding deep down in the clay beneath; the station was put completely out of action for a week and partly until 7th June.

Main lines out of Marylebone were blocked when, on 26th September 1940, a bomb penetrated so deeply as to demolish about 35 yards of the St. John's Wood tunnel roof. In a second raid only five nights later a bomb exploded only a quarter of a mile away at the tunnel mouth. Damage was so extensive that repairs were not finally completed until August 1941.

Just before midnight on 19th April 1941, a parachute mine demolished the 100 ft. span steel girder bridge carrying four electrified lines and four sidings over Southwark Street, Blackfriars, in the City of London. It was a busy route serving the south-east suburbs and was re-opened in stages between 1st May and 29th June. Permanent reconstruction of this large bridge began in January 1942 and was finished in December.

A daylight raid by enemy aircraft on 25th May 1943 on the Brighton station area damaged a nearby viaduct and halted train services east from Brighton. Most of the reconstruction was completed within four months.

All the main railway companies, and London Underground, were badly hit by the flying bombs, Hitler's "secret weapons". They struck intermittently, day and night, from the middle of June 1944 to the end of August. Over 1,000 "incidents" were recorded; but because of the density of lines in the south-east, the Southern Railway suffered as much as all the others put together. The Great Western Railway suffered the least from aerial bombardments.

One of the first German pilotless aircraft (flying bombs), known as "doodle-bugs" or "buzz-bombs", in the small hours of 13th June, seriously damaged a bridge at Coborn Road, L.N.E.R., carrying both main and local line trains. A temporary bridge for the main lines had been erected within two days.

Much credit was earned by the railway engineering departments throughout the war as breakdown trains, cranes, equipment and gangs of men who often worked round the clock, in all weathers, rushed to the scene of devastation to get trains moving again.

Losses from Enemy Action

Throughout the war, 9,239 incidents of damage and delay were recorded by the railways, well over half of them serious. Much rolling stock was destroyed or damaged:

	locomotives	*passenger vehicles*	*freight vehicles*
destroyed	8	637	3,321
damaged	484	13,487	20,294

The worst year by far was 1940. Unexploded bombs, the source of anxious suspense, accounted for 1,165 occasions of railway interruption. The total number of "enemy incidents" that affected railway operations for one week or more numbered 909.

Gallantry in Service

Railwaymen and railway families mourned the loss of 3,562 comrades who had served on the battlefield in all services and in all theatres of war. Over 400 serving men received honours, and 200 were mentioned in despatches. On the home front many suffered death and injury in the performance of their daily duties, or while serving with the Home Guard or as fire-watchers. Among the many senior railway managers who lost their lives either in battle or in civilian occupations was Lord (Josiah) Stamp, President of the London Midland & Scottish Railway, who died when his home was bombed in an air raid in April 1940.

Up to 1st January 1946, 402 railway employees of every grade from vice president and chief engineer to girl telephone operator (12 of the recipients were women), station master and porter, had received awards including the George Cross, George Medal, C.B.E., O.B.E., M.B.E., and B.E.M. Of this total 276 were honours awarded for railway work, and 126 for gallantry on the railways. In addition, 81 awards were made to railway staff employed on requisitioned railway steamers. Countless others carried on with their daily tasks in the worst operating conditions they had ever known, to maintain vital supply lines and to keep Britain on the move until final victory was won.

When V.E.-Day and V.J.-Day brought the long agony to an end, the railways worked quickly to get back to normal. Restaurant car services resumed, sleeping cars were re-instated, and the travelling post offices from London to Aberdeen and Penzance went back to work. Plans were made to restore some "named" trains. The companies stated that they were "determined to regain and surpass their peacetime standards of public service. Their intention is to equip their properties and train their staffs so as to enable the finest railway service in the world to be offered to the British public. That, in a nut-shell, is their post-war plan."

Staff training was an urgent problem, for about two-fifths of the staff were temporary and their competence was well below pre-war standards. As had happened after the First World War, railwaymen from low grades who had discovered hidden qualities in themselves while serving with H.M. Forces and had risen to middle and high rank, returned to the railways in more responsible positions. Finance was the other major problem: the railways had to take their turn in the industrial queue for the enormous capital sums required by the targets they had set themselves.

POST-WAR

In the general election of 1945, a Labour Government under Clement Attlee was returned to power and the railways for the first time in their history became totally embroiled in politics. That year, the four railway companies declared:

"Whilst a discourse upon the pros and cons of private versus public or national control and ownership is not appropriate here, this can at least be truly said – thanks alone to the constant pursuit of the courageous and enlightened policy of modernisation and improvement before the war, the railway companies, with the splendid tradition of their staffs behind them, were able to give the nation and its allies a machine of supreme national and strategic importance when the call came in 1939 and to sustain and operate it throughout the long years since then."

In 1946, a Bill was presented to Parliament proposing that the inland transport system should become publicly owned; and as a portent of technical changes to come, the London Midland & Scottish Railway in 1947 built a diesel-electric locomotive.

Chapter 8

State Ownership: A New Phase

A wintry dawn at Taplow, near Maidenhead, Western Region, in January 1962. (Photo: British Rail)

AT the beginning of 1948 the railways of Britain, now in their 123rd year, entered a new phase in their chequered history: they were "nationalised", and became the property of the State. This momentous and virtually irrevocable change was made by Parliament on behalf of a democratic nation. State ownership was carried through by the first post-war Labour Government under Prime Minister Clement (later Earl) Attlee. (Incidentally, his son Martin, Lord Attlee, nearly a quarter of a century later, became a public relations executive for the Southern Region of British Rail.)

State ownership of some sectors of industry had formed part of the political mandate which put Attlee's Party into power, to the great personal disappointment of the rejected war-time Prime Minister Winston Churchill, who, however, returned to rule another day (1951–55), retiring at the age of 81. Before the 1923 amalgamations, he himself had campaigned for State ownership of the railways, a system already operating in most other major countries. So, too, had Prime Minister David Lloyd George in 1918. The Government of 1844 under Sir Robert Peel had obtained authority to purchase railway companies in specific circumstances, an option never taken up. In this century, the railways had been taken over by the Government "for the duration" of two World Wars in the national interest: emergency and expediency then, reality and permanence now.

Although the Second World War had ended in 1945, the railways had still remained subject to certain measures of control which the Minister of Transport had exercised through the Railway Executive Committee; this facilitated State takeover. Statutory authority for the gigantic task of transferring the assets was contained in the Transport Act, 1947. Financial interests already held by the railway companies in other forms of transport added to the complexity. To understand fully its 176 pages of statutory provisions and schedules, necessarily couched in Parliamentary phraseology, needed a trained legal mind steeped in public transport affairs.

The Act repealed, superseded or absorbed most of the previous railway statutes relevant to the properties, services and business involved. It also included other organisations. In a nutshell, it meant transferring into public ownership the principal forms of inland transport: railways, with their hotels and ships; docks, inland waterways, road haulage, coach and bus undertakings; and absorbing London Transport rail and services into a single entity. Former shareholders became the owners of a new issue of British Transport Redeemable Stock which carried a fixed rate of interest.

A new body – the British Transport Commission – was created to run the conglomerate of State transport. By far the largest single part consisted of the four main line railway groups: London Midland & Scottish Railway, London & North Eastern Railway, Great Western Railway, and Southern Railway; joint lines were included.

Integration of the many separate undertakings into one organisation was the clear objective of the Act, and for this purpose, a new public authority was created:

"An Act to provide for the establishment of a British Transport Commission [BTC] concerned with transport and certain other related matters, to specify their powers and duties, to provide for the transfer to them of undertakings, parts of undertakings, property, rights, obligations and liabilities, to amend the law relating to transport, inland waterways, harbours and port facilities, to make certain consequential provision as to pensions and gratuities in the case of certain persons who become officers of the Minister of Transport, and for purposes connected with the matters aforesaid – 6th August 1947.

"Be it enacted by the King's most Excellent Majesty [George VI], by and with the advice and consent of the Lords Spiritual and Temporal, and Commons, in this present Parliament assembled and by the authority of the same . . ."

In selecting members for the Commission, the Minister had to satisfy himself that such a person "will have no such financial or other interest as is likely to affect prejudicially the discharge by him of his functions . . ."

Meanwhile, as new "think-tank" executives were formulating directives on new notepaper, the trains still continued to run. What would the effect of nationalisation be on the life of the ordinary railwayman and on his numerous customers? Only time would tell as the new policy was unfolded stage by stage.

A phrase in the Transport Act 1947, Part I, Section 3, clause (4) was contentiously debated beforehand in parliamentary committees and long afterwards in the Houses of Commons and Lords. Nationalised transport should pay its way. Clause (4) gives chapter and verse: "All the businesses carried on by the Commission, whether or not arising from undertakings or parts of undertakings vested in them by or under any provision of this Act, shall form one undertaking, and the Commission shall so conduct that undertaking and, subject to the provisions of this Act, levy such fares, rates, tolls, dues and other charges, as to secure that the revenue of the Commission is not less than sufficient for making provision for the meeting of charges properly chargeable to revenue, taking one year with another."

Many debating attempts were made to define clearly how many years should be considered in "taking one year with another." Taking railways alone, few large networks anywhere in the world, whether privately or publicly owned, were showing an overall profit. The sentiment was noble; but where was the evidence that the great railway system of Britain, legacy of the Stephensons and Brunel, could do better? Certainly railway unification should produce economies by standardisation of assets and operations, but two urgent problems loomed.

First, the railways still suffered from the wear and tear of the Second World War, the lack of maintenance and investment, and from having to manage with rolling stock that was already old and worn out. Second, there was the task of welding together the separate parts of the former group companies. A strong element of public accountability, the subject of much political argument, had been built into the general policy.

Under the control of the Commission were separate management bodies for the other inland transport services taken over. "There shall be public authorities known as Executives," states the Act, "to assist the Commission in the discharge of their functions in the manner specified in this section . . . there shall be executives known respectively as the Railway Executive, the Docks and Inland Waterways Executive, the Road Transport Executive, and the London Transport Executive and, from an appointed day, an Executive known as the Hotels Executive."

The Hotels Executive was formed on 1st July 1948 to be responsible for the 55 railway hotels (ten of which were closed), and train and station catering. At a later stage, road passenger and road haulage operations had their own separate managements – Road Passenger Executive and Road Haulage Executive, the latter trading as British Road Services.

Docks acquired were mainly former railway-owned docks and port facilities, including those at Hull, South Wales, Southampton, Holyhead, Barrow-in-Furness, the Hartlepools, Grimsby, Goole, King's Lynn and Grangemouth (Scotland); together they represented about one third of Britain's total port facilities. The transport services on canals and navigable rivers were also included. Under the Act, Transport users' consultative committees were formed, to represent the interest of users of any of the services.

The New Railway Managers

Individual members of the several Executives were appointed by the Minister after consultation with the Commission. Qualifications required were broadly similar to those for members of the Commission. Most members of the new Railway Executive had been in the management of the former railway companies. The first chairman was Sir Eustace Missenden, O.B.E., formerly general manager of the Southern Railway Company. His fellow members were:

Full-time Members:

- Mr. W. P. Allen, C.B.E. – formerly General Secretary, Associated Society of Locomotive Engineers & Firemen (ASLEF)
- Mr. V. M. Barrington-Ward – formerly Divisional General Manager, Southern Area, London & North Eastern Railway
- Mr. David Blee – formerly Chief Goods Manager, Great Western Railway
- Mr. R. A. Riddles, C.B.E. – formerly Vice-President of the Executive, London Midland & Scottish Railway
- Mr. J. C. L. Train, M.C. M.Inst.C.E. – formerly Chief Engineer, London & North Eastern Railway
- General Sir William J. Slim G.B.E., K.C.B., D.S.O., M.C. (Slim resigned on 1st November 1948 to become Chief of the Imperial General Staff, and was succeeded by General Sir G. Daril Watson).

Part-time Members: Sir Wilfrid Ayre and Mr. C. Nevile

"The Railway Executive," states the first annual report of the B.T.C., "has the status of a public authority and deals with the public, is the employer of the staff, and the body which enters into contracts and sues, or is sued, in the courts of law."

It was stated that the system must provide for the needs of the public, for agriculture, commerce and industry; that it must be reliable, speedy and safe; sufficient means should cover peak loads, seasonal demands and special occasions. Where regular goods services of different kinds were provided between the same points, any customer must be allowed free choice. This statutory requirement was expected to encourage competition, for example between rail and road, on a particular route.

UNIFYING THE FOUR MAIN GROUPS

Clearly, the railways of Britain, for the first time in their history, were not on their own; they had to bow to the statutory requirements of an integrated inland transport service. Inevitably there would be clashes between opposing interests of road and rail in the business of carrying both passengers and freight.

Britain's railways now had both feet in the jungle of party politics. For the first time, political decisions were to be paramount in railway managing, to replace the comparatively independent policy-making enjoyed by the former railway companies. It had been generally accepted, however, that with the fading fortunes of the old railway companies because of motor vehicle competition, with the prospects for internal air lines, and finally the serious war-time damage to the railways, the old companies could never have survided without enormous financial assistance from the Government. Inevitably, strings would be attached. State money had been infused in the railways in the 1930s to help them to modernise: a portent of the times. Whether the railways had been nationalised or not, independent company management and self-financing had clearly had its day.

Meanwhile, the function of the new Railway Executive was to integrate the four main-line companies into one railway, as well as to take into account "the general duty of the Commission to secure the provision of an efficient, adequate, economical and properly integrated system of public inland transport and port facilities for passengers and goods . . ."

Under the new railway regime, six new geographical "regions" were formed as follows:

Title of New Region	*New Territory*
London Midland	Former L.M.S.R. in England and Wales
Eastern	Former southern area of L.N.E.R., Doncaster and Leeds to London
North Eastern	Former north eastern area of L.N.E.R., Doncaster and Leeds to Berwick
Scottish	Former L.M.S.R. and L.N.E.R. lines in Scotland
Southern	Former S.R.
Western	Former G.W.R.

Five of the new regions were geographically little disturbed; Scottish Region consisted of two former powerful companies that had been commercial "enemies" throughout their stormy history. Competition had been highlighted by the famous "Races to the North" towards the end of the last century; and again in the 1930s when the

L.N.E.R. steam locomotive *Mallard* won with its world record speed for steam, and the L.M.S.R. achieved some outstanding speeds. Time alone, with old railwaymen retiring and new people joining the service, would blur the old company loyalties which had been built up from the days when careers in the railway lasted up to fifty years.

A certain amount of regional identity was preserved by a number of techniques. Though the original coats of arms and other insignia which had adorned rolling stock, and the printed material and various visual signs of the old companies were abandoned in favour of a new British Railways totem, a certain old-time flavour was retained by the use of different standard colours for the six regions:

Eastern	dark blue
London Midland	maroon
North Eastern	orange
Scottish	light blue
Southern	dark green
Western	chocolate

The Western Region had to make do with chocolate instead of the traditional chocolate-and-cream, long admired on West Country trains.

Members of the Railway Executive, and their management teams down the line were acutely conscious of the old loyalties as they set about their task of unification. A vast programme lay before them. Eighty years earlier, George Hudson, the Railway King, villain though he turned out to be, would have been highly gratified to see the railways unified under one central control; although his philosophy had emphatically not envisaged State ownership, but a gigantic private enterprise. Throughout the history of the railways much basic standardisation had been accomplished; but there was yet much to be done. Locomotives, carriages, wagons, track, signalling, operating methods and administration systems needed reshaping into nation-wide conformity. Most railwaymen, at whatever level, took it in their stride. The daily job still had to be done. Younger executives saw new career opportunities opening up. A few, who had occupied high posts, and who could not stomach nationalisation, had campaigned unsuccessfully against it; but wisely they had made their departure by an earlier train to enjoy their pensions.

The problem of standardising rolling stock was highlighted by a table produced by British Railways:

Assumed useful lives	
locomotives	30 to 50 years
carriages	20 to 40 years
wagons	25 to 40 years

Changes in rolling stock fleets could not therefore be made quickly.

Over half a million privately-owned wagons (POs) had been taken over. Many were old, of low capacity and unsatisfactory in service, especially those fitted with grease-lubricated axle-boxes. Maintenance costs were high. Within about five years, over 200,000 had been withdrawn and some replaced by more modern wagons fitted with oil-lubricated axle-boxes.

Within some three years, the locomotive fleet had fallen from 20,459 to 19,112. Unification meant that locomotives could be interchanged more widely from route to route and could be more effectively rostered for time-tabling.

Members of the Railway Executive described achievements and future plans in a publication entitled *Unification of British Railways*; it was issued jointly with *Modern Transport* in May 1951. Chairman John Elliot, who succeeded Missenden in January, writes in the foreword:

"One is conscious of the magnitude of the job, that a great deal has been achieved, and that what has been done has been accomplished in the face of unprecedented difficulties."

Under Elliot, members of the Railway Executive, in addition to their corporate responsibility, also continued to head separate departments: operating, mechanical and electrical engineering, permanent-way and signalling, passenger and goods commercial, stores, and personnel.

In charge of operations, V. M. Barrington-Ward reports: "To some extent, a similar state of affairs existed in 1923 after the grouping (of 120 separate companies) which followed the passing of the Railways Act 1921. But as each of the group companies maintained many differences in organisation and operating methods, which clearly could not be perpetuated under unified working, the problem then was not in any way comparable with that facing the railway administration in 1948".

Lines of demarcation were also drawn up for the operating and commercial departments for both goods and passenger traffic. It was the commercial man's job to get the business, and the operating man's job to see that it was conveyed. The principal departments with headquarters at regional or central level were served by divisional and district offices for geographical supervision

Above: Midland Railway 4–4–0, No. 1000, built in 1902 by Johnson who was outstanding as a designer of beautiful locomotives, the expresses finished in the handsome Midland lake livery. (Photo: By courtesy of J. M. Jarvis, Esq.).
Below: Thundersley, *4–4–2, No. 80, London Tilbury & Southend Railway, of 1909. Preserved today at the Bressingham Live Steam Museum, Norfolk. (Photo: By courtesy of John Adams, Esq.)*

down to station and depot level. Specialised committees at various administrative levels co-ordinated departmental activities and future planning.

Horse and Harness

In the age of mechanical devices, the humble horse – first motive power for the original railways – was still in harness. In 1948, the total stud was over 8,700; most of the animals were used for hauling drays, vans and carts in towns and cities throughout Britain in local collection and delivery services; about 230 were used for shunting purposes. In the reorganisation of 1949, a chief veterinary surgeon and horse superintendent was appointed with subordinate offices in London, Birmingham, Manchester and Glasgow. Horse purchases and sales were centralised, and facilities for horse and harness maintenance for all regions co-ordinated. The concentration of veterinary hospital and shoeing and harness services reduced overheads and staff costs. At that time, David Blee forecast that the horse stud, which was part of his department, would have disappeared about 1959, which in fact it had. Long after the power of the horse had faded from railway and general transport, horse power (hp), taken as 550 foot-pounds per second (about 1½ times the actual power of a horse), had survived as a unit for measuring the work of a prime motor.

R. A. Riddles, the Railway Executive member responsible for mechanical and electrical engineering, had the challenging task of bringing together into some common pattern the multifarious items of rolling stock.

In the unification report, Riddles writes: "With the coming into force of the Transport Act on 1st January 1948, the four main-line railways, with their four chief mechanical engineers and two chief electrical engineers, were to be amalgamated and worked as one. The need was to utilise as quickly as possible the best methods in design and works practices.

"The magnitude of the task is apparent in the fact that the maintenance bill for locomotives is approximately £27 million, and for carriages and wagons £35 million, with a renewal programme of roughly £4½ million for locomotives and £25 million for carriages and wagons and a staff of 100,000."

Four functional departments came under the direction of Riddles:

(1) locomotive construction and maintenance
(2) carriage and wagon construction and maintenance
(3) electrical engineering, particularly traction
(4) motive power

With a legacy of the original 400 types of steam locomotive, the Railway Executive concentrated on a very small number of types in a building programme from 1951, Class 7 being the most powerful:

Type or class	*Wheel arrangement*	*Axle load in tons*
7	4–6–2	20¼
6	4–6–2	18½
5	4–6–0	19
4	4–6–0	17
4	2–6–4T	18
3	2–6–2T	16¼

In later years, four additional types as required would be introduced:

4	2–6–0	16¾
3	2–6–0	16
2	2–6–0	13
2	2–6–2T	13

Those marked "T" were tank engines without a separate fuel tender; all were for "mixed" traffic – both passenger and freight, a policy which would make for greater versatility in daily operation.

At a later stage, it was proposed to build a heavy express passenger locomotive with 22½ ton axle-load, and a heavy freight locomotive with 17 ton axle-load. These new standard locomotives were to become the work-horses of the railways and were to see the nationalised network through further stages of development. Meanwhile, the old types had to be phased out and scrapped.

With the advantage of hindsight, the really astonishing feature was that this elaborate programme came only three years before the decision to phase out steam altogether.

As with locomotives, the numerous types of carriages were to be much reduced, and most of the building programme from 1951 onwards, to the new B.R. standards for corridor vehicles, would consist of twelve different body styles:

third class corridor
third class corridor brake
first class corridor
composite corridor (first and third)
composite corridor brake
third class open, fixed seating
third class open, loose seating (movable chairs)
first class open, fixed seating
first class open, loose seating

kitchen car
restaurant car with kitchen and loose seating
passenger brake van

Some other types of passenger stock were to be standardised when their turn came for building.

Literally hundreds of different designs of wagon, both railway and privately owned, were taken over on nationalisation. To cope with the enormous and long-term programme, a Wagon Standards Committee was formed.

"The policy has been adopted," reports Riddles, "of selecting, where possible, the most suitable of each of the existing types of wagon as a standard for future construction." This also included standardising the numerous wagon components. In the 1951 building programme, some 34 types had been dealt with in this way, with 17 more scheduled for 1952. Whether in timber or metal, simplicity in design and construction was to be the key.

From Footplate to Boardroom

On the day that the State took over, railway staff numbered over 700,000; of these, some 50,000 were women and girls. During 1948, the usual annual staff census had been taken, a requirement stemming from the Railways Act 1921. Figures showed the average earnings for male "wages" grades as under £7 a week, and clerical and supervisory staff, under £8 a week.

As unification took place and loss-making lines were closed, the numbers employed were to fall dramatically, and even by 1951 had been reduced to some 625,000. In recent times, the number on the payroll had shrunk to about 250,000.

When the State took over, the job of looking after all staff matters was given to a man with steam in his veins, and he took his place as a member of the Railway Executive. W. P. ("Bill") Allen, fresh from his seat as general secretary of the Associated Society of Locomotive Engineers & Firemen (ASLEF), had spent many years first firing and then driving steam trains.

Allen was now negotiating on the other side of the table with his former colleagues, the railway trade union leaders. But his practical experience enabled him to bring a deeper understanding into the board room of the problems that beset the men down the line. His views are expressed in the Unification Report:

"If we accept that there is something more in railway employment than the value of the pay packet, as I think we should, we can begin to examine some of the essential features of staff development which will aid in creating the degree of contentment we all wish to see. . . . Naturally, I have learned much since I reluctantly gave up my trade union work to become a member of the Railway Executive, but I have found nothing to change my opinion on fundamental issues.

". . . the staff representatives are to be taken into full consultation, and thus a joint responsibility is placed upon all concerned to see that the plan, whatever it may be, shall succeed."

Summing up the achievements of the first few years of nationalisation, it can be seen that top managers in the Railway Executive team conducted their business with a sense of history. They introduced the best technical equipment and know-how that was available; they took the staff and unions into their confidence; and they created a new concept of unity and purpose throughout the industry. They were acutely conscious, too, that the policy decisions they were making would affect the future shape and style of the railways for several decades. With determination, they built a sound basis ready for the modernisation of the system and the high speed trains that they knew must eventually come.

While the railways were busy welding the network into one system, at the same time integrating in the operational and technical fields with the other forms of inland transport, politics again threatened to interfere. On 26th October 1951, Winston Churchill became Prime Minister for his second term of that office; and the Conservative Party were committed to dismantling some of the nationalised transport system.

In 1952, a Bill was presented to Parliament "requiring the Commission to break up and dispose of their road haulage undertaking." The Commission made it clear to the Government "that they were completely opposed to these provisions", and emphasised to the Minister "the gravely disturbing effect which in their view the proposals were likely to have upon the efficiency of their services, upon their finances and upon the staff". Commenting on the year's finances they added, "a surplus of about £4½ million was left to be applied in reduction of past deficiencies". A net balance for the first five years of nationalisation stood at £31½ million deficit, after a promising early start in surplus.

Hurcomb, as Chairman of the British Transport Commission, and the other undertakings, had worked hard for five years in the cause of "integration". This Bill, stated Hurcomb, "brought to a halt a number of schemes designed to produce a rationalised internal transport system".

Nevertheless, the new Transport Act was passed and on 30th September 1953 the Railway Executive was abolished. Hurcomb, honoured with a seat in the House of Lords, retired on 31st August and on 15th September he was replaced by Sir Brian (later Lord) Robertson, a military man with a long and distinguished career. The new chairman summed up the essence of the Transport Act 1953 in his first annual report:

"The principal consequences intended to flow from the Act were the re-admission of private hauliers into long-distance road transport and the virtual liquidation of the Commission's long-distance road-haulage organisation; greater freedom for the railways in the sphere of charging (on a more commercial and competitive basis); re-organisation of the Commission, including the abolition of the Railway Executive and the decentralisation of railway management; and changes in the general duty of the Commission."

Robertson added, "The great constitutional changes . . . had been carried through without any serious dislocation of services or organisation."

In their early years, the BTC had acquired rapidly between 3,000 and 4,000 separate road haulage undertakings predominantly engaged in long-distance haulage, most of which were disposed of by the procedures laid down by the Act.

The job of managing the railways now fell directly to the BTC, and the trains continued to run as though little had happened.

As a result of the BTC (Organisation) Schedule Order 1954, issued by the Minister of Transport, further reorganisation of the railways took place, coming into force on 1st January 1955 when new Boards were appointed to the six Regions. The "line traffic" system of management was introduced in stages, placing more co-ordinated responsibility at local levels.

MODERNISATION AND RE-EQUIPMENT OF BRITISH RAILWAYS

When Sir Brian Robertson announced on 24th January 1955 a new modernisation plan to cost £1,200 million, he ushered in a new epoch in the history of the railways of Britain. The next 15 years were to see the greatest revolution ever seen in modern times on any railway in the world, eventually to put Britain in the lead in wheel-to-rail transport.

In outlining their Plan, the BTC recorded, "An efficient and modernised railway system is essential to the economy of the country, and it should be able to attract and retain sufficient traffic to make it economically self-supporting for many years to come. . . . This Plan aims to produce a thoroughly modern system, able fully to meet both current traffic requirements and those of the foreseeable future . . . and completed within fifteen years."

Speaking in Parliament on 3rd February 1955, the Chancellor of the Exchequer said: "It is in the interests of the country that more capital should be put into transport. . . . Our policy is to proceed with the modernisation of the railways."

In anticipation of the Plan, the BTC had reported the previous year: "Diesel multiple unit sets offer many advantages of electrification including cleanliness, good acceleration, and ability to turn round quickly at the terminals.

"Operation by one man is practicable since the 'dead man's handle' is incorporated in the driving gear – a device which automatically cuts off the power and applies the brakes in the event of the driver becoming incapacitated."

Lightweight diesel trains on some branches, the report said, were being considered; and the St. Albans–Watford branch had been selected for an experimental service with lightweight diesel cars, coupled together in short trains. Before the war, both the L.M.S.R. and the G.W.R. had run trial services with diesel traction.

"The year 1954 marked the beginning of a very large programme of multiple-unit diesel car construction," stated the annual report. "Of the 34 vehicles put into service in 1953, some went into service in the West Riding of Yorkshire, and others in West Cumberland. Design would give a high degree of passenger comfort and visibility. They were built at the BR Derby Works, the diesel equipment being purchased from outside suppliers." Other areas and routes to have diesel trains in place of stopping steam trains included Lincolnshire, East Anglia, Newcastle–Middlesbrough, and Blaenau Ffestiniog–Llandudno, and Glasgow–Edinburgh.

Details of the Plan itself, listed below, represent the massive project which was to involve railwaymen in every department in all parts of the country.

FREIGHT SERVICES	£m.	£m.
Construction and re-construction of some 55 marshalling yards, resulting in the total or partial closure of about 150 existing yards . .	80	

Driving cab of a diesel multiple unit train on the Western Region close to the River Thames and Windsor Castle, seen in 1959. About this period, diesel trains were rapidly replacing steam. (Photo: British Rail)

Reconstruction and mechanisation of freight terminals while closing various old depots, so as to improve transits and speed up exchange of full-load traffic between road and rail	50	
Associated expenditure on handling equipment and road vehicles	10	
Provision of continuous brakes on freight stock, thus securing best results from new forms of motive power	75	
New and improved wagon stock	150	
	——	365

PASSENGER CARRIAGES AND STATIONS

New passenger carriages, including electric and diesel multiple-unit vehicles and refreshment cars	230	
Improvements to passenger and parcels stations, and carriage-cleaning and servicing depots ..	55	
	——	285

TRACK AND SIGNALLING

Improvements to make possible higher speeds (of at least 100 m.p.h. on the main lines) and better use of track capacity ..		210

MOTIVE POWER

Electrification:			
Main lines	120		
Suburban lines (including schemes already planned)	65		
	—— 185		
Dieselisation:			
Main lines	125		
Shunting and trip locomotives	25		
	——	150	
Steam motive power depots ..		10	
		——	345

ANCILLARY ITEMS

Improvements at Commission's packet ports	12	
Research and development work	10	
Offices and equipment, and staff welfare	13	
	——	35
Total envisaged cost of the Plan		£1,240m.

This total expenditure of £1,240m. compares with about £600m. which would in any event have had to be spent over the period of the Plan merely to maintain the existing equipment.

Of all the changes, the most revolutionary was that contained in the declared policy to bring to an end steam locomotives as the main form of motive power. In presenting their case, the British Transport Commission paid a modest tribute: "The steam locomotive has in the past served the railways well . . . many factors combine to indicate that the end of the steam era is at hand. These include the growing shortage of large coal suitable for locomotives; the insistent demand for a reduction in air pollution by locomotives and far greater cleanliness in trains and railway stations; and the need for better acceleration."

Additional anti-steam pressures came from the campaign that was gathering force against atmospheric pollution, culminating in the Clean Air Act 1956 and the introduction of "smokeless zones". Section 19 (2) stated: "The owner of any railway locomotive engine shall use any practicable means there may be for minimising the emission of smoke from the chimney on the engine, and if he fails so to do, if smoke is emitted therefrom, be guilty of an offence."

The end of steam would also bring almost an end to the frequent fires that broke out on the lineside when sparks or burning cinders flying from the chimney set the dry grass alight, especially during hot summer spells. It would reduce, too, dirt in the eyes and smuts on the clothes of passengers seated otherwise happily at an open carriage window, and enjoying the passing scene. Engine turntables and centre-track water troughs, once important technical triumphs, would relapse into railway history.

As the Plan progressed, it was re-appraised from time to time, both technically and financially, to meet changing conditions.

On the signalling side, out-dated manual signalboxes operating semaphore signal arms with oil lamps were to be replaced by "power installations" – of which a number were already in use – to operate signals and points over stretches of main line for distances up to about 100 miles, a process that is still progressing.

Main-line electrification had been considered by the railway companies before the Second World War but were unrealised because of overriding economic conditions. One of them, however, was completed in 1955 across the Pennines, an arduous main line of the old London & North Eastern Railway, between Sheffield and Manchester. Traffic was predominantly freight.

"The modernisation plan provides for the electrification of two major trunk routes," the Commission reported, "namely the main line from Euston to Birmingham, Crewe, Manchester and Liverpool; and the main line from King's Cross to Doncaster, Leeds and, possibly, York. The Shenfield electrification is to be carried on to Ipswich." But in 1975 the King's Cross and Ipswich lines were still in the future.

Another signficant decision was made in the same year, the rights and wrongs of which were argued fiercely at the time and often questioned later. Though the air brake system was being used for electrical and diesel multi-units, the British Transport Commission decided to adopt as standard the long-established vacuum brake for all freight and for other passenger train rolling stock. Expert opinion was sharply divided on the relative merits of the two systems; total conversion to air braking would have taken many years, and would have cost an additional £20 million to £30 million. Changing over would also have created immeasurable operating difficulties and delays during a long period of conversion, during which two systems would have been working at the same time. Though the B.T.C. settled for the vacuum brake at that time, the trend in later years for both passenger and freight vehicles was towards air braking.

During the changeover from steam to diesel and electric motive power, heating of carriages presented a dual problem. Paragraph 95 of the British Transport Commission's Report for 1957 gave an outline:

". . . careful consideration was given to the problem of train heating. Heating of locomotive-hauled coaching stock is at present provided by steam from the locomotive. It has been necessary therefore to investigate the problem of heating carriages which will be hauled by the new diesel and electric locomotives. This can be achieved by carrying a train heating boiler either on the locomotive or in a special heating van. Alternatively, electric heating can be supplied from the locomotive either direct in the case of electric locomotives or otherwise by means of auxiliary diesel-driven generators. It will be necessary to equip carriages with both steam and electric heating facilities during the transition period."

Mounting financial difficulties in the railways had led the Government into setting up independent enquiries into the entire working and structure of the system; and in 1962 another Act of Parliament was passed, to bring radical changes in policy and in the management organisation. At one of the Government enquiries (the Stedeford Report), Dr. (later Lord) Beeching, a director of Imperial Chemical Industries, had made some original observations. In March 1961 when aged 47 he was appointed as a part time member of the British Transport Commission and three months later as chairman, to succeed Sir Brian Robertson.

In its last annual report – for 1962, the B.T.C. stated: "The Commission's varied undertakings, employing nearly 688,000 people and comprising rail and road transport, the London passenger transport service, canals, ports, shipping, hotel and catering services and travel agencies, represented one of the largest single industrial organisations in the world."

They also noted the sad case of railways generally: "During the course of their lifetime (British Transport Commission 15 years), they had witnessed a dramatic decline in the fortunes of many railways throughout the world; and British Railways, which was by far the largest single component of the Commission's undertaking, was no exception."

About a century earlier, exactly the opposite was the case. There was even now no cause for gloom and despondency, for within a decade the rejuvenated railways of Britain were to show that they could still be world leaders; but the financial problems were to remain.

TRANSPORT ACT, 1962

The Transport Act 1962 received Royal Assent on 1st August and its main provisions came into force on 1st September. Separate Boards, under the Minister of Transport, took over from the B.T.C. the London Transport, British Transport Docks and British Waterways; and a Transport Holding Company was formed to take over some of the activities to operate in company form. The British Railways Board became responsible for the railways: in total, five separate Boards to assume former B.T.C. responsibilities.

British Railways would no longer be statutory "common carriers". The railways for many years had battled to be relieved of having to carry any traffic offered whether profitable or not; this left their unfettered competitors free to "skim the cream off the traffic". Now, they could refuse to carry traffic they did not want and use their commercial judgement as to the value of the business. Also, they were no longer obliged to publish their rates and charges; this had put road hauliers at a strong advantage, for they could quote their own rates in private. In the freight field these were valuable commercial advantages.

Financial burdens on the railways were to be reduced:

- (a) by writing off the accumulated losses amounting to some £475 million
- (b) by placing to Suspense Account some £650–£700 million which, for the time being, will carry neither fixed interest nor fixed repayment obligations.

This would still leave the railways with the responsibility of servicing a large initial capital debt to the Minister which was likely to amount to about £900 million. This debt would mainly represent investment since 1955.

The Treasury would still assume full responsibilities for existing British Transport stock and the rights of stock holders would be fully safeguarded.

Dr. Richard Beeching, the man at the helm, received massive publicity during his sojourn; much of this highlighted his salary of £24,000 a year, the rate of his former appointment as a director of Imperial Chemical Industries (ICI), which was then over twice the going rate for a Railways Board chairman. His predecessor's salary was £10,000. On 31st October 1962, Beeching used the forum of the Institute of Directors to state publicly his "vision of the future." A few extracts show the way he was thinking, in carrying out his brief from the Minister, Ernest Marples, of whom he was a close personal friend:

"With proper judgement of the right role of the railways as part of the transport system as a whole, there are prospects of operating a railway system which will carry more traffic than at present and which will flourish financially while doing so . . .

"Our vision of the future has grown out of intensive investigations and planning. The central purpose . . . was to determine under what conditions the basic characteristics of railways enable them to be the best form of transport, and to determine how much of the total traffic pattern of the country falls within this range of conditions favourable to rail . . .

"It would be an unwise manufacturer who did not assess the characteristics of his product, both merits and demerits, survey the potential market for a product with those characteristics, and then plan to provide his product in quantities to match the foreseeable need.

"How surprising, therefore, that this has not been done before in relation to our railways. How astonishing that, when it is done, so many people should view the process with suspicion and run away in fright from their own premature conclusions." (Shades of public objections to forthcoming passenger closures.)

"Rationalisation of national transport facilities appears desirable to most thinking people, but opinions differ widely as to how it can best be achieved . . .

"History has produced, and left with us, a railway system and a pattern of railway operation which was developed, very largely, in defiance of the basic characteristics of railways . . .

"Our railways were developed to their fullest extent at a time when the horse and cart was the only means of feeding to and distributing from them." (Just over two years before Beeching arrived on the scene, British Railways still had 75 horses on their books.)

"It is clear that continued operation of widespread stopping services by rail is not compatible with commercial conduct of the business as a whole. Therefore, either we must stop such services or they must be subsidised . . .

"Surveys, which we have made in the last year, show that there is something like 90 million tons per annum of traffic at present on road which is favourable for rail haulage, if the inherent advantages of the railways are properly exploited."

But positive policies became overlaid by the emotion evoked by the proposed removal of stopping trains from many lines and closures of little-used lines running mainly through the hills and dales of rural Britain. Attractive though these lines were, nobody wanted to pay for them; and before Ministerial approval was secured, each closure was fought with the vigour and acrimony of a century earlier, when the anti-railway brigade had battled so furiously against the opening of new lines. Now it was starkly revealed that mile by mile, station by station, much of the railway was vastly underused; and the next few years saw immense pruning and at the same time wide-ranging improvements on all fronts.

Chapter and verse of the new policy was contained in a document of 148 pages with many maps and entitled *The Reshaping of British Railways* (1963). It was published in March. The document became known in the Press as the "Beeching Plan"; but this was against the personal wishes of Beeching, who always regarded it as a team job shared among top railway managers.

In the pages of "*Reshaping*", a philosophy was expressed that came to have the blessing of Parliament five years later (Transport Act 1968): evidence that long-term campaigning by sophisticated railway managements eventually broke through the clouds:

"It might pay to run railways at a loss to prevent the incidence of an even greater cost which would arise elsewhere if the railways were closed. Such other costs may be deemed to arise from congestion, provision of parking space, injury and death, additional road building, or a number of other causes."

"It is a plan (*Reshaping*) based upon a new balance between road and rail. As it succeeds, it will increase road haulage slightly in areas where traffic is light, but it will reduce it greatly on trunk routes where traffic is heavy. Also, if the depots are well sited, it will help to relieve congestion within the cities."

Modestly, and aware that to some railway people he might be considered an "outsider", Beeching ended: "This is a plan based not upon the wild ideas of newcomers but on the ideas that have welled up from thoughtful railway managers."

Some astonishing revelations about the operations of the railways are found in "*Reshaping*"; and brief information is extracted upon which new thought was centred in tackling the continuous task of up-dating the system:

The duty of the British Railways Board is to employ the assets to the best advantage of the nation;

Operating losses were likely to go on increasing unless radical changes were made;

The unknown degree of cross-subsidisation involved in carrying bad traffic on the back of financially good traffic was very largely ignored;

Stopping passenger trains are by far the worst loss maker in the passenger business;

Wagon-load general merchandise which loads badly and offers little scope for through train movement is a bad loss maker;

Minerals and coal show the best margin over costs in freight;

One third of the route mileage carries only one hundredth of the total passenger miles;

Many older signal-boxes were improved after the Second World War by the addition of track circuits and indicator track diagrams. This box at Port Eglington Junction in the Scottish Region was photographed in 1956. (Photo: British Rail)

One half of the total route mileage carries about one-twenty-fifth of the total passenger miles;

One half of the mileage carries about one-twentieth of the freight ton miles;

Most of the traffics fed from the lightly loaded lines to the rest of the system are of the less favourable kinds;

One third of the passenger stations produce less than one-hundredth of the total passenger receipts, and one half of the stations produce only a fiftieth;

34 stations – less than a hundredth of the total – produce over one quarter of the receipts;

One third of the freight stations produce less than one-hundredth of the total freight receipts, and one half produce about a seventieth;

The railways would be better off financially if a high proportion of the stations was closed;

About two-fifths of the total passenger mileage serves mainly rural areas, and most of the trains carry less than a busload and lose nearly twice as much as they collect in fares;

If fares were halved, traffic would have to increase sixfold to cover the whole costs of the stopping trains as a group;

It would be folly to suggest that widespread closure of stopping train services will cause no hardship anywhere to anybody, and questions of hardships will be considered by the Transport Users' Consultative Committees;

The peak load of London suburban services, measured over half an hour, is about ten times the average level over the hours from 6 a.m. to midnight.

Having diagnosed the ailment, what did the Doctor prescribe?

(1) Discontinue many stopping passenger services
(2) Transfer modern multiple unit stock so displaced to continuing services which are steam locomotive hauled
(3) Close a high proportion of small stations to passenger traffic
(4) Improve selectively Inter-City passenger services and rationalise routes
(5) Damp down seasonal peaks of passenger traffic and withdraw corridor coaching stock held for the purpose of covering them at present
(6) Co-ordinate suburban train and bus services and charges, in collaboration with municipal authorities, with the alternative of fare increases and possible closure of services
(7) Co-ordinate passenger parcels services with the Post Office
(8) Increase "block train" movement of coal by inducing the National Coal Board to provide train loading facilities at collieries, and inducing the establishment of coal concentration depots, in collaboration with the National Coal Board and the coal distributors
(9) Reduce uneconomic freight traffic passing through small stations by closing them progressively, but with regard to the preservation of potentially good railway traffics, and by adjustment in charges
(10) Attract more siding-to-siding traffics suitable for through-train movement by operating such trains at the expense of the (single) wagon forwarding system and by providing time-tabled trains, of special stock to meet customer requirements
(11) Study and develop a network of "Liner Train" (Freightline) services to carry flows of traffic which, though dense, are composed of consignments too small by themselves to justify through-train operation
(12) Concentrate freight sundries traffic upon about 100 main depots, many of them associated with Liner Train depots, and carriage of main flows of sundries in Liner Trains, probably coupled with passenger parcels, and possibly Post Office parcels and letters
(13) Reduce rapidly and progressively the freight wagon stock over the next three years
(14) Continue replacing steam by diesel locomotives for main line traction, up to a probable requirement of at least 3,750/4,250 (1,698 already in service and 950 on order at present)
(15) Rationalise the composition and use of the Railways' road cartage fleet.

A table in the Report breaks down the route mileages:

No. of tracks	*Route miles*	*Miles open for freight only*
Route with four tracks or over	1,500	100
Route with three tracks	400	100
Route with double track	10,000	1,200
Single track	5,900	2,700
	17,800	4,100

Most of the developments proposed in "Reshaping" were brought into operation in the years that followed. At the same time, the Modernisation Plan launched in 1955 gathered momentum.

Beeching joined the railways in 1961 and

departed in 1965. Figures in the following table tell their own story:

date (year end)	*route miles*	*passenger and goods stations*	*marshalling yards*
1960	18,369	7,283	876
1966	13,721	3,803	293

Over the next decade, these assets were to be reduced much further.

Armed with the Reshaping Plan, British Railways in February 1965 produced another important report of a hundred pages entitled: *The Development of the Major Trunk Routes.* It was described as "a critical examination of a crucial part of the system – the trunk routes – and it sets out for consideration the information and forecasts necessary to establish how the through route system can best be developed to match the future pattern of rail demand." It was the last major long-term policy document to be published by British Railways under the chairmanship of Beeching, who departed three months later to be succeeded by Stanley Raymond.

Because of emotional overtones, Beeching's name naturally became closely associated with the closure of railway lines, somewhat out of proportion to his total contribution to railway progress. His proposals for large-scale closures were published on 27th March 1963. He resigned from the Railways Board on 31st May 1965. Many of his closure proposals were declined through the parliamentary procedures and from first proposal to final closure could often take two years or more. The following table presents a thought-provoking commentary on the dramatic and revolutionary streamlining of the railway network during the terms of office of alternate Governments – Conservative 1951–64, Labour 1964–70, Conservative 1970–74, Labour 1974–. Considerable study of the history, policy and procedures of railway closures is essential for any sound conclusion to be reached:

year	*route miles open at end of year*	*miles closed*	*passenger and goods stations*	*marshalling yards*
1952	19,276		8,212	956
1960	18,369		7,283	876
1961	18,214	155	7,025	867
1962	17,471	743	6,801	602
1963	16,982	489	6,382	558
1964	15,991	991	5,129	453
1965	14,920	1,071	4,295	378
1966	13,721	1,199	3,803	293
1967	13,172	549	3,498	227
1968	12,447	725	3,155	184
1969	12,098	349	3,000	151
1970	11,799	299	2,868	146
1973	11,326		2,735	53
1974	11,289			

During the Beeching regime, a number of senior marketing posts were filled by executives with specialised marketing experience in outside industry: oil products, motor industry, agriculture, chemicals, iron and steel and the like. They brought new marketing methods to ally to the experience of seasoned railway officers. In addition, commercial executives were appointed to look after the country-wide business of some 350 large individual companies. A closer liaison was established with travel agents, who the railways began to regard as "the railway booking offices in the High Street."

"British Rail", introduced in 1964, was shorter and easier to say than British Railways: though many older railwaymen shuddered at the euphemism. "Inter-City" was identified with the higher quality trains eventually linking some two hundred cities and towns; it became the mode for business executives to say they were "going by Inter-City". As the term became associated with quality, it was purloined by others, including a large outfitter who sold Inter-City gents' natty suits. Some overseas railways adopted the term, using the English version, much as the French use "week-end" and "fortnight" for which they have no convenient translation.

"Freightliner" was the brand name which evolved from the original term of Liner Train, to become well known among transport managers in industry. "Sealink" was selected for British Rail shipping services to Europe, Ireland, the Isle of Wight, and on Lake Windermere which began in 1872. British Rail Hovercraft Services were given the name "Seaspeed", for the pioneering hovercraft routes to the Isle of Wight and to France.

"Red Star" was the name chosen by Rail Express Parcels Service for packages which, for an additional charge, could be put on a specific train, supervised throughout, and met on arrival by the waiting customer.

"Motorail" was the term devised for the services by which motorists and their parties could travel on the same train as their cars; the creative media men were invited to improve on "car carrier services" and could hardly fail. For a new subsidiary company called "Transportation Systems and Market Research Limited", the name for business use was condensed to "Transmark". The company was formed "to carry out market research, general transport consultancy, and technical studies, both for managements within the Board's business, and for outside clients in this country and overseas." A new and substantial revenue has since been established.

About this time, computers were coming into greater use, also referred to in an annual report: "More than six million different point-to-point journeys are possible on British Rail. Computers are therefore used in the complex task of analysing the sales information to determine changes in passenger flows . . ."

Creating, launching and sustaining the brand image names was the result of a close partnership between specialists in marketing and in public relations and publicity. The achievements and standards of professionalism were acknowledged to bear comparison with any other large commercial enterprise in Britain, either state-owned or public company; coverage stretched across Europe, North America and to many other countries overseas. The process continues apace. Their efforts were animated by the improving quality of products they had to offer.

Fares Adapted to the Market

Within the total passenger marketing concept, the railways for years had been striving to shake off the fetters of a fixed price per mile for "ordinary" fares. It had always been that way, so why change now? In the new atmosphere of commercialism, marketing men, backed by the Board, pressed strongly the argument that the new, faster and more comfortable trains that were in heavy demand on the best routes were worth more, and could command more in the market place than those outside the top quality range.

Supported by the tenets of the Transport Act 1962, the railways set about the huge task of calculating fares in the light of the new principle. For the first time in the history of Britain's railways, the fixed price per mile method was abolished. The new "selective" prices came into operation on 8th September 1968: a triumph for the railway management. On that date, Selective Prices Manual No. 1 came into force. Compilation had been a computer exercise. It was supplied to all railway ticket issuers, including booking clerks and travel agents. It listed fares in the main categories for all journeys, except some of the shorter ones, and was simple for all who had to use it.

FRIEND OF THE MOTORIST

A sophisticated assault on competition from the private car had never been attempted nationally by the railways until some 60 years after the registration in 1903 of the first British car numberplate. In the interim, the rich man's toy had become the common man's runabout.

Concerning the motor vehicle, harsh words were published in the Report on Traffic in Towns 1963: "We are nourishing at immense cost a monster of great potential destructiveness. And yet we love him dearly." The "potential destructiveness" referred not merely to the environment, but also to the economic viability of public transport. It was an encouraging report for the railways. They were already developing a programme on four fronts: trains to carry motorists and their cars, more and larger station car parks, new stations designed primarily for the motorist, and car hire connected with rail travel.

Motorail

British Railways had pioneered car-sleeper trains as early as 1955. Motorists and their parties travelled on an overnight sleeper train and their cars were conveyed in specially fitted covered vans on the rear of the same train. Cars owned by the well-to-do had been transported by train on occasion almost from the time they were invented, just as the hunters and cobs had journeyed in railway horse boxes from the Stephensons' days.

The first car-sleepers ran between London (King's Cross) and Perth twice a week during the summer of 1955, from 15th June to 18th September. Holiday-makers in Scotland were able to travel for the main part of their journey while they slept, saving two days of motoring in each direction and a night in a hotel each way. The difference in real costs between road and rail travel was only marginal.

During succeeding years, new services were added – still somewhat tentatively, each train and route being thoroughly analysed before capacity was increased. Researches into the market potential in the 1960s led to attention to every detail that might make the service more convenient and attractive to the motorist, and it was in 1964 that the brand name "Motorail" was launched.

Meanwhile, the steadily growing popularity encouraged the railways to link more large centres of population with favourite holiday regions such as the West Country, Wales and Ireland, as well as more destinations in Scotland. Dover was later added to the network for European visitors crossing the channel by British Rail ships.

To serve London and the south-east, the world's first custom-built Motorail terminal, designed exclusively for motoring families, was opened at Kensington Olympia station in 1966. It included an attractive lounge, complete with kitchen, refreshment facilities and a bar. Nursing mothers were catered for as well. Terminals elsewhere were improved with the motoring party in mind.

Motorail business grew as roads became more congested and petrol and motoring costs rose, despite the expansion of the motorways; demands of motor vehicles seemed always to outstrip road developments.

Each year, the railways found that nearly half the customers had used the service before, many of them five or six times previously: a welcome compliment. The dramatic growth is shown in the table of figures:

Year	*Number of car journeys*	*Number of services*
1957	11,600	8
1958	16,300	12
1959	19,800	12
1960	24,800	13
1961	25,100	13
1962	25,100	12
1963	25,800	13
1964	29,600	12
1965	34,600	11
1966	43,200	15
1967	59,300	17
1968	55,700	21
1969	66,400	20
1970	71,200	22
1971	70,200	27
1972	68,600	31
1973	71,600	31
1974	90,000	36

To meet the ever growing demands of the motorist, car parking space at stations was steadily increased in the 1950s and 1960s. Numerous disused goods yards, station sidings, locomotive depots and other pieces of land released in the Beeching era were converted to car parks. Many existing parks were extended. Railway marketing men could see that station parking alone could be developed into a good revenue earning activity that would be equivalent in size to many a medium-sized private company.

Park-and-ride

It was in the 1960s, also, that another idea was germinating – park-and-ride stations – to open up new possibilities for serving the motorist. It bore fruit in 1972 when the first railway station to be designed specially for the motorist was opened for business. It cost £200,000. Named Bristol Parkway, it was located 5 miles north of Bristol city centre and close to junctions with three motorways – M4, M5 and M32. Free car parking was laid out for 600 cars. A new feature incorporated was a local chauffeur-driven car service at a flat sharge of 40p per journey and called "dial-a-ride".

The new station was found particularly useful for motorists in the area north of Bristol, who could derive the dual benefits of local motorway development and the Inter-City network. Within a year, Bristol Parkway was being used by over 800 passengers a day, and new train services were added for Devon, Liverpool and Manchester, and a new sleeper service to Glasgow and Edinburgh.

Car Hire for Inter-City Travellers

Still wooing the motorist, British Rail in the 1960s investigated the prospects of a car hire service directly associated with leading Inter-City stations. It needed to be simple and efficient to catch on. No-one knew how successful it would be; but detailed researches confirmed that the commercial risk would not be high. People drove for long distances to have the convenience of a car at the other end. A five-year contract was signed with Godfrey Davis, the largest all-British car rental company, and "Godfrey Davis–Rail Drive" began modestly in April 1969.

RAIL AIR LINKS – WITH INTER-CITY

Air-line passengers were also courted by the railways. A new service was developed in the late 1960s to save long distance Inter-City travellers bound for London Airport the inconvenience of arriving at a London rail terminus, then having to go by bus, rail, underground or taxi for the 15-mile journey from central London. Four stations were chosen outside London which were connected by express coaches daily, direct to the airport. Reading was the link station for the West of England, South Wales and the West Midlands; Woking for the South; Watford for the Midlands, North Wales, the North West and Scotland; and Luton for the East Midlands. A fifth coach link was provided at Feltham for trains from Waterloo, serving passengers from Kent and the South East and South West suburbs of London.

Chapter 9

The Last Ten Years

The first electrically hauled train, at Wigan in July 1973, on the newly electrified Crewe–Preston section, part of the electrification to Glasgow opened in May 1974. (Photo: British Rail)

ELECTRIFICATION – LONDON TO THE NORTH-WEST

OF all the large schemes in the 1955 Modernisation Plan, the main-line electrification between London (Euston) and Crewe, Liverpool and Manchester (introduced in stages) was outstanding. Full electric services began on 18th April 1966, with additionally "fixed interval" suburban electric multi-unit trains serving Euston, Bletchley, Rugby and Coventry. Other important stations phased into the electric services included Macclesfield, Stoke, Stafford, Wolverhampton and Northampton. As the service settled down, journey times were reduced by about a third.

Henry Johnson, general manager of the London Midland Region (later chairman of the Railways Board) wrote: "A fast, modern highway for passengers and freight, running through the heart of the country, is the result of eight years' hard work by railway civil, electrical and signal engineers."

Overhead wiring together with its mass of supporting equipment had been installed, stations altered, more headroom for overhead wires created under bridges and through tunnels, and track re-aligned. It was found impossible to reconstruct Harecastle South Tunnel in North Staffordshire, 1 mile 6 yards long, with sufficient clearance for electrification; so the tunnel was abandoned and the 2½-mile Harecastle diversionary line built, and inaugurated on the 27th June. As the new railway was built on the old one, much of it originally laid by Robert Stephenson, passenger and freight trains continued to run with comparatively little inconvenience to customers – certainly less than was met in the widening and modernising of a trunk road. Much of the work was executed at night and over weekends when traffic was sparser.

Throughout the building period, as lines were completed, the changeover to electric was made in stages. For example, electric trains were introduced between Crewe and Manchester on 12th September 1960, and Crewe–Liverpool on 1st January 1962. Some electric services ran between Crewe and Stafford on 7th January 1963, extended to Nuneaton on 2nd March 1964 and to Rugby on 30th November. On 14th June 1965, they ran between Cheadle Hulme and Macclesfield; and on 22nd November, some local electric trains ran between Euston and Bletchley. On the same date, the first local train ran from Euston to Rugby, and the first main line train to Liverpool, leaving Euston at 8.25 a.m.

By the time the final stages had been reached, the electric trains also served Birmingham, Wolverhampton, Coventry and Stoke-on-Trent, the additional route to Birmingham opening on 6th March 1967. Train timings were arranged when possible on the fixed interval principle: easier for passengers to remember, station staff to operate, and timetable compilers to schedule. Close to the opening date, British Railways announced that overall 151 trains daily (instead of 54) would average 70 m.p.h., with many of them reaching 100 m.p.h.

The New Euston

A fitting climax to the electrification was the opening of the new Euston station. Her Majesty Queen Elizabeth II performed the ceremony on 14th October 1968, a gala occasion that attracted enormous public attention and acclaim, both in Britain and overseas. In their annual report, the Railways Board described it as "a station which ranks with the finest of modern termini in any continent and which is an appropriate gateway to the 100 m.p.h. electric services."

The 18 platforms at Euston vary from 700 to 1,300 ft. in length; above them a fully mechanised parcels and mails depot occupies over five acres, to remove the nuisance of strings of parcels trucks sharing the busy space with hurrying passengers. Several platforms were allocated for parcels trains. Under the station, a car park was constructed to accommodate 230 vehicles, and a taxi-rank for the convenience of passengers. Escalators were installed to give direct access to Euston tube station on the Northern and – later – the new Victoria line.

Originally built by Robert Stephenson in 1837, Euston station has been extended from time to time as business grew. A hotch-potch edifice resulted. The first vast scheme for complete reconstruction was put forward by the L. & N.W.R. in 1899 and by the L.M.S.R. in the 1930s. But there was never enough money, until large-scale electrification made it imperative. A few remaining relics of the old station can still be found by the keen eye. Baily's imposing statue of George Stephenson had been removed to a temporary store from its position in the Great Hall. Robert Stephenson's statue was moved, to stand exposed to the weather on the forecourt (Piazza) to remind railway passengers of the part father and son played in building the London & Birmingham Railway from this great terminus.

Throughout the progress of the Euston scheme, comparable speeds were being enjoyed on other main lines such as the East Coast route including Scotland, Paddington–Bristol–South Wales, and on long distance cross country journeys, on trains hauled by powerful diesel electric locomotives.

Throughout the ten or so years that the Euston electrification scheme was progressing, many other lesser but vital parts of the 1955 Modernisation Plan were being rapidly converted into reality. More lines were being electrified; diesel locomotives were replacing steam in ever-increasing numbers; and diesel multiple-unit trains, mainly of two to eight car sets of new open rolling stock usually with half of the cars powered – by diesel oil engines – were replacing steam trains in many parts of Britain. Engines were similar to those used in buses and heavy lorries. And because diesel trains were quieter and often faster than the steam trains they replaced, the fronts were partially and later wholly painted yellow to be easily seen by men working on the track. "Running round the train" by steam locomotives, or turning them on turntables, was avoided, cutting operating costs and reducing congestion in busy stations. Quicker acceleration also brought faster scheduling.

Every year trains were travelling faster. The railways reported that in 1962 speeds of coaching trains had increased by 3·7 per cent over the previous year; and freight by 2·7 per cent. Now, 81 per cent of coaching trains were hauled by diesel or electric, and 26 per cent of freight, the higher figure being accounted for by multi-unit passenger train working.

Design of new coaches for the principal routes had progressed sufficiently to justify a public showing. A prototype main line eight-coach passenger train known as "Project XP 64" was put into trial service in 1964 on the *Talisman* between London (King's Cross) and Edinburgh (Waverley). Passenger comfort was a prime consideration; the train featured wider folding doors, forced air heating and ventilation, double-glazed windows, sound-proofing, improved decor, and specially designed seats. The reactions of passengers were analysed as a guide to modifications needed before the new features were generally introduced into the building programme. XP 64 marked an important stage in the development of the new breed of high-speed passenger stock.

London–Bournemouth Electrification – 1967

Electrification of the 108 miles of route between London (Waterloo) and Bournemouth via Southampton came into operation in 1967, a £15,000,000 scheme that was completed on the third rail system in three years. New 12-coach trains were built to reach a maximum speed of 90 m.p.h., for which eight stations had to be lengthened. Nearly 250 new or converted passenger coaches were assembled for the service, at railway workshops at York, Derby, Horwich and Wolverton.

Trains were faster and more frequent to meet the growing demand. Passenger travel from Southampton to London, based on population growth estimates, was expected to increase by about 25 per cent during the following nine years, with subsequently more freight.

The last scheduled steam service (with one notable exception) ran on British Rail on Sunday 4th August 1968. On the following Sunday, British Rail ran a commemorative "Farewell to Steam" rail tour from Liverpool to Carlisle via Manchester, Blackburn and Hellifield, returning by the same route. "Old Faithful" had served the nation well for 143 years since those great days of George Stephenson's first public railway. Some 12 years of intensive modernisation had seen the rapid run-down, final exit and relegation to the preservation societies of a romantic machine that had captured the public imagination to an extraordinary extent.

The only steam railway to survive on British Rail was the Vale of Rheidol narrow gauge line of 1 ft. 11 ins., running for 11¾ miles through delightful scenery between Aberystwyth and Devil's Bridge. It was opened in 1902. Train services operate in the summer months on seven days a week. More popular than ever in recent years, this unique little railway carried 167,720 people (passenger journeys) in 1973, compared with 84,064 in 1962.

Steam locomotive building was being phased out as the diesels and electrics took over, with big changes in the railway workshops. At Crewe works, for example, steam building ended in 1958, and records showed that the last one, a heavy goods engine No. 92250 with ten coupled driving wheels, was the 7,331st since the works were originally established in 1843. The distinction of building the very last steam locomotive for British Railways fell to Swindon. This, too, had ten coupled drivers. Class 9F heavy freight No. 92220 was appropriately named *Evening Star* at a special ceremony in 1960. This locomotive, which found a place in history, was destined for only a short working life, before being added to the preservation list. Swindon works concentrated on the assembly of diesel and electric locomotives and diesel and electric multiple-unit carriages, the power units being purchased from manufacturers.

Track Developments

In the modernisation era, the most outstanding development in track work was the use of large track machines: automatic apparatus which could do the work of large gangs of men when it came to such tasks as tamping to correct the level and alignment of the track, ballast-cleaning, laying new track, and laying concrete. Track recording cars were constructed. Cruising along, they unerringly detect faults not easily picked out by the human eye. Electronic data evaluating equipment was devised by British Rail, for printing out a count of any track faults discovered and for highlighting those which demanded the most immediate attention. For the first time a permanent, detailed record of the track was possible. Instruments recorded accurately three of the most important track characteristics: curvature, cant and gauge. Variations from the norm were easily identified for correction. These new techniques were introduced to cover most of the system; visual checks by men walking the track, although still necessary, were no longer adequate.

Modernising Level Crossing Gates

Over a long period, numerous level crossings have been replaced by bridges, largely because of increased road traffic. It was also increasingly difficult to find men to work as crossing keepers. Manually operated level crossings have largely given way to mechanical operation; and in the 1960s a programme was begun to introduce the more efficient automatic half-barrier types widely used on the Continent. In special cases, some level crossings operated from a signal-box some distance away were monitored by the signalman with the aid of closed circuit television in the box itself.

Automatic Warning System

The Automatic Warning System (AWS), pioneered in a simpler mechanical version as Automatic Train Control (ATC) by the Great Western early in the century, was being rapidly installed on important lines in the mid-1960s. By 1964 some 1,520 route miles had been equipped, in addition to the 1,400 miles already fitted with the former G.W.R. system. The principle, using electro-magnets on track and train, was designed to give drivers a visible and audible warning in the cab on approaching "distant" or "warning" signals on the line – a crucial signal in train operations. When the signal is at "clear" a bell sounds. When it is at "caution" a siren sounds and a dial indication appears; if the driver does not re-set the instrument a partial application of the brakes takes place. This ensures that the driver does not miss the line-side signal.

The New Signal-boxes

Some power-operated signal-boxes, and large numbers of track circuits and electric colour-light signals, had been installed between the two World Wars by the former group companies. Modern techniques employing electronics and solid state equipment have since revolutionised signalling and train control; they allow more trains through a given section of line to move at higher speeds in even greater safety. Checks and counter-checks through mechanical and electrical interlocking have greatly increased safety. Many power boxes have been erected, to operate signals and points many miles away by the push of a button or the turn of a thumb-switch. Some installations control as much as a hundred miles of railway, and have replaced several manual boxes.

The movement of trains is shown on a large illuminated diagram on the wall, the miniature lights operated by low-voltage circuits in the running rails as trains pass over them. "Running" numbers of trains are thrown up on the diagram by means of the digital displays. Meanwhile, many traditional signal-boxes with their ranks of heavy levers connected to points and oil-lighted semaphore signals will continue in service until their time comes to be replaced by power installations. The Railways Board were still anxious to speed the changeover, as expressed in the annual report for 1971:

" . . . of 3,314 signalboxes, only 222 are modern power boxes, each of which replaced many of the old manual boxes. Given adequate investment, the whole railway system in this country could in fact be operated in time by some 75 to 80 power boxes of advanced design." This would mean an average of nearly 150 route miles per power installation.

TRANSPORT ACT 1968

Under a Labour Government many radical changes, largely organisational and administrative, resulted from the Transport Act 1968. In addition to the new division for workshops, other divisions or subsidiaries were created: British Rail Shipping and International services; the pioneering British Rail Hovercraft, for services crossing the Solent and the English Channel; and the British Rail Property Board, to manage property that combined to form the sixth biggest estate in Britain. In meeting their obligations of making the best use of railway land, the Property Board's work included the developing of modern office blocks on railway sites, and selling off areas of land, unwanted for railway purposes, for the building of homes. Also managed were rented properties on railway stations and elsewhere, such as shops.

The Act created the National Freight Corporation, a body separate from the Railways Board and answerable direct to the Government. The Corporation was allocated a 51 per cent share of Freightliners Ltd., leaving the Railways Board with 49 per cent. The Railway Sundries Division, carrying small freight of up to three tons by rail and road, was also transferred to the Corporation and named National Carriers Ltd. The Act also set up the National Bus Company to control all the companies operating public bus services, except municipal services, the central buses of London Transport, and a few private operators.

Electric colour light signals at Faversham, Kent, photographed in 1969. Telephones are installed at strategic signals to enable a train driver to speak to the signalman. (Photo: British Rail)

The N.B.C. shared equally with British Rail another company – British Transport Advertising Ltd. – selling advertising space on railway properties and in other railway media, and on N.B.C. buses.

Freightliner services were extended into the industrial heart of Europe via Harwich using British Rail's purpose-built cellular container ships, thus making Harwich Britain's principal container port for short sea routes. Earlier, in 1968, Freighliner business with the Continent had been opened with the first London–Paris service using British Rail's train ferry route via Dover–Dunkirk. The British network coupled with the container trains which had been developed in Europe, were especially prized by motor manufacturers on both sides of the North Sea.

MORE MODERNISATION

The New Coaches

An important stage in passenger carriage development came in 1971 with the introduction of the Mark II D coaches fitted with air-conditioning and sound proofing. Standard coaches designed in the early years of nationalisation were approaching the end of their working life and replacements included the new stock. Filtered air, heated or cooled according to the weather, circulated through ducts in floor and ceiling, and was changed every four minutes. Windows were sealed and double-glazed, the outer panes being tinted to reduce glare. Improved wheel bogies combined with sound-proofing added to travel comfort. Wider doors at the coach ends made it easier for passengers with luggage to get in and out. A public address system for passenger information was installed. Lighting, furnishing and decor were designed to match, in accordance with the requirements of civilised travel.

The new coaches first ran on the London (King's Cross) to Newcastle route and as more came off the production lines from British Rail workshops, they were progressively put into service on other Inter-City routes. British Rail became the first railway in Europe to introduce air conditioning in standard coaches on regular services without the payment of supplementary charge, and not – as before – on luxury trains only. Soon afterwards an entirely new range of passenger coaches, the Mark III series for the High Speed Train project, went into production. These were longer (75 ft., as opposed to 63½ ft.) and required fewer coaches to make up a train of a given number of seats. By 1976 upwards of 1,500 were expected to be in service, along with many of the Mark II type. New restaurant and buffer cars were designed at the same time.

New Commuter Train

A prototype commuter train, designed by railway engineers and built in the railway workshops at York, began public service in the Southern Region in 1973. With fast acceleration and a maximum speed of 75 m.p.h., it was scheduled to complete about 250,000 miles on busy commuter lines to test every feature of performance before going into production.

Motorail train seen at St. Austell, Cornwall. (Photo: British Rail)

This prototype commuter train began public service in the Southern Region in 1973. It included many new features for test running, and was designed as a basis for study of new standard inner suburban services on all regions. (Photo: British Rail)

Refurbished Diesel Multi-Unit Coaches

Diesel multi-units, pride and joy of the 1955 modernisation plan, eventually needed bringing up to date by restyling and technical improvement. Many of them, though technically sound, were between 11 and 17 years old when, in 1974, a prototype was assembled for test running. The outside was painted white, separated by a broad rail blue waistband, to present a strikingly different appearance. Restyled interiors, a heating system more responsive to weather changes, and new designs in engine mountings and the silencer system would improve travel on local services mainly outside London. Refurbishing some 1,800 coaches, representing over half the diesel multi-unit stock, was scheduled to begin in 1975; they would continue in service well into the 1980s.

The Electric Scots

The main line between Crewe and Glasgow was electrified in 1974, providing for the first time electric services throughout from London (Euston) to Glasgow (Central). The project took only four years to carry out and cost £74,000,000. Government consent had been obtained in February 1970. For British Rail it was another historic achievement. Preparatory track and bridge reconstructions, adaptation of tunnels, overhead wire erection, alterations to stations, and the installation of new signalling and the necessary power boxes combined to present a massive and complex challenge. In its execution much was gained from the experience of the Euston – Crewe – Liverpool – Manchester project completed eight years earlier. As in that programme, a completed section – Crewe to Preston – was brought into service in advance of the main scheme, in this case ten months in advance.

Arrangements had been made with the Central Electricity Generating Board and the South of Scotland Electricity Board as early as 1970 for power supplies to be taken from the National Grid at seven railway feeder stations. A fleet of 35 Class 87 5,000 h.p. electric locomotives were built for the new service, at a cost of more than £6,500,000, to add to the 195 electric locomotives already running on the English routes. Weighing 80 tons, these locomotives could haul 400-ton Inter-City trains, and with two working in multiple, freight trains of 1,300 tons. They could take the heavy gradients, such as those at Shap and Beattock, in their stride: contributing one of the reasons for high average speeds. Many of the coaches were of Mark II stock with air-conditioning, double-glazed windows with the outer panes tinted against glare, sound insulation and improved bogies which provided smoother riding qualities. Rails were already continuously welded between Euston and Glasgow.

An increase of 30 per cent in overall speed was achieved. The fastest train was the *Royal Scot*, inaugurated (but un-named) by the London & North Western Railway in 1848. With a stop at Preston in each direction, it was scheduled to

Second class travel in the 1970s. New improved carriages are fitted with double-glazed windows, air-conditioning equipment, better spring bogies and wide doors for easier access as standard features. Compare with the picture on page 81. (Photo: British Rail)

complete the 401-mile journey in exactly five hours: it achieved a maximum speed of 100 m.p.h. and an average of 80 m.p.h. The average journey time for non-stop trains on the route was 5 hrs. 12 mins.

FREIGHT IN BULK

In the movement of freight, the railways achieved what they set out to do as outlined in their 1955 and 1963 policy plans: and that was to make the train load the predominant unit of movement instead of the wagon load. At the same time, because of the continuing market for freight in single wagon loads, operations and marshalling yard assembly were revised; this led to more effective trunking by gathering together at key points enough single wagon loads to form a train for the main part of the journey. Wasteful shunting was reduced. Local goods trains trundling slowly along the line to drop off or pick up two or three wagons at local stations had had their day.

Coal and steel products dominated the freight scene, and on average accounted for some three-quarters of the total freight tonnage carried: coal for electric power generating installations forming the largest single sector. Regular trains for this traffic ran as "merry-go-rounds", back and forth between colliery and power station, loaded there and empty back. Wagons could be used for two or three round trips daily, many of the trains carrying over a thousand tons at a time. Sidings were specially equipped for efficient and speedy handling. Coal, Britain's chief source of power, acquired a fresh importance in a world shortage of energy from all principal sources; and British Rail were carrying more than half of Britain's total coal production.

A large proportion of freight originates in private sidings; and by 1974, some 80 big companies had made heavy investment both in sidings and in their own purpose-built wagons, committing themselves to rail freight services for many years to come. From the early 1960s, many long-term contracts for up to ten years had been signed for regular freight movements, and later renewed. As is common in long-term contracts, allowances were made for the effect of inflation.

T.O.P.S.

Efficient freight train operation has always centred on the control of the wagon fleet: supplying empty wagons of all kinds where and when needed, and keeping loaded ones on the move to their destinations. In the 1930s, wagon control was administered mainly through the former district operating control offices, aided by freight rolling stock travelling inspectors; and a reasonable level of efficiency was achieved. In the 1960s, a new system managed from the centre in London direct to nearly 40 key points throughout the railways, was introduced: a simpler and better method. It was urgently needed at that time, for in 1962 wagons spent more time standing – empty or loaded – than in moving; and the "turnround time", the period from one loading to the next, averaged 12½ days.

The next important stage came in 1973 with the introduction of the Total Operations Processing System (TOPS), which was the first complete computer control for freight wagons and locomotives. Exeter–Plymouth was the first area to use the system, which was completed progressively by 1975 to serve the whole network. The computer in London was linked direct to some 200 important freight centres, such as goods stations, marshalling yards and locomotive depots. Nearly 3,000 wagon despatch and receiving points were served, and over 6,000 freight trains handled daily.

SCIENCE AND TECHNOLOGY

The Derby Technical Centre

Still more advanced scientific and technical research was needed by the new railways if they were to exploit to the full their unique potential. Dating back to the four main line companies, individual railways had long devoted their energies, fragmented though they were, to seeking the latest and best technical knowledge. Company officers maintained links with other countries to exchange information and keep abreast of new developments. Responsibility for research for the L.M.S. Railway was in the hands of a vice-president.

During those periods and since, numerous inventions by railway scientists and engineers, in seeking a better way, have now built up into a body of patents of substantial international value. They ranged from oils and paints formulae to metal fatigue data and electronic techniques. Following nationalisation, the various resources were brought together; and the 1955 modernisation plan created new and urgent demands which ideally required to be met by a single new establishment. An environment was needed in which scientists could think ahead for some decades, and in which advanced computer technology would be as widely used as operating theory is in the marshalling yard.

For the new technical era, British Rail chose Derby for its centre, where the former L.M.S. Railway laboratories were located. Geographically well situated and 120 miles from London, there were other advantages. It was the location of world-famous railway works with over a century of experience in building locomotives, carriages and wagons; and of well established technical equipment. Work went ahead. The first

A diesel-hauled coal train from Firbeck colliery to Burton Power Station near Gainsborough. (Photo: British Rail)

laboratories and offices were formally opened in 1964 by the Duke of Edinburgh. Extensions were opened in 1967, 1970 and 1971, representing a total Government-assisted investment of over £4,000,000. Occupying a site of 20 acres, it removed the handicap of a wide dispersal of several allied activities. Engineering administration and the supplies department were also accommodated in the complex of offices.

Eventually, about 2,000 men and women – more than half of them professionally qualified scientists, engineers and technicians, comprised the personnel. Some had been recruited from other organisations, including the aircraft industry.

At Derby, several methods of automatic communication between track or control centre and train were the subject of research. One of the most promising pieces of equipment, tested on the London–Birmingham route in 1974, was a mobile laboratory, called Test Coach Mercury. On the trial journeys, it was not used in effect to control the running of the trains in which it was travelling; but for testing the equipment which might be used to aid the drivers of future high-speed trains. It would send coded messages between track and train to identify the train's exact location and other information, such as the approach to a speed restriction on the route. An objective was to display in the driver's cab information about the running of the train.

Electronic "beacons" called transponders were fastened to sleepers between the rails, from which inductive signals were picked up. Each beacon could send only the message that was coded into it during manufacture; it required no maintenance because it needed no internal or external power supply. Thirty transponders were originally installed, later increased to about 150, to cover operation on the London–Birmingham route in both directions.

During the tests Mercury, adapted from a former Southern Region passenger coach, was making three round trips a day, covering some 3,400 miles a week. Accuracy of information received was checked in a mini-computer and recorded. Reliability needed to be confirmed beyond doubt, before the system could be put to practical use for high-speed trains.

The Tribometer Train

To study further the friction between wheel and rail: the crucial link through which railway vehicles are accelerated and braked, a special Tribometer Test Train was commissioned in 1973. To improve adhesion techniques and methods, an investigation was conducted into the physical and chemical conditions on the line and in the laboratory. Better adhesion would reduce damage to wheels and rails caused by wheels spinning or locking, as well as reduce operating costs. Based at the Derby Technical Centre, the train embarked upon an intensive programme in varying operating and atmospheric conditions, to collect data for future use.

The new Derby Technical Centre was claimed to be the most advanced of its kind in the world; and in its comparatively short corporate life has earned a universal reputation in transport research that is not confined only to railways. It has placed Britain's railways to the forefront in the electronic age, and will produce more significant technical improvements than had taken place throughout the previous century.

New Trains of the Future

Of all the original researches conducted by the scientific and engineering teams at Derby, their outstanding contribution was in the conception, design and construction of the new breed of high-speed trains that came to make railway history. Talented innovators found their rightful role. The early 1970s could be seen as the watershed in the saga of locomotive building and passenger and freight train operation. Britain was to keep the lead that the Stephensons had bequeathed. Judgment and confidence within the railways was vindicated as this pioneering transmutation took shape. Full Government support had been earned.

When the railways were considering the trains of the future, they faced two alternatives: to build a totally new railway, or to build new and faster trains adapted to the existing network. They chose the latter in a decision that was irrevocable for as far ahead as imagination would stretch. Tracked hovertrains and other systems which would require a totally new track, had to be discarded, mainly because of the problem of finding and financing land to build anew in congested Britain: as indeed they had been discarded in other countries.

European railways, in seeking ways of running long distance expresses, had settled for the Trans-Europe Express (TEE) approach – a network of excellent but first-class-only trains available to a limited number of passengers on payment of a supplement. British Rail's aim was to spend money on improvements in speed and comfort for all passengers on all main services, without supplementary charges.

Market researches into service characteristics had shown that the most significant factor was shorter journey time, which is, of course, achieved mainly by increasing speed. Other factors, such as better coaches, more frequent services, brighter stations and improved catering, though vital, still took second place to speed. Faster journey times would make the railways more competitive with all other forms of transport and generate much new business.

The new trains were part of a long-term programme in three clear-cut stages for Inter-City services:

Stage I – Electrification of the main rail arteries associated with the London (Euston)–Glasgow route; the development of high-performance diesel locomotives for routes not being electrified; maximum speed 100 m.p.h., average 80 m.p.h.; this stage was completed in 1974.

Stage II – Programmed introduction of the High-Speed Train on non-electrified routes; maximum speed 125 m.p.h., average 95 mp.h.

Stage III – Programmed introduction of the Advanced Passenger Train both for electrified and non-electrified routes; maximum speed 155 m.p.h., average 100 m.p.h. +.

The new fast trains would run on conventional but improved track. Capital cost would therefore be mainly for the trains.

British Rail now built two prototype trains: the High-Speed Train (HST) capable of speeds of up to 125 m.p.h., and the Advanced Passenger Train (APT) for speeds of up to 155 m.p.h. H.S.T. was to be precursor of the A.P.T. by a few years. It was calculated that between 1975 and 1990, the average speed (start to stop) on five principal routes will have been raised from over 70 m.p.h. to over 100 m.p.h.

H.S.T.

The H.S.T. prototype consisted of two streamlined diesel-electric power units (locomotives), one at each end of the train, and seven new 75 ft. long Mark III passenger coaches, including catering vehicles. Each power car was equipped with a Paxman 2,250 h.p. diesel engine and Brush electrical equipment, giving a total train output of 4,500 h.p.

Advanced technology had reduced the weight of the prototype by nearly one-fifth compared with conventional trains of equivalent capacity; the improved power to weight ratio resulted in faster acceleration and reduced fuel consumption. Air-operated disc brakes ensured smooth and comfortable deceleration from 125 m.p.h. within the stopping distances of 100 m.p.h. trains and within the present signalling system. Wheel-slide protection was fitted to all axles. Air-pressure springing fitted as secondary suspension reduced wear and tear on vehicles and track.

Coaches were of improved design: double-glazed windows with the outer pane tinted against glare, air-conditioning giving an even temperature for all seasons, and an air change every four minutes. Improved sound insulation reduced travel strain and fatigue. New seating, fittings and decor created a restful and attractive travel environment. For the first time, carpets were fitted in second class coaches: a far cry from Stephenson's wooden wagons and bench seats. All interior doors were automatic, operated by tread-mats; this was to help passengers with small children and luggage, and passengers and catering staff moving from and to restaurant and buffet cars.

A World Speed Record

Meanwhile, on test runs in June 1973, the prototype train broke two historic speed records, which news naturally was highly rewarding to the railways in general and to the engineering and design teams in particular. It became the fastest train ever to run in Britain when it reached 131 m.p.h. between Darlington and York – the route itself enshrined in rail history. This broke the 35-year-old record of 126 m.p.h. made by the L.N.E.R. steam locomotive *Mallard* in 1938. Five days later, a world record for diesel trains was created when it ran at 141 m.p.h. between Thirsk and Tollerton in Yorkshire, improving this to 143 m.p.h. the very next day. The previously unbroken record of 133 m.p.h. had been set up by a German diesel train in 1939.

With the laurels still green, 27 new H.S.T.s were ordered. The first batch was scheduled for the London (Paddington), Bristol and South Wales route in 1976; the London–Cardiff journey of 145 miles would take only 1¾ hours. A prototype was introduced on this route in 1975. In an announcement dated 30th October 1974, the Railways Board stated that an additional 32 H.S.T.s were to be built for the East Coast main line to take over services between King's Cross and Edinburgh, the West Riding, and Hull. Journey time would be cut initially from 5½ hours to 4½ hours, and by 1979 to 4 hrs. 20 mins. According to production schedules all 59 H.S.T.s will be in service by 1977/78.

In its trial running under service conditions but without passengers, the prototype H.S.T. completed about 100,000 miles during some nine months up to May 1974. On regular journeys between York and Darlington it reached 125 m.p.h., and ran for many miles at 100 m.p.h. on frequent Leeds–Edinburgh journeys. The train then returned to Derby for examination in detail by engineers and designers, and for any modifications indicated by their findings. More main line running was conducted for the familiarisation of drivers, maintenance teams and other rail staff.

H.S.T. – Comparative Speeds

Taking London as the starting point, the table compares current Inter-City speeds with the fastest timings on the routes the High Speed Trains will first run:

The Advanced Passenger Train demonstrating its body tilting capabilities during the first series of track trials. (*Photo: British Rail*)

				H.S.T.	
	miles	*time h. m.*	*average speed*	*time h. m.*	*average speed*
Bath	107	1–38	66	1–11	90
Bristol	118	1–50	65	1–22	87
Cardiff	145	2–11	67	1–46	82
Doncaster	156	2–04	75	1–39	95
York	188	2–22	79	2–00	94
Leeds	186	2–28	75	2–14	83
Darlington	232	2–52	81	2–31	92
Newcastle	268	3–38	74	2–57	91
Edinburgh	393	5–30	71	4–30	87

It is an unfortunate fact that the progress of the new fast trains was delayed for over a year by the failure to obtain the co-operation of A.S.L.E.F., either at their headquarters or at local level, for the running programme. The drivers' union was anxious to secure better rewards than were offered, for the added responsibility of driving trains at speeds of 125–155 m.p.h. This created a costly gap in the working schedules both for the railway workshops and the major suppliers from whom British Rail purchased electrical and other specialised equipment.

A.P.T.

Progress with the experimental Advanced Passenger Train continued side by side with the High Speed Train. But why two trains? Development of revolutionary techniques needed to be absorbed cautiously into the railway system at an evolutionary pace. One train was the stepping stone to the other. Remaining always was the overriding consideration that public services should continue to run with the least possible disruption.

At Derby, a special Advanced Projects laboratory was established for the new train, of which a model was constructed in 1970. In announcing details of progress, the Railways Board had emphasised: "It is not just a fast train. It is a major technological breakthrough in advance of developments on any other railway in the world."

The experimental train, dubbed A.P.T.–E, contained a mass of electronic and data measuring equipment of all kinds relating to stress, resonance and total performance; it was a mobile laboratory which would not run in public service. It consisted of two power cars, one at each end, and two trailer cars. Each of the four-wheeled bogies carried the ends of adjoining cars – "articulated" – thus making a firm train forma-

Driving cab of the Advanced Passenger Train. (Photo: British Rail)

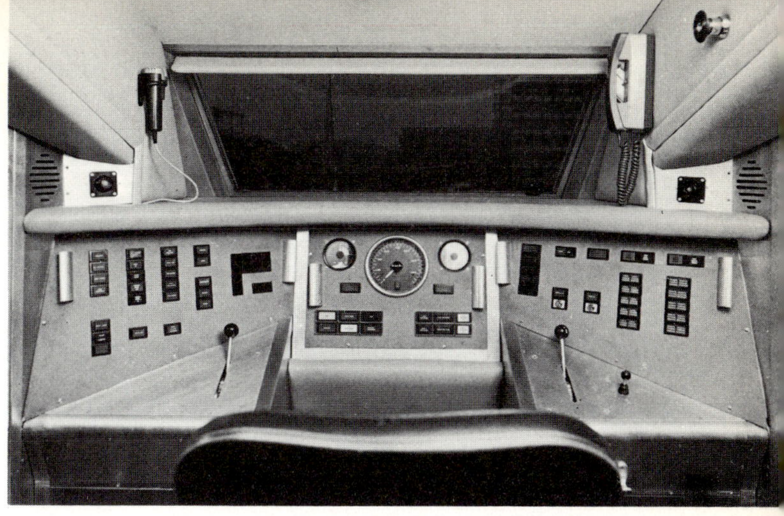

tion. Passenger doors were located above the bogies. The power cars were 69 ft. long and the trailer cars 63 ft.

Lightweight construction embodied a refined and streamlined shape. The train was designed to create less aerodynamic disturbance and to cause less track damage at high speeds than conventional trains caused at 100 m.p.h. The sealed cars would protect passengers from the air disturbance and pressure as the train rushed into a tunnel or passed another at speed. The train of thc future would weigh half as much per seat as conventional B.R. stock, itself lighter than the coaches of many other countries. The trailer cars were built with a double skin aluminium riveted structure similar to an aircraft.

A unique suspension system was built into the bogies, which were specially designed for the train. Although they appeared ordinary to the layman, they were the harvest of years of research and close study of the way vehicles ride on track and their behaviour at high speed: rail-vehicle dynamics that were dramatically new. The traditional form of rail vehicle guidance is the wheel flange; the new suspension and other bogie techniques removed almost entirely flange-to-rail friction, the finely balanced components producing a virtually self-steering characteristic. It was realised from the start that conventional braking by purely frictional means would not suffice for stopping a train from high speeds within the existing signalling distance. The power cars were fitted with a highly efficient electric braking system, and the cars with hydro-kinetic brakes, each axle containing a device resembling a fluid flywheel; rotor-stator turbine braking discs were mounted on and within the axles and high braking torque was generated, absorbing the train energy. Hydro-kinetic braking coped with the top speeds, conventional braking taking over at lower speeds.

Unquestionably the new feature of the A.P.T. which attracted greatest world-wide attention was the coach tilting mechanism to counter sideways thrust on curves at high speed. Tilt range extended to 9° on either side of centre. Centrifugal force was countered as the body leaned sideways, similar to a cyclist taking a corner. It was the first time in railway history that this technical innovation had been designed to such near-perfection. A welcome bonus was that passengers would be able to take their soup or coffee at high speeds without a spill!

Tilting allowed an increase in speed of some 50 per cent on curves, and was one of the main reasons for the continuing high speed potential: there would be no need to slow when taking a curve. Its value could be clearly seen when it was recalled that most of the railway is on curved track, however slight. Few stretches in Britain are dead straight for more than a few miles. The longest is 18 miles on the Selby–Hull line, followed by 16 miles between Boston and Burgh-le-Marsh. About a third of the London–Dover main line is nearly straight for 24 miles from Tonbridge, but only dead straight for 10½ miles as far as Staplehurst.

Tilt was not absolutely essential for the higher speeds. It was designed principally for passenger comfort. Power operated and governed by an electro-hydraulic system with accelerometer units, the mechanism could prevent unwanted tilts from heavy side winds or passengers joining and alighting at stations. Train suspension allowed for automatic height and level compensation for variations in the numbers of passengers carried – the payload. The centre of tilt rotation was about the seat height of the sitting passenger.

The driving cab, fully air-conditioned and sound-proofed, was strongly built. It had a double skin front, a hoop structure and a small thick "sandwich" windscreen.

On its maiden voyage in July 1972, the A.P.T.–E ran between Derby and Duffield at the modest speed of 50 m.p.h. Test running demonstrated a good correspondence between calculated and actual performance. The highlight of speed trials came in October 1973 when the train reached 125 m.p.h., improving later to about 130 m.p.h.

Three electric prototype A.P.T.s were ordered in 1974 for services from 1977 on the West Coast main line between London (Euston) and Glasgow. With a maximum speed of 125 m.p.h., the journey time would be reduced from five hours to four. Later, they would operate up to their current maximum speeds of 155 m.p.h.

CO-OPERATION WITH RAILWAYS OVERSEAS

One Railway for Europe

A public plea for an effective common policy for transport for all the countries in the European Economic Community (Common Market) was made in March 1974 by Robert Long, executive director of the international policy of British Rail. He was addressing students at the College of Europe in Bruges: "Without such a policy, the Common Market will never become a real European Community. . . . Within this framework, the railways of the Communities must determine their future . . . firstly with their own governments who will decide the shape of the policy, and secondly, with the other Community railways in achieving a modern, financially secure railway network.

"The opportunity for railways arose from the current realisation that we may be beginning to press up against the limits of the earth's capacity to supply its population with energy and deal with its pollution; and that the railway has a particular contribution to make in the conservation of land and energy and in improving the quality of life."

Commenting on signs of recent progress, Long said: "In 1973 a contract was signed by Eurofima (the financing company of the International Union of Railways) on behalf of six railways for the design and construction of 500 European standard coaches . . .

"Technical co-operation has always been good. It is, however, in development of research that national preferences tend to persist: individualism may be the spur, but the same individuality in application could apply brakes to the development of guided transport in Europe if incompatible systems were developed.

"The interests of railways are so interlocked by 'through' working between individual systems . . . that the dominant objective for future survival must be to place the interests of the network before the interests of the national system."

Each country had its own long history; and at the present time the statutes under which the national railways in each country work require them to meet national objectives. And until this situation is altered, Long reasoned, there can be no dramatic change: "A widespread concern for the environment and a growing anxiety over the world's resources, particularly fuel, have overshadowed the increasing burden of railway finances.

"What have railways to offer in this situation? Surely, this is the current opportunity which railways must seize within the development of the Common Transport Policy."

Environmental standards and the quality of life in the more crowded European Community of the future would require vital economies in the use of space, resources and energy. New ways of economising on water and reducing atmospheric pollution should be found.

World-Wide Railway Co-operation

A continuing process of sustaining rail links with Europe began in earnest in the 19th century when railway ships connected the railway networks. In 1872, the European Timetable Conference was formed; and ten years later a Conference for the Technical Unity of Railways which still functions, its brief to study "the regulations with which railway tracks and vehicles must comply for running in international services."

In 1885, the International Railway Congress Association was set up, followed five years later by the International Convention concerning the Carriage of Goods. The International Rail Transport Committee came into being in 1902, and in 1921, following the First World War, the International Wagon Union and the International Carriage and Brake Van Union.

Functions of these various bodies were permanently taken over and co-ordinated by a new organisation founded in 1922 – the Union Internationale des Chemins de fer (UIC), commonly known as the International Union of Railways, with headquarters in Paris. Among its wide-ranging interests were standardising vehicles, equipment and operations, automatic vehicle couplers, policy, investment, economics, research and experiments, documentation, exchange of information, Trans–Europe–Express services (TEE), and the application of cybernetics to promote automation, rationalisation and productivity.

One U.I.C. study group sought "optimum passenger comfort", with special attention devoted to vibration, noise, lighting, and other factors likely to cause fatigue. Over the years, the influence of the U.I.C. has spread widely. Its members represent more than 40 railways in many parts of the world, including those in Canada, Africa, the Middle East, India and Japan.

THE CHANNEL TUNNEL

Prospects for a tunnel under the English Channel began to look brighter when the Anglo-French Agreement was signed in 1973. The possibility of trains running through it in the early 1980s was clearly visualised. Its future would depend upon other important development programmes likely to require substantial national resources, and upon environmental factors. But talk of a tunnel had all started well before Stephenson's first railway.

In the constantly changing drama of the tunnel, the curtain rose on the French side as early as 1802 when a mining engineer named Albert Mathieu-Favier presented his proposal to Napoleon, then First Consul to the French Republic. It was intended for horses and coaches, with outlets through ventilation chimneys sticking up above the sea – and this in sailing ship days! Charles James Fox, the distinguished English politician, said of it: "This is one of the great enterprises we can now undertake together." Napoleon apparently held other views.

Another Frenchman of many talents, named Thomé de Gamond, prepared a scheme in the 1850s in the halcyon days of the new railways. The idea earned the approval of Brunel, Locke and Robert Stephenson, but came to nothing.

Nuclear weapons and closer ties with other nations have since rendered defence considerations relatively less significant. In recent years the concept of a new Channel link by tunnel has outweighed alternatives such as a bridge, or a tube laid on the sea bed. Phase II, stemming from the 1973 Agreement, included testing the equipment, digging trial borings, and boring the service tunnel for about two miles from either side.

The "tunnel" would consist of three borings: one bore in each direction between Cheriton, near Folkestone, and Sangatte, near Calais. It would be designed exclusively for electrified railways, using the 25kV a.c. overhead wire system, standard for both British and French railways. The smaller-bore service tunnel would run between, but slightly lower than, the two main bores, and would be primarily for telecommunications and ventilation equipment. The distance between the two tunnel entrances would be 35 miles, to become the longest tunnel in Europe, and the longest rail tunnel in the world.

Building costs would be shared between the two countries: and of the British share, capital would be raised on the open money market – 10 per cent of it risk capital, and 90 per cent supported by Government guarantee.

A separate project was found to be desirable to make the tunnel viable: the building of a new high speed railway between Folkestone and London.

It is only in recent years that a combination of engineering ability and volume of traffic has existed to make the project both feasible and economic. The reality could well make a lasting contribution to the economy and goodwill within Britain and Europe. However, the reality suffered another setback when the Government examined the estimated costs of a new rail link between Cheriton and London. On 26th November 1974, Anthony Crossland, Secretary of State for the Environment, made a statement in Parliament:

"The Government have now completed their examination of a revised cost estimate by British Railways. This amounts to £373,000,000 at May 1974 prices, and this excludes the additional environmental works which have been canvassed in Surrey and Kent, the greatest part of the cost of compensation under the 1973 Land Compensation Act, and the cost of enabling the link to carry freight, which was not previously envisaged.

"It is out of the question that the Government should approve or finance an investment of this magnitude. We must find some less expensive means of enabling the through rail traffic, which forms so essential an aspect of the tunnel project, to gain access to London and the British rail network. British Railways are, therefore, urgently examining a range of lower-cost options intended to achieve the greatest possible volume of through traffic, including freight, while avoiding detriment to the existing Southern system."

Yet another, more serious setback arose on 20th January 1975 when Anthony Crossland stated in Parliament: "It had become clear that we would not be able to meet the deadline for the ratification (of the Channel Tunnel Treaty and various agreements) of 1st January 1975 . . . Nor, in the current economic circumstances, and in the light of the Government's first determination to control public expenditure in the difficult years which lie immediately ahead, do I see the slightest prospect of the tunnel being taken over as a directly Government-sponsored project. The project will, therefore, be run down as soon as possible." The Minister gave assurances, however, that everything practical would be done meanwhile to enable the tunnel scheme to be revived at a more propitious time.

MANAGEMENT IN THE HIGH SPEED ERA

One of the requirements of the 1968 Act was that the Railways Board should review its organisation. The new management structure that was devised first of all separated the railway from the other business activities at Board level; secondly, it reassigned those responsibilities below Board level on a basis common to the whole system.

This was the first time since the railways had come into national ownership in 1948, that a fundamental rethink had been applied to the management mechanisms considered desirable for the new era of railways emerging in the 1970s. As this era of a modern high speed network with its supporting conurbations approached, a revised management structure was indeed seen as essential for the proper development and prosperity of the business into the next decade.

Its intention was to simplify what had grown into an over-complex organisation, and to enable the railway to be run as a single system, rather than five semi-independent railways. The five regions (London Midland, Eastern, Western, Southern, and Scottish) and the next management tier below consisting of 21 "traffic" divisions, were to be abolished; they were to be replaced by eight new geographical "territories" termed regions. Completion, through programmed stages, was expected in the mid-1970s, and to coincide with the introduction of the first High Speed Trains designed to run at 125 m.p.h.

Under the direction of David Bowick, the first chief executive (railways) in the new structure, overall policy, investment, planning, major engineering and architectural projects, planning of main trunk passenger and freight services, and the routine accounting processes, were to be centralised at rail headquarters; all such work, however, was not to be located in London. Each of the proposed eight new "territories" was to be headed by a regional director.

name of new region	*location of headquarters*
Scotland	Glasgow
North East	Newcastle
North West	Manchester
Yorkshire	York
Midlands	Birmingham
Anglia	London (Liverpool Street and King's Cross)
Western	Cardiff
Southern	London (Waterloo and Croydon)

Some offices were located in the provinces in support of Government and Railways Board policy to avoid an over concentration of management and administration in the capital; but the headquarters for the Anglia and Southern regions were to be based in London, because of the intensity of the train services and the scale of activities in London and its environs in these two new regions.

Technical departments were also to be reorganised to fit the new structure, with similar ground level area and depot engineering managements to counterpart those for train operations.

By replacing four tiers of management with three, substantial staff economies were possible as a by-product of the re-organisation. Over 4,000 posts, it was estimated, could be saved, mainly clerical, administrative and managerial; assets would be more economically employed. Such a major exercise needed close co-operation with the railway trade unions, involving full consultation at every stage, control of recruiting, retirements, and the filling of vacant posts.

However, by early 1975, because of galloping inflation, deterioration of national economic conditions, and the problems for many railwaymen who would be required to move their homes, agreement between railway management and the Transport Salaried Staffs Association for the immediate implementation of the new management structure had not been reached. The Railways Board therefore decided to change course and to proceed with only certain parts of the reorganisation, concentrating on those elements of the original plan which would avoid staff moving home.

* * *

The railways of Britain have survived into the fourth quarter of the 20th century with notable credit, the system still remaining one of the most modern and efficient among the main networks of the world. The route mileage has been progressively pruned from the peak of over 20,000 miles in the early 1930s to a little over 11,000 miles in 1975, to become the most intensively used system in the world. Every day, some 18,000 trains are carrying over 2,000,000 passengers; and 7,000 freight trains are serving trade and industry.

Britain's Inter-City trains, with a combination of speed, frequency, reliability, regularity and comfort, provide passenger services of a quality which few other countries can equal and none can surpass. Certainly, some individual services elsewhere (a few "crack" trains in Europe and – for the present, at any rate – trains on Japan's Tokaido line) can outstrip British Rail's fastest trains, but the average speeds in Britain generally are higher.

The High Speed Trains and the Advanced Trains will begin to be a common sight in the early 1980s; and another major electrification, already high on the priority list – the East Coast main line from King's Cross to Edinburgh via Peterborough, Doncaster, York, Darlington and Newcastle – may be seen as a reality.

Fuel shortage, environmental and social questions, and the tragic and growing carnage on the roads, are factors continuously working in favour of railways.

What drives the railways on? Mr. Graham Calder, Chief Mechanical and Electrical Engineer of British Rail, gave his version in a talk to rail staff at York in 1974:

"We live in a crazy, competitive world where the accent is on speed and time saving – even if we aren't sure how we are going to use the precious minutes we've saved.

"The pressures to develop equipments for high speeds come from many sources – the Government, the Railways Board, our customers and others. But it is really the threat of loss of business to our competitors, or our inability to win traffic from them, that drives us towards this goal."

The driving competition that spurred the early pioneers to find better ways of moving people and goods still remains the creative force that motivates the railway managers in the last part of the 20th century.

Power car No. 41 001 of the prototype High Speed Train (HST) which holds the World Speed Record for diesel trains.

Richard Trevithick commemorative medal of 2 inches diameter depicting the Pen-y-darren locomotive of 1804, struck by Toye, Kenning & Spencer Ltd. in 1973. Designed by Trevithick's great grandson, Richard, who died in 1973, and D. F. Payne

Chapter 10

Classic Locomotives

THE pages which follow present a chronological listing of nearly 70 important locomotives from the earliest pioneering engines to the latest diesels and electrics of a type that will virtually see the 20th century throughout. Each type is briefly described. Major characteristics are indicated in a form of specification to reflect the progressive development throughout British locomotive history.

Apart from selecting examples representative of their time, a main criterion has been that each locomotive chosen shall have its own story to tell. Choice is necessarily arbitrary and any railway author finds it difficult to resist old favourites; but the cameos take account of the interests of the general reader as well as those of the ardent and knowledgeable enthusiast. Several locomotives in the list are preserved.

Strangely enough, the magic of steam still persists, and indeed grows, as more and more locomotives are preserved. Many are lovingly restored to their former glory and set upon the rails to bring a new experience to the young and a haunting nostalgia to those still young in heart as they catch a whiff of steam and oil, a sight of gyrating coupling rods, and the sound of pounding engine and shrilling whistle.

Basic principles of the steam locomotive have not altered since Stephenson's day: a boiler of water heated by a fire to create steam for pushing a piston back and forth within a cylinder, and a connecting rod to rotate the wheels. Most engines had two cylinders, some types having three or four.

For many years, coke was the standard fuel; often timber and peat were used. Coal was found to be the most efficient, and as locomotives improved, a better quality of coal was needed. The problem of furred-up boiler tubes was overcome by the use of water softeners which were erected at motive power depots.

An excess of steam pressure often caused an engine boiler to explode, and many people have been killed and countless injured. James Fenton's spring-loaded safety valve of 1812 offered good protection. Then in 1826 came fusible plugs, introduced by Sir Goldworth Gurney (1793–1875). The plugs, of a softer metal, would be "blown", not unlike an electric fuse. Several were fitted on an engine so as to direct boiler water on to the fire to douch it, thus cutting down the incidence of outright explosion, and a safeguard against water in the boiler falling dangerously low. When a stationary locomotive "blows off", conversation in the vicinity is almost impossible.

Down the years, cylinder dimensions showed comparatively little change:

		diameter	stroke
1825	*Locomotion*	10 in. ×	24 in.
1870	*Stirling*	18 in. ×	26 in.
1938	*Mallard*	18½ in. ×	26 in.

Boiler pressure, originally about 50 lb. per square inch, had increased to 250 in the late 1920s. Tractive effort, the measure of power, was 825 lb. for the *Rocket*, and for the latest steam locomotives was in the 30,000 to 40,000 lb. range.

One of the keys to greater power was the increase in the heating surface for water; this was 60 sq. ft. for *Locomotion*, and for the largest locomotives at the peak of their performance was over 3,000. This was achieved by a complex system of steel or copper tubes which ran the length of the boiler; they were surrounded by water which was boiled by the hot gases passing through them. A refinement was the superheating system by which steam passed along the tubes twice, building up the heat. They came rapidly into use in the early 1900s, superheating the steam to about 640°; the "dried" steam was rid of tiny water droplets, giving greater driving power. Superheating could save some 25 per cent of fuel and 35 per cent of water. A simple form of superheating had been tried out as early as 1839.

A number of early locomotive inventors had used boiler tubes; but George and Robert Stephenson had improved the system to such an extent by 1829 that it was a vital factor in giving the *Rocket* the lead over all others at the time.

Robert Stephenson introduced the steam brake in 1833 and 11 years later Nasmyth and May brought out a pneumatic brake. In 1841, Stephenson had solved the long standing problem of wheel slip. Tired of watching firemen running alongside an engine with a shovel, throwing dirt on the wet and greasy rails as driving wheels raced and the struggling engine throbbed, he invented the sanding gear. Sand from a container was released to flow down a pipe fitted close to the wheel and rail. A few years later, gravity feed was aided by a steam blower, to give a better distribution of sand on the rails.

Despite various cinder-catching devices, for the first 30 or so years locomotives terrified the populace by throwing red hot cinders of coke or coal in all directions, which often caused fires and personal injury. At night, a locomotive looked something like a travelling volcano. Engineers tried to find ways of retarding the passage of the gases from firebox to chimney to give more time for combustion to be completed. Matthew Kirtley (1813–74), who was locomotive superintendent of the Midland Railway 1844–73, solved the problem in 1859 when he designed a brick arch and firehole deflector plate. This deflected the combustion gases towards the back of the firebox, causing them to circulate more freely there before entering the boiler tubes. The equipment became standard. It is stated that Thomas Yarrow had also tried out brick arches on the Scottish North Eastern Railway two years earlier, but Kirtley developed the system on a large scale. Many other techniques – introduced by countless engineers – improved the power and efficiency of the steam locomotive until it reached its peak of performance.

In the following specifications, data for some of the older engines can only be approximate and is based on early engineers' drawings, contemporary artists' sketches, old prints and documents; but they are adequate for comparison of basic technical development and power rating. From the days of the *Rocket*, both weight and tractive effort have been increased about 40 times.

The basic specifications include data under the following headings:

DWD: diameter of driving wheels

CDXS: inside diameter of cylinders and length of stroke in inches

BP: boiler pressure in lb. per square inch

THS: total heating surface of water for steaming, including tubes and superheaters, in square feet

TE: tractive effort, known also as tractive force, in lb., power or hauling capacity without driving wheels slipping in overcoming train resistance. Figure is found by multiplying total weight on coupled wheels by coefficient of friction between tyres and rail, usually about 0·25. Therefore, a locomotive with 100,000 lb. on its driving wheels will exert a pull of 100,000 × 0·25 = 25,000 lb., its tractive effort. Though an exact figure is produced, it provides only an approximate guide for locomotive engineers.

WC: water capacity, gallons

CC: coal capacity, tons

WT: weight, tons

T: after the wheel arrangement, for example: 2–4–2T, indicates a tank engine with water tanks and coal bunker instead of a separate tender for fuel, generally used for shorter journeys.

Trevithick's Coalbrookdale locomotive 0–4–0, 1803. Was probably intended for Coalbrookdale Ironworks, in Shropshire. *DWD*: 3 ft.; *CDXS*: 4¾ × 36; *BP*: 40/50; *flywheel*: 7 ft. diameter; wheels coupled by a cogwheel arrangement; horizontal cylinder enclosed in a cast iron return flue boiler; axles mounted directly on to boiler with no separate frame; protruding flywheel at the rear and extended slide rodding in the front explain the overall length of 14½ ft. for so small an engine. A large flywheel was common on stationary steam pumping engines of that period. Trevithick built his improved Newcastle locomotive in 1805, with the flywheel in front and the slide rodding at the rear. The cylinder was 9 in. wide. He proved the adhesive ability of a smooth wheel to a smooth rail for hauling wagons, thus establishing firmly the steam locomotive for railways. When he was about 26, *c.* 1797, Trevithick made three models which may have formed the basis for his locomotives.

Puffing Billy, 1813. Built by William Hedley (1779–1843). *DWD*: *c.* 3 ft. 8 in.; *CDXS*: 9 × 36; *BP*: 50; *WT*: 8¼. Motion from the two vertical cylinders and "grass-hopper" beam was transmitted to the driving wheels by cogged gearing on the early Trevithick principle. Slide valves were worked by tappets. A small tender carried fuel. This famous engine, at one time converted to eight coupled wheels, worked until 1863 and is now preserved at the Science Museum, London.

Stephenson's Killingworth locomotive 0–4–0, 1815 (travelling engine). *CDXS*: 9 × 24; *BP*: 50; *THS*: 80; *WT*: 6; *wheelbase*: 7 ft. 2 in. Each of the two vertical cylinders drove an axle. Driving wheels were coupled by a chain running on small cogged wheels on the hubs of the flanged driving wheels. A small wagon (as tender) contained fuel in the front and a water barrel at the rear. Forward and reverse movements were made possible by slide valves driven by loose eccentrics. A water colour bears the inscription: "Original drawing of Stephenson's patent locomotive supposed to have been made by himself – 1815".

Locomotion No. 1, 0–4–0, 1825, built by George Stephenson at the Stephenson Works, Newcastle, for the Stockton & Darlington Railway. *DWD*: 4 ft.; *CDXS*: 9½ (later 10) × 24; *BP*: 50; *THS*: 60; *WC*: 240; *CC*: ¾; *WT*: engine only, 7; each of the two vertical cylinders drove one of the axles and the driving wheels were connected by coupling rods. *Locomotion* hauled trains on the opening day of the new railway and could pull loads of 60 to 70 tons at five miles an hour. Sometimes the chimney became almost red hot.

In 1828 its boiler exploded and the engine was rebuilt by Timothy Hackworth at Shildon Works. It remained in service on this line until 1841, and was for the opening of the Middlesbrough & Redcar Railway in 1846. In 1892, it was placed on permanent public view at Darlington Bank Top station. In September 1875, jubilee of the first railway, it ran on local lines. The following year it was sent to the Philadelphia (U.S.A.) Exhibition, to the Liverpool Exhibition of 1886, and to the Paris Exhibition of 1889. *Locomotion* appeared again for the 150th anniversary celebrations of the Stockton & Darlington in 1975. It is counted as one of the most famous steam locomotives in world railway history.

Royal George No. 5, 0–6–0, 1826, built by Wilson & Co. for the Stockton & Darlington Railway. Rebuilt by Timothy Hackworth 1827. *DWD*: 4 ft.; *CDXS*: 11 × 20; *BP*: 50; *THS*: 141; *WT*: 8½; *wheelbase*: 8 ft. 6in. Timothy Hackworth was locomotive foreman at Shildon Works, and this was virtually his locomotive. The two inverted vertical cylinders drove the same axle directly and the wheels were connected by coupling rods. The locomotive could haul over 100 tons at about five miles an hour. It remained in service until 1842.

The Rocket 0–2–2, 1829, the most famous steam locomotive in the world, designed and built by George and Robert Stephenson in their Newcastle Works, for the Liverpool & Manchester Railway. *DWD*: 4 ft. 8½ in.; *CDXS*: (2 cyls) 8 × 16½; *BP*: 50; *THS*: 138; *TE*: 825; *WT*: engine 4¼, tender 3¼; *wheelbase*: 4 ft.; *trailing wheels*: 2½ ft.; *copper tubes*: 25 of 3 in. diameter. Driving wheels were the same dimension as the rail gauge. In a competition at the Rainhill trials near Liverpool, the locomotive won easily and went into service on the new Liverpool & Manchester Railway in 1830. The Railway paid £500 for it. Its outstanding technical features were the multi-tube boiler for a greater heating surface and the blast pipe for increased combustion, principles that remained throughout steam locomotive history. It remained in service on this line until 1837 when it was sold for £300, and is reported to have run on the Midgeholme Railway covering 4 miles in 4½ minutes – about 53 m.p.h. Probably more models, both scale and full size, have been made of the *Rocket* than any other locomotive in history. The original engine and a full scale model have been seen by countless millions of people from all over the world in the Science Museum in London.

Sans Pareil, 0–4–0, 1829, built by Timothy Hackworth. *CDXS*: (2 cyls) 7 × 18; *WT*: 4¾; *boiler*: 6 ft. × 4 ft.; competed against the *Rocket* and other locomotives at the Rainhill Trials in October but was disqualified as too heavy. After three years it was sold for £110 to the Bolton & Leigh Railway where it worked until 1844.

George Stephenson, 0–4–0, 1831, built by Robert Stephenson & Co., Newcastle, for the Glasgow & Garnkirk Railway. *CDXS*: 11 × 16; *BP*: 50; *THS*: 319; *WT*: 6½. The two cylinders were slightly inclined and drove the rear axle; wheels were coupled. Built within a "sandwich" frame, the locomotive was attractive in design and the chimney top highly decorative.

North Star, 2–2–2, 1837, built by the Stephensons originally in 5 ft. 6 in. gauge for the New Orleans Railroad of America, but the deal fell through. To the order of Brunel, it was rebuilt in the 7 ft. gauge and hauled the first train, a "Directors' Special", between Paddington and Maidenhead on the newly opened Great Western Railway in 1838. Driving wheels were the same dimension as the broad gauge rails. In describing the locomotive, Brunel wrote: "We have a splendid engine of Stephensons', it would be a beautiful ornament in the most elegant drawing-room." On 29th December 1838, it pulled a train from Paddington to Maidenhead at an average speed of 38 m.p.h., and was the most powerful engine of its day. Brunel bought several more locomotives from the Stephensons in subsequent years. *North Star* was considerably altered by Daniel Gooch in 1845 and remained in service until 1870.

Bury, 2–2–0, No. 1, 1837–39, the locomotive which Edward Bury built for the London & Birmingham Railway. Bury worked as locomotive engineer and also had his own locomotive building works. *DWD*: 5½ ft.; *CDXS*: 12 or 13 × 18; *THS*: 463; *WT*: 10; *wheelbase*: 6 ft. 5 in.; *length, engine only*: 17 ft. Bury's locomotives were considered by his contemporaries as too small; other railways had machines of more than twice the weight. By the mid-1840s, they were found to be hopelessly undersized and train services suffered.

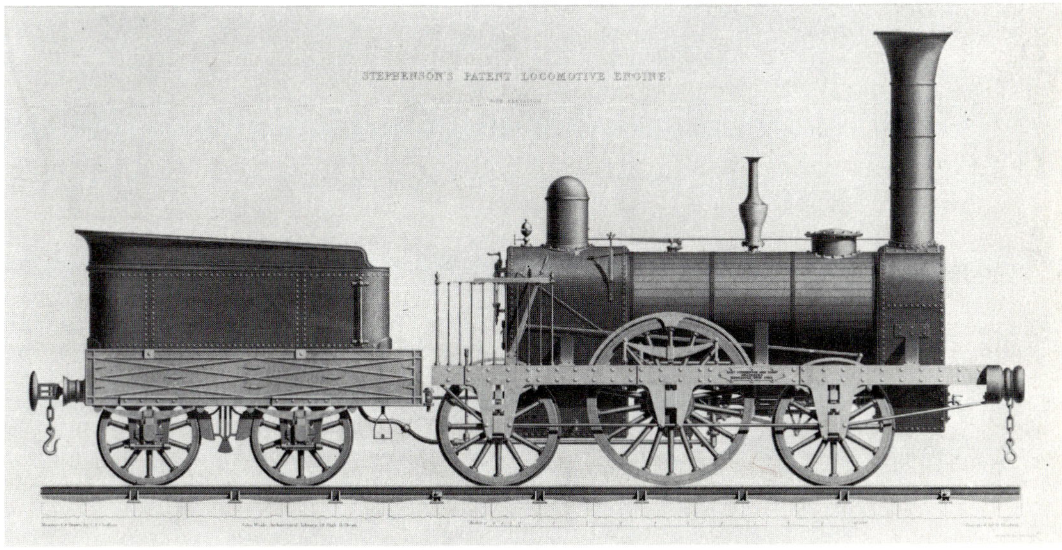

Stephenson's patent locomotive of 1838 with inside cylinders and large driving wheels for passenger trains.
(By courtesy of the Victoria & Albert Museum)

Firefly, 2–2–2, 1840, built to the design and specifications of Daniel Gooch, locomotive superintendent of the Great Western Railway under Brunel. Engines in this class had 7 ft. driving wheels and weighed about 24 tons. Design was based largely on the Stephenson *North Star*. Technical improvements included a larger boiler and a high "Gothic" firebox to increase steam space. The locomotives were built by various makers. Only five days after delivery of the first, *Firefly* hauled a directors' special train from Paddington to Reading and back, covering the 30¾ miles from Twyford to Paddington in 37 minutes at an average speed of 49 m.p.h. It was the first of the large Gooch locomotives, built when the young engineer was only 24, and was the start of a great fleet of locomotives he built for the Great Western Railway during his long service, which took him to the position of chairman of the Company.

Great Britain No. 38, 0–6–2T, 1845, by McConnell at Bromsgrove Works for the Midland Railway. *DWD*: 3¾ ft.; *CDXS*: 16 × 24; *WT*: 30. The locomotive was specially designed as a "bank" engine, to help trains from the rear up the Lickey Incline of 1 in 37·5 for over 2 miles on the Birmingham–Gloucester main line. In 1853, the locomotive was completely rebuilt and renumbered 300, and at one time carried the number 221. It worked on the incline until it was broken up in May 1901, an incredible span of 56 years.

Jenny Lind No. 45, 2–2–2, 1847, by E. B. Wilson & Co., Leeds, for the Midland Railway. *DWD*: 6 ft.; *CDXS*: 15 × 20; *BP*: 120; *TE*: 4,876; *WC*: 800; *TW*: 39¾; *length, engine only*: about 25 ft. A former Stephenson pupil and locomotive superintendent of the Midland Railway 1844–76, Matthew Kirtley was so delighted with *Jenny Lind No. 45* for expresses that he ordered a total of 20. With fluted dome and safety valve cover, lined boiler casing, pannelled firebox casing and patterned wheel shields, *Jenny Lind* locomotives were among the most attractive of the period. They were built for the London Brighton & South Coast and other railways. Later, Kirtley began to build his own engines in the *Jenny Lind* technical idiom.

Lord of the Isles, 4–2–2, 1851, Iron Duke class, designed by Gooch at Swindon Works, Great Western Railway, for expresses. *DWD*: 8 ft.; *CDXS*: 18 × 24; *BP*: 100; *WT*: engine only, 35; two whistles. At the top rear of the tender a seat was fitted for a "travelling porter" to watch for signals from the guard and to pass them on to the driver. Riding through a smoke-filled tunnel or in a storm must have tested the most hardy. It was exhibited in Hyde Park at the Great Exhibition 1851, and in 1893 was displayed at the Chicago Exhibition; unhappily, it was scrapped in 1905 along with *North Star* on the orders of Churchward. The Iron Dukes were fast runners and saw

Cornwall *with an officer's coach, built at Crewe in 1847 by Francis Trevithick, son of Richard. Long preserved at Clapham Museum, it has been allocated a site in Crewe. (Photo: British Rail)*

Lady of the Lake, *built at Crewe in 1859 by Ramsbottom.* (*Photo: British Rail*)

service until the end of the broad gauge era; they were on the road from 1847 to 1892.

Bloomer class, 2–2–2, 1851, designed by J. E. McConnell, London & North Western Railway. *DWD*: 7 ft.; *CDXS*: 16 × 22; *BP*: 120; *TE*: 6,839; *WT*: $28\frac{3}{4}$. The styling of Bloomers excluded shrouding or skirt from the outside frames; this left the driving wheels and "the works" a little more exposed, and probably earned them their name after a certain lady of fashion, Mrs. Amelia Bloomer, who had designed a certain pair of under-garments, highly favoured by Victorian ladies of style. Skirt or not, McConnell built them to run a two-hour service between Euston and Birmingham and 40 Bloomers were put on the road between 1851 and 1862. Originally painted in vermilion red with highly ornate brass boiler mountings. They were the finest engines in the Nor' West stud.

Rothwell, 4–2–4T, express tank engine, 1853, designed by J. Pearson for the broad gauge Bristol & Exeter Railway, and built by Rothwell & Co., Bolton-le-Moors. *DWD*: 9 ft.; *CDXS*: $16\frac{1}{2}$ × 24; *WT*: 42; *wheelbase*: $24\frac{3}{4}$ ft. Two unusual features distinguished this locomotive: the enormous size of the driving wheels, which were nearly as high as the top of the boiler, and the wheel arrangement of two four-wheeled bogies – one leading and the other trailing.

Lady of the Lake class, 2–2–2, 1859, designed by John Ramsbottom and built at Crewe Works for the London & North Western Railway. *DWD*: 7 ft. 9 in.; *CDXS*: 16 × 24; *BP*: 140; *TE*: 7,850. Longer non-stop journeys were possible after Ramsbottom had introduced his water troughs on the main lines starting in 1860. On a special run in 1862, one of these "dainty little singles" covered the $130\frac{1}{2}$ miles from Holyhead to Stafford non-stop in 144 minutes, an average speed of $54\frac{1}{2}$ m.p.h. For regular running, the management firmly resisted average speeds of higher than about 40 m.p.h. Some of these locomotives were rebuilt by Ramsbottom's successor, Webb, in 1895–99, and they continued in service on expresses for a further ten years or more.

Fowler's Ghost, 2–4–0, fireless steam locomotive, 1861, built to Sir John Fowler's specifications by R. Stephenson & Co., Newcastle, in 7 ft. gauge, for the Metropolitan Railway's first underground railway which opened in London in 1863. *DWD*: 5 ft. 6 in.; *CDXS*: 15 × 24; *WT*: 46; *cost*: £4,500. Fowler's objective was to run locomotives through the tunnels with a minimum of smoke and steam. Although known as "fireless", his locomotive did, in fact, contain a small furnace. Firebricks were stowed in a space in the boiler barrel and when they were almost white hot, they could steam the locomotive to run for a few miles, the fire itself then being damped down. Exhaust steam was directed into condensing tanks to convert the steam back to water; but after a few minutes, the tanks became so hot that steam and boiling water were emitted from them. Water from the condensed steam seems to have been fed back to the boiler. The whole process brought down the boiler pressure and the water level with the danger of explosion. It was intended that the furnace would be used on open sections of line and the firebrick heat in the tunnels. After a few trials, the idea had to be abandoned.

Metropolitan Railway, 4–4–0T, 1864. Designed by John Fowler and built by Beyer Peacock, Manchester. *DWD*: 5 ft. 9 in.; *CDXS*: 17¼ × 24; *BP*: 120 (later models 160); *TE*: 13,100; *WC*: 1,170; *WT*: 45. Eighteen in the first batch were built from 1863 after the Great Western Railway withdrew their locomotives which first worked the railway, because of a quarrel between the managements. Each bore a classical name:

Jupiter *Mars* *Juno* *Mercury*
Apollo *Medusa* *Orion* *Pluto*
Minerva *Cerberus* *Latona* *Cyclops*
Daphne *Dido* *Aurora* *Achilles*
Ixion *Hercules*

About 120 of this class of locomotive went into service on the Metropolitan and District railways and Fowler's originals were so successful that, with modifications, they remained the motive power of the tunnel lines until electrification, the last being withdrawn in 1905. One of them, class A No. 23, is preserved in the London Transport Collection at Syon Park, Brentford.

Stirling Single, 4–2–2, No. 1, 1870, designed by Patrick Stirling, and built at Doncaster Works to Works Order No. 50, for the Great Northern Railway. Driving wheels were as high as a suburban ceiling. *DWD*: 8 ft. 1 in.; *CDXS*: 18 × 26; *BP*: 140; *THS*: 1,165; *WC*: 2,700; *CC*: 3½; *WT*: 65; domeless boiler. This locomotive is Stirling's masterpiece and memorial, and the first of a series that made their place in history; they were known simply as "Stirling's Singles." The son of a Kilmarnock church minister, he worked for other railways before becoming locomotive superintendent in 1866 for the Great Northern, until his death in 1895. His brother James and son Matthew were locomotive superintendents on other railways, and between them they produced the Stirling family look; but Patrick's were the best. The great sweeping circles of the connecting rods on the large wheels, set against a dazzling livery of green with bold yellow, red and black lining must have presented an impressive sight. At night a column of flame from the chimney could be seen for miles, a common fault which was reduced by the development of the brick arch in the firebox. Two Stirlings made magnificent runs in the Great Race to Aberdeen in 1895: No. 668 covered the 105¼ miles from King's Cross to Grantham in 101 minutes, and No. 775 ran the 82¾ miles to York at an average speed of 65½ m.p.h. A place in history was assured for the Scottish engineer, who in 29 years had transformed the Great Northern stud. By 1907, No. 1 was pottering around Doncaster on "home" duties before being retired. Three years later it was in Shepherd's Bush, London, alongside a massive Ivatt "Atlantic". When the jubilee of the first race to the north of 1888 was being celebrated in 1938, it was brought from its second home at York Railway Museum to run local excursions, to the delight of enthusiasts.

Gladstone, 0–4–2, No. 214, 1882, designed by William Stroudley and built at Brighton Works, London Brighton & South Coast Railway. *DWD*: 6 ft. 6 in.; *CDXS*: 18¼ × 26; *BP*: 150; *THS*: 1,485; *WC*: 2,250; *CC*: 2; *WT*: 66. After training under Gooch at Swindon, Great Western Railway, Stroudley worked for other railways before becoming locomotive and carriage and wagon superintendent of the Brighton Company in 1870. He found over 70 different classes of engines of dubious ancestry, and went all out for standardisation in his new programme. He restored "pride in the job" by allocating each engine to one driver, with the driver's name painted in the cab. Stroudley also fitted a simple speed indicator in which water was splashed up a scaled glass tube; a pump driven by the engine wheels was connected to a water container and the faster the engine travelled, the higher the water splashed. No. 214 completed some 1,347,000 miles; some of this class worked until 1933. Stroudley took the

Gladstone *Edward Blount* to the Paris Exhibition in 1899; after a run between Paris and Laroche, it was awarded a gold medal. The livery was in a Scotch green which was nearer to yellow ochre, lined in black, orange and red; 214 was restored for its place in the York Railway Museum.

Experiment, 2–2–2, compound, 1882, built by Webb, Crewe Works, London & North Western Railway. *DWD*: 6 ft. 6 in.; *CDXS*: two high pressure 11½ × 24, one low pressure 26 × 24. The two pairs of driving wheels were worked by separate cylinders and were not coupled together, unique at that time. The compound principle, about which locomotive engineers argued fiercely, used the exhaust steam from the high pressure cylinders to work in the low pressure cylinder instead of being wasted. Webb was so delighted with the performance that he built 29 more of this type. In a paper read at the Institution of Civil Engineers in June 1899, Webb reported that he had been able to "dispense with coupling rods without loosing the advantages due to their use. . . . This engine was put to work on 3rd April 1882 . . . The total mileage for this class of engine up to 28th February 1899 was 15,093,758 miles." In 1899, Webb introduced the Teutonic class of improved 2–2–2 compounds with 7 ft. 1 in. driving wheels and a boiler pressure of 175 lb. On the Euston–Crewe route, they hauled trains of 250/300 tons.

Tennant class, 0–4–2, No. 1463, 1885, an engine without a designer, built at Gateshead and Doncaster, North Eastern Railway. *DWD*: 7 ft.; *CDXS*: 18 × 24; *BP*: 140; *THS*: 1,223; *TE*: 11,016; *WC*: 2,651; *CC*: 4. The Company was temporarily without a locomotive superintendent and there was a pressing need for a fast and powerful engine for the Newcastle–Edinburgh East Coast route of 124½ miles. Henry Tennant, the general manager, therefore set up a locomotive committee and supervised the building of 20 which became known as the Tennant class. The service they operated became the longest non-stop journey in Europe, and they were seen flashing up the East Coast route at high speeds. A Tennant took part in the Stockton & Darlington Railway centenary procession in 1925, and some of the class remained in service until 1927. No. 1463 is preserved.

Caledonian, 4–2–2, No. 123, 1886, designed and built for the Caledonian Railway by Neilsons of Glasgow, whose successors were the North British Locomotive Company, *DWD*: 7 ft.; *CDXS*: 18 × 26; *BP*: 150; *THS*: 1,085; *WC*: 2,850; *CC*: 4½; *WT*: 80. The only one of its kind on the Caledonian, this locomotive was built in a mere 66 days for the Edinburgh Exhibition of 1886. Its hooter was similar to those on Clyde steamers, later standardised on London Midland & Scottish Railway locomotives after the 1923 amalgamations. Dugald Drummond was the locomotive superindent and some of his fittings were incorporated. For many years, No. 123 completed daily two round trips totalling 409 miles between Carlisle and Glasgow, and frequently hauled directors' special trains. Its hour of glory came in the Race to Edinburgh in 1888, when it completed 100¾ miles in 102 minutes, this achievement later bringing material improvements on Anglo-Scottish services. About 1915, it was renumbered 1123, and in 1923 became L.M.S. No. 14140. Railway changes inflicted slights on its personal dignity; in 1923, its splendid Caledonian blue was covered by Midland red and later on by a funereal black, and it ended its days on the Perth–Dundee route before retirement in 1935. It was seen in Edinburgh in 1958 when the Scottish Tourist Board organised a special trip, with trainmen in the uniforms of 1900. The locomotive was restored for preservation in the livery of Caledonian blue, brown and black panelling and yellow and white lining, to recapture a glimpse of a great Scottish railway.

Lanky, 2–4–2T, No. 1008, 1889, designed by Sir John Aspinall, Horwich Works, Lancashire & Yorkshire Railway. *DWD*: 5 ft. 8 in.; *CDXS*: 18 × 26; *BP*: 160; *THS*: 1,216½; *WC*: 1,340; *CC*: 2; *WT*: 55. Carrying Works Order No. 1, 1008 was the first locomotive to be built at the newly opened Horwich Works, near Bolton. The works at Miles Platting, Manchester, opened in 1846, could not meet the building programme, and locomotives were purchased from outside manufacturers. No. 1008 was a new class and 330 were built at Horwich. Many were fitted with Aspinall's patent double-ended water scoop, vacuum-pressured to collect water from water troughs, whether the locomotive was running chimney first or bunker first. Even a "Lanky" enthusiast would not claim these black tankers were fast runners, but they regularly headed expresses serving the numerous mill towns in an interwoven network on either side of the Pennines, and coped well with the heavy gradients as good work horses. Heavy curves inflicted low speed restrictions, the most severe of which was 5 m.p.h. through Accrington station. Many of these locomotives continued their gruelling work for 60 years or more. Not a glamorous animal, but representative of its period, 1008 is preserved in its livery of black, with enough red, white and yellow lining to enhance its clean and business-like styling.

Hardwicke, 2–4–0, No. 790, 1892, designed by Webb, Crewe Works, London & North Western Railway. *DWD*: 6 ft. 9 in.; *CDXS*: 17 × 24; *BP*: 150; *THS*: 1,064; *TE*: 10,918; *WC*: 1,800; *WT*: 58. *Hardwicke* was among the last batch of Precedent class locomotives, of which 166 were built between 1874 and 1894. The first in the series was named *Precedent*. Their pulling power earned the nickname "Jumbos". *Hardwicke* earned fame in the Great Race to Aberdeen in 1895, with the hand of driver Ben Robinson on the regulator. Its performance helped to create a world record for steam that was not beaten until 1936 by the L.M.S. *Princess Elizabeth*. On the great night, it took over from the *Adriatic* at Crewe, completing the 141 miles to Carlisle in 126 minutes at an average speed of 67 m.p.h. Three years earlier, *Hardwicke* had collided with a Midland engine near Birmingham and toppled over a viaduct into the street below. It was retired to its birthplace on 30th January 1932 after recording 1,326,470 miles, and restored for preservation in its livery of black, lined in red, yellow and white. *Charles Dickens* in the Precedent class is reputed to have completed an incredible 2,500,000 miles.

Bulkeley, 4–2–2. Great Western Railway, hauled the last broad gauge train which left Paddington at 5 p.m. for Plymouth on 20th May 1892, ending a colourful and dramatic chapter in locomotive history.

Adams, 4–4–0, No. 563, 1893, designed by William Adams, Nine Elms Works, London, for the London & South Western Railway. *DWD*: 6 ft. 7 in.; *CDXS*: 19 × 26; *BP*: 175; *THS*: 1,320; *WC*: 3,300; *CC*: 3½; *WT*: 82. Adams built 30 locomotives in this class, probably the most handsome and efficient of his entire output of 500 locomotives in his 17 years with the Sou' West. He believed that locomotives should be beautiful to look at as well as able in performance, and he achieved this skilful blend. His 4–4–0s were fitted with improved front bogies with a wheelbase of 7 ft. 6 in., the longest in Britain; a rotating design allowed roomy sideplay and virtually guided the engines along the metals, and smoothly through points. In the absence of the pressures of competition found on routes to the north, Adams locomotives broke no important speeds records, but regularly achieved some good runs. The pleasing lineal proportions of the preserved No. 563 are enhanced by a livery in an olive green, with black smokebox and chimney, and enough lining in black, brick red, yellow and white to set off this splendid Victorian example.

Ivatt, 4–4–2T, 1893, built for the Great Southern & Western Railway of Ireland. *DWD*: 5 ft. 8½ in.; *CDXS*: 16 × 20; *BP*: 150; *TE*: 9,530; *grate area*: 16 sq. ft. Trained at Crewe, Ivatt moved to Ireland and was promoted to locomotive engineer of the Company in 1886 at the age of 35. A few years earlier, in the office at Cork, he kept a revolver in his desk, for they were troubled times in Ireland and remnants of the Fenian gangs were still roaming around. Later, Ivatt moved to the Great Northern Railway where he made a name for himself with his 4–4–2 wide firebox locomotives.

Jones, 4–6–0, Atlantic, No. 103, 1894, designed by David Jones and built by Sharp Stewart & Co. for the Highland Railway, the first of this wheel arrangement in Britain. *DWD*: 5 ft. 3 in.; *CDXS*: 20 × 26; *BP*: 170; *THS*: 1,763; *TE*: 24,556; *WC*: 3,000; *CC*: 5; *WT*: 94. Fifteen of this class were built – tough and powerful machines designed for sharp curves, gradients as steep as 1 in 60, altitudes of nearly 1,500 ft. above sea level and for driving through some of the roughest weather in the British Isles. They were the most powerful locomotives of their time. The centre coupled driving wheels were flangeless, to ease negotiation of sharp curves. The Highland Railway of some 500 route miles was mostly single line, running through some of the finest scenery in Britain – towards Perth in the south, Kyle of Lochalsh in the west, Keith in the east and to Wick branching off to Thurso, the most northerly station in the country. This locomotive, and many of the Adams design, incorporated louvres in the front of the chimney to direct steam and smoke away from the driving cab windows. Jones was locomotive superintendent for the Highland from 1869 to 1896, and was trained under his distinguished predecessor, William Stroudley. He retired prematurely after a severe fall from one of his engine

Empress of India, *4–4–0, Great Western Railway, 1894.* (*By courtesy of the Science Museum*)

tenders. The preserved No. 103 in Highland olive green, lined in red, white and black, honours his memory.

Johnson, 4–2–2, No. 118, 1897, designed by S. W. Johnson, Derby Works, Midland Railway. *DWD*: 7 ft. 9 in.; *CDXS*: 19½ × 26; *BP*: 170; *THS*: 1,233; *WC*: 3,500; *CC*: 4½; *WT*: 83¼. The Midland sported the best passenger coaches of any main line railway but though their locomotives were good, they were well matched by other leading companies. Johnson reigned as locomotive superintendent for 30 years (1873 1903), long enough to make his mark with the famous "Johnson singles". He had held a similar post with the Great Eastern Railway for seven years. He built 95 singles, with varying driving wheel diameters. Wheel slip was a perpetual problem with single driving axle engines, which he overcame by placing sand pipes closer to the wheels near the rails. Johnson is best remembered for his compounds and his singles, and at the turn of the century his singles were well into their stride at a time when coupled driving wheels for express trains were rapidly gaining ground.
No. 118 is preserved in the livery of which the Midland were so proud: Midland red, black smokebox, and lined in yellow. Four coats of grey lead paint formed the base, followed by four of purple-brown, then a coat of crimson lake mixed with a dash of purple-brown; five coats of varnish produced a glowing sheen: a total of 14 coats, exactly the number used on modern Rolls Royce cars.

Atlantic, Henry Oakley, 4–4–2, No. 990, 1898, designed by H. A. Ivatt, Great Northern Railway. *DWD*: 6 ft. 7½ in.; *CDXS*: 18¾ × 24; *BP*: 175; *WT*: engine only, 58. The first Atlantic type locomotive with 4–4–4 wheel arrangement in England,

Henry Oakley, *No. 990 4–4–2 express passenger locomotive built in 1898 at Doncaster, Great Northern Railway, withdrawn from service in 1937 and now preserved.* (*Photo by courtesy of B. Matthews*)

which became popular in succeeding years. It had a capacity for being thrashed, and could haul much heavier loads than the 4–4–0 types. Finish was in Great Northern green, with dark red below the top framing, and lines picked out in black.

Long Tom, 0–8–0, No. 401, 1901, built by Ivatt, Doncaster Works, Great Northern Railway. *DWD*: 4 ft. 8 in.; *CDXS*: 20 × 26; *TE*: 27,600; *WT*: 95½. This was one of a series of powerful goods engines which had plenty of steam and no nonsense. They were built to handle the growing mineral traffic between Yorkshire and London. Normal loading on the Peterborough–London run was 50 trucks and a goods brake-van, and a 700-ton train was no problem. The first modest 0–8–0 types had been built for the Great Northern some 50 years earlier by Archibald Sturrock who had retired in 1866 on coming into a fortune, and died in 1909 aged 93.

City of Truro, 4–6–0, No. 3440, 1903, designed by William Dean, Swindon Works, Great Western Railway, the first steam locomotive in the world to break the 100 m.p.h. speed record. *DWD*: 6 ft. 8½ in.; *CDXS*: 18 × 26; *BP*: 200; *THS*: 1,818; *TE*: 17,790; *WC*: 3,500; *CC*: 5; *WT*: 95. Churchward became locomotive superintendent in 1902, but Dean must have prepared the basic design and drawings before he retired. The City class, named after cathedral cities served by the Great Western, was the first new design on this railway to have tapered boilers, considered highly unorthodox at the time; advantages included increased water space where the barrel joins the firebox, and better water circulation. "Hot spots" were less likely to develop on firebox tube plates which often caused leaks in the joints between flue tubes and plate. World fame came to the *City of Truro* on 9th May 1904 when it reached a speed of 102·3 m.p.h. down Wellington bank hauling the Ocean Mail from Plymouth to Bristol, with driver Clements on the footplate. The distance of 128 miles was covered in 123 minutes. At Bristol, the *Duke of Connaught* quickly took over, completing the 118 miles to Paddington in 100 minutes. Consisting of five bogie mail vans, the train weighed about 148 tons. The record was held by the *City of Truro* until 1935 when Gresley's Pacific type *Papyrus* reached 108 m.p.h. on the L.N.E.R. Immediate publicity was withheld lest it frightened passengers away. The locomotive is preserved in its original livery of green and brown, lined in red and yellow.

Cardean, 4–6–0, No. 903, 1906, designed by McIntosh, Caledonian Railway. *DWD*: 6 ft. 6 in.; *CDXS*: 20 × 26; *BP*: 200; *TE*: 22,630; *WT*: 129½. Built for passenger services, this and similar types in the class were the most famous to come from McIntosh. Following the distinguished Dugald Drummond in 1895 as locomotive and carriage and wagon superintendent, he determined to build larger and more powerful locomotives for the growing business on Scotland's second largest railway. His first successful series was the *Dunalastair* class, launched in 1896, from which he developed the Cardeans. His locomotives worked hard, kept good time and were massive yet neat in outline, and rejoiced in the beautiful Caledonian blue livery, with blue wheels, and running-plate valences in deep rich purple. McIntosh became something of a legend in his lifetime. Born at Montrose in the mania year of 1846, he started railway life at the age of 14 in the workshops at Arbroath on the Scottish North Eastern, rising to fireman and driver, then moving to the Cale in 1876 as a locomotive inspector. In 1911, he was created a member of the Royal Victorian Order by King George V, the same year becoming President of the Association of Locomotive Engineers.

Great Bear, 4–6–2, Pacific, No. 111, 1908, built by Churchward, Swindon Works, Great Western Railway. *DWD*: 6 ft. 8½ in.; *CDXS*: 15 × 26; *BP*: 225; *TE*: 27,800; *WT*: 143. As the first Pacific 4–6–2 in England, *Great Bear* with four cylinders caused something of a sensation among locomotive engineers; and at 71 ft. overall, it was one of the longest locomotives of the day. It had an enormous boiler and a wide firebox and was fitted with Walschaert gear. In 1924 it was converted to a 4–6–0, was fitted with a new boiler and with other improvements took its share on all the fast routes. In its renewed form, it was grouped with the Castle class type which began a whole new series of splendid engines in the G.W.R. tradition. Livery was in Brunswick green, liberally lined in black throughout, and the number and name plates were in raised brass.

Sir Gilbert Claughton, 4–6–0, No. 2222, 1913. Designed by Bowen–Cooke, London & North Western. *DWD*: 6 ft. 9 in.; *CDXS*: 15¾ × 26; *BP*: 175; *TE*: 23,683; *WT*: 118. Named after the L. & N.W.R. chairman, this was the first of 130 locomotives in this class known as "Claughtons". These famous engines were still among the best in the L.M.S. stud over ten years later.

Butler-Henderson, *4–4–0 express locomotive No. 506 built for the Great Central Railway in 1920 and now preserved. It was named after the last director of the Company appointed before amalgamation in 1923.* (*Photo: British Rail*)

Cacrphilly Castle, 4–6–0, No. 4073, 1923, designed by Collett, Swindon, Great Western Railway, and forerunner of a class built for over twenty years. *DWD*: 6 ft. $8\frac{1}{2}$ in.; *CDXS*: 16 × 26; *TE*: 31,626; *WC*: 3,500; *CC*: 6; *WT*: 126. The four-cylinder Castle class locomotives were among the best of the day, with reduced wheel slip, the highest average speeds and good coal economy. Their excellent performance caused raised eyebrows in L. & N.E.R. locomotive circles, and Gresley was to see for himself in the exchanges of 1925, when a Castle took the Leeds expresses from King's Cross and a Gresley Pacific tackled that formidable G.W.R. express, the Cornish Riviera. *Caerphilly* was the first locomotive from Swindon after the First World War, in a livery of sparkling green, artistic lined-out panels and boiler bands, and polished brass cab and splasher beadings, safety valve cover and upper chimney rim. It had recorded 1,910,630 miles by its retirement on 10th May 1960. The only locomotive to start and finish its career in museum surroundings, it went straight from Swindon to the British Empire Exhibition at Wembley, and now rests in shining splendour in the Science Museum in London.

Lord Nelson class, 4–6–0, No. 850, 1926, designed by Maunsell and built at Eastleigh Works, Southern Railway. *DWD*: 6 ft. 7 in.; *CDXS*: $16\frac{1}{2}$ × 26; *BP*: 220; *THS*: 2,365; *TE*: 33,500; *WT*: engine 86, tender 58. Locomotives in this class, fitted with four cylinders, were of a higher tractive effort than any other express engine in Britain, and they were the most powerful on the Southern Railway for 15 years until out-done by the Merchant Navy class. They were designed to haul trains of some 500 tons at speeds averaging 55 m.p.h. One of the locomotives in the series was fitted with 6 ft. 3 in. driving wheels and had a tractive effort of 33,300 lb.

King George V, 4–6–0, No. 6000, 1927, built by Collett, Swindon Works, Great Western Railway. *DWD*: 6 ft. 6 in.; *CDXS*: $16\frac{1}{4}$ × 28; *BP*: 250; *TE*: 40,300; *WC*: 4,000; *CC*: 6; *WT*: 136. It had been proposed originally that the driving wheels of the King class should be 6 ft. $8\frac{1}{2}$ in., but Sir Felix Pole, the general manager, suggested that if they could be slightly smaller, tractive effort would be greater, and this was done. The Kings were great engines, direct descendants of Churchward's *Star* class, and they performed excellent service, particularly on the London–Plymouth and London–Birmingham Snow Hill routes. The

Company ran 5*s*. excusions to Swindon for enthusiasts to see them being built. *King George V* was shipped to America for the centenary "Festival of the Iron Horse" of the Baltimore & Ohio Railroad from 24th September to 15th October 1927, and Stanier rode on the footplate. Livery was in the much-loved Great Western Brunswick green, lined out, and liberal polished brass – wheel splasher beading, number plates, the two whistles and safety valve cover. The chimney was copper capped. This locomotive was loaned to H. P. B. Bulmer Ltd., of Hereford, the cider makers.

Garratt type, 2–6–0+0–6–2 articulated, No. 7999, 1927, designed by Sir Henry Fowler, London Midland & Scottish Railway. *DWD*: 5 ft. 3 in.; *CDXS*: 18½ × 26; *BP*: 190; *TE*: 45,620; *WC*: 4,500. Thirty-three of this class of locomotive were eventually in use, designed mainly to haul heavy trains from the Midlands to London and to avoid double-heading. They could haul loads of up to 1,400 tons. Their throbbing power and vigorous multi-wheel movement made a memorable moment for the bystander. Beyer Peacock & Co., were the leading builders of the articulated type of locomotives, usually known as Beyer-Garratts. They were exported to African countries, India, Russia, Australia and elsewhere. The variety of wheel arrangements included the 4–8–2+2–8–4.

Royal Scot class, 4–6–0, 6P, No. 6100, 1927, designed by Sir Henry Fowler, London Midland & Scottish Railway. *DWD*: 6 ft. 9 in.; *CDXS*: 18 × 26; *BP*: 250; *THS*: 2,497; *TE*: 33,150; *WC*: 4,000; *CC*: 9; *WT*: 138 (engine only, 85). Fifty of the class were built by the North British Locomotive Co. and 20 at Derby Works, all within about three years. No prototype trials were held or considered necessary: a tribute to the confidence of Fowler and his Derby team. In tests of performance on the Euston–Carlisle route, No. 6158 of the series consumed coal at about the rate of 40 lb. per mile, and water 33 gallons. The Royal Scots did their best work on the Euston–Glasgow service, and in autumn 1927 daily non-stop running on the stretch of 299 miles between Euston and Carlisle was introduced. At this stage of locomotive development, the boilers were so large to pack every ounce of power into every cubic inch of space that chimneys and domes had shrunk to mere inches.

Silver Link, 4–6–2, Pacific type, class A4, No. 2509, 1935, designed by Sir Nigel Gresley, London & North Eastern Railway, the first streamlined locomotive in Britain. *DWD*: 6 ft. 8 in.; *CDXS*: 18 × 26; *BP*: 250; *TE*: 35,455; *WT*: 168. This was the first of four of this class for working the new streamlined Silver Jubilee express. On a trial run, it reached 112½ m.p.h. The train was named to mark the silver jubilee of the reign of King George V. Tenders on some of Gresley's Pacific type locomotives were fitted with corridors so that enginemen on long journeys could be changed, and have access to the train itself.

Union of South Africa, class A4, streamlined, Pacific 4–6–2, No. 60009, power classification 8P/6F, 1937, designed by Sir Nigel Gresley, built in Doncaster Works, London & North Eastern Railway. *DWD*: 6 ft. 8 in.; *CDXS*: 18½ × 26; *BP*: 250; *THS*: 3,325; *TE*: 35,455; *WC*: 5,000; *CC*: 8; *WT*: 168. This three-cylinder locomotive was one of a class of 35 built to haul the fastest expresses on the East Coast route between London (King's Cross) and Aberdeen. From July 1937, it worked along with four sister locomotives to haul the Coronation Express between London and Edinburgh. During the Second World War, its record load consisted of 26 coaches. In the 1950s it frequently hauled the Royal train to Scotland. Withdrawn from British Rail service in 1966 and bought by the Lochty Private Railway Company, which was formed in the same year.

Coronation, 4–6–2, Pacific, No. 6220, 1937, streamlined, designed by Sir William Stanier and built at Crewe Works, London Midland & Scottish Railway. *DWD*: 6 ft. 9 in.; *CDXS*: 16½ × 28; *BP*: 250; *TE*: 40,000; *WC*: 4,000; *CC*: 10; *WT*: 161½. On a trial run on 29th June 1937, this four-cylinder locomotive hauled a train at 114 m.p.h., with Stanier and other officials aboard. On alighting at Crewe, C. R. Byrom, operating superintendent, commented testily: "How foolish to come in so fast!" Coal from the tender was propelled into the firebox by means of a steam operated coal pusher. *Coronation* was one of the great locomotives in that period just before the Second World War, which brought to a halt such exciting innovations. The streamlined locomotive and train – the Coronation Scot – was in a striking livery of blue with strong white lining. King Boris of Bulgaria, who held a steam locomotive driver's certificate, in immaculate white boiler suit and supported by a galaxy of top L.M.S. officials, drove the train from Euston to Bletchley on 5th November 1937 to add to his other train driving successes. This locomotive and three sets of coaches of the Coronation Scot were shipped to America in 1939, its return being delayed until 1942.

Mallard class A4, streamlined, Pacific 4–6–2, No. 4468, 1938, designed by Sir Nigel Gresley, built in Doncaster Works, London & North Eastern Railway. Holds the world record for steam. *DWD*: 6 ft. 8 in.; *CDXS*: 18½ × 26; *BP*: 250; *THS*: 3,325; *TE*: 35,455; *WC*: 5,000; *CC*: 8; *WT*: 168. This three-cylinder locomotive, along with others in the class, was fitted with a Kylchap double blast pipe and double chimney, and a tender with eight wheels. Streamlining saved appreciable power at high speeds and proved a masterstroke of publicity. The world record for steam of 126 m.p.h. was achieved with a train of seven coaches weighing 240 tons on 3rd July 1938, when the locomotive was only a few weeks old. The top speed was held fleetingly for a distance of 185 ft. at 4.36 p.m. just north of Little Bytham near Peterborough. An average speed of 120·4 m.p.h. was maintained for five miles between mileposts 94 and 89 (Essendine). The hand of Driver Duddington was on the regulator and Gresley, his usual impassive self, rode with his team in the dynomometer car. The 35 A4 Pacifics were at their best on the East Coast route and proved to be the fastest steam locomotives anywhere in the world. To make way for diesel traction, *Mallard* was withdrawn from active service in April 1963 having registered 1,426,261 miles; and the end of the romantic days of steam was in sight.

Merchant Navy class, 4–6–2, 1941, designed by Bulleid, Southern Railway. *DWD*: 6 ft. 1 in.; *CDXS*: 18 × 24; *BP*: 280; *THS*: 3,273; *TE*: 37,500; *WC*: 5,000; *CC*: 5; *WT*: 143. *Channel Packet* was the first locomotive in this class of three-cylinder machines for Southern express passenger trains. Among new features were high boiler pressure, steel welded firebox, thermic syphons for rapid circulation of water, and continental style wheels. The air-smoothed outer casing was completely different from any other locomotive and became closely identified with Bulleid. To reduce wear and maintenance, Bulleid enclosed the valve gear and the inside connecting rod in an enclosed container of oil. It was the first British locomotive to be lighted throughout by electricity.

WD (War Department) Austerity locomotive, 2–8–0, 1943, built by the North British Locomotive Co. in conjunction with the Ministry of Supply and British Railways. Of the variations in design construction, including a 2–10–0 version, the following are basic specifications: *DWD*: 4 ft. 8½ in.; *CDXS*: 19 × 28; *BP*: 225; *THS*: 1,990; *TE*: 34,215; *WT*: 126. Several hundred Austerity types were built, including a batch in America. Their design needed a minimum of tooling and casting, and avoided the use of materials in short supply. As well as serving in Britain, many were shipped overseas as part of the war effort – to Europe, Iran, Palestine, Egypt and the Western Desert. Shorn of all fal-de-lals, windshields and useless finery their naked austerity caught the eye and gave an impression of throbbing power, as though they had taken their jackets off to get down to business. An Austerity Q1 class 0–6–0 with the simplest exterior lines, not unlike a giant toy engine, prompted Stanier to ask its designer, Bulleid, "Where's the key?"

Winston Churchill, 4–6–2, No. 34051, Battle of Britain class, 1946, designed by Bulleid, and built at Brighton Works, Southern Railway. *DWD*: 6 ft. 2 in.; *CDXS*: 16½ × 24; *BP*: 280; *TE*: 31,000; *WC*: 4,500; *CC*: 5; *WT*: 129. Of similar design to the Merchant Navy class, this locomotive was one of 50 of the class bearing the names of personalities, R.A.F. stations and squadrons associated with "our finest hour" of the Second World War. On 30th January 1965, No. 34051 hauled the special train, with Driver Alf Hurley of Nine Elms Depot on the footplate, which conveyed the body of Sir Winston Churchill and family mourners from Waterloo to Handborough for the burial ceremony at Bladon Church. For this historic occasion, the locomotive had been painted in Southern green livery with orange and black piping and bore the Marlborough family crest.

W. P. Allen, class A1, 4–6–2, Pacific, No. 60114, 1948. *DWD*: 6 ft. 8 in.; *CDXS*: 19 × 26; *BP*: 250; *TE*: 37,400; *WC*: 5,000; *CC*: 9; *WT*: 164. This fine three-cylinder locomotive, built in the Gresley tradition, was named in honour of "Bill" Allen, who started as an engine cleaner at 2*s*. 6*d*. (12½p) a week, progressing to fireman, driver, union officer, general secretary of the Associated Society of Locomotive Engineers & Firemen (ASLEF), and was appointed as a member of the Railway Executive on nationalisation in 1948. Norman McKillop, "top-link" express driver and railway author, described the appointment as an

British Rail class 4 standard mixed traffic type No. 75000 built in 1951 – one of the early standard locomotives designed after nationalisation in 1948. (*Photo: British Rail*)

"almost miraculous climax to the career of a member of the drivers' union."

Beyer-Peacock of Manchester, 4–4–0, 1948, designed by H. R. McIntosh. *DWD*: 6 ft. 7 in.; *CDXS*: 15¼ × 26; *BP*: 220; *TE*: 21,469; *WC*: 4,000; *CC*: 6; *WT*: 110. This locomotive was built for the 112½-mile Dublin–Belfast route of the Great Northern Railway of Ireland in the standard Irish gauge of 5 ft. 3 in. Livery was in blue and lined out.

Britannia, class 5, 4–6–0, No. 70,000, 1951, designed by R. A. Riddles, the first British Railways standard locomotive after nationalisation in 1948. *DWD*: 6 ft. 2 in.; *CDXS*: 19 × 28; *BP*: 250; *THS*: 2,019; *TE*: 26,120; *WC*: 4,250; *CC*: 7; *WT*: 123¼ (went into service on 30th January). After nationalisation, a Locomotive Standards Committee was set up and eight guiding principles were set out: (1) maximum steam raising capacity; (2) simplicity, the least number of working parts and all readily visible and accessible; (3) each new class to handle a wide variety of mixed traffic; (4) high standard of bearings; (5) simplified shed preparation, by wide use of mechanical lubricators and grease lubrication; (6) more rapid disposal; self-cleaning smokeboxes; rocking grates; self-emptying ashpans; (7) high factors of adhesion to minimise wheel slipping; (8) high thermal efficiency, through large grate areas, high degree of superheating, long-lap valve gear. The best features from private enterprise locomotive practice were included. Six new standard classes were at first undertaken, and four others planned, the emphasis being on "mixed traffic" classes to handle both passenger and freight trains.

Evening Star, class 9 freight, 2–10–0, No. 92220, 1960, built at Swindon Works, Western Region, the very last steam locomotive ever to be built by British Rail. *DWD*: 5 ft.; *CDXS*: 20 × 28; *BP*: 250; *THS*: 2,550; *grate area*: 40 sq. ft.; *TE*: 39,667; *WC*: 5,000; *CC*: 7; *WT*: 139T 4 cwt; *diameter of pony truck wheels:* 3 ft.; *tender wheels*: 3 ft. 3½ in.; *adhesion factor*: 4·38. There had to be a "last one" and this was it: a really beautiful locomotive in the best traditions of the master-builders of steam: two large cylinders, wide Belpaire firebox, Walschaert gear, double chimney and double blast pipe like Gresley's memorable A4s, and a new-pattern spark arrester basket which was fitted between the blast pipe top and the chimney petticoat. Western Region type Automatic Train Control apparatus was included. Welcome evidence that a warm heart and not a diesel engine was still beating in the breast of British Rail came when it was decided to give the animal a name and to celebrate the occasion in style. At the behest of his masters, Fred Stone, editor of the Western Region staff magazine (and later of *Rail News*), publicised a competition for the choice of a name. The cash prize was shared by T. M. Phillips, engine driver, Aberystwyth;

J. S. Sathi, boiler washer, Old Oak Common, London; and F. L. Pugh, general manager's office, Paddington. Keith Grand, Railways Board member and former Western Region general manager, performed the naming ceremony in the presence of a large company and in a setting of historic locomotives and carriages (shades of Brunel and Gooch). During its short working life, *Evening Star* busied itself hauling heavy freight trains on main lines. Following a spell on loan to the Keighley & Worth Valley line private railway, then reliving its old glory in the Stephenson anniversary celebrations of 1975, it was destined to its rightful and permanent home, the new National Railway Museum in York.

Significant Stages in the Development of Modern Rail Traction

1924 **Diesel locomotive, 1924.** First in Britain, a small German-built diesel-hydraulic unit tested on London & North Eastern Railway.

1925 **Diesel railcar, 1925,** first in the British Isles, the vehicle consisting of a 3 ft. gauge car, driven by a converted Fordson paraffin-driven tractor engine. It could be driven from either end, weighed ten tons, travelled ten miles to one gallon of fuel, and was capable of 30 m.p.h. It went into service on the Castlederg and Victoria Bridge line of the County Donegal Joint Committee, in Southern Ireland. It was withdrawn in 1928. Six years later, orthodox diesel cars of the Walker-Gardner type appeared on the same railway.

1928 **Diesel electric four-car passenger train set, 1928,** the first in Britain, introduced by the L.M.S., under the direction of Sir Henry Fowler. A 500 h.p. Beardmore diesel engine drove a 340kW 600V English Electric generator, the power being fed to electric motors to drive the wheels. The set weighed 144 tons. It consisted of a four-car electric set from the Manchester–Bury line and had been converted at Horwich Works. The new train set ran between Blackpool and Lytham. A similar train, with cars built by Armstrong Whitworth, was first operated on the L.N.E.R. in November 1931.

1931 **Experimental diesel hydraulic locomotive, 1931,** 400 h.p. This was a steam tank locomotive which was converted to diesel traction by L.M.S. at Derby Works. Subsequent experiments showed that diesel-electric traction was the most efficient method.

1938 **Three car diesel train,** 750 h.p., built by L.M.S. at Derby Works, an experimental set with articulated cars. Six Leyland diesel engines drove separate axles through hydraulic transmissions.

Evening Star, *the last steam locomotive built by British Rail and now preserved. (Photo: British Rail)*

1947 **Diesel electric locomotives 10000 and 10001, 1947.** Britain's first main line types, virtually power houses on wheels. *Power*: 1600 h.p.; *WT*: 128; *Wheel arrangement:* Co-Co; *TE*: 41,000. They ranked in power with the largest steam locomotives, were nearly 30 tons lighter, but cost several times more. Noting diesel developments elsewhere and realising that the steam locomotive was reaching the limits of its potential within the British loading gauge, Ivatt, acting chief mechanical engineer, L.M.S., Derby, in 1945 began to turn his mind to the new power medium. English Electric built the power units at Stafford, and the locomotives were built and assembled at Derby. Ivatt himself drove No. 10000 out of the diesel shop at Derby on 8th December 1947 and a well reported Press trip from St. Pancras to Manchester took place in mid-January. After the two locomotives coupled together had worked the return Euston–Glasgow express trip six times weekly for six months in 1949, Ivatt, satisfied, gladly released the purchase money to the manufacturers. Six years later, the end of steam was officially foreshadowed.

1950 **Gas turbine locomotive No. 18000, 1950.** British Rail, Western Region. *P*: 2500 h.p.; *WA*: A1A–A1A; *TE*: 32,500; *WT*: 116. Built by the Swiss firm Brown-Boveri, it used a gas turbine engine to drive an electric generator which provided power for the electric motors. The "gas" consisted of burnt atomised oil under air compression in the combustion chamber, the released gas rotating turbine blades. Like all gas turbine machines, it used a great deal of oil fuel. The world's first gas turbine locomotive was built by Brown-Boveri in Switzerland in 1941.

1952 **Gas turbine locomotive No. 18100, 1952.** British Rail, Western Region. *P*: 3000 h.p.; *WA*: Co-Co; *TE*: 60,000; *WT*: 120. Power equipment was built by Metropolitan-Vickers. The locomotive was later withdrawn after a number of failures and converted into a straight electric locomotive for test running.

1954 **Diesel multiple-unit trains 1954,** consisting mainly of fixed sets of four or eight cars, half of which were powered, and half non-powered "trailer" cars. Typical specifications: *P*: power cars, 300 h.p.; *WT*: 35. First introduced in this year, the diesel mechanical units (DMUs) became the backbone of local passenger services throughout Britain. Some sets ran in other formations, such as three or six cars. Many designs were produced in railway workshops, the power units coming from various manufacturers,

The first main line diesel electric locomotive, 1947. (Photo: British Rail)

One of the diesel electric Deltics, No. 9004. (Photo: British Rail)

using mechanical transmission with gearboxes. British Rail has since stated that their replacements, not expected before the early 1980s, will be diesel electric.

1958 **Diesel hydraulic locomotives, 1958.** *P*: 2200 h.p.; *WA*: B-B; *TE*: 48,000; *WT*: 80. The famous *Warships* were introduced and named after distinguished fighting ships. They used two Bristol-Siddeley-Maybach diesel engines and hydraulic transmissions through single torque converters and four speed automatic gearboxes. Their merits were the subject of much controversy and they were subsequently withdrawn.

1959 **E1000 electric locomotive No. 18100, 1959.** *WA*: A1A-A1A; *TE*: 40,000; *WT*: 109. The first 25kV industrial frequency a.c. locomotive to be designed for the new British Rail main line electrification from Euston, the first section between Crewe and Manchester opening on 12th September 1960. It was formerly one of two experimental gas turbine locomotives in which rotating turbines generated electricity for the traction motors. In its rebuilt form, the turbo-generating set and associated equipment were replaced by a transformer and rectifiers, and the number of traction motors reduced from six to four of 625 h.p. each. Many long-service steam locomotive drivers were trained on this and similar locomotives ready for the new electric services.

1959 **Electric locomotive No. E3001, class 81 (originally AL1), 1959.** *P*: 3300 h.p.; *WA*: Bo-Bo; *TE*: 48,000; *WT*: 80. This was the first of a fleet of new generation electric locomotives. They were required for the Euston–Manchester–Liverpool lines for which approval to electricity had just been given. The bold decision to electrify at a standard of 25kV called for some pioneering design in the locomotives.

1961 **Deltic diesel electric No. 9000, 1961.** *P*: 3300 h.p.; *WA*: Co-Co; *TE*: 50,000; *WT*: 100. The first diesel electric locomotive in the world to house a power plant as high as 3300 h.p. on a single Co-Co chassis. They were called Deltics because the two Napier 18-cylinder diesel engines had three banks of cylinders arranged in the form of the inverted Greek letter delta. Twenty-two Deltics in 1975 were still operating the services on the East Coast main line which had previously required 55 steam locomotives. Their maximum allowed speed is 100 m.p.h. A magnificent machine, it is British Rail's most powerful diesel.

1962 **Brush type 4 diesel electric No. 1100, 1962.** *P*: 2750 h.p.; *WA*: Co-Co; *TE*: 55,000; *WT*: 117. This was the first of what are now the standard heavy duty diesel locomotives for main line passenger and freight trains. Over 500 were built, and in 1974 British Rail announced that an updated version would be built to provide 60 freight locomotives urgently required; power will be increased to 3000 h.p.

1965 **Electro-diesel locomotive, Type JB, No. E6007, 1965,** to work on electrified and non-electrified lines. *WA*: Bo-Bo; *DWD*: 3 ft. 4 in.; *TE*: 42,000; *WT*: 75; *length*: 53 ft. 8 in. The first of 43 dual purpose types Nos. E6007–49 for the Southern Region, including the London–Southampton–Bournemouth lines.

1965 **Electric locomotive, class 86, No. 3101, 1965.** *P*: 3500 h.p.; *WA*: Bo-Bo; *TE*: 58,000; *WT*; 80. This was the first of 100 built for the London Midland Region electrified main lines. They were developed to incorporate the best features of classes 81 to 85 and using the latest technology such as solid-state rectifier equipments. They have proved to be excellent work horses with heavy trains at speeds of up to 100 m.p.h.

1968 **Kestrel diesel electric, No. HS 4000, 1968.** *P*: 4000 h.p.; *WA*: Co-Co; *TE*: 70,000; *WT*: 126. This was the world's most powerful single engined diesel. It was built as a private venture by Hawker-Siddeley and contained a 16 cylinder 4000 h.p. engine. A magnificent animal, it was tested on British Rail track but was not favoured because of its heavy axle loadings. In 1974 it was sold to Russia.

1972 **APT-E gas turbine train, 1972,** power unit at each end. *P*: 2400 h.p.; *WT*: 49. The Advanced Passenger Train – Experimental –is strictly speaking a multiple-unit train, and this four-car set is virtually a rolling test-bed built by British Rail Research & Development Division at Derby to prove the fundamental principles for trains of the future. It is articulated between the coaches and its two power cars contain four Leyland 300 h.p. gas turbine engines which rotate generators to produce power for the electric traction motors. A unique body tilting system aids passenger comfort as the train takes curves at high speeds.

1973 **High Speed Train, 1973.** *P*: 5000 h.p.; *WA*: Co-Co; *WT*: 66. This is a diesel electric multiple-unit train designed to operate 125 m.p.h. Inter-City services. Each of the two power cars – one at each end – contained a 2250 h.p. Paxman "Valenta" engine, later uprated to 2500 h.p. The prototype holds the world speed record for diesel traction at 143 m.p.h. In 1974, 59 new H.S.T. trains were ordered, the first sets running on the Western Region main lines from London to South Wales and Bristol starting in 1976.

1974 **Electric locomotive, No. 87–001, 1974, class 87.** *P*: 5000 h.p.; *WA*: Bo-Bo; *TE*: 50,000; *WT*: 80. This is the first of 35, class 87, electric locomotives built, British Rail's most powerful, to haul express trains between London and Glasgow in five hours when the West Coast main line electrification was opened in May 1974. They were developed from the class 86 versions, an extra locomotive No. 87–036 being used for research into new types of electrical control systems.

Electric locomotive class 87. (*Photo: British Rail*)

George Stephenson (*Photo: British Rail*)

Chapter 11

Great British Railway Personalities

IT is a responsibility if not a presumption to select but a handful of names from the rich harvest of great men to whom the world is indebted for its railways. In any great and continuing human endeavour, it is inevitable that there will always be those whose extraordinary talents and dedication will lead them to exceptional achievements; and a few who will neglect family and home comforts, and work themselves through long days and sleepless nights to a premature death. A limited number were men of true genius – of complex character like Brunel, or simple, in the best sense of the word, like George Stephenson. Too many, in the George Hudson mould, desired only money, power and prestige; others were anxious to see the old country still taking the lead at the centre of her great empire.

All were men of ideas and brilliant ingenuity, with the drive and single-minded purpose to carry them through danger, political storms, social ostracism and public ridicule. But when a man gets an idea in which he deeply believes, he becomes a self-motivating entity that no force can stop. These men, in their separate life spans, have left the world a vastly different place from when they entered it. Selection from such a wealthy store of outstanding personalities is representative of countless others who played their part in numerous facets of railway development, but whose names have long faded from view.

No single railway maintained a continuous and total lead, for engineers and managers moved from one railway to another, spreading knowledge and furthering their own careers. From the short biographies, it will be gathered that life on the railways was a family life. Sons followed fathers and nephews followed uncles, a pattern that went right down the line. Even today, railwaymen are still conscious of a unique comradely and family atmosphere that has always been part of the tradition.

ADAMS, William Bridges (1823–1904) built 500 locomotives while locomotive superintendent, London & South Western Railway 1878–93. His 30 4–4–0s were among the most handsome of the period, and No. 563 is preserved. A Londoner, he was also a talented singer and brilliant musician.

ALLPORT, Sir James (1811–92). General manager, Midland Railway 1857–80 and one of the great railway managers of Victorian times. He was the driving force behind the building of Midland's first line into London and of the hotel and station at St. Pancras. He pioneered amenities in travel, scrapped most of the third class carriages and redesignated second to third, giving the poorer passengers upholstered seats. After a visit to America, he imported the first Pullman luxury carriages, introducing sleeping carriages and bringing more elegance and comfort into Victorian travel: a style which his competitors were forced to follow.

ARMSTRONG, Joseph (d. 1901). Locomotive superintendent, Great Western Railway, Stafford Road Works, Wolverhampton 1854–64; Swindon Works 1864–77. Born Newburn village, Northumberland. One of five Armstrongs of the G.W.R. The Company built a fine residence, "Newburn", for the family on the line side at Swindon.

ARMSTRONG, George. Brother of Joseph. Divisional locomotive, carriage and wagon superintendent, Wolverhampton 1864–97.

ARMSTRONG, Joseph junior. Engineer at Swindon. Designed an improved vacuum brake. Killed on the track 1888.

ARMSTRONG, John, son of Joseph. Divisional locomotive, carriage and wagon superintendent, G.W.R., London 1882–1916.

ARMSTRONG, R. J., son of John. Divisional locomotive, carriage and wagon superintendent, G.W.R., Worcester 1929–46.

ASPINALL, Sir John Audley Frederick, Kt., M.I.C.E., M.I.Mech.E., M.I.S.I., D.Eng. General Manager, Lancashire & Yorkshire Railway 1899–1919 and later a director of the Company. Introduced many fine locomotives. Promoted from chief mechanical engineer. Locomotive engineer, Great Southern & Western Railway of Ireland 1882–86. Introduced the first inter-urban electrified service in Britain between Liverpool and Southport in 1904. President, Institution of Mechanical Engineers, 1909; President, Institution of Civil Engineers, 1918. Retired 1919.

Dr. Richard Beeching (Photo: British Rail)

BEECHING, Dr. Richard, Ph.D. (Baron, 1965). Chairman, British Transport Commission 1961–63 and of the British Railways Board 1963–65. Formerly a director of Imperial Chemical Industries. Educated Maidstone, Kent, Grammar School and Imperial College of Science and Technology, to begin a highly distinguished career. Best remembered in the railways for his "Beeching Plan" of 1963 which visualised vast changes to develop the railways' strongest features – the mass movement of people and goods – and the closing of little-used lines.

BOUCH, Sir Thomas (1822–80). Civil engineer. Designed spectacular viaducts in north east England and the first Tay Bridge, the world's longest, which opened in 1878. In the following year, on her way to Balmoral Castle, Queen Victoria knighted Bouch after the Royal train had travelled over the bridge. In December the bridge was blown down in a fierce storm and the train passing over it fell into the Firth, with a total loss of life. Before its opening a Board of Trade official had inspected it. Several factors contributed to the disaster, but Bouch became the scapegoat, his

Above: The Gordon Highlander *4–4–0, No. 49, built in 1920 for the Great North of Scotland Railway serving the Inverness and Aberdeen areas. (Photo: By courtesy of J. M. Jarvis, Esq.). Below:* King George V, *4–6–0, No. 6000, one of the Great Western Railway's outstanding King class locomotives, seen at Bulmer's sidings, Hereford. (Photo: By courtesy of John Adams, Esq.)*

fortunes being swiftly and pitilessly eclipsed. The heartbreak of it all broke his health and within ten months he was dead. At 17, Bouch assisted the engineer in building the Lancaster & Carlisle Railway and at 21 was one of the resident engineers of the Stockton & Darlington Railway. In 1849 he became the manager and engineer of the Edinburgh & Northern Railway, noticing the breaks of the route to the north by the Firths of Forth and Tay. Later he went into private practice and built nearly 300 miles of railway in the north of England and in Scotland, including the South Durham & Lancashire of 50 miles and the 10-mile Peebles Railway. His brother William was for many years associated with the locomotive department of the Stockton & Darlington and the North Eastern railways, and in 1860 built a 4-4-0 locomotive for the S. & D.R.

BOWEN-COOKE, Charles John (1848–1920). Chief Mechanical engineer, London & North Western Railway 1909–20. Trained under Francis Webb. Introduced superheating of locomotives at Crewe and designed *George the Fifth*, *Prince of Wales* and *Claughton* class express locomotives. During the First World War he organised large-scale production of munitions for military use. A monument to him stands in the village churchyard at St. Justin-in-Roseland, Cornwall, where he died.

BOWICK, David Marshall (b. 1923). The first Chief Executive (Railways) in the new management structure in 1971. Responsible to the British Railways Board for the successful operation of the whole of the British Rail system. Joined the Railways in Scotland 1940, Fleet Air Arm 1942–46, traffic apprentice London & North Eastern Railway 1947. After holding various appointments, became planning officer closely associated with the 1963 Reshaping Plan under Beeching, rising to General Manager, London Midland Region.

BRADSHAW, George (1801–53) originator of monthly railway guides, born in Salford, Manchester. At 14 he was apprenticed to an engraver, five years later moving with his parents to Belfast as an engraver. He returned to Manchester and from 1827 engraved maps of canals with much success. Attracted by the new railways, he began producing *Bradshaw's Railway Time Tables* in 1839 at 6*d*. (2½p), renamed the next year as *Bradshaw's Railway Companion*. The first regular monthly guide appeared on 10th October 1839 and the last on 10th March 1961. They were always known simply as "Bradshaw". A highly religious man, he gave much money to the needy and established schools for the poorer classes over 20 years before compulsory elementary education became law.

BRUNEL, Isambard Kingdom (1806–59). One of the most brilliant engineers of his period. His finest railway was the line between London (Paddington) and Bristol. As the first chief engineer of the Great Western Railway 1833–58 was virtually the creator of the main parts of that great line. Outstanding civil engineering works include Box Tunnel, Wiltshire, Maidenhead railway bridge, and timber trestle bridges in Devon, Cornwall and South Wales, his most famous viaduct being the Royal Albert Bridge on the main line near Plymouth. Also designed the Clifton Suspension Bridge for road traffic over the River Avon at Bristol. His fame spread to the Continent and he surveyed two routes for Italian railways. Made an international reputation by building three of the greatest ships in the world, *Great Eastern*, *Great Western* and *Great Britain*. At the age of 20, under his distinguished French father Sir Marc Brunel (his mother, née Kingdom, was English) he became resident engineer of the Thames Tunnel, to be cut from Rotherhithe to Limehouse, and which

Brunel photographed at Millwall Docks, London. (Photo: British Rail)

Trevithick had tackled earlier. In 1855 he designed a sectional hospital for shipment overseas for the wounded from the Crimean War 1853–56, as a result of campaigning by Florence Nightingale. Brunel never sought public honours and was stimulated more by creative achievement than by wealth. "I am not making money," he wrote in his journal for April 1836. "I have made more by my Great Western shares." He hated bureaucracy, statutory restriction, advance official approval and Government inspectors. This short, dynamic man, always seen in tall chimney-pot hat and smoking a big cigar, literally worked himself to death at the age of 53.

BUCKTON, Raymond William (b. 1922). General Secretary, Associated Society of Locomotive Engineers & Firemen (ASLEF) from 1970. Motive power department, British Railways, 1940–60. After being a part time union officer he became full time, progressing to district organiser York, and assistant general secretary. Educated at Appleton Roebuck School. Active in Labour Party work since 1940, holding several leading positions in York and district. Elected to York City Council 1952 and Alderman in 1955.

(After long battles with the Victorian railway companies, particularly concerning extremely long hours, cash fines as a disciplinary measure and wages below £2 a week, ASLEF was formed in 1880. Head office was at Holbeck, Leeds, and Charles H. Perry the first general secretary. About the time of formation, the *Daily Telegraph* described railway enginemen as having "a noble sense of enormous trust imposed upon them . . . who had not permitted abuse, tyranny, or oppression to impoverish their integrity or honesty." On 26th February 1882, the Union "resolved that the general secretary give up his job as an engine driver and work full time for the Union at £2 a week." Six years later, the Union began its own magazine, *Locomotive Journal*. In 1917 the Union proposed nationalisation of the railways to which the Government subscribed. Two years later, an eight-hour day was secured. The head office was transferred to the present premises in Hampstead, London, in 1921. John Bromley was the longest serving general secretary, 1914–36.)

BURY, Edward (1794–1858). First locomotive superintendent of the London & Birmingham Railway, opened in 1838, and later partner of Bury, Curtis & Kennedy, locomotive builders. Many of his 2–2–0 and 0–4–0 engines used on the L. & B.R. His engines were characterised by their rounded "haycock" fireboxes, and *Coppernob*, which he built for the Furness Railway is preserved.

CALDER, Graham, B.Sc.(Eng.), C.E., M.I.E.E., F.I.Mech.E. (b. 1920). Chief mechanical and electrical engineer, British Railways Board, from 1971; director, British Rail Engineering Ltd. Closely involved in the development of electrification and the new breed of high speed trains. Born Prestwich, educated North Manchester School and Salford Technical College. In Second World War served in the Royal Engineers. Joined the railways as a technical assistant, electric traction, in 1950, progressing to the top through various engineering posts to chief mechanical and electric engineer, Scottish Region 1966 and traction engineer, British Railways Board, 1970.

CHAPLIN, William James (d. 1859). Pioneering chairman, London & South Western Railway. Before opening the project was heading for failure, but was saved by his drive and financial backing. By pushing into the West of England in the Stephenson gauge, stifled the advance of Brunel's wide gauge.

CHURCHILL, Viscount, G.C.V.O. (1864–1934). Chairman, Great Western Railway 1908–34, one of the greatest of the 20th century chairmen.

Viscount Churchill (Photo: British Rail)

G. J. Churchward

Guided the Company through Edwardian expansion, First World War, and the depression and unrest of the following decades. God-son of Queen Victoria, and an Eton scholar.

CHURCHWARD, George Jackson, C.B.E., M.Inst.C.E., M.I.Mech.E. (1857–1933). Locomotive superintendent Great Western Railway 1902–21, title changed to chief mechanical engineer 1916. Created standard G.W.R. locomotives with tapered boilers, high boiler pressure, long travel valves. Most had two outside cylinders and inside Stephenson link motion. Built Star class with four cylinders. Launched Dean's *City of Truro* which broke the world record in 1904. An innovator whose influence was felt throughout the steam era.

CLAUGHTON, Sir Gilbert Henry, Bt. (1856–1921). Chairman, London & North Western Railway 1911–21, whose name was honoured by Bowen-Cooke's locomotives. A greatly loved man, he had the rare gift of earning high esteem from trade unionists and rank and file staff as well as from his senior officers. His father was Bishop of St. Albans.

COCKSHOT, Francis P. (1824–96). Superintendent of the line, Great Northern Railway 1865–95. He believed that speed encouraged good business and made the G.N.R. the fastest railway in the world, achieving his greatest successes in the first Race to the North, when he kept the East Coast route ahead of his rivals.

COLLETT, Charles Benjamin, O.B.E., M.I.Mech.E., M.Inst.C.E. (1871–1952). Chief mechanical engineer, Great Western Railway 1921–41, designer of the *Castle* and *King* classes, extended standardisation of boilers and fittings, and introduced higher standards and improved methods of technical testing.

COOK, Thomas (1808–92). The first travel agent and founder of the personally conducted railway excursion system. Ran his first excursion train on 5th July 1841, conveying 570 passengers in open wagons from Leicester to Loughborough, a distance of 12 miles, for one shilling return. The line had opened only the previous year as part of the Midland Counties Railway. A renowned temperance worker when common drunkenness was a social scourge, he took his party to a temperance meeting. Cook, born in Melbourne, Derbyshire, had been in turn gardener's help, wood turner and printer, and was a keen Bible reader and local missionary. In 1840 he founded a children's temperance magazine. His first pleasure trip was to Liverpool and Snowdonia in 1845. That year he also organised the first excursion to Scotland – via Fleetwood, Ardrossan, to Glasgow and Edinburgh – which continued for 15 years. Ten years later (1855) he arranged "through tickets" to Belgium and France, and in 1866 organised his first

C. B. Collett

tour to America. The year before, he transferred his business from Leicester to Fleet Street in London. In 1872 he personally conducted his first world tour. His connections with hotels enabled him the following year to found the travellers' cheques system. Later, his name was immortalised in a popular song: "Follow the Man from Cook's". In 1928, the business was fused with overseas companies and in 1948 under a Labour Government Thomas Cook & Son was nationalised along with the railways. Under a Conservative Government in 1972, the business was purchased by a consortium: Midland Bank (70 per cent of shares), Trust Houses Forte (23 per cent), and the Automobile Association (7 per cent). Plans were made to transfer its headquarters in 1976 from Berkeley Square, London, to Peterborough.

CUBITT, Sir William (1785–1861). Civil engineer from Norfolk. Engineer in chief, South Eastern Railway. On 26th January 1843, he used 18,000 lb. of gunpowder to blow up the Round Down Cliff face between Folkestone and Dover, to avoid a costly tunnel, building the railway along the beach and a tunnel beneath Shakespeare Cliff. Worked hard to make the Croydon Atmospheric Railway a success. Consulting engineer to the Great Northern Railway where he introduced modern methods of construction and locomotion. He was adviser to the Hanoverian Government on the harbour and docks at Harburg and built water works in Berlin. He surveyed and reported on the projected Paris-Lyons Railway, improved the port of Boulogne and was consulting engineer to the Boulogne-Amiens Railway. He built two landing stages at Liverpool docks and the Medway bridge at Rochester. Eerected the Crystal Palace at the Great Exhibition of 1851, for which he received a knighthood. His son, Joseph (1811–72) constructed much of the London & South Western Railway, built the Great Northern Railway, the London Chatham & Dover Railway, the Rhymney Railway, the Oswestry & Newton Railway, Colne Valley Railway and the pier at Weymouth. Another Cubitt – Lewis – also from a Norfolk family, was the architect who built the Great Northern Railway terminus at King's Cross.

DELL, R. Signal engineer, London Transport, in 1942 and later chief signal engineer. Introduced programme machine working at junctions, automatic train operation installed on the new Victorian line, designed the systems of automatic ticket reading and automatic fare collection, and many other innovations for the intense underground services.

FLETCHER, Edward (1807–89). Locomotive superintendent, North Eastern Railway 1854–82 from the Company's formation. An apprentice to George Stephenson, he helped father and son to build the *Rocket* and took a hand with them on the Canterbury & Whitstable Railway. He drove Stephenson's *Invicta* locomotive (still preserved at Canterbury) on the opening day in 1830, when aged only 23. Of the many locomotives he designed for the N.E.R., his best were the "901" class 2–4–0s of 1872 which hauled expresses between York and Edinburgh; they were fast runners and economical on fuel. No. 910 of the class is preserved.

FORBES, James Staats (1823–1904). General manager, London Chatham & Dover Railway 1862–73 and chairman 1873–98. Chairman London District Railway 1872–1901. Forbes pursued a strategy of expansion and ruthless competition against the South Eastern Railway, while over the years his Company was tottering on the edge of bankruptcy; he gave his customers a good service and his shareholders a poor dividend. A great "character" in his day, he was once described as "a past master in the art of bunkum". His nephew, Sir William Forbes, was trained on the L.C. & D.R., rose to traffic manager, then was general manager of the London Brighton & South Coast Railway where he reconstructed Victoria station, introduced the 60-minute London–Brighton service and inaugurated the suburban electrification of the South London line in 1909.

FOWLER, Sir John, Bt., K.C.M.G. (1817–99), noted for his steam locomotive "*Fowler's Ghost*", so called for its quietness and lack of smoke, built by Stephenson's to his design in 1861 for the projected underground Metropolitan Railway, which he also executed. A celebrated civil engineer born at Sheffield, he built railways in many parts of Britain: Stockton & Hartlepool, London Brighton & South Coast (with Rastrick), Manchester Sheffield & Lincolnshire, St. John's Wood line, Edgware Highgate & London, Oxford Worcester & Wolverhampton, Severn Valley, Mid-Kent, London Tilbury & Southend, Great Northern & Western of Ireland, Much Wenlock (Shropshire), Isle of Wight, Launceston & South Devon, Moretonhampstead (Devon), Weymouth & Portland, Wellington & Chester, Essex and Cambridgeshire extension of the Great Eastern

Railway, and the Victoria & Pimlico which included the first rail bridge across the Thames in London. He supervised the construction of the Forth Bridge, and visited Norway, Egypt and India to advise on railway construction.

FOWLER, Sir Henry, K.B.E., D.Sc. (1870–1938). Chief mechanical engineer, Midland Railway 1909–22 and London Midland & Scottish Railway 1925–30. Introduced locomotive superheating on the Midland, designed the heavy 2–8–0 freight engines for the Somerset & Dorset Joint Line, and the large 0–10–0 "bank" engine for the Lickey Incline on the Birmingham–Gloucester line. He was responsible for the three-cylinder 4–6–0 Royal Scots and the articulated Beyer-Garratt 2–6–0+0–6–2 engines handling long trains of coal between Toton and Cricklewood.

GIBB, Sir George Stegman, Kt. (1850–1925). General manager, North Eastern Railway 1891–1906). Devised "passenger-mile" and "ton mile" statistics (ten passengers travelling 10 miles = 100 passenger miles; 10 tons of goods conveyed 10 miles = 100 ton miles) to improve train loadings. Inaugurated the Tyneside electric train service in 1904. Appointed a director of the Company. In 1906 he became managing director of the London Underground Railways.

Sir Daniel Gooch

Sir Henry Fowler

GOOCH, Sir Daniel (1816–89). Rose from assistant to George Stephenson to chairman of the Great Western Railway. At age of 21, under Brunel, was locomotive superintendent of the G.W.R. until 1864. He built his first locomotives in the Stephenson idiom and created some fine performers which later engineers developed into the famous *Kings* and *Castles*. He resigned to lay a cable across the Atlantic using one of Brunel's ships, the *Great Eastern*, for which he received a knighthood. He was invited to become chairman of the G.W.R. to pilot the Company through the financial crisis of the mid-1860s which shattered Britain. As a powerful supporter of Brunel's wide gauge, he had the unhappy task of planning its total abolition.

GRANET, Sir William Guy, G.B.E. (1867–1943). General manager and a director, Midland Railway 1906–18 and chairman London Midland & Scottish Railway 1924–27; one of the most dominant personalities in the negotiations from which the L.M.S. emerged in 1923. A barrister by profession, he remodelled the management structure of both Companies.

GRESLEY, Sir Herbert Nigel, Kt., C.B.E., D.Sc., M.Inst.C.E., M.I.Mech.E., M.I.E.E., M.Inst.T. (1876–1941). Son of a church minister; locomotive, carriage and wagon engineer, Great Northern Railway 1911–22; chief mechanical engineer, London & North Eastern Railway 1923–41. One of the world's greatest steam locomotive designers, whose *Mallard* A4 Pacific brought him everlasting fame by creating a world record. Designed articulated carriages, twin sleeping-cars and triple dining car sets.

HACKWORTH, Timothy (1786–1850). Railway pioneer, best known for his locomotive *Royal George* with six coupled wheels and originally having four cylinders. His locomotive *Sans Pariel* competed against the *Rocket* and others at the Rainhill Trials of 1829. Worked under both Stephensons at their Newcastle factory. He was appointed resident engineer for the locomotives of the Stockton & Darlington Railway on opening and brought many improvements. Later, he contracted privately to maintain all the Company's engines and rolling stock; and at his Shildon works he built locomotives for railways in Britain and overseas. Engineers trained under Hackworth were in much demand at home and for new railways abroad. Hackworth is still revered in the Darlington and Shildon areas and his tiny cottage at Sedgefield was restored in 1975 as a permanent museum.

HAWKSHAW, Sir John (1811–91). Designed and built Lockwood Viaduct near Huddersfield, and Charing Cross and Cannon Street railway bridges across the River Thames. Engineer to the East London Railway and to the Inner Circle line of the London Underground. As early as 1838, he counselled the Great Western Railway to reject the broad gauge.

HAWKSWORTH, Frederick William (b. 1884). Chief mechanical engineer, Great Western Railway 1941–49, which railway he served throughout his working life. A drawing board man, he trained under Churchward and Collett, made the drawings for the *Great Bear*, personally supervised design work for *King George V*, successfully converted locomotives from coal to oil burning, and introduced the first gas turbine locomotive to run in Britain.

HEDLEY, William (1779–1843). Famous for *Puffing Billy* which he built in 1813–14. An ingenious inspector at Wylam Colliery near Newcastle, he experimented to confirm the adhesive ability of a smooth wheel to a smooth rail by adjusting the weight of an engine in relation to its power. To establish claim to his locomotive improvements, he registered Patent No. 3666 on 13th March 1813.

HOLDEN, James (1837–1925). Locomotive superintendent Great Eastern Railway, 1885–1907. Spent previous 20 years at Swindon. On the G.E.R. he introduced some splendid engines such as the *Claud Hamilton* for Cromer expresses and the three-cylinder 0–10–0 tank *Decapod.* Among the carriages he introduced were palatial corridor dining car trains, and in 1893 he built the first dining cars for third class passengers on the Harwich-York route. He was born in Whitstable, Kent, and died in Bath. His third son followed him as G.E.R. locomotive superintendent 1908–12.

HUDSON, George (1800–71). The "Railway King" who created the Midland Railway Company, rose to great power and wealth during Railway Mania, speculated fraudulently in railway shares, was publicly disgraced, sent to prison and ruined. Son of a farmer, he was born in Howsham village near York. At 15 was apprenticed to a linen draper in York and later was made a partner in the firm. This brought him some wealth. In 1827 he inherited from a distant relative a fortune of £30,000 and he bought shares in the North Midland Railway. Six years later he formed the York Banking Company, made it a success and in the same year was appointed head of the York Conservative Party. In 1835 he was made a town councillor, an alderman in 1836 and Lord Mayor of York in 1837 and again in 1846.

He subscribed £500 to a new railway project, the York & North Midland, which was carried out in 1837 with himself as chairman, and he helped to promote the Great North of England Railway. In 1842 he was made chairman of a company to build a line to connect York with Darlington and Newcastle; he subscribed five times as much as any other director and personally guaranteed a dividend of six per cent. His masterstroke was to form the Midland Railway in 1844 by amalgamations, to make it the biggest railway in Britain with himself as chairman. By that time, 1,016 miles of railway were largely under his control. All his companies developed good business and paid liberal dividends and the influence he acquired was unparalleled. Admirers made him a gift of £16,000 and his directors from time to time presented him with shares. As Member of Parliament for Sunderland from 1845,

Captain Mark Huish

and deputy lieutenant and magistrate in County Durham, his personal stock soared. He bought Londesborough Estates from the Duke of Devonshire to prevent the land falling into the hands of another railway, the Manchester & Leeds, and he acquired Newby Hall.

In amalgamating the Newcastle & Berwick Railway with the Newcastle & North Shields he increased the authorised shares, pocketing 9,956 shares from which he made about £145,000 for himself, by omitting them from the account books. Similar fraudulent transactions followed. After the railway boom eased, investigations into his companies began. The main companies of which he was chairman included the Midland, Eastern Counties, York Newcastle & Berwick, and York & North Midland. It was found that he was in debt to all of them. Angry shareholders' meetings resulted in his being stripped of his power and on 17th May 1849 he made a personal statement of explanation in Parliament, where he was heard in stony silence. Later he went to Europe and tried his hand in Continental finance, but without success. Practically for the rest of his life he was involved in a long law suit with the North Eastern Railway, who tried to force him to sell his estates to pay his creditors. On 10th October 1865 he was sent to prison in York Castle for three months as a debtor. He was married, had a large family and died in London.

HUISH, Captain Mark (d. 1867). First general manager of London & North Western Railway 1846–59. A forceful character of the pioneering days, he was skilled in negotiating financial deals and traffic agreements with competing companies. His railway political in-fighting prompted Sir Richard Moon to describe him as "an intriguing web-weaving protocoller."

HURCOMB, Sir Cyril (Baron, 1950) G.C.B., K.B.E. (b. 1883). First chairman of the British Transport Commission, controlling the newly nationalised inland transport services, 1947–53. Educated Oxford High School and St. John's College, Oxford. Held a number of senior posts in Government departments. In an outstanding career, received public honours in Britain and overseas. Worked with drive and dedication to integrate inland transport services but was eventually frustrated by the 1953 Transport Act which broke up the original organisation and sold off most of British Road Services.

IVATT, Henry Alfred (1851–1923). Locomotive superintendent, Great Southern & Western Railway of Ireland, then of the Great Northern Railway 1895–1911. Designed the pioneer Atlantic type locomotive 4–4–2 in 1898, later named *Henry Oakley* after the general manager, No. 990 for East Coast expresses, the first of its kind and now preserved.

IVATT, Henry George, C.Eng., F.I.Mech.E., M.I.Loco.E. (b.1886), son of Henry Alfred, chief mechanical engineer L.M.S. 1945–47, then of the London Midland Region after nationalisation. Trained at Crewe, L.N. & W.R., later serving on the North Staffordshire Railway before joining Stanier on the L.M.S. He introduced modern aids to maintenance including rocking grates, hopper ashpans and self-cleaning smokeboxes. In 1947, he introduced the English-Electric built diesel electric locomotives Nos. 10000 and 10001, the first to work main line expresses.

JOHNSON, Sir Henry Cecil, K.B.E. (b. 1906). Chairman, British Railways Board 1968–71. After leaving Bedford Modern School, was a traffic apprentice for three years, learning the work of all departments of the London & North Eastern Railway. Promoted to various posts, mainly operating, rising to general manager London Midland Region in 1962 and chairman and general manager 1963–67, during which time

Sir Henry Johnson

he launched the new station at Euston and the main line electrification to Birmingham, Crewe, Liverpool and Manchester.

JOHNSON, Samuel Waite (d. 1912). Locomotive superintendent, Midland Railway 1873–1903, Edinburgh & Glasgow Railway 1864–66, Great Eastern Railway 1866–73. Best remembered for his famous three cylinder compounds of 1902, 4–4–0s which formed the basis of 2–4–0 locomotives on the L.M.S., of which one is preserved. A great locomotive man of his day, his style and finish on the 2–4–0, 4–2–2 and 4–4–0 made his name as a designer of beautiful locomotives for Midland expresses. He also built some powerful 0–6–0s for goods working.

JONES, David (1843–1907). Locomotive superintendent, Highland Railway 1870–96. Trained under Ramsbottom, at 21 he obtained a post at Inverness, and served under Barclay and William Stroudley. He created his own corner in locomotive history by introducing the very first 4–6–0 in Britain, one of which is preserved in Glasgow. After a serious fall from one of his locomotive tenders, he resigned in 1896.

JOY, David (1825–1903). A lovable character, he will be remembered for his original work on the *Jenny Lind* locomotives while with E. B. Wilson & Co. of Leeds. Worked largely as a consultant engineer and designer. In 1879 he invented the radial valve gear that bears his name; he reduced working parts by dispensing with eccentrics and securing the valve movement from the connecting rod working through a curved slot link. From 1880, Webb adopted the Joy valve as a standard for inside cylinder 0–6–0 goods for the L. & N.W.R.

KEEN, Peter (b. 1928). Director, Channel Tunnel, British Rail, from 1974. Educated Kingston-on-Thames Grammar School and Queen's College, Oxford. Joined London Transport in 1950 as a trainee and later the British Transport Commission working on the British Railways Modernisation Plan 1955, followed by operating, commercial and traffic costing appointments in the London and Sheffield divisions of the Eastern Region. In 1962, took charge of the initial planning of the new Freightliner network, then to the London Midland Region as commercial research officer, passenger manager, then freight manager. In 1968, appointed assistant general manager, Southern Region. Two years later, he became chief passenger planning manager, British Railways Board, to develop high speed train strategy

Peter Keen

and to participate in a detailed study of the London rail network. Keen's career is quoted as representative of the new breed of top managers who are running the modernised railways and planning for the long term future.

KIRTLEY, Matthew (1813–74). The first locomotive superintendent of the newly formed Midland Railway from 1844 to 1873, typical of the practical men who rose to take charge of locomotives and crews in early days. At 13, he joined the Stockton & Darlington Railway and was taught by Stephenson, later becoming a locomotive fireman on the London & Birmingham Railway, then locomotive superintendent of the Birmingham & Derby Junction Railway, the smallest of the three companies constituting the Midland. His brother Thomas held a similar post with the North Midland, finishing his career with the London Brighton & South Coast Railway. Thomas' son William worked for his uncle Matthew at Derby. Of Kirtley's many excellent Midland engines, his 2–4–0 expresses were outstanding, one of which is preserved. His sound engines lasted through many boiler renewals. He is particularly remembered for his development of the brick arch and firehold deflector plates which improved performance. His distinguished successors at Derby included Johnson, Deeley, Fowler, Anderson and Paget.

LOCKE, Joseph (1805–60) ranks high among the great pioneers. Son of a Barnsley colliery manager, he was an articled pupil of Stephenson's whom he helped to construct the Liverpool & Manchester Railway. In his early twenties he took part in locomotive experiments and later built his "Crewe" engine, bringing great mathematical accuracy and introducing standard components. Alone or with partners, he built at least 16 railways – Grand Junction, London & Southampton, Sheffield & Manchester, Lancaster & Preston, Greenock Paisley & Glasgow, Lancaster & Carlisle, East Lancashire, Scottish Central, Caledonian, Scottish Midland, Aberdeen Railway and Greenock Docks. He built the first railway in Spain, after an earlier visit by Robert Stephenson to advise, the Barcelona & Mattaro line of 17 miles; three railways in France – Paris & Rouen, Rouen & Havre, and Mantes, Caen & Cherbourg; and the Dutch-Rheinish Railway. In 1835, he had designed an improved track to carry heavier trains at higher speeds. He was a Fellow of the Royal Society from 1838, and President of the Institution of Civil Engineers in 1858 and 1859. All Locke's work was carried out with the greatest economy. In 1847 he bought Honiton Manor in Devon and in that year became a Liberal Member of Parliament for that borough, holding it until his death. He received honours at home and abroad. To his home town of Barnsley, he presented Locke Park where a statue was later erected, and an endowment to his old grammar school.

MACKENZIE, David A. (b. 1922). General secretary, from 1973, Transport Salaried Staffs' Association, the trade union for nationalised transport clerks, supervisors, administrative and management staff and for travel trade staff. Son of a railwayman and trade unionist. On leaving school, began as a junior clerk at Inverness station, moving to Strathpeffer and Alness before joining the Royal Navy. On demobilisation after the Second World War he worked at Camden, London. As a full time officer of the Union, he was promoted to line secretary for the Southern Region, then the Western, followed by the largest Region, the London Midland. He then became senior assistant secretary and assistant general secretary before obtaining the senior national post.

MARSH, Rt. Hon. Richard William, P.C., F.R.S.A., F.C.I.T. (b. 1928). Chairman, British Railways Board from 1971. Launched the programme for the new breed of high speed trains; campaigned consistently for a national transport policy in the interests of a better use of the country's resources, and for a bigger share of transport investment for railways. Educated Jennings School, Swindon, Woolwich Polytechnic, Ruskin College, Oxford. Contested Hertford 1951, Labour M.P. for Greenwich 1959–71, Privy Councillor 1966. Health Services Officer, National Union of Public Employees 1951–59, Member various Whitley Councils for Health Service 1953–59, promoted the Shops, Offices and Railway Premises Bill which was passed on 31st July 1963. Member Select Committee Estimates 1961, chairman of Interdepartmental Committee to Co-ordinate Government Policy on Industrial Training 1964. Parliamentary Secretary, Ministry of Labour 1964–65, Joint Parliamentary Secretary Ministry of Technology 1965–66. Minister of Power 1966–68, Minister of Transport 1968–69, President Council of Association European Coal and Steel Community 1968. Joint deputy chairman British Railways Board May 1971 and chairman in September. Fellow Royal Society of

Rt. Hon. Richard Marsh (Photo: British Rail)

Arts, Fellow Chartered Institute of Transport, Fellow British Institute of Management.

MAUNSELL, Richard Edward Lloyd, C.B.E., M.A. (1868–1944). Chief mechanical engineer, South Eastern & Chatham Railway 1913–23, Southern Railway 1923–37. Previously Great South & Western Railway of Ireland, the country of his birth. His rebuilt Wainwright E1 4–4–0s were a highlight in British locomotive history. On the S.R. he introduced the *King Arthur*, *Nelson* and *Schools* classes, the Schools being the most powerful 4–4–0s in Europe in their time.

McCONNELL, James Edward (1815–83). Locomotive superintendent, southern division, London & North Western 1846–64, formerly Birmingham & Gloucester Railway, the man who made a *Bloomer* and made his name by making many more. He built these 2–2–2 express engines in three sizes for versatility. Some of his locomotives were covering the London–Birmingham journey of 113¼ miles in two hours as early as 1852. Four of his 0–4–2 locomotives were shipped in parts to Sydney for Australia's first railway, opened in 1855.

MEYNELL, Thomas. The first chairman of the world's first railway, the Stockton & Darlington. Appointed on 21st May 1821, 4 years before the railway opened. A wealthy Durham landowner, he subscribed £3,000 to the Company. Resigned in 1828 as he opposed an extension from Stockton to Middlesbrough. Some 20 years later, after the breach had been healed, his son became chairman.

MISSENDEN, Sir Eustace James, Kt., O.B.E. (b. 1886). Rose from clerk, South Eastern Railway, to be the first chairman of British Railways (Railway Executive) on nationalisation in 1948. As acting general manager (later, general manager), Southern Railway, during Second World War, handled with his team the problems of the Dunkirk evacuation, widespread railway damage during the Battle of Britain and the night raids (Blitz) of 1940/41.

MOON, Sir Richard, Bt. (1815–99). Chairman of the London & North Western Railway at the age of 46 from 1861–91 and one of the greatest railway personalities of the Victorian period. A shrewd and successful administrator, within about ten years of his appointment he had cut down expenditure by about a fifth of the figures for receipts. Money saved was ploughed back into developments; one of the oldest established railways in the world carried the heaviest traffic in the world, was the largest joint stock company, and fully deserving of its description "The Premier Line". Moon built up a brilliant team of senior officers who dedicated themselves to "The Company". A street in Crewe is named after him.

NEELE, G. P. (1825–1920). Superintendent of the line, London & North Western Railway 1874–95, a top officer brought on by Moon. His job was to "run the trains", and he mastered every detail of train operation. He personally interviewed practically every guard before appointment (the guard is still in charge of the train), selecting guards for important main line expresses. Neele's book of reminiscences, written in retirement, is an excellent railway documentary.

NEWCOMEN, Thomas (1663–1729), of Dartmouth, Devon, was the inventor of the first practical (stationary) steam engine, a reciprocating type with cylinder and piston used in 1712, originally for pumping water from tin mine workings. He is said to have invented his first engine in about 1698. In an unbroken succession it was improved by James Watt in 1769, developed and converted into a "travelling engine" by Richard Trevithick in 1803, further improved by George Stephenson in 1814 and established by him for the world's first proper steam-operated railway in 1825.

Except for the clock, the world had never before seen the like of Newcomen's automatic action. After an apprenticeship at Exeter, Newcomen returned to Dartmouth as a blacksmith or ironmonger. As a dealer in mining tools, he visited tin mines and noticed that water was raised by horses operating gins – simple pumping machines – a system both costly and slow, and spent ten years in inventing a steam operated pump. About the same time, Thomas Savery invented a suction and forcing pumping machine worked by steam, and later the two men worked together on improvements. In 1725, by which time Newcomen's engines were highly successful, Joseph Hornblower helped him in Cornwall, and in 1753 his son, Josiah Hornblower, sailed to New Jersey and there erected the first stationary steam engine in America, then a British colony. For over 60 years, Newcomen's engine was the only powerful and economical agent for draining mines. Without its aid, the great industrial developments of the 18th century – which opened up a new era of material progress for the world in general – would certainly have been much retarded. Newcomen was a modest and highly religious man and his great invention of the steam engine, like the man himself, has been obscured by such brilliant inventors as Savery, Watt, Trevithick and Stephenson, who all benefited from his pioneering work.

NEWLANDS, Alexander, C.B.E., M.Inst.C.E., (1870–1938). Chief engineer, London Midland & Scottish Railway 1927–34, formerly assistant engineer then engineer-in-chief, Highland Railway 1902–22. Among the heavy civil engineering works he carried out in Scotland was the extension of the Dingwall–Skye line of 10¼ miles through beautiful and rugged scenery from Stromeferry to Kyle of Lochalsh, connecting with ferries to the Isle of Skye.

OAKLEY, Sir Henry, Kt. (1823–1912). General manager, and later director, Great Northern Railway 1870–98, and chairman, Central London Railway 1900–11. One of his greatest achievements was to persuade his fellow general managers at York and Edinburgh to join him in the Great Race to Aberdeen of 1895 against their rivals on the Euston route, and to overcome the caution of his colleagues. H. A. Ivatt's locomotive *Henry Oakley* was named in his honour, and remained in service until 23rd November 1937.

PAGET, Lt.-Col. Sir Cecil Walter, Bt., C.M.G., D.S.O., R.E. (1874–1936). Cambridge scholar and general superintendent, Midland Railway, 1907–19. To cope with the enormous goods and mineral traffic, he introduced the traffic control system with "nerve centres" in districts connected by telephone to every station, signalbox and depot for a minute-by-minute regulation of the flow of all traffic round the clock. Movements were controlled centrally at the Derby control office. The system formed the basis for other railways, adapted in modern times to high-speed passenger and freight train movement. During the First World War he commanded the railway operating division in France, using a train as his headquarters.

PETO, Sir Samuel Morton (1809–89). One of the greatest railway contractors of the Victorian age. In business with different partners, he and his gangs of navvies built railways for many companies including the Great Western, Great Eastern, Great Northern, Eastern Counties, London Tilbury & Southend, East Lincolnshire, South Eastern, London Chatham & Dover, London & South Western, Oxford, Worcester & Wolverhampton, Hereford Ross & Gloucester, and London underground lines. He built Norway's first railway between Christiania and Eidsvoll, the Lyons–Avignon in France, and railways in Russia, Algiers, Australia and Canada. In 1847 he became a Member of Parliament for Norwich. A devoted Baptist, he found time for church work and money for the deprived. In the financial crisis of 1866 Peto's business collapsed leaving heavy debts, but he survived to a great age and saw the railways grow. (His father built Nelson's Column London, in 1843.)

PETTIGREW, W. F. Carriage and wagon superintendent, Furness Railway 1897–1918, formerly with the London & South Western Railway. Was with the Furness at a time of expansion of local industry bringing good business to this tiny railway. In pioneering days when train crews could neither read nor write, they were taught by example, but as locomotives became increasingly complex, the time came for correct printed technical material; Pettigrew was one of the first engineers to produce a comprehensive locomotive textbook which others followed.

POLE, Sir Felix John Clewett, Kt. (1877–1956). Rose from junior telegraph clerk aged 14 at Swindon station to general manager, Great Western Railway 1921–29. He brought tremendous enterprise into goods and passenger traffic development and the achievement of express train speeds that set high standards for his successors. Guided the Company through the traumatic general strike period of 1926 and personally developed the G.W.R. staff magazine. He was a hard task master but was fair and just. Left the Company to become chairman of Associated Electrical Industries Ltd., which post took him to most parts of the world. He later lost his fading sight.

RAMSBOTTOM, John G. (1814–97). Chief mechanical engineer, London & North Western Railway 1862–71. In his twenties appointed locomotive superintendent 1842–45, north eastern division based at Longsight, Manchester, 1846–57, and northern division 1857–62. Combined exceptional organising ability with inventive skill, designing a locomotive safety valve, split piston ring, and the water-pick-up scoop apparatus and water troughs to save trains stopping to take water. At Crewe he produced some excellent classes of locomotive including the *Newton*, *Samson*, *Lady of the Lake* and the DX six-coupled goods engines. He built the steel works at Crewe, using the world's first Bessemer steel producing process. President, Institution of Mechanical Engineers 1870–71, then retired from the Company to become a consultant.

RASTRICK, John Urpeth (1780–1856). Civil Engineer, builder of locomotives and railways; he could well have become a second George Stephenson, but later moved into the heavy engineering field with works at Stourbridge, Worcestershire. He was born at Morpeth, Northumberland, in Stephenson country. In 1814 he registered Patent No. 3799 for a steam locomotive, and conducted experiments in that year of Stephenson's first engine. In pioneering days, he supported the idea of railways before many Parliamentary Committees, as a witness showing shrewdness and coolness. In 1826/7 he constructed a line of some 16 miles between Stratford-on-Avon and Moreton-in-Marsh in the Cotswolds, and in 1829 opened the Shutt End colliery in South Staffordshire, operated by one of his locomotives. That year, he was one of the judges who awarded the prize to the Stephensons for the *Rocket*. With George Stephenson, he surveyed the Grand Junction Railway from Birmingham and he marked out a line between Manchester and Crewe. In 1835 he was appointed engineer to the Manchester & Cheshire Junction railway. With Sir John Rennie, he built part of the London & Brighton Railway and personally supervised the construction of the Merstham, Balcombe, and Clayton tunnels and the Ouse viaduct (still in use) of 37 arches at an elevation of 100 feet, completed in 1840. Later, he built several branches including the Shoreham line, which comprised the London Brighton & South Coast Railway. In the 1830s, he sold some of his locomotives to the first American railways. With James Walker, he published a paper in 1829 entitled: *Report on the Comparative Merits of Locomotives and Fixed Engines as a Moving Power* which played an important part in promoting early railways. Retiring in 1847, he was buried at Brighton.

RAVEN, Sir Vincent Litchfield, K.B.E., M.Inst.C.E., M.I.Mech.E., M.I.E.E. (1859–1934). Son of a church minister; last chief mechanical engineer, North Eastern Railway 1910–22, and assistant from 1895. Developed an early cab signalling system, at first audible, with visual indication later. The Pacifics of 1922 were his best locomotives, which were named after cities on the routes. A leading advocate of railway electrification, he electrified the Newport-Shildon, Northumberland, goods line. President, Institution of Mechanical Engineers in centenary year of 1925.

RAYMOND, Sir Stanley Edward, Kt., F.C.I.T., F.B.I.M. (b. 1913). Chairman, British Railways Board 1965–67. Educated at an orphanage and Hampton, Middlesex, Grammar School, then entered the Civil Service. War service 1939–45, rose to lieutenant-colonel. London Transport 1946, British Road Services 1947, British Transport Commission 1955, rising through various senior appointments to chairman and general manager, Western Region 1962–63. At historic Paddington headquarters, he ordered the removal of 19th century pictures and their replacement with modern illustrations, his maxim being: "We must move into the second half of the twentieth century." In 1968 he was appointed chairman of the Gaming Board and four years later of the Horse Race Betting Levy Board.

RIDDLES, R. A. (b. 1892). Member, Railway Executive on railway nationalisation, 1948–54, formerly a vice president London Midland & Scottish Railway, involved in designing the highly successful War Department austerity 2–8–0 and 2–10–0 locomotives during Second World War. His crowning success was to design excellent standard locomotives and rolling stock from 1951. After retirement, became chairman of Stothert & Pitt Ltd., crane builders of Bath.

ROBERTSON, General Lord (Brian Hubert Robertson) of Oakridge, G.C.B., G.B.E., K.C.M.G., K.C.V.O., D.S.O., M.C. (1896–1974). Chairman, British Transport Commission 1953–61, appointed by Sir Winston Churchill. He launched the British Railways Modernisation Plan of 1955 which was to phase out steam in favour of diesel and electric traction. He joined the Commission in a period of readjustment to the Government's new policy for transport, which involved the decentralisation of management and the disposal of most of the road haulage services. Robertson had seen action in two World Wars and earned outstanding distinction as had his father before him.

RUSSELL, Charles (d. 1856). Chairman of the Parliamentary Committee that examined the Great Western Railway Bill which received the Royal Assent in 1835, chairman of the G.W.R. 1839–55, M.P. for Reading. Fought hard with Brunel, Gooch and Saunders during the "Battle of the Gauges". The pressures of office had weighed heavily upon him and in 1856, after his retirement, he took his own life.

SAUNDERS, Charles (1796–1864). Secretary and general superintendent of the line, Great Western Railway 1840–63. Skilful negotiator in spreading the broad gauge lines. A man of honesty and integrity in all his dealings who enhanced the standing of the Company in Victorian railway politics. In the battle over the gauge, this conscientious man suffered a battering and virtually died broken-hearted.

SAXBY, John. Signalling pioneer who, after working in the locomotive department of the London & Brighton Railway, founded the firm of Saxby & Farmer Ltd. in 1856. Prolific inventor of railway safety devices, particularly signalling. His interlocking frame was the first successful apparatus of this kind, which prevented signals being placed to "clear" in a wrong sequence and permitted points to be changed only when the signal reading through them was in the right position. His firm designed, built and supplied various equipment for railways in all parts of the world, signalling apparatus in general becoming known in France as "Le Saxby". Saxby's company was absorbed into the Westinghouse Brake & Signal Co. which was incorporated in 1920.

SMILES, Dr. Samuel (1812–1904). Railway official and author whose books and articles celebrated the work of the great railway pioneers, many of whom he knew personally. Born in Haddington some 15 miles east of Edinburgh, he became a doctor and practised locally. Going to England, he met George Stephenson at Leeds in 1840 at the opening of the North Midland Railway, and five years later became assistant secretary of the projected Leeds & Thirsk Railway, remaining associated with the Company for 21 years. He took a prominent part in the amalgamations which formed the North Eastern Railway in 1854. Moving to London in that year, he was appointed secretary of the South Eastern Railway, a post he held for 12 years. He negotiated the extension from Charing Cross to Cannon Street in 1858–9. Among his published works was a paper of 1849 entitled: *Railway Property, its Conditions and Prospects*. Smiles wrote brilliantly about the developing railways, his *Life of George and Robert Stephenson*, first published in 1858, being a classic in its own right. He published books about Boulton, Watt, Telford, Brindley and other pioneers of the Industrial Revolution. He became internationally famous for his book *Self Help*, which sold 120,000 copies and was translated into all the main languages of the civilised world. Smiles, who had visited Ireland, France, Italy and Scandinavia, lived long enough to enjoy watching the dreams of the great railway pioneers come true.

STAMP, Josiah Charles, Baron, of Shortlands, G.C.B., G.B.E., Hon.D.Sc. (1880–1941). Chairman and President of the Executive, London Midland & Scottish Railway 1926–41. Engaged to reorganise the management on modern lines. He introduced systematic costing, eliminated inefficient processes, plant and equipment, and created an executive of vice-presidents, each responsible for specific major activities with departmental heads reporting to a vice-president instead of to the general manager. Civil Service and the Inland Revenue was his main background; he was a Director of the Bank of England, member of a Royal Commission, author of several books and the recipient of 23 honorary degrees in Britain, America, Canada and elsewhere. Stamp was respected as a man of honesty and simplicity and a lifelong friend said of him: "Religion pervaded his whole life." Stamp, his wife and eldest son were killed when their home was almost destroyed in an air raid on 16th April 1941. His father was a railway bookstall manager at Wigan station.

STANIER, Sir William Arthur, Kt., F.R.S., M.I.Loco.E. (1878–1966). Chief mechanical en-

Lord Stamp

gineer, London Midland & Scottish Railway 1932–44, formerly of the Great Western Railway. His brief on the L.M.S. was to "scrap and build", a tempting option for any engineer; the locomotives he built included the *Black Five* 4–6–0 and the *Duchess* 4–6–2 classes and formed a splendid fleet. He joined two important missions to Indian Railways and during the Second World War served as scientific adviser to the Minister of Production.

STEPHENSON, George (1781–1848). Inventor and founder of railways. Born at Wylam, eight miles from Newcastle, the second of six children. In his spare time he mended boots and repaired clocks and watches. He married in 1802, his only son Robert was born in 1803 and his wife died in 1806. Setting off on foot with his kit upon his back, he spent most of 1807 tending a Boulton & Watt stationary steam engine at Montrose, Scotland. Returning to Killingworth colliery on similar work, he took the engine to pieces every Saturday to see exactly how it worked. After repairing a large Newcomen steam pumping engine in 1812, he was appointed enginewright at £100 per annum. In 1815 he invented a miner's safety lamp for which he was awarded £1,000 three years later. During that period he examined experimental steam locomotives designed by Blenkinsop and Hedley, building his first – the *Blücher* – in 1814. The following year, he took out a patent for an improved locomotive incorporating steamblast, and was the first to use this system with a full knowledge of its important influence on the steam locomotive.

In 1819, he started building an eight-mile railway at Hetton colliery, to be worked by horses and stationary engines with cables, the line opening in 1822. His first real step to fame came the next year when he was appointed engineer to the projected Stockton & Darlington Railway at £300 per annum. It opened in 1825 to become the world's first proper steam locomotive railway hauling goods and passengers. The year before he had opened, with his son, the locomotive factory at Newcastle, in which locomotives were built for railways in Britain and overseas. At the Rainhill trials near Liverpool of 1829, the Stephenson *Rocket* set the stage for rapid railway development, and the *Scotsman* reported: "The experiments at Liverpool have established principles which will give a greater impulse to civilisation that it has ever received from any single cause since the Press first opened the gates of knowledge to the human species at large."

Even before he had built his first railway, he visualised a national network in a standard rail gauge serving the whole of Britain. Apart from railways he himself built, he was consulted about nearly every major pioneering railway in Britain and many overseas. Though he did not in fact invent the first "travelling engine", he improved it out of all recognition. He had to manage with few tools and fewer skilled men. The brighter young mechanics whom he trained became railway builders in their own right, and those established engineers who worked with him gained from his experience. In this way, the original work of Stephenson fanned out across the civilised world into a massive building boom. Of gentle disposition but great strength of character, he remained aloof from the "Mania" and used his influence to discourage reckless schemes. His talented son worked with him throughout his life. Robert survived his father by only 11 years, and by that time the Stephensons and other engineers had built in Britain about 9,000 route miles of railway, which is nearly half the total mileage ever built and a little over 2,000 miles short of what remains today. He started many mechanics' institutes and founded the Institution of Mechanical Engineers in 1847, becoming its first president. He refused many offers of public honours, including a seat in Parliament.

After completing the Liverpool & Manchester Railway in 1830 he moved to Alton Grange near Ashby-de-la-Zouch, Leicestershire, and opened large collieries in the area, which brought him much additional wealth. Later he moved to Tapton House, near Chesterfield, with his second wife, and retiring from business he took up farming and horticulture. As cucumbers by nature were curved, he took great delight in growing straight ones by covering them in specially made glass cylinders! His second wife died in 1845 and he remarried early in 1848, only seven months before his death. Of great physical strength and endurance, his life's work places him among the world's greatest benefactors.

STEPHENSON, Robert (1803–59). Civil engineer, only son of George. Attended village school and Bruce's Academy, Newcastle. Assisted his father in 1821 with the projected Stockton & Darlington Railway and the following year spent six months at Edinburgh University, returning to manage the new locomotive factory of Robert Stephenson & Co. established in 1824. His health broke down and in June he went to Colombia, South America, to supervise gold and silver mining, hoping the climate would benefit his health. On his journey home to help his father in 1827, he met Richard Trevithick, who was stranded and penniless, and lent him his fare home. After a tour of the United States he returned to his factory, where he took detailed charge of the construction of the *Rocket* and helped his father build the Liverpool & Manchester Railway. Next he built the Canterbury & Whitstable Railway, opened in 1830. When in 1833 the Act for the London & Birmingham Railway was passed he was appointed engineer and was wholly responsible for the construction of this first main railway into the capital. Outstanding works were the Kilsby Tunnel, and Blisworth and Tring cuttings. The railway was completed throughout in 1838 and was one of his finest accomplishments.

Robert Stephenson

In 1840, he succeeded his father (then nearly sixty) and took over from him most of his current railway and other business activities. He was appointed engineer of the projected Chester & Holyhead Railway and built the famous tubular bridge, the Britannia, across the Menai Straits – a unique structure. In 1852 he took Queen Victoria and Prince Albert to inspect it. He also built other outstanding bridges including the High Level Bridge over the Tyne at Newcastle and the tubular bridge at Conway, North Wales, and designed the Royal Border Bridge to cross the Tweed at Berwick. He went to Canada to build the Great Victoria Bridge over the St. Lawrence at Montreal, for many years the longest bridge in the world. It played a key part in the development of Canada's new railways. In 1836, his factory had built the locomotive *Dorchester* for the first railway in Canada and a few years earlier had built the *John Bull* for an early American railway, which formed the basis of considerable locomotive building in that country. Stephenson spent much time in Europe building or advising about new railways, and the Newcastle factory built locomotives for new lines in France, Belgium and Russia. Stephenson designed two tubular bridges to cross the Nile in lower Egypt. He also built the railway between Cairo and Alexandria. By this time, he had become one of the leading bridge builders in the world, and wrote "Iron Bridges" for the 8th Edn. of Encyclopaedia Britannica.

He was consulted about a projected Suez Canal and in 1846, accompanied by a French and an

Austrian engineer, he surveyed a route from the Red Sea to the Mediterranean. He considered the scheme too costly to justify at that time and forecast a commercial failure; the canal, however, was opened in 1869.

George Stephenson's death in 1848 brought Robert the inheritance of his father's valuable collieries, his share in the Newcastle locomotive factory and his accumulation of capital. This, plus the fortune he had amassed from his own railway and engineering work, made him the first railway engineering millionaire. He received various honours at home and overseas, becoming Member of Parliament for Whitby in 1847 and President of the Institution of Civil Engineers for both 1856 and 1857. He married in 1829 and was devoted to his wife, who died in 1842. There were no children. Like his father, he was offered a knighthood but did not accept it. Smiles, who knew him well, described him as modest and gentle; he used his great wealth unobtrusively to help worthy causes and needy people; he had great personal charm and earned respect from all. In his professional life, he was cautious and experimental, a pre-eminently "safe man"; like his father, he recognised that a railway could be a dangerous thing with lives at stake and always urged care and caution in signalling, track, maintenance and operations.

His hard working life and extensive foreign travel took a toll of his indifferent health, but he found time to enjoy sailing in his yacht *Titania* off the east coast of Scotland. Like Brunel, he was a heavy cigar smoker. He died on 12th October 1859, 27 days after Brunel and four days before his 56th birthday. Robert Stephenson was buried in Westminster Abbey beside his fellow-pioneer of transport, Thomas Telford.

STIRLING, Patrick (1820–95). Born in a manse at Kilmarnock, Patrick Stirling was celebrated for his fine locomotives with 8 ft. single driving wheels for the Great Northern Railway, 1870. Apprenticed to his uncle at the Dundee foundries of James Stirling & Co. in 1837, he worked later at both the Vulcan Works and Neilsons of Glasgow. His first railway appointment was as superintendent of a short line between the Clyde and Balloch on Loch Lomond, at the age of 31. He was locomotive superintendent of the Glasgow & South Western Railway from 1853–66, and of the G.N.R. from 1866–95. A fountain was erected to his memory at Doncaster by his drivers and firemen.

SYKES, William Robert (1840–1917). Pioneering signal and telegraph engineer, joined the London Chatham & Dover Railway in 1862 as a maintenance man on watches, clocks and telegraph instruments. Studied ways of improving equipment and in 1875 patented his "Lock and Block" system, by which signals were electrically connected to the signal-box telegraph instruments which had magnetic needles and dials; this was to avoid a second train entering a "section" between two signal-boxes until the train ahead was clear of it. "Lock and Block" system fitted throughout London Chatham & Dover Railway from 1878, introduced on the London & Brighton Coast, London & South Western and on Great Eastern suburban lines. Sykes Interlocking Signal Co. Ltd. incorporated in 1889. Sykes developed a miniature slide lever for electrical operation of signals.

TATTERSALL, A. E. Pioneering electrical signal engineer. Held various signal engineering posts, Lancashire & Yorkshire, Great Southern & Western Railway of Ireland; and from 1907: assistant signalling and electrical engineer, Metropolitan Railway; signal superintendent, Great Northern Railway 1921; signal and telegraph engineer, north eastern area, London & North Eastern Railway; then in 1936, of the southern area. He pioneered the use of electric relay interlocking to replace mechanical, and introduced thumb-switch panel operation of signals in place of heavy manual levers. Responsible for the early panel interlocking systems at Thirsk and Leeds which led to the installation of "power" signal-boxes at Hull and York. He introduced the complete resignalling for the complexity of lines in and approaching Liverpool Street and the sequence-switch interlocking installation at Doncaster, in which the turn of one switch by the signalman operated all the points and signals in progressive sequence for the route of a train. The spadework of Tattersall formed the basis for "power installations" of modern times from which over a hundred miles of route could be controlled from one signal-box.

TREVITHICK, Richard (1771–1833). "Father of the steam locomotive", he is generally accepted as the inventor of the steam locomotive using smooth wheels able to grip smooth rails sufficiently to hauling wagons. Born at Illogan near Redruth, Cornwall, the only child of a tin mining bursar. Of outstanding mechanical gifts, he saw the future of his travelling locomotive on the roads of Britain and left others to develop it for railways. Apprenticed to a James Watt man, William Murdock, who had built a model locomotive about a foot high in 1786, he learnt much about the steam pumping engine, and himself made three models of locomotives when he was about 25. He later began to build and sell steam pumping engines. He took out a patent, jointly with his cousin, Andrew Vivian, for "an improved steam carriage" using a high pressure. It weighed 1½ tons and ran through Cambourne Cross, Cornwall, on 24th December 1801; he registered a patent the following year. His next locomotive, the *Coalbrookdale*, built in 1803, ran on the Coakbrookdale, Shropshire, iron tramway opened in 1760. Another Trevithick locomotive was tested on the Pen-y-darran wagon-way at Merthyr Tydfil on 15th February 1804; a few days later, it hauled a train of five wagons carrying 10 tons of iron ore, and 70 people, covering 9 miles at about 5 m.p.h.

Four years later he demonstrated a locomotive hauling a passenger carriage round an enclosed circular railway track near Euston; while in London he lodged at No. 1 Southampton Street, Strand. From the rhythmic sound of steam exhaust, his locomotives were nicknamed "puffers". In 1815 he took out another patent for further improvements. Earlier, he had been engaged in dredging the Thames by steam power, and in 1807 was appointed to build a tunnel under the River Thames in London. He was promised £1,000 on its completion, but flooding caused its abandonment and he received only £105. (Some 20 years later, Sir Marc Brunel, father of Isambard, undertook the task.) Trevithick continued designing and building pumping engines for home and overseas. He sold nine in 1814 for use in silver and gold mines in Peru, a source of wealth threatened by flooding. He designed coining apparatus for the Peruvian mint and furnaces for purifying silver ore. With these, and more pumping engines ordered, he set sail from Portsmouth in October 1816, reaching Lima four months later to an almost royal welcome. The Government Gazette announced the arrival of "Don Ricardo Trevithick, an eminent professor of mechanics, machinery, and mineralogy, inventor and constructor of the engines now at work in Pasco."

In 1818 the Peruvian revolution broke out, lasting for some years, and he and his mining partners were ruined. It was reported that he joined the patriotic party and invented an ingenious gun carriage. He finally escaped from Peru. Aiming for Panama, he and a friend crossed mountains, slept in the forests by night, travelled on foot by day and swam rivers, covering many hundreds of miles. At an inn in Cartagena, gaunt, wasted and ragged, he met by chance Robert Stephenson, who had heard of his Peruvian exploits and was himself homeward bound from South America. Stephenson lent him money and they sailed the long journey together to New York. When Trevithick reached home via Falmouth in October 1827, his only remnant from the "torrents of silver" was a pair of silver spurs.

He registered a patent in 1831 for heating rooms and another in 1832 for a steam-powered ship. He persuaded Halls, engineers of Dartford, Kent, to allow him to build and test his new invention, water ejected through a tube providing the propulsion. A year passed without significant progress, and in 1833 he died in poverty. His other inventions included an oscillating engine and screw propellor, a patented superheating system, and designs for wrought iron ships and wrought iron floating docks to rise and fall with the tide. Throughout his life he had been absorbed in new ideas, failing to pursue them to a logical conclusion, and his imagination often outran his judgment.

VIGNOLES, Charles Blacker (1793–1875). Civil engineer. Following a military career at home and abroad, he prepared the plans for the Liverpool & Manchester Railway which Stephenson built, and worked with Rennie in building the London & Brighton Railway. Designed an improved rail with flat bottom. Engineer of the Dublin & Kingston Railway 1834, the first railway in his homeland of Ireland. During Railway Mania was engineer to a number of railway companies; built the first railway in Switzerland; built railways in Spain and surveyed a route for a line in Brazil. Visited Russia several times for civil engineering works and built a bridge at Kiev. Helped with the railway from Warsaw to Terespol, which opened in 1865. Died at Hythe, Hampshire.

WALKER, Sir Herbert Ashcombe, Kt., K.C.B. (1868–1949). One of the great general managers in British railway history. Served under George Neele and Sir Robert Turnbull, London & North Western Railway; general manager London & South Western Railway 1912–22; and of Southern Railway 1923–37; chairman of Railway Executive Committee during First World War; after the 1923 grouping, fused the constituent companies into a single railway. Great driving force behind the development of electrification and of colour-light signalling schemes, electric trains reaching Brighton, Eastbourne, Hastings, Portsmouth and Gravesend and many others to form the great Southern Electric, the busiest network of its kind in the world.

WATKIN, Sir Edward William, Bt. (1819–1901). One of the most go-ahead railway managers of his time. Chairman of the South Eastern Railway 1866–94, the Manchester Sheffield & Lincolnshire, and the Metropolitan; a director of both the Great Western and the Great Eastern, and at one time President of the Grand Trunk Railway of Canada. He was chairman of the first Channel Tunnel Company and became a Member of Parliament for Hythe, Kent. He thrived on rivalry and controversy and revelled in the sustained "war" with his Kent competitor, the London Chatham & Dover Railway. Retired from all his railway posts in 1894 when aged 75.

WATT, James (1736–1819). Improved Newcomen's stationary steam engine by a system of condensation, making it much more efficient and economical in the use of water and fuel. His engines were a great commercial success, at home and overseas, and led directly to the "travelling locomotive". Born in Greenock, he was of delicate health and suffered throughout his life from severe attacks of headache. The engines of Watt, and his partner, Boulton, made an enormous contribution to the prosperity of Britain during the Industrial Revolution, putting her well ahead of any other country in the world.

WEBB, Francis William (1835–1906). One of the greatest engineering administrators of the 19th century. As chief mechanical engineer, London & North Western Railway 1871–1903, he built Crewe Works into a highly efficient production unit turning out new main line locomotives at the rate of five or six a month, using assembly line techniques similar to the modern car industry. He invented the compound engine, designed a radial axle box for passenger carriages, and signal interlocking frames for greater safety; he also invented numerous detail features for locomotives and other rolling stock. In 1888, on behalf of Beyer Peacock & Co., he personally supervised the building of a 2–2–2–2 three-cylinder compound locomotive for the Pennsylvania Railroad of America. It was fitted with a bell and cowcatcher and carried the number 1320 on a standard Webb number plate. Of the hundreds of locomotives he built, the Precedent class 2–4–0s were outstanding. One of them, *Hardwicke* No. 790, now preserved, made record time in the Race to the North of 1895 by averaging 67 m.p.h. from Crewe to Carlisle. Webb was proud, arrogant, bridled at criticism and became almost a law unto himself.

WEIGHELL, Sidney (b. 1922). General Secretary, National Union of Railwaymen (NUR) from February 1975. Succeeded Sir Sidney Greene, C.B.E., who held the position for a record 17 years. His father, now 83, served as an unpaid union official at Northallerton, and his grandfather was a founder member of the N.U.Rs' oldest parent union. Rose from engine cleaner and fireman to locomotive driver in the north-east before becoming a full time union official. A keen footballer, he played for Sunderland reserves, earning more in a Saturday afternoon match than his fireman's pay.

WESTINGHOUSE, George (1846–1914). Inventor of the automatic air brake. From the 1870s, the Westinghouse brake was adopted on various railways including the London Brighton & South Coast, Great Eastern, North Eastern, North British, Caledonian and some Welsh lines. An American, he demonstrated his compressed air braking system on the Panhandle Railroad, U.S.A., in 1868 when he was only 22. He came to England three years later to interest railway engineers, including William Stroudley, then locomotive superintendent, L.B. & S.C. Response was at first lukewarm. Then the magazine *Engineering* published an article specifying in detail the requirements for a sound braking system for railways vehicles. Returning to America with the article, Westinghouse secured a patent for his automatic brake in 1874. Specifications and detail were virtually worked out in Britain and the system eventually came into wide use.

WHITELAW, William (1868–1946). A great Scotsman who was a railway director for nearly 40 years and a chairman for 36. In 1898, at the age of 30, he became a director of the Highland Railway, and chairman four years later, holding the post until 1912. Meanwhile, he became a director of the North British Railway in 1908, and its chairman in 1912. When the N.B.R. was absorbed into the London & North Eastern Railway, he remained with the parent Company during the years of severe financial pressures between the wars, relinquishing office in his 70th year.

Appendix A: Some Railway Accidents

IN pioneering days, the new railways had to learn from their mistakes. Acts of Parliament in 1840 and 1842 gave the Board of Trade power to appoint railway inspecting officers who were recruited from the Corps of Royal Engineers. They were to report on newly built lines, which could not be opened for public use without their inspection and approval. They were also to investigate the causes of accidents. The first was conducted at Howden on the Hull & Selby Railway in 1840. Six people lost their lives when a casting fell from a wagon and derailed a "mixed traffic" train consisting of wagons of goods and carriages with passengers. Inspecting officers have always been thorough in investigation, fearless in criticism and forthright in their recommendations. In safety regulations and techniques, the leading railway companies were ahead of the Statutes which brought recalcitrant railways up to the required standards. Over the years, "fail safe" systems and modern technology have increasingly removed the "human element" from train operations, with the continuing objective of higher standards of safety.

In the following pages, the mishaps that have been selected portray a variety of causes and situations on different railways from the early pioneering days.

PARKSIDE, Liverpool & Manchester Railway, 15th September 1830

The first fatal railway accident of historic significance occurred at the official opening of the Liverpool & Manchester Railway. At Parkside, the engines had stopped to take water. George Stephenson had just driven the *Northumbrian* hauling the carriage containing the Prime Minister, the Duke of Wellington, and his party. His Minister of State, Sir Robert Peel and William Huskisson, Member of Parliament for Liverpool, were in attendance. Huskisson had used his strong influence only a few years earlier to get the Bill through Parliament for the new railway serving his constituency. The Prime Minister's carriage was drawn up on one line for trains on the other line to pass before him in review. Then, on the track, he chatted with Huskisson and they were shaking hands when the *Rocket* came along the line. Joseph Locke was its driver that day. Huskisson tried to jump out of its path but it knocked him down and crushed his leg; he cried out, "I have met my death!" He was taken to a parsonage where he died that evening. The accident threw a dark shadow over the day's proceedings, and the fatality dramatically called the attention of the Government to the potential dangers inherent in the new railways.

BAGWORTH, Leicester & Swannington Railway, 4th May 1833

The locomotive *Samson* is said to have crashed into a market cart loaded with eggs and butter on Thornton level crossing at Bagworth. Ashlin Bagster, manager of the railway and the first manager of the London & Birmingham Railway, asked George Stephenson if the engines could be fitted by a whistle blown by steam to warn of their approach. Stephenson thought the idea an excellent one and a Leicester musical instrument maker designed one for *Samson*. It was known then as a "steam trumpet".

SONNING CUTTING, near Reading, Great Western Railway, 24th December 1841

At 4.30 a.m. the regular goods train left Paddington for Bristol, headed by *Hecla* of the Leo class 2–4–0. It was a "mixed train" consisting of 17 goods wagons, a covered parcels van and two passenger carriages, one a six-wheeler and the other a four-wheeler. In the winter darkness, heavy rain had disturbed the sides of the deep two-mile cutting and a great mound of earth had fallen on to the line. The train plunged deep into it, and the goods wagons at the rear rammed the passenger carriages into the engine tender, resulting in the loss of eight lives and injury to 17 other passengers. Most were workmen who had been building the new Houses of Parliament, and were returning home for Christmas. The accident resulted in strong criticism of the third class carriages which were open-sided and exposed to the weather, with wooden plank seats and buffers without springs. Protection against accident was negligible. The journey from London to Bristol took nine and a half hours. The practice of running trains composed of goods wagons, often loaded with cattle and pigs, and passenger carriages, also used on some other railways, was strongly condemned at the inquiry. Gladstone's Act, passed three years later, brought many long overdue improvements for third class passengers.

STAPLEHURST, Kent, South Eastern Railway, 9th June 1865

On a bright and sunny afternoon, Charles Dickens (1812–70) narrowly escaped with his life when the boat train of 13 carriages from Folkestone crashed. A gang of men was repairing a small bridge spanning the Beult stream near Staplehurst and John Benge, the foreman, had to get the work done between trains. Unfortunately, he misread his timetable and had less time than he thought. The boat train ran at different times daily according to tides. In addition, he sent a platelayer with a red flag and detonators, insufficient in number, up the line only about 550 yards, instead of 1,000 yards as prescribed by the rules, to warn an approaching train. The express suddenly appeared, travelling at about 50 m.p.h. On seeing the red flag, the driver applied his brakes but found it impossible to stop within the short distance. The engine and the first coach, in which Dickens was travelling, ran across the rail-less timbers of the bridge, leaving the first coach hanging at a perilous angle. Five carriages fell through the bridge gap into the stream and broke up. One of them stood on its end and another lay on its roof. Ten people were killed and 49 injured. When the accident happened, Dickens had been reading the manuscript of *Our Mutual Friend*, and he added a postscript:

"On Friday, the ninth of June," he wrote, "in the present year, Mr. & Mrs. Boffin . . . were on the South Eastern Railway with me, in a terribly destructive accident. When I had done what I could to help others, I climbed back into my carriage – nearly turned over a viaduct, and caught aslant upon the turn – to extricate the couple. They were much soiled, but otherwise unhurt . . . I remember with devout thankfulness that I can never be much nearer parting company with my readers for ever than I was then, until there shall be written against my life the two words with which I have this day closed this book – The End."

The terrifying experience affected his health and he avoided train travel for some time. He later described the memory of the accident as "inexpressibly distressing." John Benge's fatal error may even have curtailed Dickens' contribution to English literature and left still unsolved *The Mystery of Edwin Drood.*

ABERGELE, London & North Western Railway, 20th August 1868

The station master at Llandulas was strongly criticised by the investigating officer for allowing a dangerous shunting operation which caused a violent collision and train fire. The Railway was also condemned for their rules which allowed shunting to take place on a main line with insufficient margin of time ahead of a train. In the shunting operations, the local goods train from Crewe to Holyhead placed six wagons and the brake van on the main line, the guard securing the brakes of the van. Two of the wagons contained drums of paraffin oil. These stationary vehicles were bumped in the shunting operations and started to move backwards down the gradient. The guard frantically ran alongside, hoping to pin down wagon brakes, but the wagons gained speed and he was quickly outpaced. It was found afterwards that the van brakes had already been damaged, probably in rough shunting.

Meanwhile, the *Irish Mail*, the oldest "named" train in the world, on its Euston–Holyhead journey, had left Chester at 11.47 a.m. and ran through Abergele station at 12.39 p.m. at about 40 m.p.h. A minute or so later, driver Arthur Thompson saw the runaway wagons rapidly approaching him round a bend only 200 yards away. It was too late to avoid disaster and he shouted to his fireman, "For God's sake, Joe, jump for it!" He leapt out, but Joe did not follow him. Paraffin deluged the front van and the first three coaches, and, ignited by the flying coals from the engine firebox, the vehicles, tender and wagons blazed furiously, bringing almost instantaneous death for 31 passengers and two railwaymen. The Press strongly criticised the Railway for locking carriage doors, but the collision and fire were so sudden that this made little difference to the outcome.

WIGAN, London & North Western Railway, 2nd August 1873

High speed alone was almost certainly the cause of a derailment that tore up Wigan station in the dead of night. Touring in Scotland had become more fashionable following Queen Victoria's frequent visits to Balmoral. A tourists' special for Scotland left Euston at 8 p.m. on the night in question. From Crewe, the train consisted of 25 four-wheeled carriages, some of them family coaches carrying distinguished travellers, and hauled by two locomotives. Speeding at over 40 m.p.h. through Wigan station, the train broke loose between the 15th and 16th carriages, the rear portion becoming derailed at facing points.

The front portion stopped after a short distance, but the rear carriages crashed through the station at about 1.20 a.m., strewing wreckage all over the platforms. Some carriages had run on to the platform, dragging along the awning. The 18th carriage landed on the platform upside down. Thirteen people were killed and 30 injured. The front portion eventually departed at 2.53 a.m., and it is said that the passengers remained unaware of the disaster until they reached their destination. Keen competition between the main routes to Scotland encouraged the companies to run trains of flimsy four-wheeled wooden carriages faster than was safe. The precise cause of the derailment remained a mystery but the inspecting officer strongly criticised running at such high speed through a station.

ABBOTS RIPTON, near Huntingdon, Great Northern Railway, 21st January 1876

A terrific snowstorm, north-easterly gale and severe frost which froze early slot-type signals in the clear position, caused the southbound *Flying Scotsman* to crash into a goods train, and a northbound express to plough into the wreckage. The goods train of 37 coal wagons travelling south from Peterborough passed signals at Holme which were frozen incorrectly in the clear position. It had been intended to stop it and have it shunted clear of the main line for the *Flying Scotsman* to pass. The coal train proceeded to Abbots Ripton where the signals were similarly frozen to the clear position, but the signalman there stopped the train with a red handlamp. It was being shunted clear of the main line when the *Flying Scotsman* passed the faulty signals at high speed and crashed into the wagons, strewing them across the lines.

The 5.30 p.m. express from King's Cross to Leeds approached at speed on the down line, could not be halted, and ploughed into the wreckage of the other two trains, killing 14 people and injuring 24. The Board of Trade investigating inspector criticised the station master at Holme, when told the coal train had passed signals at danger, for not taking preventive action which could have averted the first collision. He also condemned the signalman at Abbots Ripton for not having the Leeds express stopped further south. He said that fog signalmen should have been posted at the signals. He proposed improvements to the signals themselves and in the signalling system. Signals were placed to danger usually to protect a train that had passed, then replaced to remain in the clear position. They should normally be kept in the danger position, and placed to clear only for the passage of a train. Block signalling methods should also be improved. His recommendations were widely adopted, marking an important stage in safe train operation.

TAY BRIDGE, North British Railway, 28th December 1879

On a stormy Sunday evening in exceptionally heavy gales, the first Tay Bridge collapsed under the fierce side-winds and the weight of a crossing train which dropped into the Firth of Tay. Every soul was drowned in the rushing waters below; 73 were passengers and four were railwaymen. Only a few months before, Queen Victoria had stopped on her journey to confer a knighthood on the designer, Thomas Bouch. Carrying a single line of railway, the lattice girder bridge had been opened in May 1878, to shorten the journey and avoid the rough ferry crossing connecting Edinburgh and Dundee. It was then the longest railway bridge in the world and acclaimed as a masterpiece of Victorian engineering skill. Before its opening, a Board of Trade inspector had thoroughly examined it and had run six coupled locomotives of 73 tons each, travelling at 40 m.p.h. In his report, he recommended a maximum speed of 25 m.p.h., adding a warning about high winds. After a detailed inquiry, the investigating committee reported:

"We find that the bridge was badly designed, badly constructed and badly maintained and that its downfall was due to inherent defects in the structure which must sooner or later have brought it down. For these defects both in design, construction and maintenance Sir Thomas Bouch is in our opinion mainly to blame."

The new Tay Bridge was opened in 1887. The only "survivor" of the catastrophe was the locomotive, No. 224 4–4–0, which was hauled out and taken on its own wheels to Glasgow Works for overhaul; but for many years, no driver would take it over the bridge, a taboo that was not broken until 1908. The locomotive was finally scrapped in 1919.

ARMAGH, Northern Ireland, 12th June 1889

A special day excursion train mainly for schoolchildren left Armagh station for Warren Point. Before departure, driver Thomas McGrath complained that his four-coupled engine was inadequate to haul the train of 15 carriages packed with some 940 passengers up the heavy gradients;

but the stationmaster at Armagh overruled him, and anxiously he drove off. Climbing to the summit at Dobbins Bridge, the stalwart little engine finally stalled. James Elliot, chief clerk to the superintendent of the line, was in charge of the excursion and rode on the footplate with the driver; and there were two guards – one in the front guards van and one in the rear. As the train stood on the rising gradient, there were two options: either to take a few carriages over the summit to nearby sidings, the engine returning for the remainder; or to secure the whole of the train on the gradient, protect it in the rear, and await the assistance of the following lightly loaded regular train, which could give a push. This was the 10.35 a.m. from Armagh, with driver Patrick Murphy. Elliot made the decision, a fatal one, to divide the train in two, between the fifth and sixth carriages. The carriages were fitted with non-automatic vacuum brakes which were not effective without an engine in steam. Brakes in the guards van were secured and stones put under the wheels of the sixth carriage.

As driver McGrath eased back his engine for uncoupling, the nudge was enough to start the rear portion moving. The sixth coach crunched over the stones and the separated carriages started to move backwards down the gradient. The men tried to halt it by throwing stones under the wheels, which crushed them to powder. Panic stricken, Elliot shouted, "Oh, my God. We'll all be killed!" then tried to blame driver McGrath. The ten runaway coaches holding about 600 passengers began to gather speed, outpacing the pursuers. All the carriage doors had been locked before departure from Armagh, and there was no escape, although some passengers had been crowded into guard Henry's rear guards van and these lucky ones jumped for their lives. Meanwhile, Patrick Murphy's train was labouring up the gradient at about 30 m.p.h. when his fireman suddenly spotted the runaway approaching in the distance. Murphy had managed to reduce his speed to little more than walking pace when the two trains crashed.

The first three carriages of the runaway were completely shattered and scattered down the 40 ft. embankment, the other vehicles piling up. Murphy's engine rolled over on its side, his train became separated and it in turn began to run backwards in two portions: first the three coaches, then the horse box and the tender of the engine. Murphy clung to the tender and applied the hand-brake. The whole of his train eventually came to a stand without further mishap. In the appalling catastrophe, 80 lives were lost including many young children, and an estimated 250 were injured. In the Board of Trade inquiry blame was attached to several railway officials, the heaviest share resting on James Elliot. One of two technical features, already in use on many railways, would have avoided the accident: continuous automatic train braking, and absolute "block" signal working. Both were incorporated in the Act of Parliament passed on 30th August in the same year.

AISGILL, Midland Railway, 2nd September 1913
Poor quality of coal contributed to one night express running into the rear of another in the wild fell country of Westmorland. The 1.35 a.m. from Carlisle to St. Pancras consisted of ten coaches, of which three were sleeping cars, totalling 243 tons – which was 13 tons above the maximum weight for the locomotive. The driver had complained, but was overruled. He also grumbled about the poor quality of coal in the tender. For over 40 miles the gradients were heavy, the line climbing to more than 1,000 ft. above sea level. Time was lost, and in the last stiff climb up the Aisgill Summit boiler pressure had fallen severely and the locomotive wheezed to a halt. At this moment, the guard should have walked back with detonators and red handlamp to protect his stationary train from the rear, but was assured by the driver that the engine would soon be on the move. Some miles behind, the 1.49 a.m. night express from Carlisle was following, with a train of only six coaches; the driver and firemen were distracted as they tried to coax the locomotive along on the poor coal. They both missed seeing the signals at danger at Mallerstang signal-box and their train rammed into the rear of the standing express, demolishing coaches in a violent collision. The gas-lighted coaches quickly caught fire, bringing the death roll to 16, and many more injured. The signalmen concerned smartly carried out their emergency operations but were unable to avert the disaster. All those at fault, including the management, were castigated by the inspecting officer and again gas lighting for carriages was condemned. He also recommended Automatic Train Control for distant signals, as used so effectively on the Great Western Railway.

QUINTINSHILL, Caledonian Railway, 22nd May 1915
Britain's worst railway disaster was caused by the criminal neglect of two signalmen. Their box, Quintinshill Loop, lay in the countryside ten miles

north of Carlisle just over the Scottish border. On each side of the two main lines was a lay-by loop. A crossover junction connected the two main lines. When the Scottish express from Euston was running late, the 6.10 a.m. local train from Carlisle was usually shunted off the main line at Quintinshill to let it pass by. This was such an occasion, and the day turn signalman, James Tinsley, travelled on it from Gretna Junction, where he lived, to save walking 1½ miles. This made him late for his 6 a.m. duty, so his mate, signalman Meakin, from 6 a.m. entered train signalling details on a slip of paper for Tinsley to copy into the train register book to cover up his late arrival. A goods train was already standing in the down loop and another was shunted into the up loop, so Meakin shunted the local train from the down line to the up for the express to pass.

Tinsley entered the box about 6.35 a.m. Absorbed in copying details into the train book and distracted by the two guards of the goods trains and by the fireman of the local passenger train, all of whom should have left the box, he incredibly forgot about it and accepted the Scottish express from the next box south, and a few minutes afterwards accepted a fully loaded troop train from the next box north; it was travelling from Larbert to Liverpool. The troop train came first and ran straight into the local, engine to engine, in a violent collision. About a minute later, the Scottish express at high speed ploughed into the wreckage, running down survivors of the first crash who were helping fellow passengers. Carriages on the troop train were gas-lighted and the mountain of wreckage became a blazing inferno, which the Carlisle fire brigade and railway men tackled manfully. The fire raged throughout the day and night to the following morning. Ultimately, the death roll was estimated at 227, with 246 injured. At the official inquiry, most of the blame was laid on the two signalmen who were imprisoned for manslaughter; Colonel Druitt recommended the abolition of gas lighting which had caused train fires elsewhere, and all-steel coaches, which were gradually adopted.

CASTLECARY, London & North Eastern Railway, 10th December 1937

Bad visibility of signals, which were passed at danger in a heavy snowstorm, was the main cause of a serious collision when an express from Edinburgh to Glasgow ran into the back of the 2 p.m. express from Dundee to Glasgow while it was stationary. The Dundee train was stopped at Castlecary as a goods train further ahead was unable to run into sidings to clear the main line for the Dundee train because points were blocked with snow. The Dundee driver had passed signals at danger, but managed to stop past Castlecary signal-box but just out of the signalman's sight. Mistakenly, the signalman thought the train had continued on its journey and accepted behind it the Edinburgh express. Unfortunately, the Edinburgh train also passed signals at danger in the snowstorm, and at about 60 m.p.h. crashed into the rear of the stationary Dundee train.

The Edinburgh train was hauled by a class A3 of the Grand Parade series, which alone weighed about 150 tons. The Dundee train was pushed about 50 yards and the driver in front was badly injured. The driver of the rear train was uninjured and his fireman only slightly hurt. Constructed in steel, the coaches did not telescope. Even so, 35 people were killed and 179 injured.

NORTON FITZWARREN, Great Western Railway, 4th November 1940

The driver of the 9.50 p.m. sleeping car express from Paddington to Penzance, which was running 68 minutes late, found he was unexpectedly diverted at Taunton from the down main line to the down relief line at 3.45 a.m. Unknown to him, it was to keep the main line clear for an express newspaper train shortly due. In error, he read the signals for the main line instead of the adjacent relief line, and did not realise his mistake until he saw the newspaper express overtaking him on his right. Shocked, he applied his brakes, but too late to avert a derailment through catch points which protected a crossover road to the main line. His train of 13 coaches, including one sleeping car, was estimated to be carrying about 900 passengers, and was headed by a powerful King class locomotive No. 6028, *King George VI*. The engine was thrown on its side and the first six coaches were flung across all four tracks. Twenty-six passengers and the fireman lost their lives and 75 were injured. It was a miraculous escape for the driver. The newspaper train, also with a King class locomotive, must have speeded by only seconds before the wreckage was flung across the rails, otherwise the death roll might well have been much worse.

SOHAM, London & North Eastern Railway, 1st June 1944

Driver Gimbert and fireman Nightall were aboard the 2–8–0 WD locomotive No. 7337 hauling the 11.40 p.m. freight train from Whitemoor to Ipswich, the 51 open wagons conveying heavy aircraft bombs and components covered with wagon sheets. Approaching Soham station, the driver looked back and saw that the first wagon was on fire. Both men could have been forgiven if they had jumped and run away fast. Instead, they carried out their correct duty by bringing the train gently to a stand, uncoupling the first blazing wagon and drawing it clear of the rest of the train. The driver stopped at Soham station and shouted to signalman Bridges who telegraphed adjacent signal-boxes to protect other trains. Guard Clarke had already protected his lethal train from the rear. Then the wagon exploded. It blew a crater 66 ft. across and 16 ft. deep. Fireman Nightall was killed instantly and signalman Bridges died the next day. Driver Gimbert,though badly injured, survived. The courageous action of the two enginemen averted the whole train blowing up, which would have been a major catastrophe. As it was, the station buildings, signal-box and 15 houses in Soham were destroyed and 36 others made uninhabitable. The exploded wagon was completely destroyed and the tender reduced to splintered metal. Though the locomotive was derailed, it sustained little damage. Cause of the fire was never completely established, but it was considered that the wagon, which had previously contained sulphur, had not been thoroughly cleaned out and became ignited by sparks from the locomotive. The George Cross was awarded to Driver Gimbert and posthumously to Fireman Nightall.

HARROW, 8th October 1952

About 800 passengers off to London to work as usual were sitting in the local train at Harrow – the 7.31 a.m. from Tring – when it was struck violently in the rear by a sleeping car express from Perth travelling at 55 to 60 m.p.h. The damaged trains sprawled across the crowded station. Seeing what was coming, the shocked signalman had showed the presence of mind to slam all signals to danger, to send "obstruction danger" on his telegraph instruments to adjacent signal-boxes in each direction, and to pull the detonator lever putting explosive detonators on the rails. The Perth driver applied his emergency brakes, but it was too late. Almost immediately, the 8 a.m. express from Euston to Liverpool and Manchester, headed by two steam locomotives and travelling at about 60 m.p.h., ploughed into the wreckage in a double collision. In the worst train accident ever experienced in England and the second worst in Britain's railway history, 112 people were killed, 167 seriously injured and taken to hospital, and 187 suffered minor injuries. Four of the train crews were killed. Ten of the injured died later. Thirty-six of the killed and 67 of the injured were railway staff of the London Midland Region. The Perth express, running late in patchy fog, had passed a colour-light distant and two semaphore signals at danger. As the driver and fireman were killed, it was almost impossible to establish exactly why the signals had been passed at danger.

LEWISHAM ST. JOHNS, 4th December 1957

On a foggy evening, the 4.56 p.m. to Ramsgate, headed by Battle of Britain class Pacific locomotive No. 34066, left Cannon Street station three-quarters of an hour late. Because the tender was only half full of water, the driver had arranged to make an unscheduled stop at Sevenoaks to fill up, and was anxious to make up time on the journey. His train was closely following a crowded ten-car electric train, the 5.18 p.m. from Charing Cross to Hayes. The electric train was brought to a stand at Parks Bridge Junction home signal. Unfortunately, the driver of the Ramsgate train had missed seeing a double yellow signal, which tells him the next signal may be a single yellow, then missed the single yellow which means the next signal may be expected to be red. Halting from his firing, the fireman looked out in time to see St. John's home signal, and shouted to the driver, "You've got a red". The driver instantly applied emergency braking to his train, but it was then too late and the Ramsgate train crashed into the back of the electric train, which had its brakes firmly on. The collision took place under the girder bridge carrying the Nunhead–Lewisham loop line. A steel column was struck by vehicles and the bridge crashed down on top of the wreckage below, adding to the disaster. Ninety people were killed and 109 seriously injured.

HITHER GREEN, Southern Region, 8th November 1967

A serious derailment to a passenger train occurred at Hither Green because of a fractured rail at a joint connected with standard fishplate fittings on a heavily used line. Forty-seven lives were lost. Following the official inquiry, it was recommended that continuously welded rail on main lines and heavily worked commuter lines would prevent this kind of accident. British Rail were already well ahead in a national programme of continuously welded track replacement with flat bottom rails and most of the important routes have since been completed.

Appendix B: London Underground Railways

The Metropolitan Railway under construction ready for the opening in 1863. King's Cross mainline station with clock tower is seen in the background. (Photo: London Transport)

WHEN Charles Pearson in the 1830s proposed a railway to run under the ground in London, people said he was mad. They feared that the vibration would bring buildings crashing down into the tunnels and on top of the trains. He was convinced it was a good idea, however, and he was joined in his campaign by John Hargrave Stevens, who later was appointed City architect and surveyor. Pearson's influence grew after he became a City solicitor. He published a pamphlet proposing an atmospheric railway to run underground along the Fleet Valley; but failure of this type of railway elsewhere discouraged him.

In those days, congestion in the London streets was mounting with horse-drawn omnibuses, stage coaches, pack-horses, street traders' handcarts and a variety of goods vehicles. Conditions were worsened as the new provincial railways began to reach London, bringing more people and goods to the Metropolis and building their own terminus stations.

It was clear to City authorities that as more railways came into London, the equivalent of town planning would have to be considered. In this new climate, Pearson and Stevens pressed their arguments. In the late 1840s, Pearson worked hard in promoting his "Railway Terminus and City Improvement Plan", and it was considered in 1851 by a special committee.

The opening of main line stations at Paddington, Euston and King's Cross increased the traffic movements between the Paddington area and the City along the New Road, later named Euston Road, and made it a promising route for an underground railway. Competing schemes and routes were projected; finance was offered from the City, landowners, contractors and main line railways. A company called "The Metropolitan Railway" won the day, Parliamentary sanction being obtained in 1854. John (later Sir John) Fowler was appointed engineer and John Hargrave Stevens the architect. Pearson was in the thick of the developments. Money was hard to find during the Crimean War years 1853–56, and work finally began in March 1860.

In stages, a wide trench was dug along Praed Street, Marylebone Road, Euston Road, King's Cross Road and Farrington Road for an underground railway to run between Paddington and Farrington, some 3¾ miles. Cut-and-cover construction was used, the trench being roofed over with brick arches or iron girders to make the street good again. Some parts would be in the open. Masses of underground pipes – water, gas and sewers – and some electric telegraph equipment to be re-aligned to make way. Traffic was redirected through nearby side streets. In wet weather, mud and clay were trodden into adjacent houses and shops and passers-by had to walk across planks of wood "over a yawning cavern underneath the pavement."

Costs for cut-and-cover excavations worked out at only £50 to £60 per yard, but enormous expenses had to be met for demolishing buildings and for accidental damage to properties on the route. For example, Sir Edward Watkin, the famous chairman of the Met., told shareholders that repairs to the cracked fabric of a chapel which excavations had disturbed would cost £14,500. The only serious accident was when the Fleet River burst at the Clerkenwell end, flooding the workings to about 10 ft.

As work progressed, the Great Western Railway were anxious to be connected with the new line and it was agreed that the new railway would be in the wide gauge of 7 ft.; the G.W.R. also agreed to supply locomotives and carriages. The Great Northern Railway wished to use the railway and eventually a second rail was laid for the Stephenson gauge of 4 ft. 8½ in., to run a "mixed gauge".

In 1862, Daniel Gooch built 2–4–0 locomotives with 6 ft. driving wheels for the new railway and supplied 49 long eight-wheeled carriages which were reasonably comfortable and known as "Long Charleys." Spagnoletti, telegraph superintendent of the G.W.R., devised disc block signalling instruments.

On 24th May 1862, a short trial run was made. Two contractors' wagons with temporary bench seats conveyed an official party including William Gladstone (later Prime Minister), railway officials, contractors, influential men of rank, and John Fowler, the engineer.

The first underground city railway in the world opened on Saturday 10th January 1863 and the public crowded into the decorated stations to see this latest "wonder of London". Members of the aristocracy jostled among the "lower orders" in an undignified rush to have a ride. The trains were filled to capacity and about 30,000 passengers were carried on that first day, fares taken exceeding £850. Intermediate stations were Baker Street, Portland Road (Great Portland Street from 1917),

A momentous occasion on 24th May 1862 for the smiling engineer, John Fowler (15), seated next to W. E. Gladstone (16), and accompanied by nobilities of the day. They were inspecting the first underground railway, then under construction. (Photo: London Transport)

Locomotive 0–4–2T No. 1 built in 1865 for the Talyllyn narrow gauge railway, seen here taking water at Dolgoch Falls in 1963. (Photo: By courtesy of John Adams, Esq.)

Gower Street (Euston Square from 1909), and King's Cross.

All was not sweetness and light, however, for before the year was out quarrels about the working arrangements blew up between the G.W.R. and the Metropolitan. The Great Western threatened to withdraw their engines and carriages; but as this produced no panic, the date was brought forward by seven weeks. Not to be brought to heel, the Met. hired locomotives from the London & North Western and carriages from the Great Northern until they could have their own built. Fowler designed 4–4–0T engines and had them built by Beyer-Peacock of Manchester. They proved so successful that with modifications they remained the motive power of the tunnel lines until 1905.

Fowler had earlier designed a steam locomotive that emitted very little steam and smoke and tested it in 1862, but this quiet engine called "Fowler's Ghost" was not a success. Apart from a number of technical shortcomings, explosion of the boiler was possible.

In the first year, the new railway carried about 10,000,000 passengers and the numbers steadily increased. In winter, passengers brought their own travelling rugs and hired "foot warmers" from the stations. Smoking was strictly forbidden because of the danger of fire in the tunnels. Carriages were lit by dim oil or gas lamps, gas being stored in bags in the ceilings. Passengers often stuck candles to the side of the carriage to supplement the meagre lighting as they read their morning or evening papers.

Fowler built another underground line, the Hammersmith & City, backed by the G.W.R. and the Met., laid with mixed gauge and opened in 1864; expansion was already on the way. A new company, the District Railway, was formed, its first section from South Kensington to Westminster being opened in 1868. Extension by the two leading companies took the underground, some sections in the open, into central London and the City, to Richmond, Ealing Broadway, Putney Bridge, Hounslow and Harrow. By 1884, the Inner Circle was completed, connecting with the main line stations; and within eight years, extensions reached out to Rickmansworth, Chesham and Aylesbury.

An almost insoluble problem was still bothering

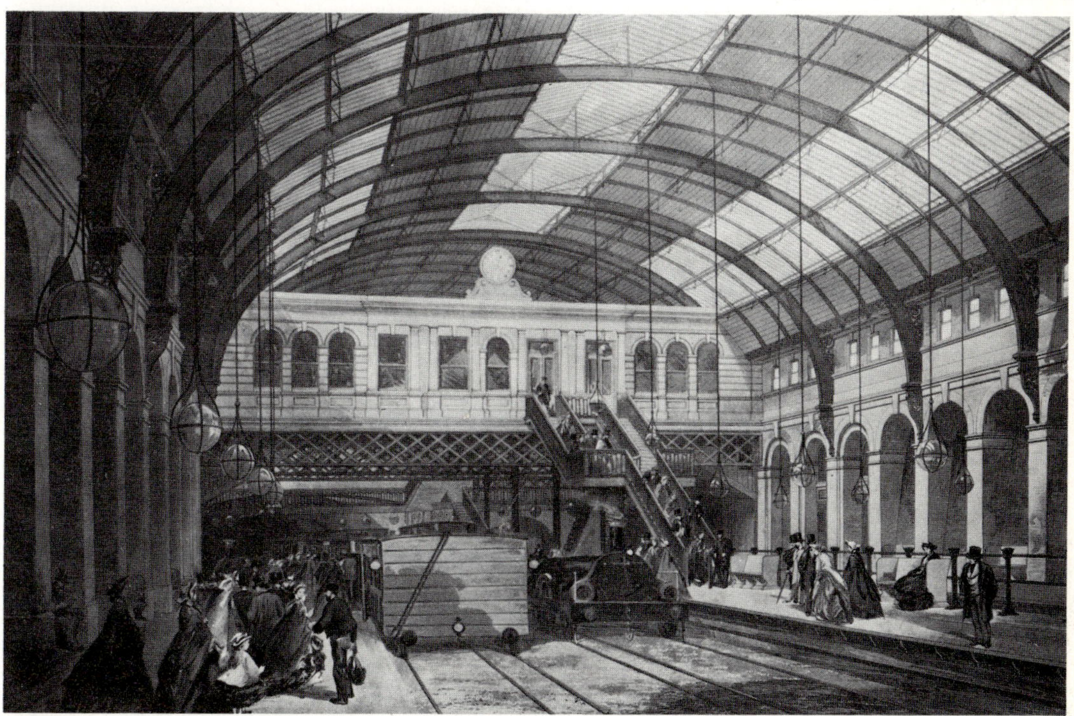

King's Cross underground station showing a wide-gauge steam locomotive on double-gauge track. (*Photo: By courtesy of the Science Museum*)

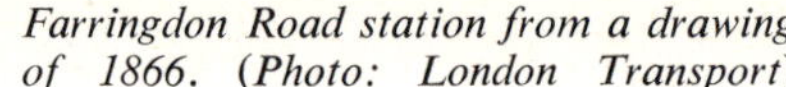

Farringdon Road station from a drawing of 1866. (Photo: London Transport)

the tunnel railways. Dirt and grime thrown out by the smoky steam locomotives besooted stations, carriages and door handles. Even on the shortest journeys, the white linen shirts of city gentlemen and the long dresses of Victorian ladies were soon soiled with sticky black smuts. Tunnel ventilators were not the real answer for the fumes sent up through iron gridding to the streets above brought complaints from passers-by; and many a bashful Victorian damsel with her swain was publicly embarrassed as a sudden gush from a ventilator below blew up her skirts to reveal long pink drawers. It was the problem of smoke that made railway engineers consider an alternative – electric power. Cut-and-cover presented difficulties, too, in extending the underground, and deep tunnelling was found to be the answer.

Schemes for a tunnel under the Thames were put forward as early as 1798 and 1802, the 1802 version to link Rotherhithe with Limehouse. Though intended for a roadway, it was a forerunner to tube railways. Richard Trevithick and a team of Cornish miners were commissioned for the work in 1808, but flooding closed the preliminary works. A distinguished French engineer named Marc Brunel (father of Isambard, born 1806, the railway engineer) patented a shield for tunnelling and a new Thames Tunnel Company engaged him to cut a tunnel between Rotherhithe and Wapping. The son was resident engineer 1825–28. Marc Brunel's tunnel-boring shield was the first in the world, and developments of it made London's deep tube railways possible many years afterwards. It was designed to move forward a few inches at a time, and supported the tunnel section while brickwork was completed.

Problems occurred with regularity. Water from the Thames above flooded through the roof. The money ran out. Accidents happened, and men lost their lives. Down in the dark depths, Isambard Brunel himself damaged his leg and had a narrow escape. Delay upon delay earned for the tunnel the derisive name "The Great Bore". But the bore was finally made in 1841 and the first person to pass through it was an excited little boy – the three-year-old son of Isambard Brunel. Final completion and official opening came in 1843, and a procession was led through by a band of musicians. Marc Brunel, now ageing and sick, received a knighthood for his great achievement, and lived for another six years.

Originally, the intention had been to dig approaches to the tunnel for horse-drawn vehicles to pass through, but the cash could not be raised, and stairways were built. For many years the Thames Tunnel remained as a pedestrian subway, bringing virtually no return on the huge costs and the many years of work entailed. In time, however, it came into its own, and earned its place in history as "the first tunnel for public traffic ever to be driven beneath a river."

The next tunnel under the Thames was the

result of a most astonishing idea for a labyrinth of deep tube miniature railways in a network serving the whole of London. Peter Barlow thought it up and presented it in a pamphlet in 1867. When he was sinking the iron cylinders for the Lambeth suspension bridge, of which he was the engineer, in 1862, the idea struck him that if cylinders were laid horizontally in a deep tunnel, trains could run through them. He described it in detail: diameter would be 6 ft. 8 in., rail gauge would be 2 ft. 6 in. and a single car would hold twelve passengers and would be hauled by a cable from a stationary steam engine.

Location of the tunnel was to be between Great Tower Hill and Southwark, for a length of about a quarter of a mile, and cast iron segments would form the lining. Developing Marc Brunel's tunnelling shield system, Barlow designed a circular shield which he had patented in 1864. Four years later the Tower Subway Company was formed. Work began in 1869, with Barlow as engineer and his young pupil, James Henry Greathead, the contractor. Two 4 h.p. steam engines were installed to pull the cables, the rails were laid, the car was provided and tests were made for several months before the public opening on 2nd August 1870. Rattling steam-driven lift cages took anxious passengers up and down the shafts to the tunnel railway. Fares were 1*d.* and 2*d.*, so nobody was going to make a fortune. And when the machinery went wrong, the lifts jammed and the tiny 10 ft. car ground to a halt, revenue was nil. This could not go on; neither did it. Within a few months the whole paraphernalia was uplifted, stairways replaced the steam lifts and pedestrians used the tunnel as a footway for which they paid a toll of a halfpenny. Londoners found the subway tolerable until they were lured away to a walk with a view – across the magnificent Tower Bridge, which opened in 1894. Today the Tower Subway is still earning its keep, carrying hydraulic piping, and water mains of the Metropolitan Water Board.

On an epic page in the saga of travel deep under the swarming streets of London, this modest project can be truly described as the first tube passenger railway in the world. But more than that: it set alight the fires of ambition in the young Greathead, who improved the tunnelling shield to such standards that the modified version used today is still known as the Greathead shield.

Though the railway through the Tower Subway closed in 1870, still more new schemes were put forward. Parliamentary and public objections were as fierce and numerous as those met by railway builders in the provinces, involving legal wrangles and large payments of compensation. Battle-scarred but triumphant, the City of London & Southwark Subway Company emerged in 1884 with Parliamentary approval; Greathead's performance in committee had confounded the opposition. It was natural that he should become the engineer and Sir John Fowler of Metropolitan fame a consultant. Optimistically, the company promised a high dividend of 12 per cent, encouraged by the success of the Metropolitan and the District.

It was settled that the new tube should be built, passing under the Thames, between the Monument and Stockwell, just over 3 miles. Greathead had been impressed in 1883 by the cable tramway in San Francisco. He had discontinued electric trains. Contracts were placed and work began in 1886. Cable apparatus was ordered. Then the advantages of electric traction began to be aired and followed up strongly in the technical Press. Volk's electric railway at Brighton had been working well since 1883, and that of the Bessbrook & Newry Railway in Northern Ireland had opened in 1885. Why should not the new London tube be electric?

Experimental running with a small electric locomotive and two coaches began in December 1889; but there were many mechanical and power failures and minor mishaps as the engineers strove to complete the line. At last it was finished and a great gala day was planned, to match anything seen in the Midlands and the north; for, after all, it was the first electric underground railway in the world.

Large crowds gathered at the stations for the formal opening of the railway, on 4th November 1890, by the Prince of Wales, later King Edward VII. The Royal party travelled all the way hauled by a cream and grey locomotive, and celebrated at a lunch held in a marquee in the rolling stock department at Stockwell.

By that time, the railway had changed its name to the City & South London, with an extension south to Clapham its next aim. Fourteen locomotives were built for the new line, each on two axles and weighing about 10 tons; one of them is preserved in the Science Museum, London. The 30 wooden cars that were built, running three to a train, sat 30 people facing each other on long seats. Upholstery almost reached the ceiling, leaving narrow slits for ventilation, hence their nickname "padded cells." There were no windows, presumably on the assumption that there was nothing

Third class wooden carriage used on the District Railway in the days of steam. (Photo: London Transport)

to see. Passengers were strictly forbidden to ride on the roof. One car in each train was provided for smokers, but on no account, the railway notices said, could ladies enter. The cars were lighted by electric lamps of somewhat low power. An attendant at the end of each car operated the sliding lattice gates. Travelling at about 12 m.p.h., the new railway showed great promise and was soon popular.

Greathead shields were busier than ever as extensions and new lines were built. Moorgate and Clapham Common were reached in 1900, and electric lamps replaced oil and gas in the line-side signals; new lines reached the Angel in 1901 and Euston in 1907. Meanwhile, the Met. and District and other railways were steadily burrowing under London and spreading out in the open to the suburbs. One of them was the 5¾-mile Central London Railway which opened in 1900 from Shepherds Bush to the Bank. Greathead had been appointed engineer soon after the Parliamentary Act was passed in 1891, but he died after the work was begun. An ingenious track design at the stations had the effect of getting a train away smartly and aiding the braking of an incoming train: the approach to the stations was on a rising gradient of 1 in 60.

INTO THE TWENTIETH CENTURY

In a splendid start for the new century, the Prince of Wales officially opened the line, the first really modern tube. The smart trains were hauled by locomotives sporting a bright livery of crimson lake, gold lining and polished brasswork. The eyes of Londoners were opened to the great possibilities of underground railways, and the Press had a field day. The *Daily Mail* reported: "Yesterday the crowds swayed and surged to get on to the trains. It was a cosmopolitan throng. Nearly every civilised nation under the sun was represented among the humanity that was struggling to experience London's latest sensation."

Vibration from the locomotives, however, disturbed residents and business people so much that a Board of Trade inquiry was set up and the locomotives were modified. Some years later, locomotives were abandoned and electric motors were installed in some of the cars in each train.

In 1902, an American financier named Yerks became chairman of the Metropolitan & District Railway Company and followed a policy of expansion.

Spagnoletti's son introduced the first automatic signals on the Great Northern & City line so that when a train passed a signal at "clear", it automatically placed it to "danger". Later, track circuiting was installed to connect with signals; and train stops were fitted on the track so that if a driver mistakenly passed a signal at danger, the train stop would operate the train brake. These techniques, in modified form, are still in use and account for the remarkable safety record of the Underground.

New railways were opening in rapid succession and the Bakerloo line from Baker Street to Waterloo was in service in 1906, complete with automatic signalling. An up and coming politician named David Lloyd George opened the Charing Cross, Euston and Hampstead tube in 1907, by which time the main central London underground network was completed very much in its present shape. Later extensions were mainly surface lines into the suburbs.

In 1910, a number of companies were amalgamated to form the London Electric Railway. In that year, two Pullman cars – *Mayflower* and *Galatea* – serving refreshments at the armchair seats went into service on the Metropolitan lines between the City and Baker Street and Chesham and Aylesbury. They were withdrawn in October 1939.

To promote travel, the Metropolitan Railway formed a subsidiary in 1919 called Metropolitan Railway Country Estates Ltd. to buy land in the outer suburbs and develop housing estates. Before the Second World War the Company had built

4,600 houses in "Metroland" as far out as Amersham.

All the underground railways, along with the bus services, were absorbed by the London Passenger Transport Board in 1933.

THE SECOND WORLD WAR

When war broke out, the underground railways, along with the main line companies, were taken over by the Government, and most of the first class accommodation was abolished. Tube stations were regarded as prime shelters during air raids, and 79 were fitted with bunks, clinics and sanitary facilities. To guard against flooding, electrically operated flood gates were installed especially at stations near the Thames, which could be closed in an emergency in one minute.

Extensive damage was suffered during the war and in October 1940 a bomb penetrated the tunnel at Balham on the Morden line. Flooding from water mains and sewers quickly followed, and 68 people lost their lives. Three months later, a dropped bomb burst in Bank station; the entire roadway collapsed on to the platforms below, killing 56 people and injuring 69.

Of all the personalities of the 20th century, Derby-born Albert Stanley (1874–1948) – later Lord Ashfield – is the man most closely associated with the development of London Transport. He was still very young when his family moved to America, where he entered a railway career and by 1904 had risen to manager, then general manager, of the Public Service Corporation of New Jersey. In 1907, he became general manager of the London Underground group of railways, and managing director in 1911. He was knighted in 1914.

Two years later he entered the Government and became President of the Board of Trade, returning to the Underground Group in 1919. When the London Passenger Transport Board was created in 1933, Ashfield was chairman, a post he held until he joined the British Transport Commission which took charge of the newly nationalised transport services in 1948. His hand had guided the fortunes of transport in London for 41 years until his death.

Long-term planning had been his forte and a broad look was taken at London's underground even before the war ended. It was finally decided to build a new tube railway – the first new route across London since 1907 – from Walthamstow to Victoria, later extended to Brixton, a total of 14 miles served by 16 stations. An Act of Parliament was passed in 1955 and work began in 1962 when pneumatic drills broke the surface of Oxford Circus. The new route was named the Victoria Line. Most stations would connect with other

Map of the Inner Circle of the Metropolitan and District railways, showing the year in which each section was opened.

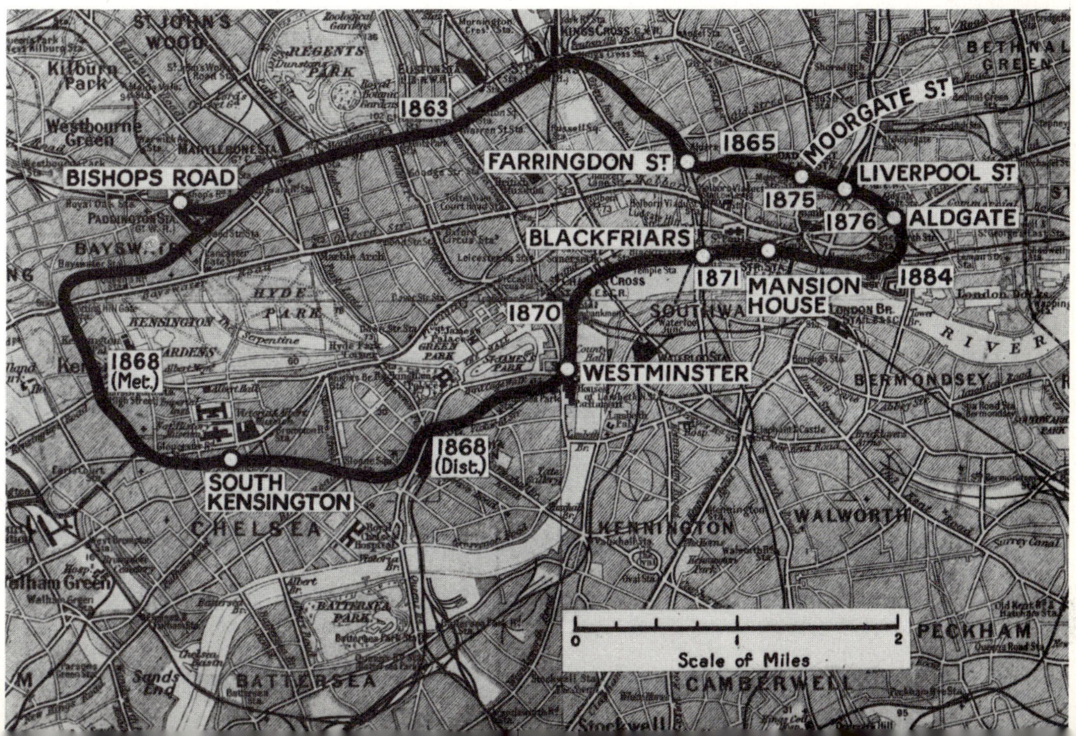

A new underground train with automatic doors introduced on the Central Line in 1926

underground routes and would provide interchange with British Rail.

Technology had made enormous strides since 1907. A Greathead-type shield known as a Drum Digger cut through the earth much faster and the railway itself was to be better than any other of its kind in the world: automated throughout. For the first time in such a service the trains were automatic, although a motorman remained in the driving cab. Car windows were double-glazed for sound insulation, and door windows were high enough for tall passengers to read station names without stooping. Carrier wave links enabled the motorman to speak direct to the central control at Cobourg Street, Euston. Loudspeakers were installed in all the cars. A closed circuit television system with 74 cameras and 42 monitor screens enabled the controllers at Euston and at stations to view any of the platforms or key pedestrian areas in the stations at any time. To enable motormen to see just above the heads of passengers before closing the automatic doors, a screen was mounted at the front end of each platform, the picture for which was transmitted by a camera at the rear end of the platform. Such technicalities invariably escape the attention of scurrying passengers. Automatic ticket systems were introduced at the new and rebuilt stations.

Queen Elizabeth II officially opened the new line on 7th March 1969. Her Majesty travelled from Green Park to Oxford Circus and back to Victoria, and the most highly automated underground railway line in the world was in full commission. Three years later, the extension from Victoria to Brixton was completed.

More changes in the management structure took place as a result of the 1962 Transport Act, giving the London Transport Board direct access to the Minister of Transport instead of the British Transport Commission; and in 1970 a further change vested London Transport in a new Executive whose members were appointed by the Greater London Council. The G.L.C. became responsible for overall policy and financial control, including the road services.

During this time, two more major projects were progressing. An extension of 3½ miles was built from the Piccadilly Line at Hounslow West to the heart of London Airport, with a station at Hatton Cross mainly to serve airport staff, and at Heathrow Central with platforms 44 ft. below ground. Part of the extension to Hatton Cross was cut-and-cover and part in the open; deep tube was bored to the Airport. Work began in 1971 and the line was opened to Hatton Cross in 1975, and scheduled for completion to Heathrow

Central by 1978. At peak times, trains were timed to run every 4 minutes, but never falling below 7½ minutes.

The other project is the Fleet Line. It will operate on the Stanmore branch to Baker Street, then by new deep tube via Bond Street, Green Park, Trafalgar Square, Aldwych, Ludgate Circus, Cannon Street and Fenchurch Street; then – if the scheme is eventually approved – using the present East London line route to New Cross and Lewisham, with a short branch from Surrey Docks to New Cross Gate. The station in Trafalgar Square/Strand will be renamed Charing Cross, and the present Charing Cross will be called Embankment.

Preliminary work began in 1971. Stage 1 to Trafalgar Square is scheduled to open in 1977; Stage 2 to Fenchurch Street rates as "high priority". Stage 3 for the remainder, however, is a "low priority" project and could possibly be preceded by a proposed "River Line" through London's dockland to Thamesmead in co-operation with British Rail in a London Rail Plan. Stations on the Fleet Line will provide interchange to other underground routes and connect with British Rail at Charing Cross, Cannon Street and Fenchurch Street. The one-man-operated trains of a new and advanced design will be automated. A fast and direct link will be provided between the north-west suburbs and the City.

London's underground, which has formed a model for many cities in the world, has come a long way since the smoky days of 1863. But the new technocrats were not too absorbed in automation to spare a nostalgic thought for the pioneers who started it all; and the last day of the steam locomotive was well celebrated on 6th June 1971. A pannier tank 0–6–0 hauled a commemorative train of engineers' vehicles from Moorgate to Neasden. Some 2,000 enthusiasts saw and heard the train steam along at Moorgate, Barbican and Farringdon stations, then followed it to Neasden in four modern electric trains. Another railway era had ended.

Stages in the progress of London Underground Railways of various companies

1863	Opening of the first underground railway, cut and cover Paddington to Farringdon Street
1868	First section of the District Line opened, South Kensington to Westminster
1877	Extension to Richmond
1879	Extension to Ealing Broadway
1880	Extension to Putney Bridge
1880	Extension Baker Street to Harrow
1884	Inner Circle completed
1884	Extension to Hounslow
1887	Opening Harrow to Rickmansworth
1889	Extension to Chesham
1890	Opening of first electrified deep tube railway, City & South London Line, King William Street, near the Monument, to Stockwell
1892	Extension to Aylesbury
1899	Extension to Quainton Road to join the Great Central Railway
1900	Central London Railway opens from Shepherds Bush to Bank
1900	Extension to Clapham Common
1901	Extension to Angel
1902	Extension Whitechapel to Bow
1905	Electric operation, Baker Street to Uxbridge
1905	Inner Circle electrified and steam locomotives withdrawn
1906	Bakerloo Line tube opened, Baker Street to Waterloo
1906	Great Northern, Piccadilly and Brompton tube opened
1907	Charing Cross, Euston and Hampstead tube opened
1910	Electrification to South Harrow
1920	Extension Shepherds Bush to Ealing
1922–24	City & South London tube extended northwards to Edgware and southwards to Morden
1925	Electrification extended to Rickmansworth
1934	Piccadilly Line extended to Cockfosters
1939	Bakerloo Line extended from Baker Street to Finchley Road
1939	Highgate Line extended to East Finchley
1940	Highgate Line tube trains extended to High Barnet
1946	Central London Line extended to Stratford, to Leytonstone 1947 and Hainault 1949
1961	Electrification extended to Amersham
1971	Preliminary work begins on the Fleet Line
1972	Victoria Line completed by extension to Brixton
1975	Piccadilly Line extended from Hounslow West to Hatton Cross, and scheduled to Heathrow Central 1978

Appendix C: Railway Enthusiasts' and Preservation Societies

Blue Peter, *Pacific type A4 4–6–2, Doncaster-built in the Gresley tradition, went into service in 1948. Withdrawn in the twilight of steam in 1966 after service on the heavy gradients on the Edinburgh-Aberdeen main line. Later it was bought by two enthusiasts for preservation in its apple-green livery and was adopted by the BBC television programme of the same name.* (*Photo: British Rail*)

ENTHUSIASM for steam locomotives and steam railways has grown at an astonishing pace over the past two decades, until there are now in the late 1970s about 500 societies. Of the following selected list of nearly 100 societies, some two-thirds have been founded since 1955, the year that British Railways decided that steam inevitably would have to go, to make way for diesels and electrics.

The Railways Board has welcomed the growing interest in steam and in November 1974 announced that over 1,000 miles of line had been "approved" for the consideration of steam running, including the addition in 1975 of the Shrewsbury–Chester route. During the Stockton & Darlington Railway 150th anniversary celebrations from spring to autumn 1975, railway managements have supported many steam projects. Throughout the year, a new impetus was given to the devoted work of the societies to bring the excitement of steam to countless people from all over the world, serving as a reminder that a great Englishman, George Stephenson, started it all. Once again, historic locomotives such as the *Flying Scotsman*, *King George V*, *Sir Nigel Gresley* and *Pendennis Castle*, have thundered along the tracks.

Each of the societies and private companies has its own individual story to tell. To add to private donation, some have successfully called for subscription, and on 2nd October 1972 the Dart Valley Light Railway Ltd. offered to the public up to 250,000 ordinary shares at £1 each to run their trains. In these hectic days, millions of passengers are enjoying the leisure and magic of steam and catching a nostalgic glimpse of the glorious past. Some narrow gauge railways have come into their own, a number of which were built as a result of the Light Railways Act of 1896 to serve rural areas for passengers and goods. A thriving society is now active in many areas.

About 500 steam locomotives are now preserved in museums and elsewhere, together with carriages, wagons, track, signals and every type of relic that recreates the historical scene. Steam preservation is far from the prerogative of the middle-aged or the wealthy. Many young men who barely remember the steam age don overalls at the weekend to wield paint brush and oil can. In 1974, 25-year-old Andrew Goltz, a Birmingham University student, led the Swanage Railway Society to gain the support of the local council in a plan to re-open the picturesque line of about 10 miles between Swanage and Wareham. Steam ventures have attracted people from all walks of life and recently H.R.H. Prince Philip, the Duke of Edinburgh, became Patron of a leading society. At the centre of things, Capt. Peter Manisty, R.N., as the chairman of the Association of Railway Preservation Societies, continues his stirling promotional work.

RAILWAY ENTHUSIASTS' AND PRESERVATION SOCIETIES

Association of Railway Preservation Societies (*1960*)
(*Sec.*) M. D. Crewe, 34 Templegate Road, Leeds LS15 0HE

A4 Locomotive Society Ltd. (*1967*)
(*Sec.*) G. R. Pope, 49a Townshend Road, London NW8 6LJ

Bala Lake Railway Society (*1973*)
(*Sec.*) M. Martin, Yr Orsaf, Llanuwchllyn, Bala, Merioneth

Battle of Britain Locomotive Preservation Society (*1973*)
(*Chmn.*) A. W. T. Fielding, 137 Tuffley Lane, Gloucester GL4 0NZ

B1 Locomotive Preservation Society Ltd. (*1967*)
(*Sec.*) R. Hadingham, 30 Brook Crescent, Chingford, London E4 9EP

Birmingham Locomotive Club (*1930*)
(*Sec.*) Eric S. Tonks, 87 Sunnymead Road, South Yardley, Birmingham B26 1LL

Bluebell Railway Preservation Society (*1959*)
(*Sec.*) J. E. Potter, 16 Govett Avenue, Shepperton, Middlesex, TW17 8AR

Blue Peter Locomotive Society (*1968*)
120 Holgate Road, York

Branch Line Society (*1955*)
(*Sec.*) N. J. Hill, 15 Springwood Hall Gardens, Gledholt, Huddersfield HD1 4HA

Bristol Railway Circle (*1934*)
(*Sec.*) J. P. Simons, 20 Wades Road, Filton, Bristol BS12 7EE

Bristol Suburban Railway Society (*1970*)
(*Sec.*) I. S. Bishop, 32 Henfield Crescent, Oldland, Bristol

Britannia Locomotive Society (*1967*)
(*Sec.*) Mrs. K. A. Swinger, "Ambleside", Finborough Road, Stowmarket, Suffolk IP14 1PY

Brockham Museum Association (*1972*)
(*Sec.*) J. L. Townsend, Didley Cottage, New Mills, Clehonger, nr. Hereford

Bulleid Society (*1965*)
(*Sec.*) R. T. Price, 61 Kempshott Road, Stretham, London SW 16

Cambridge University Railway Club
(*Sec.*) F. Marsden, Clare College, Cambridge

Dart Valley Railway Association (*1965*)
(*Sec.*) R. D. N. Salisbury, Forelands, Redwood

Lydham Manor, *No. 7827 4–6–0 express locomotive built at Swindon in 1951 and now owned by the Dart Valley Light Railway Company in Devon.* (*Photo: By courtesy of the D.V.L.R.*)

Locomotive No. 4588 2–6–2T built at Swindon in 1927 and now owned by the Dart Valley Light Railway in Devon. (Photo: By Courtesy of the D.V.L.R.)

Road, Sidmouth, Devon EX10 9AD

Dean Forest Railway Preservation Society (*1970*)
(*Sec.*) J. S. Metherall, 15 Sudbrook Way, Gloucester GL4 9QP

East Lancashire Railway Preservation Society (*1968*)
(*Sec.*) H. Brierley, 4 Richmal Terrace, Carr Street, Ramsbottom, via Bury, Lancashire

Electric Transport Development Society (*1953*)
(*Sec.*) E. Relton, 37 Wellesley Road, Ilford 1GI 4JX

Festiniog Railway Society (*1954*)
(*Sec.*) W. R. Holton, 42 Hanbury Road, Dorridge, Solihull, Warwickshire

Foxcote Manor Society (*1973*)
(*Sec.*) D. Norman, 4 Yew Tree Court, Gresford, Wrexham, Denbighshire LL12 8ET

Great North of Scotland Railway Association (*1964*)
(*Sec.*) *Great North Review*, 14 Gordon Road, Bridge of Don, Aberdeen AB2 8PT

Great Western Society Ltd. (*1961*)
(*Sec.*) W. J. Smith, Didcot, Berkshire

Gresley Society (*1963*)
(*Sec.*) P. Holmes, 9 Broadmead, Willow Wong, Burton Joyce, Nottingham

"H" Class Trust (*1965*)
(*Sec.*) R. G. D. Ranson, Braeside Cottage, Beechcroft Road, Orpington, Kent BR6 9NR

Hampshire Narrow Gauge Railway Society (*1961*)
(*Sec.*) J. G. Davis, 57 Alresford Road, Winchester, Hants

Historical Model Railway Society (*1950*)
(*Sec.*) S. N. Adam, 18 Beverley Gardens, Great Woodley, Romsey, Hants SO5 8TA

Huddersfield Railway Circle (*1946*)
(*Sec.*) J. K. Morton, Room 5, Top floor, Railway Station, Huddersfield

Hull & Barnsley Railway Stock Fund (*1968*)
(*Sec.*) M. F. Haddon, 508 James Reckitt Avenue, Hull HU8 0LQ

Industrial Locomotive Society (*1937*)
(*Sec.*) J. R. Rainbow, 7 Gipsy Lane, Warminster, Wilts

Industrial Railway Society (*1949*)
(*Sec.*) T. Riddle, 14 Harcourt Street, Kettering, Northants

Isle of Man Steam Railway Supporters' Association (*1966*)
(*Chmn.*) J. R. Evans, Manx Museum, Crosby, Isle of Man

Keighley & Worth Valley Railway Preservation Society (1962)
(*M.Sec.*) D. Moorehouse, "Hest Bank", 4 Moss Carr Road, Long Lee, Keighley, Yorks

Lakeside Railway Society (*1960*)
(*Sec.*) A. Middleton, Haverthwaite Station, Ulverston, Lancs

Lee Moor Tramway Preservation Society (*1964*)
(*Sec.*) R. E. Taylor, 32 Honicknowle Lane, Plymouth, Devon

Leighton Buzzard Narrow Gauge Railway Society Ltd.
(*Sec.*) M. A. Lilley, 5 Springside, Springfield Road, Linslade, Leighton Buzzard, Beds

Light Railway Transport League (*1938*)
(*Sec.*) D. F. Russell, 64 Grove Avenue, London W7 3ES

Liverpool Locomotive Preservation Group (*1968*)
(*Sec.*) E. Wheelwright, 1 Merton Drive, Roby, Nr. Liverpool L36 4NS

Liverpool University Public Transport Society
(*Sec.*) C. M. Whitehouse, Students' Union, 2 Bedford Street North, Liverpool L7 7BD

Locomotive Club of Great Britain (*1949*)
(*Sec.*) J. M. Cramp, 8 Lovatt Close, Edgware, Middlesex HA8 9XG

London Underground Railway Society (*1961*)
(*Sec.*) S. E. Jones, 113 Wandle Road, Morden, Surrey

Main Line Steam Trust Ltd. (*1971*)
(*Sec.*) M. J. M. Whithouse, 13 New Street, Leicester

Manx Electric Railway Society (*1973*)
(*Sec.*) Mrs. J. Coblett, Sunnybank, Laxey, Isle of Man

Merchant Navy Locomotive Preservation Society (*1965*)
(*Sec.*) A. C. Clare, 331 Uxbridge Road, Acton, London W3 9RA

Middleton Railway Trust (*1959*)
(*Sec.*) J. D. Edwards, 55 Village Way, Pinner, Middlesex HA5 5AB

Midland & Great Northern Circle (*1959*)
(*Sec.*) I. R. Dack, 38 Holway Road, Sheringham, Norfolk

Midland Railway Locomotive Fund (*1964*)
(*Sec.*) B. S. Ashby, 18 Robinson Crescent, Harlington, Beds

Model Railway Club (*1910*)
(*Sec.*) J. E. Geach, Keen House, Calshot Street, London N1

Monmouthshire Railway Society (*1956*)
(*Sec.*) J. D. Thorne, Lyn Orchard, Undy, Magor, Newport, Mon. NP6 3EN

Narrow Gauge Railway Museum Trust
(*Sec.*) Mrs. H. W. Clarey, The Wharf Station, Towyn, Merionethshire

Narrow Gauge Railway Society (*1951*)
(*Sec.*) Yorkshire area, R. N. Redman, 14a Oliver Hill, Horsforth, Leeds LS18 4JF
London & Southern, P. R. Lemmey, Herons Ghyll, Uckfield, Sussex
East Midlands, G. Holt, 22 Exton Road, Leicester LE5 4AF
North Staffs, A. K. Rogers, 68 Maythorne Road, Blurton, Stoke-on-Trent
South Devon, A. H. Mazonowicz, 187 Exwick Road, Exeter, Devon

Newcomen Society (*1920*)
(*Sec.*) R. J. Law, Science Museum, London SW7

North Eastern Locomotive Preservation Group (*1966*)
(*Sec.*) C. J. Lawson, 27 Cairnsmore Close, Cramlington, Northumberland NE23 6LE

North Norfolk Railway Co. Ltd. (*1959*)
(*Sec.*) D. P. Madden, Sheringham Station, Sheringham, Norfolk

North York Moors Historical Trust (*1967*)
(*Sec.*) A. K. Peterson, 12 Staindrop Drive, Middlesbrough, Teesside TS5 8NX

Oxford University Railway Society
(*Pres.*) J. G. Griffith, Jesus College, Oxford

Plymouth Railway Circle (*1948*)
(*Sec.*) B. Mills, 17 Birchfield Avenue, Beacon Park, Plymouth PL2 3LA

Princess Elizabeth Locomotive Society (*1963*)
(*Sec.*) P. Walker, Flat 1, 34 Elmdon Road, Acocks Green, Birmingham

Quainton Railway Society Ltd. (*1969*)
(*Sec.*) R. B. Miller, 25 Loudham Road, Little Chalfont, Bucks

Railway & Canal Historical Society (*1967*)
(*Sec.*) J. B. Harding, 174 Station Road, Wylde Green, Sutton Coldfield, Warwicks, B73 5LE

Railway Club (*1899*)
(*Sec.*) 122 High Holborn, London WC1V 6JS

Railway Correspondence & Travel Society (*1928*)
(*Sec.*) J. E. Baker, 95 Chestnut Avenue, Forest Gate, London E7 0JF

Railway Enthusiasts' Club (*1953*)
(*Sec.*) P. D. Hingley, 5 Wynford Close, Southcote, Reading, Berks RG3 2HX

Railway Photographic Society (*1922*)
(*Sec.*) M. W. Earley, 4 Beechwood Avenue, Tilehurst, Reading, Berks

Railway Preservation Society
(*Sec.*) B. J. Bull, 144 Freer Road, Birmingham B6 6NB

Ravenglass & Eskdale Railway Preservation Society Ltd. (*1960*)
(*Sec.*) D. B. Webb, Bindon, 29 Cedar Lane, Cockermouth, Cumberland CA13 9HN

Romney Hythe & Dymchurch Railway Association (*1967*)
(*Sec.*) L. Adams, 43 Eliot Road, Dagenham, Essex RM9 5XT

Scottish Railway Preservation Society (*1961*)
(*Sec.*) Ian Gordon, 4 Beech Crescent, Larbert, Stirlingshire

Scottish Tramway Museum Society (*1951*)
(*Sec.*) I. L. Cormack, 46 Wellshot Drive, Cambuslang, Glasgow G72 8BN

Severn Valley Railway Co. Ltd. (re-opened *1970*)
(*Sec.*) Head Office, 12 Sansome Place, Worcester

Shackerstone Railway Society (*1971*)
(*Sec.*) D. F. Pratley, 127 Loughborough Road, Whitwick, Leicestershire

Society of Model & Experimental Engineers
(*Sec.*) George Corderoy, 3 Warwick Square, London SW1

Somerset & Dorset Railway Circle (*1965*)
(*Sec.*) D. A. Martin, 7 Montrose Avenue, Redland, Bristol BS6 6EH

Southern Electric Group (*1970*)
(*Sec.*) B. W. Rayner, 18 Higher Drive, Purley, Surrey CR2 2HE

Southern Mogul Preservation Society
(*Sec.*) R. Packham, 68 Braemar Avenue, Croydon, Surrey CR2 0QB

Southern "Q" Fund (*1973*)
(*Sec.*) Lyn George, 9 Springmeadow, Lydney, Glos.

Standard 4 Loco. Preservation Society (re-named *1971*)
(*Sec.*) S. Taylor, 6 Greenwoods Terrace, Colne, Lancs

Stanier Black 5 Locomotive Preservation Society (*1968*)
(*Pres.*) David J. Porter, c/o Flying Club, Terminal Block, Civil Airport, Biggin Hill, Kent

Stanier 8F Locomotive Society Ltd. (*1968*)
(*Sec.*) A. Wilkinson, 42 Westlands Road, Middlewich, Cheshire CW10 9HN

Steamtown – Lakeside Railway Estates Co. Ltd.
(*Sec.*) Mrs. E. A. Beet, Warton Road, Carnforth, Lancs

Stephenson Locomotive Society (*1909*)
(*Sec.*) C. K. J. Kerley, 34 Durley Avenue, Pinner, Middlesex HA5 1JQ

Stour Valley Railway Preservation Society (*1968*)
(*Sec.*) T. Kearney, 145 Linnet Drive, Chelmsford, Essex

Strathspey Railway Association (*1972*)
(*Sec.*) J. Scott, 1 Church Grove, Sauchie, Clackmannanshire FK10 3BU

Swanage Railway Society (*1972*)
(*Sec.*) A. Goltz, 31 Waldeck Road, London W13 8LY

Tayllyn Railway Preservation Society (*1950*)
(*Sec.*) R. A. Hope, Olinda, 78 Bridgewater Road, Berkhamsted, Herts

Tenterden Railway Company (*1971*)
(*Sec.*) G. N. Bennett, Tenterden Town Station, Tenterden, Kent

Tramway & Light Railway Society (*1938*)
(*Sec.*) E. R. Oakley, 27 Dickens Close, Hartley, Dartford, Kent

Tramway Museum Society (*1955*)
(*Sec.*) G. B. Claydon, 23 Baron's Keep, West Kensington, London W14

Transport Ticket Society (*1945*)
(*Sec.*) J. E. Shelbourn, 18 Villa Road, Luton, Beds LU2 7NT

Transport Trust (*1964*)
(*Sec.*) J. T. Webb, 18 Ramillies Place, London W1V 2BA

Wainwright "C" Preservation Society (*1962*)
(*Sec.*) R. F. Stephens, 51 Downs Avenue, Chislehurst, Kent

Welsh Highland Light Railway Ltd. (*1964*)
(*Sec.*) R. W. Dutton, 118 Colmore Row, Birmingham 3

Welshpool & Llanfair Light Railway Preservation Co. Ltd. (*1960*)
(*Sec.*) A. R. Douglas, Llanfair Caercinion Station, Welshpool, Mont.

Wight Locomotive Society (*1966*)
(*Sec.*) R. E. Burroughs, "Spring Vale", The Grove, Ventnor, Isle of Wight

Yorkshire Dales Railway Society (*1969*)
(*Sec.*) G. Brogden, 31 Otley Old Road, Leeds LS16 6HB

Owain Glyndwr '*No. 7 2–6–2T built at Swindon in 1923, seen on British Rail's only steam line, the Vale of Rheidol Railway. The narrow gauge track of 1 ft. 11 ins. runs for 11¾ miles between Aberystwyth and Devil's Bridge, and was opened in* 1902. (*Photo: By courtesy of A. Robey, VORRSA*)

GENERAL INDEX

Page numbers shown in *italics* refer to illustrations or their captions. Counties shown against place names are those in being prior to the passage of the Local Government Act 1972 as being relevant to the period in which reference is made.

INDEX TO RAILWAYS

The word *Company* has been omitted from the titles in the interests of space

INDEX TO PERSONS

INDEX TO LOCOMOTIVES AND TRAINS

(See also list on page 170)